The Technique of Television Production

Eleventh Edition

THE LIBRARY
OF COMMUNICATION TECHNIQUES

FILM
THE TECHNIQUE OF DOCUMENTARY FILM PRODUCTION
W. Hugh Baddeley

THE TECHNIQUE OF EDITING 16 *mm* FILMS
John Burder

THE TECHNIQUE OF THE FILM CUTTING ROOM
Ernest Walter

THE TECHNIQUE OF FILM EDITING
Compiled by Karel Reisz and Gavin Millar

THE TECHNIQUE OF PROFESSIONAL MAKE-UP FOR FILM,
TELEVISION AND STAGE
Vincent J-R Kehoe

THE TECHNIQUE OF SPECIAL EFFECTS CINEMATOGRAPHY
Raymond Fielding

TELEVISION
THE TECHNIQUE OF LIGHTING FOR TELEVISION
AND MOTION PICTURES
Gerald Millerson

THE TECHNIQUE OF SPECIAL EFFECTS IN TELEVISION
Bernard Wilkie

THE TECHNIQUE OF TELEVISION NEWS
Ivor Yorke

THE TECHNIQUE OF TELEVISION PRODUCTION
Gerald Millerson

SOUND
THE TECHNIQUE OF RADIO PRODUCTION
Robert McLeish

THE TECHNIQUE OF THE SOUND STUDIO
Alec Nisbett

The Technique of Television Production

Eleventh Edition

Gerald Millerson

Focal Press

London and Boston

Focal Press
is an imprint of the Butterworth Group
which has principal offices in
London, Boston, Durban, Singapore, Sydney, Toronto, Wellington

First published 1961
Second edition 1963
Third edition 1964
Fourth edition 1966
Fifth edition 1967
Sixth edition 1968
Seventh edition 1969
Eighth edition 1970
Ninth edition 1972
Tenth edition 1979
Eleventh edition 1985
   Reprinted 1987

© Gerald Millerson, 1985

British Library Cataloguing in Publication Data

Millerson, Gerald
  The technique of television production.—11th ed.
  —(The Library of communication techniques)
  1. Television—Production and direction
  I. Title II. Series
  791.45′0232 PN1992.75

ISBN 0-240-51252-9

Library of Congress Cataloging in Publication Data

Millerson, Gerald.
  The technique of television production.
  Bibliography: p.
  Includes index.
  1. Television—Production and direction. I. Title.

PN1992.75.M5 1985   791.45′0232   85–4391
ISBN 0-240-51252-9

Photoset by En-to-En, Tunbridge Wells
Printed by Anchor-Brendon Ltd., Tiptree, Essex

Contents

To
my wife, Pamela

Preface

You cannot learn TV production direct from any book! It is essentially a very practical process, and there is no substitute for personal experience. But knowledge through experience alone can take a long time to acquire. In any craft you find a blend of proven principles and practices that support the free expression of the artist. Without a systematic study, it is all too easy to work hopefully but ineffectually. The more quickly you master these background facts, the sooner you will build up confidence and expertise.

This is essentially a *practical* book, discussing from first principles the process behind effective production techniques. It has been designed to be adapted to introductory, intermediate and advanced studies.

Do not be daunted by technicalities! As you will see, the basics are simple enough. Included here are easy reference digests, compact diagrams, and quick-guide tables. You will find guidance rather than 'rules'; advice rather than instructions. Reminder lists summarize operational 'know-how'.

This book will not only provide you with 'how-to', but explain 'why'. It discusses not only production *mechanics* and *techniques*, but the *aesthetics* of the medium; the power to persuade and the nature of its audience appeal. This book aims to encourage experiment and individuality, as well as showing how the various facets of production come together.

Television is a dynamic expanding medium, and this new volume has been fully updated and extended to reflect current developments in production techniques and technology. In the Glossary, you will find not only definitions, but also a selection of useful explanatory digests of the more technical aspects of the medium. Combined with practical experience, it can help you develop a firm understanding of the most important contributory features of TV production.

Throughout the book, the masculine gender rather than the more laborious 'persons' has been used for convenience and consistency, although the various jobs are carried out by women and men.

I would like to thank the Director of Engineering of the British Broadcasting Corporation for permission to publish the original book.

Gerald Millerson

Typical development for a complex production

PROGRAM IDEA	Subject research
DRAFT SCRIPT	
PRELIMINARY PLANNING	*Preliminary discussion* of production interpretation, initiation of staging designs (sketches, rough plans); perhaps consider lighting, make-up costume, technical facilities.
FINAL SCRIPT	Casting, performer booking.
TECHNICAL PLANNING	*Firming* of production treatment. *Detail planning* of above contributions. *Arrange* graphics, properties, special effects (scenic and video). *Initiate* organizational paperwork (requisitions). *Construction:* scenic, properties, graphics, effects. *Inserts:* obtain library film and graphics; location filming/videotaping.
REHEARSAL SCRIPT	*Make/obtain:* properties, costume, hairwork, models.
PRE-STUDIO REHEARSALS	*Performers practise:* lines, performance, action, business, etc. *Consolidation* of production treatment. *Finalize organization:* lighting, facilities. *Select/devise:* audio effects, background music. *Review/edit* inserts (film, VT) graphics.
CAMERA SCRIPT	*Prepare:* breakdown sheet, show format, camera cards, cue cards, prompters. *Transport:* hired equipment, scenery, props, graphics, costume, etc.
PREPARE STUDIO	*Set up* staging, dress sets, rough light. *Readying services:* telecine, videotape.
* CAMERA BLOCKING	*Adjust:* camera treatment, fine lighting, audio pick-up, make-up, costume, set-dressings, effects.
* RUN THROUGH	Finalize above.
* FINAL REHEARSAL	*Assess:* performance, treatment, operations, etc. Polishing revisions.
* VIDEOTAPING	Record or rehearse/record. Log time-code for required sections (as guide to editing). Check timing, durations. Retakes.
OFF-LINE EDITING DECISIONS	Examine tape (with log/notes from videotaping). Select required shots, shot order and edit points.
ON-LINE EDITING	*Dub off* required shots in order, introduce transitions. *Add* titles, audio sweetening, audio effects, background music, video effects. Post-syncing.
REVIEW	Airing schedule, promotion.
TRANSMISSION	Copying, distribution, archives.

*When 'Rehearse/Record' production techniques are used, these steps merge, as separate shots or sequences are individually blocked . . . rehearsed . . . taped.

1 Studio tour

Video productions today are shot anywhere and everywhere, with facilities ranging from 'state-of-art' to shoestring! But the same purposeful spirit pervades them all. So let's do the obvious, and begin our exploration by visiting a typical TV studio, where so many crafts blend to provide the daily miracle of television.

The television studio

As you push through the soundproof entry doors, the empty TV studio has a strangely inhospitable complexity. The stark expanse of smooth floor with lifeless equipment huddled in one corner. The acoustically padded walls bespattered with technical paraphernalia. A ceiling of dormant lamps clustering above. It has the impersonal silence of a deserted warehouse.

But introduce the scenery, switch on those lamps to bathe the settings in light and shade . . . and the atmosphere becomes expectantly transformed. And with this magic comes a feeling of urgency; a purposeful tension conveyed to performers and crew alike.

A hundred and one jobs converge. The furniture, drapes and bric-a-

Fig. 1.1   The television studio
A typical view of the empty studio: with uncluttered staging area, surround safety lane, overhead lighting battens and control-room observation window.

brac begin to clothe the scene as the sets are dressed. Cameras and sound booms are pushed into their opening positions. Lamps are selectively adjusted. Last-minute rearrangements of sets and props . . . By a daily organization miracle, the various pieces of the production combine to provide the complete TV show we have been planning and preparing. The cameras set up their shots. Now, on the picture monitor screens, the illusion begins to live!

Yet, within a time span of hours, the production will have completed rehearsals; the crew will have learned and practiced the director's treatment; performances hopefully reached their peak . . . and the program been recorded or transmitted. And then the whole 'magic cave' will be dismantled. Unbelievably quickly, the settings will be 'struck' and tucked away for stock or junking; equipment stored; and floors cleaned off. The original emptiness will return.

These are the conditions in which our theories and hopes become reality. And it is only when we relate our aspirations to the relentless pressure of practical conditions that we see TV production in its true perspective.

The television studio in action

Turn back the clock now, to earlier in the day when camera rehearsal was in progress for a drama production. The illuminated wall signs show that the studio is in closed-circuit rehearsal. So, although all the equipment is *hot* (operating), its output is only being monitored locally. At scheduled time, the studio video (pictures) and audio (sound) signals will be fed via the coordinating *master control room* (the central switching/routing control point) to the videotape recorders or immediately to the transmitters for *live* telecasting.

Around the studio you can see examples of the *set designer's* art: the three-walled rooms, a section of a street scene and a summer garden.

Fig. 1.2   **Contributory video sources**

Fig. 1.3   Contributory audio sources

After surprise at the colorful realism of these sets, the first impression is one of endless lights! Suspended, clamped to sets, on floor stands . . . it is hard to appreciate that each has been placed and angled with precision, for a particular purpose.

At the moment, action is in a 'living room' (an *interior*). Despite the number of people working around, everywhere is surprisingly quiet. There is little reverberation, thanks to the dampening effect of the acoustically treated walls. A camera moves silently over the specially leveled floor – where the slightest bumps could judder the picture. Its long cable snakes away to a wall outlet. Through headsets, the studio crew hear the coordinating instructions from the production director. The technical and operation staff overlook the studio from the control room(s).

Outside the 'living room' you see the 'sunny garden' (an *exterior*). Close

Fig. 1.4   Contributory services

scrutiny reveals that the convincingly flowering trees are really plastic blossoms wired to lopped-off branches and the turf is grass matting laid over sandbags. But on camera, the effect is idyllic. Quiet birdsong fills the air (from a nearby *playback* or *foldback* loudspeaker).

The *floor manager* (FM), the director's link with the studio floor, hand cues an actress to enter the garden. The sound boom's telescopic arm swings, its microphone following her as she speaks. The cameras within the room pull away quickly and move to the next set.

The director, from behind the tinted glass of the *production control room*, is watching a series of picture monitors (high-quality TV displays) continuously showing each camera's shot. He hears the *program audio* (all sound sources blended together) on an adjacent hi-fi loudspeaker system. His continuous *intercom* (*talkback*) instructions to the crew's headsets are unheard by the actors or the studio microphones. The FM cues performers, guiding and advising them where necessary; diplomatically relaying the director's instructions and observations.

The director has just seen a bad shot, as a foreground actor *masks* (obscures) another. He asks the FM to stop action. 'Hold it please,' calls the FM. Action pauses while he explains the problem. A slight position change is crayon-marked on the floor (*toe/location marks*). Actors go through the revised moves, and all is well. But the director feels that the shot now looks too close. 'Can you pull back on Two?' Camera Two's cameraman shakes the camera's head to signal 'No.' 'Can you zoom out a

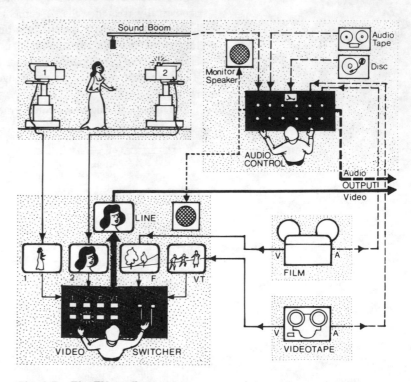

Fig. 1.5   The TV studio system
This simplified diagram shows how video and audio sources are routed to their respective selection points.

little?' And with a wider lens angle, picture composition improves. On the director's go-ahead, the FM calls for silence. 'Right, back to Shot 54, as Joe enters.' His arm moves cueing action, and the game of make-believe springs back to life ... as if no mere technicalities had interrupted. The rehearsal continues.

The production control room

Here in the production nerve centre, the director and his staff of specialists control the production. There are two basic approaches to control room design: communal and sectionalized layouts. Each has its merits and shortcomings.

■ *The communal layout*   This uses open-plan arrangements in either a single-level or split-level forms. Here everyone concerned with production control, sits at a long central desk: the *production director*, his *assistant* (who checks program timing, calls shot numbers and standby cues), the *switcher* (*vision mixer*), the *technical director* and *audio engineer*; and perhaps the *video control engineer* (*shader*). (As you will see the jobs, titles and names vary considerably!)

The desk faces a row of picture monitor screens. The *preview* (*channel*) *monitors* show the outputs of the various video sources and continuously display each camera's output as well as film, videotape, slide scanners and remote sources. Any source may be selected and switched (or faded) by the *production switcher* to the *studio output* (line output to master control.) The *master monitor* (*line, main channel, transmission*) displays the result.

The director's attention is divided between the various preview monitors, the selected output on the master monitor, and the *program audio* from a nearby loudspeaker. Via his headset, the director instructs his team – cuing action, assessing, guiding, explaining, coordinating their various contributions. All members of the team are joined into the communal intercom circuit; this can involve a fair amount of extraneous talk when participants hear others' instructions and exchanges.

For straightforward interswitching, the production director may operate the production switcher (video switching panel, vision mixer) – particularly on remotes (OBs). But for more complex operations, a specialist switcher (vision mixer) or the technical director usually does this job, enabling the production director to concentrate on controlling the many other aspects of the show.

The technical director's responsibility can vary between one organization and another. He may direct cameras, actively assisting in production treatment, and he may carry out video switching. As a supervisory engineer, he may oversee the engineering aspects of the production such as aligning effects, checking shots, ensuring source availability and monitoring quality.

At the far end of the desk the audio specialist (*audio engineer, audio control*) sits at his audio console (board, panel) adjusting and blending the various sound sources.

Depending on the show and its organization, others directly involved in its presentation may include:

1. The *set designer* (*scenic designer*) responsible for the *scenic treatment* (*staging*).
2. The *lighting director* who designs and arranges the studio lighting.
3. The *producer, editors* (script, film, videotape), *sponsor*, special assistants, researchers . . . and so on ad infinitum.
4. Where a program uses elaborate *video effects*, these can take some time to prepare. So an extra operator may be needed to devise and control them. Otherwise the person at the production switcher has to arrange these, in addition to the regular inter-source transitions (!).

The technical quality of pictures is controlled by a *video engineer* (*shader, video operator*) who continually monitors and adjusts video equipment, either within the production control room or in a separate technical area (*apparatus room* or in *master control*).

There may be a small adjacent *announce booth* from which announcements and commentaries can be read *out of vision (off camera)*.

■ *The sectionalized layout* Here the control area is subdivided into separate rooms:

1. Production control – where the director, assistant, switcher and technical director are located.
2. Sound control – audio coordination and control.
3. Vision control – video quality and lighting coordination.

Large glass panels and intercom circuits link these separate rooms. This layout has the advantage that their various activities and discussions do not impinge. No one in these control areas wears headsets and the intercom is of the local mike/loudspeaker type. The director's desk mike relays the general (communal) intercom (talkback) which is heard over

Fig. 1.6 part 1   The 'communal' production control room
All production operations are concentrated at a central desk. Video and lighting may be controlled locally or elsewhere.

other control rooms' loudspeakers. Individual specialists have their switched *private wire* (*party line*) circuits, for example from audio console to sound-boom operator, as well as being able to break into the general intercom system.

■ *Video control – vision control room*   In this area, the picture quality of all the local video sources is controlled and matched (cameras, slide/film scanner). Each studio camera's cable is plugged via a studio wall outlet to its main video apparatus – the *camera control unit* (CCU). These units, one per camera, are usually housed in an engineering area (master control, apparatus room) where they may be controlled directly by a video engineer.

In a more sophisticated arrangement, all the video operational controls are extended to a central console, where a single operator continually

Fig. 1.6 part 2   The 'sectionalized' production control room
Production control, audio control and video/lighting control functions are located in separate rooms to prevent interaction.
Preview picture monitors show: Cameras 1, 2, 3, 4; F film; VT videotape; E video effects; S slides; CG character generator/titles; R remote source; PV switchable preview monitor; L line monitor (transmission).
Personnel: D Director; DA director's assistant; SW switcher (vision mixer); TD technical director/technical manager; LC lighting control; VC video control; A audio control; O audio operator (disc/tape).
Equipment: AT Audio tape; DT disc turntable; MS monitor speaker; C clock; I on-air indicator lights.

monitors and adjusts picture quality from video cameras, slide, film sources. Lighting and pictorial effect are closely interrelated, so the video operator usually sits next to the *lighting console* operator, and shares the same picture monitors. These operators, guided by the lighting director, can therefore work in harmony.

■ *Audio control – sound control room* At his *audio console* (*sound desk, mixer, board*) the *audio engineer* (*sound mixer, sound supervisor*) monitors and adjusts sound dynamics and quality, blending the sources to suit the production's artistic and technical requirements. As well as the studio microphones, he is controlling various additional audio sources including discs, audio tapes (reels, cassettes, carts), film and videotape tracks, announce booth and remotes.

The audio control man guides by intercom his sound crew on the studio floor. He helps then to avoid mikes or their shadows appearing in shot, warns them of subject moves or shot changes, etc., and assists them in achieving sound perspective to match the pictures. Whether he operates disc and tape recorders himself, or is assisted by an operator, depends on production complexity and control room layout.

Master control

The *Master Control Room* is the engineering coordination center for a TV station. It provides a master control point where a *routing switcher* interconnects the various production units – e.g. studios, film chains, VTRs, remotes, etc. Because of the technical complexities of source routing, switching is increasingly automated.

The Master Control Room houses such items as synchronizing generators, distribution amplifiers, camera control equipment (CCUs), and may include audio equipment, film chains VTRs, slide scanners, etc., when these are not located in separate areas elsewhere.

Television programs from larger studio centers are often routed to a transmitter, via a *Continuity/Presentation suite*. Arranged rather like a production control room, it may have a small studio (and/or announce booth) for station announcements, newscasts, weather, interviews.

Table 1.1 Typical approximate TV studio sizes

			Typical	*Ceiling*
Local TV/campus studios	Small	150 m² (1600 ft²)	15 × 10 m (50 × 30 ft)	3.5 m (11 ft)
	Medium	216 m² (2400 ft²)	18 × 12 m (60 × 40 ft)	7 m (23 ft)
Network studio center	Small general purpose	330 m² (3500 ft²)	22 × 15 m (70 × 50 ft)	9 m (30 ft)
	Medium	672 m² (7200 ft²)	28 × 24 m (90 × 80 ft)	10 m (33 ft)
	Large	1024 m² (10 000 ft²)	32 × 32 m (100 × 100 ft)	13 m (43 ft)

Continuity control is mainly concerned with providing a smooth-flowing program output from the station: switching between program sources at the scheduled times, inserting commercials, trailers/promos (promotions) for upcoming shows, station idents (channel identification logos), covering breakdowns, etc. In addition there will be liaison with program-sources (studios, remotes, VT and film channels) relative to go-ahead cues, scheduled timing, introductory announcements, etc.

2 How television works

Considering its technical complexity, the basic principles involved in producing a TV picture are surprisingly simple.

The video signal

In a monochrome TV system, an image of the scene is focused onto a *camera tube*. A *target* inside the tube builds up a pattern of electrical charges corresponding to light and shade variations in the image. A continuous *electron beam* generated within the camera tube reads across this charge pattern line by line and at the same time discharges it. The net result is a fluctuating voltage which is the *video* or picture signal.

In the receiver, a *picture tube* (*kinescope*) has a glass screen coated with a fluorescent powder. This glows according to the strength of an electron beam scanning across the screen and is synchronized with the camera tube's scanning process. As this beam's strength fluctuates, controlled by the video signal, it traces a light and shade pattern corresponding with the image of the original scene.

The brief period during which the scanning process returns (re-traces) from bottom-right to top-left of the field (the vertical interval/field blanking period) contains no picture information. It is used for various identification, test and control signals (perhaps including *teletext* information).

Color television

Any color can be analyzed into various proportions of red, green and blue light. Therefore to televise a scene in color, we analyze it into these three *primaries*. Although color TV cameras may use one, two or three camera pick-up tubes to do this, the principles of operation remain the same. The

Fig. 2.1   The camera tube (Photoconductive types)
The inside of the camera tube's glass face-plate is covered with a fine metallic coating (signal plate), on which a layer of photoconductive material is deposited. The scene's image is focused onto this target (T). The electrical resistance of the layer varies at each surface point, with the light and shade of the scene, so building up a corresponding charge-pattern. The constant electron-beam (E-B) from the tube's gun (G) scans across the target in a series of close parallel lines, neutralizing each point (element) in turn. The resultant re-charging currents constitute the camera's video signal.

single lens image is split into three identical light paths which incorporate red, green and blue filters respectively. A normal monochrome camera tube behind each filter responds to the light and shade in its particular filtered image, producing a corresponding video signal. (A single-tube camera uses a multicolor striped filter instead.) So the camera provides information about red, green and blue proportions of the scene (*chrominance*), and the brightness (*luminance*) of each point.

In the TV receiver or picture monitor, the color picture tube's screen has a close pattern of three different phosphors emitting red, green, or blue light respectively, when scanned by an electron beam. These phosphor dots or stripes glow according to the strengths of their relative

Fig. 2.2   The monochrome picture tube
A gun in the picture tube produces an electron beam (E-B), which fluctuates in intensity with the video signal. As the beam scans across the screen in a series of close parallel lines, it causes the fluorescent coating to glow correspondingly, building up the light and shade pattern of the original image. The picture (frame) is scanned in 525 lines (485 active) 30 times each second (Europe – 625 lines, 25 per second). To conserve bandwidth and decrease flicker effects, the odd lines (*odd field*) are scanned, and then the even lines (*even field*) fitted between them (*interlacing*). In simple TV systems, this interlacing varies (*random interlace*) and definition deteriorates.

Fig. 2.3   The picture and its video
Showing a typical scanned line and its corresponding video signal.

video signals. The eye blends these colors, interpreting them as a reproduction of the original scene.

Some color receivers include special compensatory circuits that automatically correct for signal distortions arising between the transmitter and the set. These circuits adjust tint and screen color automatically to the levels specified by the station's VIR (vertical interval reference) signals.

Fig. 2.4   The parts of the video signal

1. Peak white (peak modulation).   2. Peak black.   3. Color burst.   4. Front porch.
5. Horizontal (line) sync pulse.   6. Back porch.   7. Synchronizing level.   8.
Blanking level.   9. Set-up (pedestal).   10. Reference black (black level).   11.
Reference white (white level).

The picture information (video) is suppressed (blanking) at the end of each line (and each field) and a synchronizing pulse inserted – this ensures that the entire TV system from camera to picture tube scans in step. The brief color burst (of sub-carrier frequency) provides a color-reference signal.

Fig. 2.5   Color TV principles

The focused image is split by a prismatic block (or dichroic filter-mirrors) into three light paths –covering the red, green, and blue regions of the spectrum. Camera tubes (3, 2, or 1) produce corresponding video signals. These signals could be transmitted in this form, and recombined to recreate the original color image (as in color printing processes). However, to provide a *compatible* color TV picture (that will reproduce on monochrome receivers) a complex intermediate system is necessary – NTSC, PAL or SECAM. This involves *coding* to derive special *luminance* (brightness) and *chrominance* (hue, color) video signals. (Monochrome receivers respond to the luminous component of the signal.)

In the color picture-monitor or receiver, the separate RGB components are recovered by a *de-coding matrix* (decoder), each video signal being used to control their respective electron-beam strengths in the picture tube.

Fig. 2.6   Color picture-monitor or receiver
The tube screen comprises three patterns of phosphors (dots or stripes) that glow
red, green, or blue when energized by their associated electron beam. The eye
merges these tiny RGB patterns, seeing them as color mixtures; when
proportionately activated they appear white to gray.
The color picture tube may take three forms: (1) delta-gun dot mask (shadow mask);
(2) self-converging precision in-line (PIL) slot-mask design, or (3) single-gun (three
beams) aperture-grille type (Trinitron). The last two avoid the convergence color-
fringing problems of 1.

Fig. 2.7 part 1 Light mixtures –Additive primaries

Light can be analyzed into red, green, and blue components. Suitable mixtures of these *additive primaries* can reproduce most colors. Equal proportions of two such primaries produces a *secondary* color – magenta (purple), cyan (blue-green), yellow; also known as *subtractive primaries*. This mixture is often termed a 'minus' of the third primary hue: hence yellow is *minus blue*, cyan is *minus red*, and magenta is *minus green*.

Fig. 2.7 part 2

Hue derives from the *proportions* of red, green, and blue present. *Luminance* (brightness) results from their *quantities*. 1. If only one phosphor is activated, the screen appears of primary hue. 2. Two or three phosphors produce additive color mixtures (e.g. R + G = Yellow). 3, 4. If three phosphors are combined, various shades or degrees of color dilution (saturation) result (e.g. Diluted red = pink; Dim orange or yellow = brown).

Fig. 2.7 part 3 Pigment mixtures –Subtractive primaries

When pigments are used (ink, paint, dyes), the apparent surface color is actually the light remaining after surface absorption. So the mixing process becomes a subtractive one.

Fig. 2.8 Picture detail

The TV system's ability to resolve detail (its resolution) is checked with standard test charts. These contain *gratings* (1) or *resolution wedges* (2). The finest information that can be discerned, reveals the system's maximum resolution. (The calibrations indicate the 'number of picture lines' that could be resolved in the picture width.) In a 525-line system, typically '320 lines' (4MHz) represents maximum transmitted detail. Maximum closed-circuit resolution may be '640 lines' (8MHz).

Fig. 2.9   The gray scale
The standard gray scale takes the maximum-to-minimum tonal range readily reproduced by the TV system (overall 20:1 contrast), and divides it into 10 steps. (Relative light reflectance 70–3½%.) Each step is √2 times brightness of the next, the logarithmic scale looking linear to the eye. (What appears mid-gray is only 17½% reflectance, not the 50% you might expect.)

Picture detail

The finest detail that can be resolved in a TV picture is determined by how rapidly the system can change from one tone to another during the scanning process. This rate of change is measured as frequency (4 MHz for a 525-line system; 5 MHz for 625 lines).

All systems (video and film) have a maximum detail limit (*definition, resolution*). In TV this is initially influenced by the number of transmitted picture lines. But ultimately it depends also on the performance of the whole video chain, from lens to receiver picture tube. Various factors affect picture clarity including lighting contrast, lens flares, dirty lens or prompter, focusing, video equipment design, alignment, and so on. Hence an unsharp picture can have many causes!

Tonal contrast

The reproduced tonal range of the TV picture (*contrast range*) lies between the picture tube's maximum brightness (without defocusing) and the 'black' represented by the screen face. In practice, ambient light spilling on the screen, circuit design and adjustment, and eye adaptation, often limit the available range on many TV receivers to as little as 10:1 to 15:1, if halftones are to be clear. Under good conditions, however, an adjacent tone contrast of 20:1 (30:1 on widely spaced areas) is achieved, with a maximum contrast of 50:1.

Fig. 2.10   Exposure
The camera tube can only handle a limited *contrast range* (e.g. 20:1). Within these limits, tones are reproduced proportionally. If tones in a scene are relatively restricted, the *f*-stop can be adjusted to accommodate them. If subject tones or lighting contrast exceed the TV camera's range, detail and gradation are lost in lightest and/or darkest areas. (They appear as solid tone.)
Adjusting lens aperture (*f*-stop) selectively moves camera's 'exposure segment' up or down the scenic tonal scale, determining which tones are to be reproduced successfully. *Opening up* (e.g. *f*/2) progressively improves shadow detail, but increasingly overexposes detail in lightest tones (blocking off to white). *Stopping down* (e.g. *F*/16) progressively improves detail in lightest tones, but increasingly underexposes dark tones (crushing them to black).

Fig. 2.11   Exposure curve
Only within the straight part of the exposure curve (with unity gamma) will relative tonal values be reproduced accurately. When the video signal is weak (mainly lower tones), inherent system noise is prominent ('snow' in dark tones). When video strength is high (lightest tones), it can reach the system's upper limits, and block off to a blank white.
If the *knee* of the curve is made more gradual (*soft*) by circuitry, highlights are reproduced more realistically. The camera tube's overall exposure range can be effectively increased by beam-enhancement circuits (see Glossary –*Highlight overload*).

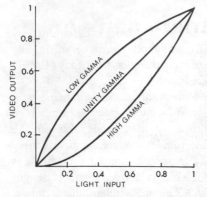

Fig. 2.12   Gamma
The *gamma curve* reveals how a video system reproduces tonal gradation. Where a device is linear (gamma of 1) its output is proportional to the input. A *low gamma* device accepts a wide contrast range, compressing it into the system's limits; resulting in reduced tonal contrast (thin). A high gamma device accepts only limited subject contrast, expanding it to fit the reproduction limits; giving exaggerated coarsened tonal values.

When you shoot a scene involving a considerable contrast range, due to extreme scenic tones and lighting contrast, you must recognize that although the eye can accommodate about 100:1, the camera tube can only handle a range of some 20:1 to 30:1. The reproduced picture therefore has its limitations.

Where you can control contrast of subjects (scenic tones, costume, lighting), it is best to keep these within the camera's tonal limits, unless you are prepared to lose extreme tones (highlights or shadows).

Tonal contrasts between subjects and backgrounds are important, too. If they are of fairly similar tone (their *contrast ratio* is small), they will tend to merge and the picture appear flat and lifeless.

A special microscopic coating on the surface of lenses (blooming) reduces internal reflections and light scatter, so improving the tonal contrast in the picture. On the other hand, dust on the lens surface (or deliberate diffusion through suitable filters) can reduce overall tonal contrast.

Tonal gradation

For most pictorial subjects, we are concerned not only with a picture's tonal extremes, but how well the system reproduces intermediate tones (gray scale values) between these limits. And this is directly affected by camera channel design and operation, and by the receiver or picture monitor's performance.

Table 2.1   Color terms

Hue	The predominant sensation of color i.e. red, blue, yellow, etc.
Saturation/chroma/purity/intensity	The color strength; how far it has been 'diluted'. *De*saturation produces pastel colors, such as pink.
Luminance/brightness/value	A color's apparent brightness (lightness or darkness).
Tint	A hue diluted with white.
Tone	A grayed hue.
Shade	A hue mixed with black.
Achromatic/gray scale	Intermediate tonal steps (*values*) from black to white.
Monochrome	Generally refers to 'black-and-white' (achromatic) reproduction. (Strictly means varying brightnesses of *any* hue.
Primary colors	Three colors (usually red, green, blue) which, when mixed in correct proportions, produce any other colors of the spectrum.
Complementary colors	In *light*, two colors which, when added together, produce white light, e.g. blue and yellow: cyan and red; magenta and green. In *pigment or dye*, complementary colors produce black. If the visible spectrum is filtered to hold back one primary color, e.g. red, the result is a *minus red* mixture, called cyan (blue, green). Similarly, minus-green is magenta (red, blue); minus -blue is yellow.

The terms Hue, Chroma, and Value are used in the Munsell system of color notation.

3 What your camera can do

Whether your TV camera produces color or monochrome pictures, is hand-held or fitted to a giant crane, the basic operating principles remain the same.

The lens

The camera's lens is actually made up of a series of individual lenses, referred to as *elements*, set within a tubular barrel. These elements have been carefully designed and combined for optimum overall performance, minimizing various inherent optical defects (aberrations). This lens arrangement focuses a small sharp image of the scene on to the camera's pickup tube(s).

There are two basic lens types: those with fixed optics (fixed focal length) and those with an adjustable focal length (*zoom lens*). Fixed focal length lenses are fitted to most photographic cameras, to film and TV cameras of simpler design. The fixed focal length lens (focus and *f*-stop are adjustable) is designed to cover a certain segment of the scene – known as the *angle of view* or *lens angle*. The zoom lens on the other hand, has variable coverage.

The impressions of distance, space and size that your picture conveys, will be strongly influenced by the angle of view of the lens used. While a 'normal' or 'standard' lens will show the scene in reasonably natural proportions, other lens angles will modify effective perspective. A *wide-angle* ('*short-focus*') lens seems to exaggerate distance; a *narrow-angle* ('*long-focus*') lens appears to compress it.

The lens system

Your camera's lens system will influence how you use the camera.

■ *A fixed focal length lens* (also called *prime lens, primary lens,* or *fixed focus lens*) This provides you with a certain image size at a given distance. If you want a larger image of your subject you must move the camera closer or bring the subject nearer.

■ *A zoom lens* This has a variable focal length, and so can be continuously adjusted to provide any shot size you wish within its range, without interrupting the picture or needing to move the camera at all. So you can select the camera lens angle to suit the size of shot required, instead of having to move the subject or the camera. But as you will see, this technique has its disadvantages because it can introduce perspective distortion and handling problems for the cameraman.

Fig. 3.1   The television camera
The TV camera consists of:

A. *The camera head.* Z, zoom lens. T, camera tubes. V, viewfinder. C, camera cable (taking technical supplies to the camera, and the resultant video to the camera control unit/CCU). A quick-release *wedge-mount* under the head slides into a corresponding recessed plate on the panning head.

B. *The panning head (pan head).* This enables the camera head to tilt and turn (*pan*) smoothly. These movements can be restrained by deliberately introduced friction (*drag*), and can be *locked off* to hold the head rigid. *Tilt balance* positions the head horizontally, preventing it being nose- or tail-heavy. One or two attached *pan (panning) handles* (H) enable the cameraman to direct and control the camera head.

C. *The camera mounting.* This can take many forms, e.g. camera-clamp, monopod, tripod, pedestal, crane.

31

Whenever we deviate from a more or less 'normal' lens angle, there is a certain amount of compromise – both artistically and technically (see Table 3.3).

Focal length and lens angle

When we want to identify which particular lens (or zoom setting) is being

FRONT

REAR

Fig. 3.2   The camera head

1. Tally light (on-air selected) with camera number.
2. Zoom lens.
3. Lens hood (sun shade, ray shade).
4. Beam-splitter prism block.
5. Camera tubes.
6. Zoom-control cable.
7. Zoom focus cable.
8. Zoom focus control (integrated in camera head).
9. Zoom control (thumb lever).
10. Viewfinder (monochrome) with magnifier.
11. Camera cable.
12. Panning head.
13. Pan head controls (Pan and tilt

lock. Adjust pan drag/friction).
14. Adjust tilt drag/friction.
15. Tilt balance.
16. Panning handle (pan bar).
17. Adjust pan-handle angle.
18. Clip for camera card.
19. Zoom lens indicator meter (for lens-angle).
20. Lens aperture (*f*-stop) indicator.
21. Lens range-extender.
22. Viewfinder controls (including hi-peaker crispening viewfinder detail).
23. Shot box (integrated in camera head or on pan bar).
24. Headset jack-points (intercom and program), with volume controls.
25. Mixed viewfinder feeds switch.

used, we can quote either its *focal length* (*F*) or its *lens angle* (horizontal angle of view).

■ *Focal length* For many years, film and TV cameramen using fixed lenses have found the focal length (*F*) inscribed on each lens in millimetres or inches a very convenient method of identification. (Focal length is defined as the distance from the camera tube target to the lens' optical center when the lens is focused on infinity.)

A lens' coverage (its angle of view) and the subject image size it

Camera controls
A. *Lightweight zoom lens* showing focus (distance) control, zoom lever (focal length/lens angle), *f*-stop (lens aperture).

B. *Forms of focus control*
1. Spoked capstan control
2. Twist-grip
3. Camera-head focus control.

C. *Forms of zoom control*
On studio cameras:
1. Twist-grip.
2. Hand-crank.
3. Thumb-lever.
4. Push-rod (also focuses).
On lightweight cameras, thumb-operated switches by the handgrip operate the zoom motor.

D. *Shot box* (integrated into camera head, or clamped to a pan handle). This provides pre-selected zoom settings; overridden by pan-bar thumb control.
1. Zoom meter shows focal length/lens angle.
2. Buttons select pre-set angles adjusted by knobs at 3.
4. Auto-zoom switch, zooms the lens in/out towards narrowest/widest angles when pressed.
5. Adjusts auto-zoom speed.

Fig. 3.3   Camera controls for focus, zoom and *f*-stop (lens aperture) can take several forms

■ *Direct lens adjustment* – by turning a sleeve ring, lever or handle.

■ *Pushrod system* (through the camera head) – turn to focus; push-pull to zoom.

■ *Direct cable control* – flexible cables from lens to pan handle controls; focus on left, zoom control on right handle. (Aperture/*f*-stop control by sleeve ring on lens barrel, or remotely adjusted; manually or automatically.)

■ *Motor control* – small motors adjust the lens settings (local or remotely controlled).

■ *Servo control* – adjusting a control unit produces corresponding changes in slave units adjusting the lens settings. Turning a twist-grip or thumb-lever on a pan-bar, zooms in/out (zoom speed increases with angle of twist).

With direct manual control, adjustment often feels coarser at longer focal lengths. Compensated servo systems have a similar response at all lens angles.

Fig. 3.4 part 1   Fixed optics lens (prime lens)
Adjustable focus (distance) and lens stop. Fixed lens angle (focal length).

Fig. 3.4 part 2   Zoom lens
Adjustable focus, stop, and focal length (lens angle). Altering focal length varies the field of view. Usually set at a pre-selected angle. Changing the angle in shot produces 'zooming in' (as angle narrows, F increases), or 'zooming out' (angle widens, F decreases). Typically 12–120 mm focal length adjustments.

provides vary with the focal length of the lens. If you change to a lens with double the previous focal length, the subject now appears twice as large in the frame, but the shot covers only half the previous scene width/height. A lens of half this original focal length reproduces the subject as half the size with the scene width/height being double the original.

Knowing the focal length of any lens, you can check with tables for your particular *format* (e.g. for 35 mm film or 25 mm [1 inch] camera tube) to see the area it will show at the required distance. Where the lens has a focal length equal to the diagonal length of the format used, it will provide 'natural' perspective and be termed a *normal* lens.

Providing you continually use cameras of the same format, the operational practice of identifying lenses by their focal length is very convenient. You become accustomed, for example, to the subject distance at which a 25 mm (1 inch) lens gives a 'waist shot'. But what happens if you then use a camera with a different size camera tube? Now you may find that a 25 mm (1 inch) lens at this distance provides a 'large-head shot', and your previous associations between shot size and focal length are upset! This is because the lens' coverage or angle of view depends on both the focal length *and* the film or camera tube format. As there are now several formats in use, these shot variations can be confusing, especially as lens designs of identical focal length can have dissimilar coverage anyway!

Fig. 3.5   Basic lens characteristics
Focal length – The distance from the lens' optical center (rear nodal point) to the tube target when focused at infinity. *Back focus* – The distance from the back lens surface to the target, when focused at infinity.

■ *Lens angle* To overcome such problems, some TV organizations refer to their lenses operationally by the *horizontal angle of view*.

This convention has several practical advantages. The *cameraman* gets used to the shots various lens angles provide, and these will be the same whatever the camera system's format. All '25° lenses' give the same shots; whereas a '25 mm (1 inch) lens' gives different shots from different size camera tubes.

For the *director*, there are many bonuses. You do not need tables to determine shot size. Simply by drawing a 'V' of the chosen angle on a scale plan, or better still using a protractor, you can judge exactly what the camera has in shot. You can determine whether unwanted subjects will be seen, the shot size, relative proportions in the shot, and so on.

Perspective distortion

The strange pictorial effects arising from perspective distortion have become familiar to most TV audiences. Examples of this are grotesquely distorted closeups, squashed-up cardboarded images of distant subjects, and the bent architecture portrayed by the fisheye lens. Used deliberately for a special purpose, they can have a dramatic impact. But how do you control this distortion and use it selectively?

Fig. 3.6 part 1   Angle of view
The TV camera lens 'sees' 4 by 3 proportions. The vertical angle of view is therefore ¾ of its horizontal angle. The angle a lens covers depends on its *focal length* relative to the size of camera-tube used.
For a given camera position, the longer the lens focal length (narrower lens angle) the closer the subject appears; but less of the scene is visible. The shorter the focal length (wider lens angle), the more distant the subject appears.

Fig. 3.6 part 2   Lens angles
Changes are proportional as the lens-angle alters. Using a lens of three times the present angle (i.e. ⅓F), the subject now appears ⅓ of former size and × 3 of scene width is now visible. The effect is that of increasing the camera distance by 3 times. Changing to a narrower angle has the opposite effect.

Fig. 3.7   Viewing distance
Ideally, a photograph should be viewed so that the image subtends a similar angle to that of the original camera lens. The perspective (relative distances, sizes, depths, proportions) will than appear *natural*. Viewing distance, therefore, should really be adjusted to suit the screen size.

Fig. 3.8   Natural perspectives
When the viewing angle equals the camera's lens angle our impression of the picture's perspective will be similar to that of the original scene. Viewing the picture from too far away or using a camera lens of too wide angle for normal viewing conditions gives a false impression of perspective. Depth and distance are exaggerated; distant subjects unduly small. Viewing the picture too closely or using a too narrow angle lens for normal viewing conditions again gives a false impression. Depth and distance are compressed; distant subjects unduly large.

Perspective distortion arises whenever your camera's lens angle differs considerably from the audience's *viewing angle*, which is around 24° from the eye to either side-edge of the screen. Their impression of perspective – space, distance, proportion – will be inaccurate (Fig. 3.7).

■ *Normal perspective* In practice, 'normal' perspective is a fairly arbitrary concept. We are least likely to notice inaccuracies in shots of open spaces, such as seascapes or deserts, and are most critical of perspective for familiar architectural surroundings.

Although the ideal distance is where line detail just disappears, people watch TV screens of various sizes at various distances. Even a photograph shot on a 'normal' lens will produce different perspective effects as the print is enlarged.

However, for most purposes, if we use a lens around 20–27° the results are natural enough. In practice this means for a:

30 mm (1.25 in) camera tube a lens focal length of about 20–25 mm (0.8–1.0 in) gives a 'normal' lens angle.

25 mm (1.00 in) camera tube a lens focal length of about 16–20 mm (0.6–0.8 in) gives a 'normal' lens angle.

18 mm (0.67 in) camera tube a lens focal length of about 11 mm (0.4 in) gives a 'normal' lens angle.

Long-focus lens (narrow-angle lens)

The long-focus (telephoto) or narrow-angle lens enables you to select small parts of the subject from a distance. This is a particular advantage when you cannot move the camera nearer the subject because of obstructions, terrain, static camera, etc. Outside the studio, at remotes or

TOTAL SCENE

Wide Angle Lens   Normal Angle Lens   Narrow Angle Lens

Fig. 3.9   Perspective distortion *(see Glossary)*
Reducing the lens angle (increasing F) provides a magnified image of part of the scene. This emphasizes perspective effects normally associated with distant subjects, and produces an illusion of space compression.

Table 3.1 Typical lens coverages *(see Table 4.2)*

	Focal length (F) mm (in)	Hori- zontal angle	Vertical angle	Horizontal field of view at distances of		
				1.5 m (5 ft) m (ft)	6 m (20 ft) m (ft)	30 m (100 ft) m (ft)
25 mm (1 in) camera tube	12.5 (0.5)	54°	40°	1.53 (5.0)	6.1 (20.0)	30.5 (100.0)
	25 (1.0)	27	20	0.76 (2.5)	3.1 (10.0)	15.3 (50.0)
	50 (2.0)	13.5	10	0.40 (1.3)	1.5 (5.0)	7.6 (25.0)
	75 (3.0)	9	7	0.24 (0.8)	1.0 (3.3)	5.2 (17.0)
	150 (6.0)	4.5	3.5	0.12 (0.4)	0.5 (1.6)	2.5 (8.3)
32 mm (1.25 in) camera tube	17 (0.6)	50°	37.5°	1.46 (4.8)	5.80 (19.0)	29.0 (95)
	35 (1.5)	26	19	0.64 (2.1)	2.56 (8.4)	12.8 (42)
	52 (2.0)	17	13	0.49 (1.6)	1.95 (6.4)	9.8 (32)
	90 (3.5)	9.5	7	0.28 (0.9)	1.10 (3.6)	5.5 (18)
	135 (5.3)	6.5	5	0.18 (0.6)	0.73 (2.4)	3.7 (12)
	215 (8.5)	4	3	0.12 (0.4)	0.49 (1.6)	2.4 (8)

outside broadcasts, these lenses often prove the only means of getting 'detailed' shots.

■ *Distortion effects* Purists argue that no lens *distorts* perspective, but this is true only if the viewer adjusts his distance from the screen to compensate for perspective changes. Under practical conditions we find when using a narrow-angle lens, that depth appears remarkably compressed and foreground to background distance seems much shorter than it really is. Solid objects look 'depth-squashed'. People seem to take an interminable time, even when running, to move toward or from the camera. Distant objects are shown disproportionately large:

Seen end-on, a jumbo jet looks only a few meters long.
At the race track, horses gallop towards us but appear to cover little ground.
Flat cramped figures of a rowing eight, squat in a foreshortened boat.
Shots along piano keyboards appear strangely foreshortened.

Even in the studio, at much shorter distances using lenses around 5–10°, people can appear quite distorted as 'closeups' show unpleasantly flattened features, flat chests and reduced modeling (contouring). This is particularly noticeable in three-quarters face and full-face views.

■ *Camera handling* Even if you chose to disregard such effects productionally, the cameraman cannot overlook that camerawork becomes more difficult as the lens angle narrows (focal length increases). Even slight camera movement, caused by a wavering hand-grip or

Table 3.2 Camera tube sizes

Diameter	Image size	Diagonal of image
1 ¼ in 30 mm	17.1 × 12.8 mm	21.4 mm
1 in 25 mm	12.8 × 9.6 mm	16 mm
⅔ in 18 mm	8.8 × 6.6 mm	11 mm
½ in 12.5 mm	6.4 × 4.8 mm	8 mm

Typical applications: ENG cameras 18 mm tubes; EFP/OB cameras 25 mm tubes; studio cameras 18 mm to 30 mm tubes.

dolling over uneven floor, produces disturbing picture judder. On remote (OBs) where lenses of ½–5° become essential to see otherwise inaccessible action, such problems become acute. The camera may even have to be rigidly *locked-off* on its panning head to ensure picture steadiness, rather than held ready to tilt and pan.

In hot weather, the diffraction due to heat haze may cause an overall

Fig. 3.10 part 1   Lens angles and camera movement
Here we see the effect of moving the camera (positions 1, 2, 3) with wide-angle, normal, narrow-angle lenses.

Fig. 3.10 part 2   Maintaining foreground subject size
If lens is changed, and camera distance altered to maintain the same foreground subject size, proportions change too. (1) Narrow; (2) normal; (3) wide-angle lens.

shimmering on 'close' shots of distant subjects. The only remedy is to move closer to the subject.

Focusing too, can become a problem as the available depth of field becomes quite shallow on long-focus (narrow-angle) lenses.

Short-focus lens (wide-angle lens)

This lens can provide you with a wide overall view of a scene, even when the camera is relatively close. A boon when shooting in confined or congested surroundings, where you cannot move away sufficiently to obtain a shot on a normal lens, or after moving closer to exclude unwanted foreground objects.

■ *Distortion effects* However, the wide-angle lens appears to *exaggerate* perspective, making subjects seem further away than they really are. A small room may look quite spacious – even impressively extensive when shot on this type of lens. This is a great facility when we want to emphasize space or make smaller settings appear large. But in naturally small surroundings, such as a cell or a hovel, this can destroy scale and realism.

Shooting people on wide-angle lenses results in bizarre distortions;

Table 3.3   Lens angles *(see Table 4.2)*

	Advantages	Disadvantages
'Normal' lens *(20°–27°)*	Perspective appears natural. Space/distance appears consistent when intercutting 'normal' lenses. Camera handling feels natural and is relatively stable. Focused depth is generally satisfactory, even though fairly shallow for closer shots.	Inadequate width-coverage in confined spaces. Camera must move close to subject for detail; so may be seen by other cameras taking longer shots of the same subject.
Narrow-angle long-focus lens *(less than 20°)*	Brings distant subjects closer. Permits 'closer' shots of inaccessible subjects. Can flatten or reduce emphasis on surface contours. Enable objects spaced-out away from the camera to be compressed into a more cohesive group (e.g. a string of automobiles). Can suggest aborted effort in subjects moving quickly to/from the camera (e.g. running). Defocuses distracting background.	Depth appears compressed. Heat haze may shimmer the picture. Flattening of subject modeling can appear unnatural. Camera handling is considerably more difficult (pan, tilt, smooth dollying). Restricted depth of field makes focusing critical.
Wide-angle short-focus lens *(greater than 30°)*	Can obtain wide views at closer distances, especially in confined space. Camera handling causes negligible judder. Because of extended depth of field, focusing is less critical. Enables modeling and space to be exaggerated. Impressive spatial effects possible. Useful for grotesque or dramatic shots. Provides considerable depth of field.	Depth appears exaggerated. (Confined spaces cannot be shown in correct proportions.) Pronounced geometric distortion, at widest angles. Susceptible to lens flares. On close-ups, problems with camera shadows falling on subject.

Barrel   Pincushion

Fig. 3.11   Geometrical (curvilinear) distortion
Optical distortion in which lines parallel to the frame edges appear progressively bent
outwards (barrel distortion) or inwards (pincushion distortion).

puffed-up bulbous heads, large protruding noses, stumpy legs, and
enlarged chests. Fine for grotesques but totally unacceptable for
flattering portraiture.

Very wide-angle lenses can produce geometric distortion that is
particularly noticeable on graphics, music and printing. When the
camera pans, straight verticals bend as they approach the picture edge.

The wider the lens angle (shorter focal length), the more pronounced
will all these effects be. The fisheye lens (between 140° and 360°) can
only be used for special applications.

The wide-angle lens exaggerates speed of movement along the lens
axis, so that camera dollying looks faster than it actually is and people
coming up to camera seem to cover distance remarkably rapidly.

■ *Camera handling* On the plus side, smooth camerawork is much
easier when using a wide-angle lens, for any movement or unevenness is
less liable to cause picture judder. Moreover, focusing is less critical as
the available depth of field is much greater.

Supplementary lenses

By attaching a supplementary lens to the front of your lens, you can
modify its focal length and hence its angle of view. Although mainly used
for fixed lenses, these add-on lenses are employed in flip-in *range
extenders* on zoom lenses.

A *positive supplementary lens* reduces the effective focal length and
therefore widens the lens angle. It also means that the lens can be focused
on closer subjects than normal. Held at arm's length, the positive
supplementary lens shows a small inverted image.

A *negative supplementary lens* has the opposite effect, recognizable by
its tiny upright image when held at arms's length. When used normally
this lens will therefore narrow the lens angle. However, if placed beyond
the main lens' focal length, the result is an increase in lens angle. The
power of a supplementary lens is quoted in diopters.

The zoom lens

The practical disadvantage of a fixed lens is that it covers only one
particular angle of view. If you want to see more or less of the scene you

must either alter your distance from the subject or replace the lens with another of more suitable focal length.

■ *Zoom range* Zoom lenses are now widely used on video, cine, and photographic cameras. Ingenious optical design enables the lens' focal length to be adjusted over a range. The lens can be left at any setting within this range, when it will behave similarly to an equivalent fixed (prime) lens. If adjusted on shot, the picture *zooms* in or out, i.e. the image size grows/reduces – depending on whether you are increasing or decreasing the effective focal length. If the focal length when fully zoomed in (narrowest lens angle/longest focal length) is three times that when fully zoomed out, it has a ×3 or 3:1 zoom ratio. So the subject image size can be changed by a factor of 3. This lens could zoom from a close-up to a knee-length shot. A high-ratio zoom lens on the other hand (e.g. 44:1) might fill the screen with a person's eye, then zoom out until he becomes a dot in the landscape.

Studio cameras fitted with 30 mm (1¼ in) pickup tubes require larger zoom lens systems, typically with a range of 10:1 (e.g. 5–50°). Bigger EFP cameras may use a similar range, but different angles (e.g. 1–10°), or extended ranges up to 44:1. Hand-held ENG cameras with 18 mm tubes are often fitted with 10:1 (12 mm–120 mm) or 13:1 zoom systems.

■ *Zoom performance* The zoom lens has certain limitations: higher cost, greater complexity, increased light losses (due to absorption and inter-lens reflections), with greater bulk and weight. Overall performance may well be below that achievable by fixed lenses especially where optical quality has to be compromised for compactness. But technically and operationally, the zoom lens has many merits.

Wide Angle   Narrow Angle
Zoomed Out   ←————ZOOMING OUT————   Zoomed In
                       ————ZOOMING IN————→

Fig. 3.12   Zooming
Zooming in progressively fills the screen with a smaller section of the scene. (Narrowing lens angle, increasing focal length.)

■ *Zoom advantages* Any chosen lens angle can be selected quickly (manually or by push-button – *shot box*) without losing picture. The automatic zoom-rate is adjustable with a preset control. Lens angle can be adjusted specifically to frame a subject without moving the camera.

Adjusting the lens angle alters the image size, simulating camera movement to/from the subject. For *flat* subjects, the effect is identical to dollying. But for three-dimensional scenes, the effect is artificial owing to the absence of spatial displacement movements between planes (*parallactic movement*). Smooth zooming is easier to achieve than smooth camera moves; particularly over long distances, or for fast shot changes.

■ *Zoom disadvantages* Unfortunately, it is all too easy to select lens angles indiscriminately, so that perspective becomes inappropriately distorted and intercut shots give different spatial impressions. Shot sizes may not be repeated accurately, unless the cameraman notes his exact position and the angle used.

Remember, a zoom lens handles like a fixed-angle lens of the focal length you have selected. Consequently, at a *narrow-angle* (long focal length) setting, camerawork is more difficult and focusing is more critical. At a *wide-angle* (short focal length) setting, operation is easy and focusing less critical. The 'feel' of a zoom lens continually alters therefore, over its range.

Many zoom lenses do not have a constant performance throughout their range – focus may not remain sharp and the image brightness may vary (aperture losses).

Some zoom lens systems do not have meters or reliable indicators showing the selected angle (or focal length). So the zoom lens has to be used entirely empirically and production standards fall.

■ *Zoom range extender* Continuous zooming over a wide range poses considerable lens design problems, so some systems introduce a cable-controlled flip-in supplementary *extender lens* to change the normal range by a factor of 1½, 2 or 3 times. To zoom over its entire available range therefore requires resetting the system midway; often with a short overlap in between. Unfortunately, such extenders can cut down light considerably (to ¼ perhaps), and degrade picture definition.

Fig. 3.13   Depth of field
Within the depth of field, subjects appear sharp; although definition is optimum at the *focused distance* (FD). Beyond the furthest acceptable distance (Df) and closer than the nearest limits (Dn), subjects are defocused.

Close-up attachment lenses are sometimes added similarly, to reduce the minimum focusing distance (closest point at which an object can be focused).

Focus controls

When you focus a camera, you adjust its lens to produce the sharpest possible image of your subject. With a fixed focal length lens this involves altering the distance between the lens and the camera tube; in a zoom lens, focusing is achieved by internal readjustments of lens elements.

Fig. 3.14 part 1   The effect of aperture on depth of field
Keeping the focal length and focusing distance (FD) constant, the depth of field increases as lens aperture is reduced (stopped-down).

Fig. 3.14 part 2   The effect of subject distance on depth of field
Keeping the focal length and aperture constant, the depth of field increases as the camera gets further from the subject; but image size decreases.

Fig. 3.14 part 3   The effect of focal length on depth of field
Keeping the aperture and subject distances constant, the depth of field increases as focal length decreases (lens angle is widened), but image size decreases.

Fig. 3.15   Constant depth of field
If the camera distance is adjusted for each lens angle to keep the same subject size, the depth of field will remain the same (for a given *f* stop).

Fig. 3.16   Zoom lens focusing problems
Unless the camera has been pre-focused, the close-up after zooming it may be unsharp. *Zoomed out* '–Although the focused distance is incorrect, the subject appears focused due to the considerable depth of field available (wide lens angle). *Zoomed in* – Without re-adjusting focusing, we zoom in. Now the depth of field has become shallower (narrower lens angle) and it no longer includes subject, which appears defocused.

■ *Focusing methods*   (Fig. 3.3)   Lens focus can be operated by:

1. A *focus ring* on the lens barrel (screwing the lens in/out).
2. A *knob* at the side of the camera head.
3. A *twist grip* on a panning handle.
4. A *focus/zoom rod* at the rear of the camera.

Some cameras use a mechanical focusing system, in which the focus cable is directly linked to the lens. Although simple, this method has disadvantages. Adjustment feels critical when focusing at narrow lens angles, while at wide angles appreciable control movement is needed before differences in focus are apparent.

Where electrical *servo systems* are used, the focus control directs a motor which adjusts the lens focus, and its 'feel' can be maintained irrespective of the lens angle (focal length).

Cameras fitted with *auto-focus systems* (i.e. distance sensors that adjust focus automatically) have had some limited use on remotes, to ease camera operation. But such devices are quite undiscriminating. So if, for instance, something suddenly intrudes into the picture, the camera is quite capable of refocusing itself there, and ignoring your real subject!

■ *The need to adjust focus*   A lens can only provide maximum sharpness at the distance to which it has been focused (focused plane). Sharpness gradually falls off nearer and further than this focused distance, until the image is too blurred for us to accept as sharp or 'in focus'.

The range of distances over which subjects are apparently sharp, is called the *depth of field* (*not depth of focus* which refers to focal plane tolerances). How far sharpness can deteriorate before you notice it, depends on your subject's detail and the system's limits (definition, resolution). Given a vague subject (detailless, plain) or a low-definition system, you have difficulty in seeing what *is* in focus!

Providing a subject remains within this depth of field, you do not need to readjust the focus control. The focused depth may be considerable, especially when the lens is focused at the *hyperfocal distance*; but it can also become embarrassingly shallow, particularly in close-shots.

If you change focusing distance, focal length (lens angle), or the lens *f*-stop (aperture), the available focused depth in the scene will alter (Fig. 3.14).

■ *Focusing problems*   When using the zoom lens you may, for instance, find focus drifting as you zoom (bad focus tracking) due to design or incorrect setting-up adjustments. But even with a high performance zoom lens there is always a major operational hazard (Fig. 3.16):

The cameraman is zoomed out showing a sharp focused long shot of a crowd (using a wide angle – short focal length). He zooms in to a big closeup of a person (to a narrow angle – long focal length setting) . . . and the shot is now *completely out of focus*. Why!

Focusing with any zoom lens is uncritical when it is zoomed out. This is because the depth of field is considerable so the exact focused distance is not easy to see. Most subjects in the scene appear sharp. But when you zoom *in*, focused depth becomes progressively limited as the lens angle narrows, so you may well find that you have been focused at the wrong distance! Apart from corrective refocusing while on shot (often unavoidable in ENG camerawork), the only solution is anticipatory *prefocusing* – while off-shot, you zoom in, sharp focus, and zoom out to the required wider angle, so that you are now ready for a subsequent zoom in on shot.

■ *Minimum focusing distance* Any lens can be focused over a range from *infinity* (far distance) to a plane a short distance from the camera. Nearer than this *minimum focusing distance* (mfd) the shot remains defocused, the control having reached its limit. This minimum distance varies with the type and design of the lens. While wide-angle (short-focus) lenses can focus down to a few centimeters away, the mfd for a very narrow-angle (long-focus) lens may be several meters from the lens. For a zoom lens therefore, this distance varies with the angle selected.

With *macro-focus zoom lens* design, focusing is possible right up to the front lens surface.

■ *Setting up a zoom lens* In principle, you can regard the zoom assembly as a fixed-focus lens with a telescope of variable magnification in front of it. While its field of view changes, its back-focus distance (rear-lens to tube target) remains constant and sharply focused.

To ensure that the zoom lens maintains focus as its focal length is changed, the system has to be set up, as follows. First zoom in to distant detail and adjust the normal operational *zoom focus* control (*lens focus, rough* or *coarse focus, front focus*) for greatest clarity. Then zoom out and adjust the internal preset focus control (*camera focus, back* or *fine focus*) for sharpest image. Ideally you can now zoom in/out without focus drift (i.e. correct *focus tracking*). If necessary, repeat this setting-up for optimum results. When the subject's distance changes, you may need to readjust the zoom focus control to maintain sharpness (Fig. 3.16).

Lens aperture – *f*-stop

Looking into a lens, you will see a variable circular diaphragm comprising a number of overlapping metal blades. This device (*diaphragm, iris*) alters the effective diameter of the lens opening over a wide range. The *aperture* (*stop*) is adjusted by a marked ring on the lens barrel – either directly or by remote control.

Changing the aperture (stop) does two quite separate things simultaneously:

1. It adjusts the amount of light (image brightness) falling on the camera tube (or film).
2. It alters the depth of field.

Fig. 3.17   Lens aperture
Lens aperture is adjustable from a maximum (e.g. *f*2 for a fast lens *f*5.6 for a slow lens) to a minimum (e.g. *f*22). *Large aperture* – Small *f*-number, shallow depth of field, but less light needed. *Small aperture* – Large *f*-number, increased depth of field, but more light needed.

■ *Over- and underexposure* If the camera tube receives excessive light from any part of the scene, those tones become *overexposed* and merge into unmodeled detailless areas (block off, crush out).

Insufficient light results in *underexposure*. Lighter tones are reproduced at too low a level, and darker tones mass as black detailless areas (*clog, crush*).

Over- or underexposure can also cause technical defects in the TV picture.

The lens aperture enables you to regulate exposure to suit the lighting intensities and subject tones. *Correct exposure* involves adjusting the aperture for optimum pictorial effect. For bright lighting and light-toned scenes, you reduce the lens aperture (*stop-down*); while for dimly lit surrounding or darker tones, you *open-up* the lens.

■ *f-numbers/f-stops* The lens aperture is graduated in *stops*. These are marked as *f-numbers* (*f-stops*) or *transmission* (*T*) numbers. The amount of light the lens lets through will be doubled for each complete stop you open (halved when stopping down). As a whole stop is an inconveniently large calibration, subdivisional *f*-numbers are normally used.

The standard series of lens markings is:

$$1.4/2/2.8/3.5/4/5.6/8/11/16/22/32.$$

The larger the aperture, the smaller will be the *f*-number.

To calculate the difference in light passed at two apertures, you use the formula:

$$\frac{(\text{First } f\text{-no.})^2}{(\text{Second } f\text{-no.})^2} = \text{light change}$$

Thus, from *f*/4 to *f*/8 the image brightness changes to ¼. If, therefore, you stop the lens down from *f*/4 to *f*/8 to increase the depth of field, you must increase lighting fourfold to maintain the same exposure.

■ *Working apertures* The highest grade lenses will still provide sharp pictures at their maximum aperture (e.g. *f*/2) when opened up for low light levels, or to achieve a deliberately shallow depth of field (to isolate a subject). But clarity (*definition, resolution*) falls off discernibly towards the frame edges at large apertures.

Many lenses produce optimum picture quality at around *f*/5.6 to *f*/8.

Stopping down to small apertures (f/16) does not provide maximum definition, although increased focused depth may improve subject clarity.

Neutral density filters

When the scene is too bright for the aperture you want to work at, a *neutral density filter* is used to cut down the overall intensity. These transparent gray-tinted (neutral) discs are usually fitted in a filter wheel behind the camera lens. Typical values range from 1/10 (10 per cent) to 1/100 (1 per cent) transmission. A 10 per cent filter will, for example, cut light down by nearly three stops (e.g. f/5.6 to f/16).

Neutral density (ND) filters may be used when shooting in very strong sunlight, to prevent overexposure or the need for unduly small apertures. Again, should you want to open up the lens of a particular camera to restrict focused depth for artistic reasons, while perhaps other cameras use smaller stops, a ND filter can be used to compensate exposure.

Camera-tube sensitivity

All TV cameras require a certain minimum general light level to produce clear, crisp pictures with good tonal gradation. The actual intensities needed depend on the camera tube's inherent sensitivity, scenic tones, the atmospheric effect required, and suitable depth of field (hence the f-stop).

Camera-tube sensitivity varies with design and lineup. High tube sensitivity allows you to get satisfactory pictures under lower light conditions, when otherwise you would have to increase video gain (amplification) despite greater picture noise, to try to strengthen the dim underexposed shot.

In the studio, however, very dim lighting provides depressing and uncomfortable working conditions. Artistic lighting balance becomes difficult, as the eye cannot evaluate light values accurately, or detect extraneous shadows or spill light that are very evident on camera. Instead, when using high-sensitivity tubes, we normally find ourselves lighting to comfortable intensities and stopping down or filtering to prevent overexposure.

Cameras are quoted as needing a certain incident-light level at a particular stop. But much depends on the scenic tones (mainly light or dark), light direction, video amplification, lens system, etc. Light levels (intensities) are measured in lux (lumens per square meter) or in foot-candles (lumens per square foot); 1 fc = 10.74 lux. Light levels are only an indication of camera sensitivity when related to the working aperture (f-stop).

Typical light levels required for modern camera systems are around f/4 at 2000–3500 lux (186–325 foot-candles).

The relative amount of light needed on the scene at various lens apertures (taking f/4 as unity) varies:

f/1.4	f/2	f/2.8	f/3.5	f/4	f/4.5	f/5	f/5.6	f/6.3	f/8
1/8	1/4	1/2	3/4	1	1¼	1½	2	2½	4

← Less light   More light →

Mountings for lightweight cameras

A camera's operational flexibility is considerably influenced by the mounting you use. Over the years a variety of devices have been developed, each providing its particular opportunities and limitations.

Lightweight cameras are of two kinds. Simpler designs are usually employed in closed-circuit TV (CCTV), classroom TV and for demonstration and surveillance purposes. More sophisticated mountings are used for broadcast work – for mobile location shooting and electronic news gathering (ENG).

Lightweight TV cameras have increased production opportunities considerably. They can move within the action, along the touchline, amongst the crowd and generally provide a new immediacy, covering events as they happen.

Lightweight cameras are mainly hand-held, and to avoid undue camera shake, jitter and unsteady handling, a *body-brace (shoulder harness)* is usually worn. Elaborate harnesses (Steadicam, Panaglide) provide outstanding compensatory stabilization, even for violent running and climbing! But underneath it all there is a human cameraman whose arms tire and back aches. Shots waver and standards become difficult to maintain.

Even when capable of the sustained broadcast quality of larger studio cameras, hand-held lightweights do not lend themselves to long days of continuous exacting rehearse/record production techniques. Although they are ideal for mobility over difficult terrain and confined conditions, it is not easy to sustain high-grade camerawork for long periods with hand-held cameras, particularly when using narrower lens angles.

Fig. 3.18   Lightweight camera stabilizers
To increase stability of hand-held cameras, (1) a body brace or (2) an elaborate stabilizing spring harness may be worn (Steadicam, Panaglide).

Fig. 3.19 part 1   The tripod
A simple 3-legged stand with independently extensible legs. Height is
preset. Unlike other mountings it can
be set up on sloping or uneven ground.
A *spider* (spreader) may be used to
prevent tripod feet slipping.

Fig. 3.19 part 2   Camera clamps
The panning head may be clamped to
a firm tubular-rail structure at a
vantage point.

Static mountings

For certain applications (e.g. remotes or isolated camera positions) a
totally static mounting provides the safest and simplest method of
securing a camera. Particularly where extreme narrow-angle (long-focus)
lenses are used, this ensures complete rigidity for stable shots.

Typically, a fixed tripod is used, alternatively a scaffold clamp fastens
the camera panning head to tubular steel scaffolding, or a *camera
frame/camera tower* structure.

The rolling tripod

The simplest wheeled camera mounting, known as the *rolling tripod*
(*tripod dolly*), comprises a collapsible metal or wooden tripod fitted to a
three-castered base (*skid; skate*). This makes wheeling easy, but not
always accurately controlled. The wheels have adjustable guards to
prevent overunning floor cables. Screw-jacks lock-off (immobilize) the
mounting when required. The tripod height is preset, and not quickly
altered. Suitable for simpler studio operations, the rolling tripod is
extremely useful for remotes.

← Caster Foot Brake

**Fig. 3.20   The rolling tripod/
tripod dolly**
The tripod can be mounted onto a
castered base (skid/skate/rolling
spider). Height is preset (pneumatic or
hand-crank). Easily wheeled on a flat
smooth floor (although steering may
be imprecise). Caster foot-brakes, and
cable guards may be fitted.

The studio pedestal

The *pedestal* (*ped*) is the most widely used TV camera mounting. Designs
range from preset lightweight hydraulic columns on casters to
heavyweight monstrosities requiring assisted operation. The well-
designed pedestal is stable, flexible, easy to move and controlled quickly
by one person. During complex moves, a cameraman might need to
zoom, focus, pan, tilt, change height, push and guide simultaneously; so

controlled movement is essential! At his eye level, this can be a difficult feat. At maximum or minimum height, it becomes impractical.

Using the pedestal, the camera height can be adjusted smoothly while on shot and held firmly in position at heights from about 1–2 m (3–6 ft). A large *ring steering wheel* around the central extendable column, usually serves to raise/lower the camera as well as guide dolly movements. Pedestal designs include pneumatic, hydraulic, counterbalanced and hand-cranked versions; they can be operated manually or with motor assistance.

The pedestal's three base wheels are guided by the steering wheel and/or a handle (*tiller*) in an interlinked or single wheel mode.

Fig. 3.21   The studio pedestal
1. A surround wheel or ring at the top of the column is used to adjust column height (hence the lens height) and to steer the pedestal. A second ring may be fitted, to lock-off the column.
2. The lens-height range is typically 1–2 m (3–6 ft).
3. The camera can be moved around and repositioned in various ways.'
4. The rubber-tired tricycle wheels can be steered in either of two ways (foot-pedal selection). *Dolly (tricycle tracking) mode:* single wheel steered, other two fixed. Used for general dolly moves and curved tracks (arcs). *Crab (parallel) mode:* all three wheels interlinked, steered simultaneously. Used for trucking – crabbing, sideways movements, moving into confined spaces.

The small crane

The small crane (Panoram or Vinten dolly, velocitor, small boom) in various forms is widely used for filming and TV remotes (OBs). They also have some TV studio use. The crane offers greater height variations than the pedestal, for example 0.6–2 m (2–7 ft), and unlike the pedestal, can overreach foreground obstacles. Some versions permit the boom (crane arm, jib) to slew left/right for tonguing movements.

However, the small crane requires a crew of two or three and a fair amount of floor space to move around. The cameraman uses finger movements to coordinate assistants (grips, pusher, tracker) in pushing, steering and elevating the mounting.

A level even floor surface is essential to ensure smooth dollying (less critical for pneumatically tired dollies); but special rails or tracks are desirable on rough terrain.

Larger cranes

Large cranes range from the Motion Picture Research Council crane

Fig. 3.22   The small crane
Lightweight versions of the small crane are increasingly used. 1. Particularly for remotes, the height range (0.6–2 m, 2–7 ft) with 360° seat and camera-mounting rotation, offer improved shot flexibility (Vinten – 'Kestrel'). 2. A counterbalanced crane-arm attached to a pedestal, tripod, or wheeled base again provides a variety of viewpoints for portable and ENG cameras.

Fig. 3.23 Larger cranes
Heavy-duty cranes are normally used where extensive camera viewpoint changes,
high-angle or swooping shots are required for large-scale action. Thanks to precision
counter-balancing, the boom can be swung manually by a single operator (guided by
a picture monitor and cameraman's finger-signals).

(Academy Mole crane) which covers heights from 0.45–2.7 m (1½–9 ft),
to the truck-mounted giants of the large studio that are used at heights of
1–8.2 m (3½–27 ft).

Needing considerable maneuvering space and a three/four man crew,
we find cranes come into their own for production numbers, mass
spectacles and large-area displays.

In all cranes, the camera and panning-head remain level irrespective of
the boom (crane-arm) angle. The cameraman can often rotate his seat
with the camera through 360°.

Owing to their size, weight and balance problems, cranes require
highly skilled operation for smooth safe movement. A heavy moving
crane attains speeds up to 40 kph (25 mph) and therefore any
misjudgements can be highly dangerous. The cameraman must take all
precautions, including use of a helmet and harness, and have total
confidence in his crew. He also needs a good head for heights!

Motorized dolly

To relieve the tedium of manual effort and improve coordination, two-

Fig. 3.24   Crane movements
Upward/downward movements of the boom (crane arm, jib) are *craning, booming, jibbing*. Swinging the boom sideways is *tonguing left/right*. Swinging the boom to/from action is *tonguing in/back*. The base may be steered, using a tracking line to/from action (*dollying, tracking*), or across the action (*trucking, crabbing*).

man camera cranes with motorized controls were introduced into larger TV studios. Foot pedals for height control and camera-platform direction are operated by the cameraman, while a dolly operator (tracker) on a rear-platform controls speed and direction. During operation, the cameraman must take care not to depress the jib onto anything beneath its overhang or crush himself against scenery (ceiling, arches).

Fig. 3.25   Motorized dolly
A 2-man crane in which all operations are motor-controlled, reducing crewing requirements and operational fatigue.

Fig. 3.26   Low angle dolly
Gives height-mobility for low-angle shots, together with considerable maneuverability.

Fig. 3.27 Hydraulic platform
Considerable platform-height variation is possible (even while on shot), giving a high stable viewpoint.

SkyCam Here a remotely-controlled camera (gyro balanced) is suspended in the center of an X-pattern of overhead cables. Independent computer-controlled winches simultaneously adjust cable-lengths, to rapidly reposition the camera anywhere over the action area (e.g. a sportsfield). The result is a 'flying camera', capable of wide-ranging aerial views, zooming in to detail, out to vista shots, at rates of up to 27 mph.

Low dollies (creepers)

This is basically a steerable wheeled platform. The camera head can be raised/lowered from around 0.5 m to 1.1 m (1½ ft to 3½ ft) for moving low-angle shots. However, for static set-ups, a mirror periscope attached to a pedestal may suffice instead.

Hydraulic platforms (cherry-pickers; Simon crane)

Truck-mounted hydraulic lifting platforms can raise a camera from 1.8–26 m (6–85 ft) above the ground for high overall shots. It is also useful for positioning microwave dishes (radio links) for remote telecasts or ENG work. If you want to go higher than 26 m (85 ft) then you require the services of a helicopter – with a special camera-stabilizing device to avoid rhythmic vibration.

Remotely controlled cameras

For semi-static presentations, such as newscasts, or from small announce studios or unmanned reporting studios; a remotely controlled pedestal camera can be operated from a master control room several miles away. A keyboard control system can store up to 100 shots with detail variations of pan, tilt, zoom, focus, aperture and pedestal height. Lighting, cueing and equipment switching can be similarly operated.

Pre-rehearsal camera checkout list

■ *1. Preliminaries* Camera switched on, warmed up, and lined up?
■ *2. Camera cable* Are the cable plugs at the camera and wall (or equipment) socket tight? Is the cable secured to the camera mounting? Is there sufficient cable for camera moves, and is it suitably routed?
■ *3. Camera-head* Is the pan-bar/panning handle(s) firmly attached, at a comfortable angle? Unlock the tilt secure control, and check the camera-head balance. It is nose or back heavy, or needing readjustment? Check (and adjust) vertical drag/tilt friction. Unlock pan-secure. Is the action smooth, with just sufficient friction? (Adjust horizontal drag/pan friction.)
■ *4. Column* For a rolling-tripod, check column height and adjustment. For a pedestal, unlock column, and raise/lower it. Check the ease of vertical movement (balance), and adjust if necessary.
■ *5. Steering* Check freedom of movement in all directions, in dolly (track) and truck (crab) modes.
■ *6. Cable guards* Adjust guards to prevent cable-overrun or floor scraping.
■ *7. Lens* Remove the lens cap. Switch lens electrical capping out. Check that the lens is clean.
■ *8. Viewfinder* Check its focus, brightness, contrast, picture shape (aspect ratio), edge cut-off, image-sharpening (crispening). Are internal

Fig. 3.28

indicators working (re: zoom, *f*-stop, exposure, etc.)? Are tally and indicator cue-lamps OK? Check mixed viewfinder feeds.

■ *9. Focus*   Check focus control smoothness from nearest to furthest distance (infinity). In a lens servo system, is there any spurious focus overrun or hunting (rhythmical changes) occurring? Is the zoom action smooth throughout? Focus at the widest and narrowest angles. Check that focus is constant throughout the zoom range (tracking correctly).

■ *10. Lens aperture*   Check the *f*-stop no., selected during camera line-up with chart/diascope under standard illumination. (This indicates system's sensitivity.)

■ *11. Zoom*   Check zoom meter or indicator. Adjust shot-box if any, to preset angles. Check operation.

■ *12. Intercom (talkback)*   Check intercom circuits (general and private-wire). Is the program sound feed OK?

■ *13. Filters*   Check filters (filter wheel), making sure that one is not accidentally left in position.

Preparing portable cameras
In addition to the above, check out the following:

■ *14. Cable*   Do you have enough cable for the job? Has the camera cable compensation control been set to suit the cable length? Are cable joints firmly screwed together? Route the cable to protect it from feet, vehicles, etc. (sling, hide, cover, bury).

■ *15. Battery*   Check that the fitted battery and standby batteries are fully charged.

■ *16. Viewfinder*   Is the fitting secure? Check warning lights, including tally-light, exposure, low battery, VTR on, tape left, etc.

■ *17. Microphone*   Is the mike secure and functioning? Check connections. Cable for announcer/commentator mike.

■ *18.*   Check out video and sound recording.

Basic camera operation

Good camerawork is a mixture of know-how, dexterity, observation and anticipation. Here is a digest of the most important points to look out for:

■ *1. Tally light*   Be aware of your tally/cue light. Do not move off shot (*clear*) unless instructed, or until light goes out.

■ *2. Posture*   Avoid having a tense stance or gripping controls too tightly.

■ *3. Pan head*   Always be ready to pan or tilt on shot. Only lock off the head during breaks or when repositioning the mounting or when shooting captions and floor titles.

■ *4. Viewfinder*   Ensure that it is at a comfortable angle and not diluted with spill light. Make sure you have a sharp and bright image.

■ *5. Lens angle*   Be aware of your lens angle (focal length). This helps you to anticipate handling problems or depth of field limitations.

■ *6. Checking your shot*   Make sure you are *focused* on your subject and

Fig. 3.29

that you have sufficient depth of field. Be ready to follow focus as subject moves. Always anticipate the need to prefocus lens (for close shot) before zooming in from a wide shot.

Check your *framing* for such things as headroom. Remember to off-center your shot for angled, profile, or moving people ('looking-room').

Recheck your *composition* (for unity, balance, subject importance, clarity, etc.).

It is best to mark the dolly base floor position. This will help to give *consistent* shots.

Always try to match other cameras' shots to maintain similar headroom and height. Where several cameras' shots are combined (for 'supers' or effects) watch floor monitor or use mixed viewfinder feeds.

■ *7. Spurious items in shot*   Check that scenic lines are not 'growing out' of subjects. Take care that the mike (or its shadow), lamps, or other cameras are not visible. Guard against shooting off settings. Avoid strong specular light reflections. If lens flares arise, raise your viewpoint, or stretch tape across top of lens shade. Always be ready to compensate composition, if a performer moves unexpectedly out of position, or others intrude into your shot.

■ *8. Shot changes*   Anticipate subject movements and prevent it passing out of frame or becoming defocused in close shots. Be aware of people 'breaking' (moving apart).

Maintain focus and framing on moving subjects.

Also reframe (recompose) shot as a person repositions, or an extra person enters frame.

Be ready to alter shot size (by zooming or dollying) for wider action or new grouping. Avoid overwidening and then having to correct on shot.

■ *9. Dolly movement*   Check that the mounting is in correct mode to dolly (track) or truck (crab). Be ready to steer in a new direction. (Turn and slightly push while off-shot, to prevent wheel jerk as you move.)

Start dollying with gentle pressure and have your foot ready to push pedestal base. Always be ready to 'ped' up or down, which means that the column must be unlocked. Avoid hitting upper or lower column limits. Be aware of obstructions before dollying. Dolly smoothly and do not overshoot your floor marks.

■ *10. Intercom*   Listen to all instructions during rehearsal, including those for other cameras. In rehearsal visual signals may be used such as 'Yes' (tilt up and down); 'No' (pan left and right); 'I've a problem' (pan and tilt in circles); 'I've focus problems' (rapidly rock focus); and 'I want to speak on the private wire' (quick in and out zooms).

Inform the director of *problems* such as subject masking, insufficient time for dolly moves, composition, focusing, that need his reorganization. But avoid undue intercom chat.

■ *11. Shot sheet*   Check your next shot, move to the new position and then be ready.

■ *12. Cable*   Ensure that you have sufficient cable and that it is not trapped around objects. Never pull cable tight. Route cable in anticipation of moves. To avoid cable drag noise you may need assistance.

■ *13. Obstacles*   Anticipate obstructions such as cables, scenery, people, cameras and booms. Avoid elevating or depressing on nearby obstacles.

■ *14. Problems* Be calm. If you are late on shot, try not to lose it altogether. Do not lose the next! If you misjudge then correct as unobtrusively as possible.

4 The persuasive camera

Anybody can do the obvious, and point a couple of cameras at the subject. One takes an overall *cover(ing) shot*, while the other shows closer detail. Subjects and cameras move around for the sake of variety, and to interlink areas. TV and film cameras can be used at this level. But this is making pedestrian use of a persuasive tool.

The selection of the right techniques at the right time, distinguishes the creative artist from the hack.

1. Good techniques are meaningful and apt. They add persuasively and significantly to the raw program material.
2. Poor techniques are mechanical conveniences, often unmotivated, ambiguous, unstimulating.

Fig. 4.1   Shots of people

Shots are classified by the amount of a person taken in:

ECU Extreme close-up (detail shot) – isolated detail.
VCU Very close-up (face shot) – from mid-forehead to above chin.
BCU Big close-up (tight CU, full head) – full head height nearly fills screen.
CU   Close-up – just above head to upper chest (cuts below necktie knot).
MCU Medium close-up (bust shot, chest shot) – cuts body at lower chest (breast-pocket, armpit).
MS   Medium shot (mid-shot, close medium shot, CMS, waist shot) – cuts body just below waist.
KNEE Knee shot, three-quarter length shot – cuts just below knees.
MLS Medium long-shot (full-length shot, FLS) – entire body plus short distance above/below.
LS   Long shot – person occupies ¾ to ⅓ screen height.
ELS Extra long shot (XLS), extreme LS.

58

Defining the shot

In defining the *length of shot*, we are really considering how much of the screen the subject fills – how close it appears to be. Some descriptions are quite general.

1. *Long shot* or *full shot* – a distant view of an unspecified coverage.
2. *Wide shot* or *cover shot* – a broad view taking in all action.
3. *Close shot* or *tight shot* – a detailed view, often excluding other nearby subjects.
4. Shooting people, we have the approximations: single, 2-shot, 3-shot, group shot.

A shot is classified according to its *effect*, irrespective of how you achieve it. It is still a *close shot* for example, whether you use a close wide-angle lens, or a distant narrow-angle (long-focus) lens; although you will find the effective perspective, distortions, camera handling, etc. can vary considerably between these extremes (but depth of field remains similar).

Selecting the length of shot

The TV screen's size limitations do not prevent you from presenting effective variations in shot size. Although a small screen does less than justice to panoramic or spectacular situations, the TV camera can

Fig. 4.2 part 1   Restricted framing
In close shots, action must be kept within the frame area. Avoid moving items in/out of frame (it draws attention to limited viewpoint).

Fig. 4.2 part 2   Limited depth of field
Confine movement for big close-ups (use firm, marked position) as depth of field is extremely restricted.

Fig. 4.2 part 3   Combined close-up and wide shot
Combined shots can show detail and wider view simultaneously. This can be achieved by *detail insert* (left) or showing foreground detail (right). The latter method requires considerable focused depth.

successfully explore the scene and action, from vista shots to microscopic close-ups.

Longer shots reveal location, establish mood, show interrelationships, or follow broad action. But sustained long-shots can deprive the viewer of detail he is anxious to see (e.g. individual paintings in a wide view of an art gallery).

Closer shots lay emphasis, dramatize, reveal reactions, demonstrate detail. But sustained close-ups can be very restrictive. They can prevent the viewer from looking around the scene, from seeing the response of other performers, from watching action, or observing other aspects of the subject.

By using the wrong type of shot you may frustrate the viewer, leaving him uninformed, leading him to wrong conclusions, underplaying important information, or simply depriving him of what he wants to see at that moment. Occasionally you can arrange a combination picture to show a wide view of the scene and close detail simultaneously (Fig. 4.2).

The very long shot (vista shot)

Here the environment predominates, and the viewer often develops an impersonal, detached attitude to people within the scene, or a feeling of surveillance. In most studios, such wide views are only achievable by using a distant wide-angle lens and electronic insertion into a pictorial background.

Appropriately used, the very long shot enables you to establish broad location, provide an overall atmospheric impression, to coordinate several small action groups, or to accommodate widespread activity.

The long shot

Often used at the start of a scene, the long shot establishes location and atmosphere, and enables you to follow the pattern and purpose of movement.

As the shot tightens (less of the scene shown) the influence of setting and lighting will lessen. The impact of people within the scene grows. They become more important; their gestures and facial expressions become correspondingly more forceful.

Instead of beginning a sequence with a long *establishing shot*, you can build up impressions gradually, shot-by-shot; satisfying curiosity a little at a time. This encourages a sense of expectation, speculation.

But take care that delayed piecemeal introductions do not confuse; especially where the locale is unfamiliar. There must be sufficient pointers for our audience to be able to interpret the time, place and action correctly. Where action has been seen from closer viewpoints for some time, longer shots may be desirable to remind, or re-establish the locale in the viewer's mind.

Medium shots

These range from full-length to mid-shots; their value lying somewhere between the environmental strength of the long shot and the scrutiny of closer shots. From *full-length* to *three-quarter shots*, large bodily gestures (outflung arms) can be contained. But they are likely to pass out of shot if the shot becomes tighter. Then you have the option of restricting performer movement, taking a longer shot, or tightening to exclude arm movements entirely.

The closeup

An extremely powerful shot, the closeup concentrates interest. With people, it draws attention to their reactions, response and emotions. Closeups can reveal or point out information that might otherwise be overlooked, or only discerned with difficulty. They focus attention, or provide emphasis.

When introducing closeups, you have to ensure that the viewer wants to look that close, and does not feel that:

1. He has been cheated of the wider view, where something more interesting may be happening.
2. He has been thrust disconcertingly close to the subject – he may become over aware of facial blemishes in overenlarged faces.
3. Detail that is already familiar is being overemphasized.
4. Picture clarity is actually being *reduced*: because there is no fine detail, or irrelevant details have become prominent, or restricted focus has blurred details.
5. Through continually watching closeup fragments, they have forgotten how these relate to the main subject, or have become disorientated.

Where shots do not contain enough detail to sustain continued interest, take care not to hold them so long that they entirely satisfy the curiosity, or encourage attention to wander.

The prudent director remembers, and allows for, the cameraman's various operational problems when shooting closeups:

1. Restricted depth of field, which therefore requires critical focusing.
2. Handling difficulties with narrow-angle lenses.
3. Depth compression.
4. The distortions and camera shadowing hazards when using close wide-angle lenses.
5. The difficulties in framing and following close movements.

Sometimes you will need to pan over closeup detail on a large flat surface (map or photograph). Then you must avoid the geometric distortions (keystoning) of a close short-focus (wide-angle) lens, or the restricted focused depth of a long-focus (narrow-angle) lens. It is best to move the lens parallel to the surface by trucking (crabbing) past it; with a long mural this is the only successful solution.

Deep-focus techniques

As you saw earlier, the *depth of field* in a scene varies with the lens *f*-stop, lens angle, and focused distance. You can change it by altering any of these parameters.

Stopping the lens down (e.g. *f*/11), everything from foreground to far distance appears sharply focused. The cameraman has no problems in following focus and there is little danger of subjects becoming soft focused. There is an illusion of spaciousness and depth; enabling shots to be composed with subjects at various distances from the camera. (But higher light levels are necessary.)

One weakness of this technique is that where there is little camera movement or few progressively distant planes in the picture, it can appear unattractively flat. Surfaces or subjects at very different distances can merge or become confused. *Too much* may be sharply and distractingly visible.

Shallow-focus techniques

Using a wider lens aperture (e.g. *f*/2) restricts focused depth. It enables you to *isolate* a subject spatially, keeping it sharp within blurred surroundings; and avoids the distraction of irrelevant subjects. You can

Fig. 4.3. Varying the length of shot
1. *Dollying:* Forward dollying can offer a gradual build-up of interest or tension, the importance of the subject growing progressively. Dollying back allows interest, tension or importance to be released gradually. The change can be made imperceptibly or fairly rapidly, the size and rate being controlled throughout. (Zooming has a similar effect for many purposes.) Dollying avoids disruptive editing but can appear laborious when rapid viewpoint changes are needed.
2. *Cutting:* Cutting shock-excites, thrusting the second viewpoint forward forcefully. Cutting to closer shots helps to emphasize momentarily the subject's strength and importance, while cutting to longer shots tends to cause sudden drops in tension and subject-importance.
3. *Mixing* (dissolves): Mixing has something of the transitional smoothness of dollying while taking less time. It enables the viewer to interrelate two viewpoints more readily than cutting, but the double-exposure of slow mixes is highly distracting.

display a single sharply focused flower against a detailless background; concentrating attention on the bloom and suppressing the confusion of foliage. Sharply defined detail attracts the eye more readily than defocused areas.

By deliberately restricting depth of field, you can 'soften' obtrusive backgrounds, even if these are strongly patterned, so that people stand out from their surroundings.

On the other hand, restricted depth can prove embarrassing when essential details of a close object are badly defocused. The cameraman has the problem of continually refocusing to keep a close moving subject in focus. For instance close shots along a piano keyboard can demand

Table 4.1   Why change the lens angle?

To adjust framing	A slight change in lens angle:
	where you want to exclude (or include) certain foreground objects, and repositioning camera or subject would spoil proportions;
	where a normal lens would not provide the required shot size or framing, without repositioning the camera or subject.
For otherwise unobtainable shots	Using a narrow-angle (long-focus) lens:
	to shoot remotely situated subjects – where they are separated from the camera by uneven ground or inaccessible;
	where the camera is isolated – on a camera platform (tower), shooting through scenic openings;
	where the camera cannot be moved – static tripod, obstructions.
	Using a wider-angle (shorter-focus) lens:
	where the normal lens does not provide a wide enough shot – space restrictions;
	to maintain a reasonably close camera position (e.g. so talent can read *prompter*) yet still provide wider shots.
To adjust effective perspective	Altering lens angle and changing camera distance to maintain same subject size, alters relative subject/background proportions and effective distances (Table 4.3):
	using a wider-lens angle (short-focus lens) – enhances spatial impression, increases depth of field;
	using a narrower-lens angle (long-focus lens) – reduces spatial impression, compresses depth, e.g. bunching together a straggling procession.
Insufficient time to change camera distance	Altering apparent camera distance (shot size) by changing lens angle:
	during fast intercutting sequence;
	when camera repositioning would involve complicated moves.
To provide simpler or more reliable operations	Zooming in/out instead of dollying may produce smoother, easier changes in shot size (but perspective and handling effects change).
	Zooming provides rapid changes in image size more safely than fast dollying (for dramatic effect or to suddenly reveal detail).
	Zooming in/out on a flat subject is indistinguishable from dollying, but avoids focus-following problems.
	Lens angle changes can avoid close-up cameras coming into picture.
To increase production flexibility	Where dollying would distract talent or obscure action from audience.
	When using only one camera.
To produce distortion	For grotesque closeups; to flatten modeling.

considerable dexterity of the cameraman when following focus on quickly moving fingers. Where there are two or more subjects in shot, he may not be able to maintain sharp overall focus but have to split focus between them, or select one to focus on.

Occasionally, by changing focus between subjects at different distances (*pulling focus, throwing focus*), you can move the viewer's attention from one to another; however, this trick easily becomes disturbing unless coordinated with action. Blurred color pictures can be frustrating. Whereas in monochrome defocused planes merge, in color the viewer may find himself trying to decipher unsharp detail and the effect can be less acceptable.

Fig. 4.4   The problem of limited depth of field
Where depth of field proves too *limited* (1), the solutions are:
2. *Stop down* – depth of field increases, but higher light intensity necessary.
3. *Focus on one subject* – permitting other(s) to soften.'
4. *Split focus* – spread available depth between both subjects (both are now softer than optimum).
5. *Move subjects closer together* – making subjects more equidistant from camera.
6. *Use wider lens angle* – depth of field increases but subjects now appear smaller. (Moving closer for larger image, re-introduces limited depth.)
7. *Pull camera back* – depth increases but shot is smaller.

Moving the camera head

In everyday life, we respond to situations by making particular gestures or movements. These reactions and actions often become very closely associated. We look around with curiosity; move in to inspect an object; withdraw or avert our eyes from a situation that we find embarrassing, distastful or boring.

It is not surprising to find, therefore, that certain *camera movements* can evoke associated responses in our audience; causing them to have particular feelings towards what they see on the screen. And these effects underly the impact of persuasive camera techniques.

Panning the camera

Panning shows us the spatial relationship between two subjects or areas. Cutting between two viewpoints does not provide the same sense of continuity or extent. When panning over a wide arc, the intermediate parts of the scene connect together in our minds, helping us to orientate ourselves. We develop an impression of space. But avoid panning across irrelevant areas – such as the 'dead' space between two widely separated people.

Panning should be smooth; neither jerking into action nor juddering to a halt. Erratic or hesitant panning irritates. With a correctly adjusted panning head (suitable drag/friction) and a properly stanced cameraman, such unevenness usually occurs only when using very narrow lens angles or where a subject makes an unpredicted move.

■ *The following pan* This is the commonest camera movement. The camera pans as it follows a moving subject.

In longer shots the viewer becomes aware of the interrelationship

Fig. 4.5   Focus techniques
Deep focus (top illustrations) provides overall clarity. This technique allows the cameraman to compose in depth and also accommodate close shots of three-dimensional subjects. *Shallow focus* (bottom illustrations) isolates subjects from distracting or confusing backgrounds, softens off unwanted detail.

between the subject and its surroundings. Visual interaction can develop between the subject and its apparently moving background pattern, creating a dynamic mutual impact (*dynamic composition*).

In closer shots, the background becomes incidental; often indecipherably blurred.

■ *The surveying pan* Here the camera slowly searches the scene (a crowd, a landscape), allowing the audience to look around at choice. It can be a restful anticipatory action; providing there is something worth seeing. It is not enough to pan hopefully.

The move can be dramatic, with high expectancy – the ship-wrecked survivor scans the horizon, sees a ship . . . but will it notice him? But the surveying pan can build to an anticlimax too; the fugitive searches to see if he is being followed . . . and finds that his 'pursuer' is a friendly hound.

■ *The interrupted pan* This pan is a long smooth movement, that is suddenly stopped (sometimes reversed) to provide visual contrast. It is normally used to link a series of isolated subjects. In a dance spectacle, the camera might follow a solo dancer from one group to the next, pausing awhile at each as it becomes the new center of interest.

The technique has comic applications: the camera follows a bunch of sailors. They pass a pretty girl. The camera stops in mid-pan to watch her. One sailor comes running back and grimaces to the camera, beckoning it to hurry and catch them up.

In a dramatic application: escaping prisoners slowly stagger over treacherous marshland. One man falls exhausted, but the camera stays with the rest. A moment later it stops and pans back – to see only the last traces of the straggler remain.

■ *Panning speed* A slow prolonged pan can create opportunities or disappointments, according to how it is used. If the camera pans slowly over a series of objects that are increasingly interesting or significant, the movement will continually hold our attention; even build up to a climax. But a slow pan around without any real points of interest, will quickly pall, as the viewer's initial expectancy falls.

■ *The whip pan* A *fast* pan may produce nothing but a series of broken-up, half-seen images due to stroboscopic effects. But a *whip pan* (*swish, zip, blur pan*) turns so rapidly from one subject to the next, that the intermediate scene becomes a brief streaking blur.

Fig. 4.6   Pulling focus
As the subject turns his head to welcome a newcomer, the camera refocuses.

Fig. 4.7   Slow panning
To provide a dramatic development.
Panning slowly from the sleeping
victim . . . along the intruder's shadow
. . . then a rapid upward-tilt, revealing
the intruder's identity.

Whether the effect arouses excitement or annoyance, largely rests on how the preceding and following shots are developed. As our attention is dragged rapidly to the next shot, it gives it transitory importance.

The *whip pan* usually produces a dynamic relational or comparative change:

1. *Joining different viewpoints of the same scene* – The pan *direction* should be compatible with the location of these viewpoints i.e. panning right to a viewpoint located to camera right.
2. *Providing continuity of interest* – Connecting a series of similar subjects or themes.
3. *Changing centers of attention* – From one area of concentration to another e.g. a golfer drives . . . we whip pan to the awaiting hole.
4. *Showing cause and effect* – A whip pan from a cannon . . . to the demolished castle wall.
5. *Comparing or contrasting* – Relating situations e.g. wealth with poverty, old and new.
6. *Transferring in filmic time and space* – An aircraft takes off . . . whip pan to it landing at the destination.
7. *Dramatic change of direction* – Changing the viewpoint with a sudden climax e.g. the camera subjectively scans the distance, we hear a noise and it whip pans to see an intruder behind, about to attack.

A whip pan continues the pace between two rapidly moving scenes. It can provide a tempo-bridge between a slow scene and a fast one. But at all times it remains something of a stunt.

A whip pan has to be *accurate* as well as appropriate, to be successful; no fumbling, reframing, refocusing at the end of the pan! To avoid such problems, the effect may be cheated by intercutting a brief shot of 'blur' between two static cameras' shots.

Tilting the camera head

Tilting, like panning, enables you to visually connect subjects or areas that are spaced apart, and would otherwise require intercut shots or a more distant viewpoint to encompass them. This technique can be used:

1. To emphasize *height or depth* – tilting up from the mountaineer, . . . to show the steep cliff face to be climbed.
2. To denote *relationships* – as the camera tilts from the rooftop watcher

Fig. 4.8   The impact of viewpoint
Viewpoint immediately influences our response to the sleeping old man.   1. Drunk?
2. Quiet contemplation?   3. Lonely? Deserted?

. . . down to his victim in the street below; or from the victim . . . up to the rooftop, revealing that he is not alone.

Fundamentally, *tilting upward* creates feelings of rising interest and emotion, expectancy, hope, anticipation. Conversely, *tilting downward* is allied to lowering interest and emotion, disappointment, sadness, critical inspection.

Where the viewer is conditioned beforehand by dialogue or action, responses become more complex. The *downward* tilt can become an act of enquiry; the upward tilt, a gesture of despair. Again, where a subject no longer holds our interest, the relief of a downward tilt can produce an anticipatory feeling – although the movement is not itself anticipatory.

In practice, of course, you will not stop to hypothesize about each camera movement. You come to recognize the 'feel' of such treatment. In a dramatic situation, for example: A woman hears of her son's death, and the camera *tilts down* with her, as she sits. This treatment conveys her grief more convincingly than either a static shot or a depressed viewpoint.

Camera height

The angle from which you shoot a subject can have a considerable influence on the audience's attitude towards it. Intercut high and low angle shots of a person, demonstrate this immediately. In a drama you may deliberately choose the camera's height to emphasize or diminish a

Fig. 4.9 part 1 Level shots
A normal viewpoint, usually around chest height; carries no special significance. Camera height: 1.2–1.8 m (4–5 ft) for a standing person, 1.1 m (3½ ft) for a sitting person.

Fig. 4.9 part 2 Low shots
Low angle shots make most subjects appear stronger, more imposing, overpowering, strange, ominous. A person can seem threatening, pompous, authoritative, determined, dignified, benevolent, according to his attitude and environment. Dialogue and movement become significant and dramatic. The closer we are, the stronger these impressions. In a very-low-angle shot, the subject takes on a strangely distorted, even mystical, appearance. At greater distances, it appears remote and unknown.

Fig. 4.9 part 3 High shots
High angle shots give the audience a sense of strength or superiority, an air of tolerance, even condescension, towards the subject; this feeling increases with distance. Therefore high shots can be used to imply unimportance, inferiority, impotence, etc. Very high angle shots give an attitude of peering down, scrutinizing. From a height of 3–6 m (10–20 ft) surveillance gives way to complete detachment. Overhead shots emphasize pattern and movement in formation (as in ballet and dance spectacle). Reveal isolation or congestion.

person's dramatic strength, or to control the impact of dialogue. Similarly, if you shoot a piece of sculpture from a low viewpoint, it will appear imposing, forceful and impressive; while shot from above it loses vitality and significance.

How you get that viewpoint is immaterial. Shooting an architect's miniature/model of land development, for example, you could equally well obtain an overhead view from a crane shot, a suspended camera, a mirror shot, or by attaching the subject vertically to the studio wall and shooting straight on to it. The effect is the same, although in some cases camera movement will be very restricted.

■ *Extreme camera angles* Extreme angles have an unhappy knack of drawing attention to the abnormality or ingenuity of the camera's position. If our audience is left wondering how we got that shot, mechanics have intruded over artistic purpose. Similarly, during the now familiar swooping and climbing of helicopter shots, the viewer can become overaware of wind-beaten grass or tell-tale shadows of the aircraft on the ground below.

Fig. 4.10   Verticals in overhead shots
In overhead shots, the position of the camera relative to strong verticals in the scene can considerably affect shot impact. 1. Verticals at the bottom of the frame cause tension and instability.   2. This impression is absent where foreground verticals are at the top of the frame.

Where extreme angles arise *naturally*, viewers accept them readily: looking down from an upper storey window; looking up from a seated position; even an eavesdropper peering through plank flooring to the room below. But an unexplained extreme usually becomes a visual stunt; for example: a bird's-eye view of a prisoner pacing a ceilingless cell, or shooting up through glass floors.

■ *Emotional impact of extreme viewpoints* As you have seen, while *high shots* generally create an audience-strength/subject-weakness relationship, low shots reverse this influence. But the associations are often much more subtle than that. Imagine a high-angle shot of an old man trudging through rainswept streets. The audience does not feel 'strength' or 'superiority', but pities him, or feels sorry for his loneliness. But these are, of course, psychological variations on the fundamental theme of 'viewer-strength/subject-weakness' that the high shot provides.

In a very high angle shot, the viewer has an overall view; in fact, more than people on the spot. This underlying response colors their attitude to what they are seeing.

Fig. 4.11 Dollying (tracking)
Moving to or from the subject. *Dollying in* causes increased interest, build-up of tension, but the closer view may result in disappointment, disillusionment and, consequently, diminished interest. Dollying back results in lowered interest, relaxed tension; unless unseen subjects are revealed, or when curiosity, expectation, or hope have been aroused. Attention tends to be directed towards the edges of the picture. Rapid dollying is visually exciting, but space and safe speed restrict fast moves. (Controlled zooming may produce allied effects.) Dollying (like subject movement to and from camera) appears faster than it really is, on a wide-angle lens, and slower on a narrower lens angle.

In an *aerial view* we survey the extent of the landscape; we follow the course of a river, seeing houses clustered along its banks, and its toy-like boats. We feel remote, seeing it all at a glance. We see the searchers moving towards the hiding fugitive. We see the magnitude of the invading army. But there is emotional detachment in this inspectional viewpoint; none of the involvement of more normal camera positions. Dynamics are reduced. Some subjects, such as high-wire acts, juggling, balancing feats, can lose their appeal entirely if shot from above, whereas a very low angle position emphasizes their difficulty and suspense.

■ *Portraiture*   The camera's height modifies what people look like, too. *Elevated shots* (especially on wide-angle lenses) emphasize baldness and plumpness in women; also through fore-shortening and distortion, they can produce a dumpy sawn-off effect.

Low-angle shots can emphasize dilated nostrils, upturned or large noses, heavy jawlines, and scrawny necks. Men with high foreheads or receding hair may look entirely bald. Protruding ears may appear very prominent.

Moving the camera

How freely you can move the camera around is determined by the type of mounting used. Whereas a crane boom shot offers considerable flexibility, it may not be able to relocate the viewpoint as rapidly as a highly mobile pedestal. Well-chosen camera moves add visual interest and vitality, as well as engendering certain audience reactions. The intermovement of planes (parallactic changes) that takes place as the camera moves, provides an illusion of solidity and depth; a realness that no static zooming camera can achieve.

But camera movement needs to be motivated, appropriate, smoothly controlled, and at a suitable speed, or it can become restless and disturbing.

■ *Prominence of camera movement*   The effects of camera movement are most prominent when shooting a static subject. Movement impact is correspondingly lessened where the camera moves with the subject; e.g. following it in a *tail-away shot* as the subject moves away; or dollying out as the subject approaches the camera in a *head-on shot*. And if respective

Fig. 4.12 Trucking (crabbing)
Moving across the scene, parallel with it. Trucking becomes associated with an attitude of inspection, critical observation, expectancy, intolerant appraisal. The lateral displacement of planes (parallactic movement) introduces a strong illusion of depth and solidity, but the restriction of the picture's frame becomes over-apparent if trucking stops abruptly.

Fig. 4.13 part 1   Craning from a static dolly
1. When craning up from level, audience response is elation, superiority, eventual detachment as height increases; while the subject becomes less significant, even unimportant.
2. When craning down from level, the response is depression, inferiority, even a feeling of being dominated; and the subject becomes more important, impressive, significant.
3. Craning down from an elevated height with superior viewpoint will produce an effect of return to normality, with some sense of depression.
4. Craning up from low-level to level produces the same effect, but with a slight feeling of elation.

direction and speeds match in a *traveling shot*, the dynamic effect of movement will come largely from the passing background. Whenever camera and subject are heading toward or away from each other, the overall impression is considerably heightened.

■ *Move the camera – or the subject?* There are intrinsic differences between the effects of moving the *camera*, or moving the *subject*. You can see this by watching a mute TV screen in a darkened room. You will feel your peephole vision moved around, almost physically, as the moving camera *subjectively* examines the scene. Where the camera is static, the performers will seem to move to and from you; an *objective* effect.

Camera movement (or zooming) becomes 'our behavior' by proxy, towards the subject. *We* the audience are moving; going up to look at or meet the subject . . . to satisfy our curiosity or to see detail more clearly. Forward camera movement is strong and exploratory; while dollying back is usually a weak move.

When a performer moves towards or away from the camera, we the audience become recipients of 'his attitude towards us'. Our reactions to his move largely depend upon his demeanour; whether his action is forceful or casual. Circumstances may alter situations – we may experience an 'audience superiority' effect as someone walks the length of

Fig. 4.13 part 2   Craning from a moving dolly
1. Forwards and craning upwards creates an air of freedom, flight, lack of restriction, elevation, joy.
2. Dollying forwards and craning down, implies swooping, power, strength, importance relative to subject when fast; but when done slowly suggests depression, return to normality.
3. Dollying back and craning upwards gives a feeling of complete release; detachment from the subject or action.
4. Dollying back and craning down is a recessive move, often saddening disillusioning; a return to earth; no longer detached from subject or action.

a corridor to meet us, but 'inferiority' if they sit while we (the camera) have to move up to meet them.

Subjective treatment

Subjective camera movement creates a participatory effect for the audience. But if a director moves us when we do not want to do so, or fails to show us something we wish to see, we feel resentful or frustrated. The skilled director persuades his audience to want a change in viewpoint, or a move. The unskilled director thrusts it upon them.

Fig. 4.14   Arcing
1. Circling round a subject to see it from a different viewpoint, tends to be a self-conscious move, drawing attention to the action. Spurious side-slip effects can arise.
2. Slight position changes can help when one performer masks (obscures) another.

Fig. 4.15   Camera and subject movement
Someone enters a room (in long shot) and crosses to a table (arriving in close-up). There are two methods of single-camera treatment, each providing a different audience impact.
1. The entrance and walk are taken in long shot. When the subject has stopped, the camera dollies in to close-up.
2. The camera pans and trucks throughout the walk, with subject and camera arriving simultaneously in a close-up.

Table 4.2   Production uses of lens angles

About 50°	The widest lens angle generally used in the studio.
	Used for wide shots at close camera distances.
	Used to exaggerate setting size, space, distance, scale.
	Exaggerates dolly movements and speed.
	Exaggerates performer movements to and from the camera.
	Used to frame fast on erratically moving subjects.
	Facilitates very smooth camera handling.
	Provides considerable depth of field.
	Provides deliberate grotesque geometric (barrel) distortion – e.g. of CU faces, forward arm movements.
	But camera is liable to *overshoot* (*shoot-off*), and gets lens flares.
About 35°	Frequently used for close shots of small objects, but camera shadows may arise.
	Noticeable increase in spatial impressions, without the exaggeration of wider lens angles.
	Generally emphasizes dolly movements and speed.
	Provides easy camera handling.
	Depth of field facilitates easy focusing.
	Appreciable camera movement may be necessary to correct framing.
About 25°	The 'normal' lens angle, used for most purposes and providing natural perspective,
	A generally effective lens angle for good camera handling.
	Generally convenient working distances for floor title cards and closer views.
	Focusing and available depth of field suitable for longer shots (deep focus). Yet close-ups provide sufficient depth for most subjects, with background defocusing providing isolation.
About 15°	Useful narrow angle for 'close shots' from a distance – whether due to subject inaccessibility, or preventing other cameras coming in shot.
	Isolates individuals from a group.
	Noticeable compression of depth and perspective distortion.
	Camera handling is not easy.
	The lens angle is only really suitable for slight dolly movements.
	Depth of field is somewhat restricted.
About 10°	Achieves close-ups from around 3.5 m (11½ ft) but depth compression is considerable.
	Very 'compressed' perspective.
	Depth of field is very limited for close shots.
	Camera handling becomes coarse; needs skilled operation, even for limited movements.
	Movement of close subjects is often hard to follow accurately.
About 5°	Used for static close shots on a distant camera.
	Considerable depth compression.
	Mainly suitable for flat subjects, where perspective distortion is absent.
	Most unsuitable for close-ups of people, because of extreme perspective distortion.
	Camera handling is extremely coarse.
	Subject movement is very difficult to follow.
	Depth of field is extremely limited.

Focal lengths (mm)

Approx. Angle	Camera tube size 12.5mm ½ in	18mm ⅔ in	25mm 1 in	30mm 1¼ in
50°	7.5	10	15	17
35°	10	14	20	27
25°	15	20	30	38
15°	25	33	50	62
10°	37	50	75	94
5°	75	100	150	188

Fig. 4.16 part 1   Following the subject – long shot throughout
Audience impact comes chiefly from the moving environment; subject importance being limited. The pace of action is relatively slow. Varying composition or tone during the pan, can produce emotional changes – e.g. the 'uplift' on panning from low to high key. Sudden mood changes are achieved by, for example, having the actor raise window blind to let in daylight, or switching room lights.

Fig. 4.16 part 2   Following the subject – close shot throughout
The subject dominates, its strength depending on camera height. The influence of the environment is limited, and pace varies with dynamic composition. Slightly off-centering the subject in the direction of movement creates a feeling of anticipation, extectancy.
1. Profile – weak against a plain background, but an impression of speed and urgency against a detailed background.
2. Three-quarter frontal – can be dramatically strong. By preventing us from seeing the subject's route or destination, marked curiosity can be encouraged.
3. Elevated frontal – although himself weakened, the subject dominates his environment.
4. Depressed frontal – the subject is especially forceful, dominating his environment.
Rear shots introduce a subjective effect
5. Three-quarter-rear – partially subjective; the viewer moves with the subject expectancy developing during movement.
6. High rear shot – almost entirely subjective; produced increased anticipation; searching.
7, 8. In level and low shots there is a striking sense of depth. The subject is strongly linked to the setting and other people, yet remains separated from them.

Fig. 4.16 part 3   Following the subject – long shot to close-up
The subject walks up to the camera. Environment predominates at first, but the subject grows increasingly stronger as it approaches. The impact can be modified by dollying or zooming as the subject approaches.

Fig. 4.16 part 4   Following the subject – close-up to long shot
A weak, recessive movement, generally accompanied by lowering tension as the subject's strength falls and that of the environment increases. Used to depict pathos, anticlimax.

1   2

Fig. 4.16 part 5   Following the subject – then arriving at his destination before him
1. The camera moves more quickly than the subject, to his destination – the quickening pace providing an exciting introduction to the new position; but it must be sustained to be effective. The shot shows spatial relationships and gives the viewer time to assimilate the destination before the subject arrives.
2. Here the person begins to move, you cut to his destination, and he then arrives. Often mechanically convenient, the cut gives the destination shot impact. Audience-superiority can arise through foreknowledge of the subject's destination, and provide pathos, bathos, stage irony, climatic effects. It avoids lengthy dollying shots, and can imply non-existent spatial relationships. Irrelevant intermediate movement is eliminated and pseudo filmic time effect achieved, but interest and tension can flag while awaiting the subject.

Fig. 4.16 part 6   Following the subject – cutting from the static subject to his destination
A simple but weak treatment, unless dialogue or gesture has indicated that he is going to move. Spatial relationship or significance may not be clear to the viewer Static action cuts of this kind can make the viewer over-conscious of the time taken for the subject's move. On commenced-action cuts, as in part 5 above, this is less pronounced.

■ *Imitative camera movement*   Apart from the familiar ploy of moving cameras to suggest jogging vehicles or rolling ships, camera movements can provide subjective comments on the action itself. Staggering as it dollies after a drunk; copying the bounce of a dandy's gait; swaying in waltztime as we follow a girl home from her first dance.

Drawing attention to itself quite openly, the camera movement becomes a tongue-in-cheek observation between the director and his audience. When it comes off, this device has persuasive appeal.

Fig. 4.17   The canted shot
1. Canting is most pronounced with subjects inherently associated with horizontal or vertical stability. Left: slight slanting (about 10°) is ineffectual. Centre: typical tilt around 20–30° is used to convey instability, abnormality, dynamism. Right: excessively canted (50–60°) the effect is excessive overbalancing.
2. From low-angle (or high-angle) positions, canting causes subjects to lean into, or out of frame.

Using a zoom lens

As you saw in Chapter 3, the zoom lens brings both advantages and pitfalls for the unwary. It is too easy to use lens angles indiscriminately, just to change subject image size.

There is a great temptation to stand and zoom, rather than move around with a normal lens angle. It is an easy operation, demands little of the cameraman or director, and avoids problems such as keeping close cameras out of long shots. There is just the need for a prezoom focus check, before zooming in.

Zooming is extremely convenient. But it only simulates camera movement. There are no natural parallactic changes; and scale, distance, and shape become distorted through zooming. A slow zoom made during panning, tilting or subject movement may disguise these discrepancies. A rapid zoom during an exciting fast-moving ball game, would scarcely disturb even the pedant. Much depends on the occasion.

Fig. 4.18   The need to pre-focus
1. The considerable depth of field available with a wide lens angle broadens focusing, so that subjects may appear sharp although not at the focused plane.
2. However, on zooming in to a narrow lens angle (without re-focusing) depth of field becomes restricted, and the subject now falls outside the available depth of field.

Dollying

Zooming

Fig. 4.19 Comparing dollying and zooming
1. Dollying: When a camera moves through a scene, relative sizes and spacing of subjects change proportionately. This continual parallactic movement causes planes to become visible and disappear with position changes. Perspective remains constant.
2. Zooming: As the field of view alters with lens angle, the shot is simply enlarged or diminished. There is no parallactic movement, no planes appear/disapppear, or change relative proportions. So effective perspective appears to change (unless the viewer adjusts his viewing distance to compensate) and visible 'depth-stretching' or compression results.

Zooming can provide a visual bridge from the wide view to the close-up, without the time and effort involved in dollying or the interruption (and possible disorientation) of *cutting*. A *rapid zoom-in* produces a highly dramatic swoop onto the subject. An instant *crash (snap) zoom-in* flings subject detail at the audience. Such effects can be fantastically forceful – or plain annoying!

All zooming should be decisive. Avoid the nauseous results of rhythmical or jerky in-out zooms, or quick *slight* angular changes that look like an operational error.

Required Shot

1   2   3a   3b

Fig. 4.20 Adjusting proportions
Altering relative subject proportions in the picture can be achieved by changing to a different lens-angle and readjusting camera distance (see Fig. 3.10).
1. A distant narrow-angle lens provides the required subject/foreground proportions.
2. A closer position using a normal lens angle, shows required foreground proportions, but the subject appears too small.
3a. Dollying-in will correct the subject size but loses the foreground fence.
3b. Widening the lens angle now will bring the fence into shot again, but the subject image appears small and the subject-foreground distance increased.

Table 4.3   Adjustable picture proportions

Subject size	Background appears	Lens angle correction	Camera position
Too large	Too large*	Use wider lens angle (zoom out)	Keep camera still
Too small	Too small*	Use narrower lens angle (zoom in)	Keep camera still
Satisfactory	Too distant	Use narrower lens angle	Increase camera distance
Satisfactory	Too near	Use wider lens angle	Move camera closer
Too large	Satisfactory	Use narrower lens angle	Increase camera distance
Too small	Satisfactory	Use wider lens angle	Move camera closer

But relative subject/background proportions satisfactory.

Zooming on *flat surfaces* (maps, illustrations) avoids the need to *follow focus* that dollying would entail. On title cards you can produce carefully controlled size changes (titling growth or shrinkage) by zooming.

Use zoom-ins to direct attention, to increase tension, to give powerful emphasis, or to restrict the coverage. But the zooming action itself should be used discriminately for particular occasions – like wipes, star filters, diffusion discs, and similar productional tinsel. Certain effects, like that of zooming in and dollying back simultaneously (keeping the subject-size constant), are bewildering, to say the least!

5 Composing the picture

People have very diverse attitudes towards the study of pictorial composition. Some try to follow the 'laws' slavishly, with varying success; others use a few routine rules-of-thumb; others dismiss it with suspicion and arrange shots in a hit or miss fashion. Any meaningful study of pictorial composition must be realistically related to *practical working conditions*, and this is what experienced practitioners do.

A study of pictorial composition helps you to produce attractive significant pictures, that direct audience attention and influence their feelings about the subject and its surroundings. There are really three basic kinds of picture making in photography:

1. Composition by *design*.
2. Composition by *arrangement*.
3. Composition by *selection*.

Composition by design

This occurs where you have an *entirely free hand* in composing your picture. The artist approaching his blank canvas can arrange line, tone and color in any way he chooses, without concern for accuracy or feasibility. The physical limitations are minimal and are inherent in his medium.

Canaletto 'improved' his paintings of London by actually repositioning entire buildings for effect, whatever the resulting topographical errors. Only occasionally does this freedom exist for the camera (e.g. in process work).

Composition by arrangement

Here you *deliberately position subjects* before the camera to produce an appealing meaningful result. A set designer dressing a setting does this by placing furniture, flowers and ornaments to form appropriate arrangements. Sometimes even a single carefully introduced foreground object (a leafy branch perhaps), will help the cameraman to devise appropriate composition.

More usually, a designer creates *potential* rather than specific composition opportunities; an environmental package suiting the mood and mechanics of the occasion, rather than calculated composition arrangements.

There is always the danger when arranging natural situations, that the resultant effect will look deliberately contrived. You can become overaware of how 'cleverly' the picture has been manipulated.

Fig. 5.1   Why compose the picture?
The unguided eye wanders around the scene, finding its own centers of interest.

Composition by selection

This is the situation most cameramen encounter. The camera is positioned at a certain viewpoint chosen by the director (or the cameraman himself) and he composes the shot *using what is there*, to show the subject most effectively.

He can move his camera in three dimensions to select visual components. He adjusts shot size, camera height, moves slightly left/right, arranges framing, and perhaps selectively focusing.

As the camera is moved vertically or laterally, foreground subjects change frame position more markedly than others further away. By adjusting lens angle and distance he can modify proportions. In these ways, the cameraman composes his picture.

The director and composition

The director's attitude to pictorial composition varies between individuals, and with the type of production. For many shows, the director is so preoccupied with that what is being said, with performance, continuity and mechanics, that he does not arrange the composition of shots specifically. Instead, he indicates the shot size required (CU, singles, two shots, group shots) and leaves details of lens angle, framing, etc. to the cameraman.

In other types of production (primarily drama), the director deliberately groups actors to provide particular compositional arrangements – for dramatic effect, or to direct audience attention. In some cases , he (or the set designer) may have prepared a *storyboard sketch*, showing the detailed composition of certain *keyshots*.

Composition principles

Composition principles are not laws. They are indications of how people respond to distribution of line and tone. Whether you put that tone into the scene, or are selecting from whatever is already there, is not important. What *is* important, is that if you do not organize pictures appropriately, your audience may well react by looking at the wrong things, interpret the picture inappropriately, or become bored by unattractive shots. *Composing shots* is not just a matter of 'pictorial packaging', but a method of controlling continuity of thought.

The effect of the picture frame

The camera does much more than 'put a frame' round a segment of the scene. *It inherently modifies whatever it shows.* Because the screen *totally isolates* its subjects (the viewer cannot see whatever else is happening), and because the resultant picture is flat (and cannot reproduce stereoscopic depth) unique relationships develop within it, that are not present in the actual scene.

No shot directly portrays *reality*. In many cases our own experience enables us to rationalize and interpret, so that we make a pretty acccurate assessment of what we are seeing, e.g. a tourist photograph composed to make the Statue of Liberty rest on his outstretched hand . . . or is it a model after all? But this does not always happen; particularly where the viewer is not familiar with the situation.

The subjective effects that arise in the flat framed picture take several forms:

1. Although one plane may be some distance behind another, they can appear conjoined or even merge in the shot.
2. Spatially unrelated areas of tone and color are often juxtaposed in the picture; interacting and influencing pictorial balance. Simultaneous contrast effects result.
3. Seen in perspective on the flat screen, the shapes of objects and composition lines can change with camera angle.
4. A series of quite unrelated subjects at varying distances can combine pictorially to form a composition group.
5. Within the picture, *imaginary* composition relationships can seem to develop between subjects, and visual tensions form between them.
6. As subjects approach the edge of the screen, impressions of tension or compression can develop; particularly in screen-filling shots.
7. The lateral position of subjects influences their composition impact.
8. Various dynamic effects arise (dynamic composition).

Proportions

There are no formulae for beauty. But centuries ago, artists discovered a widely accepted principle guiding harmonic proportions – the Golden Section or Golden Mean. Great painters, sculptors, architects, have used these ratios in many ways (often unwittingly, perhaps) when expressing their concepts of beauty.

If you cut a straight line into equal parts providing the most pleasing relationship, you will find with incredible regularity that the line lengths are divided according to the Golden Section; in a constant ratio, so that the small part is to the larger, as the larger is to the whole. These proportions work out in practice to about 8:13 (often quoted as 3:5).

Such proportioning has quite far-reaching applications, for it gives us a guide to ratios that most readily please the eye. Be suspicious of such formulae; but see how often they seem to validate themselves.

■ *Rule of thirds* When composing a shot, you should avoid mechanically dividing the screen into regular sections. A screen cut into halves or quarters can produce a dull, monotonous balance.

You will find the 'rule of thirds' often advocated when selecting proportions. Main subjects are placed at the intersections of lines dividing the screen vertically and horizontally into three equal parts. A useful enough mechanical concept to guide in composing pictures, it should not be allowed overslavishly for it can develop a recognizable sameness.

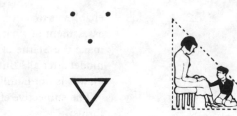

Fig. 5.2 part 1   Subjective lines
The mind tends to seek pattern and to see relationships, even where none really exist. Individual subjects seem to combine or interact to form patterns.

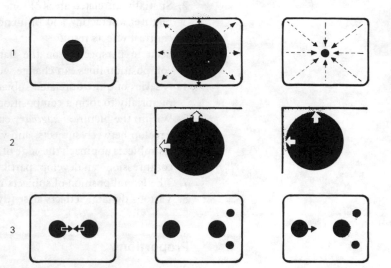

Fig. 5.2 part 2   Illusory attraction
1. A disc in the center of the frame appears at rest, surrounded by empty areas of equal tension. A change in subject size alters this reaction between the subject and its frame. An over-large subject bulges the frame, squeezing-out the surrounding space, while a too-small subject becomes compressed by the large area of empty space surrounding it.
2. This compression effect gives way to a forceful thrusting as the intermediate space lessens.
3. Tension is built up between subjects in a picture. The two close subjects convey a feeling of mutual interlinking – illusory attraction. In a more complex example, the isolated subject appears to be attracted towards the more stable supported group.

Fig. 5.3   Proportions
The Golden Section: Dividing for ideal proportions tends to produce YZ:XY in the same proportions as XY:XZ. Making several such divisions, a series appears, and this ratio of division, the Golden Section, is about 3:5. Dividing the frame: An equally divided frame allows only formal balance – usually dull and monotonous. Thirds can lead to quickly recognized mechanical proportions. Dividing the screen in a 2:3, or a 3:5 ratio achieves a far more pleasing balance.

Framing

As you frame or line up a shot, you are doing several important things:

1. First of all, you are choosing *exactly* what the viewer is going to see; what is to be included within the picture (*on-frame, in-frame*); and what is to be excluded from it (*off-frame, out-of-frame, out of shot*). You may be selecting to concentrate attention and avoid distractions, or to show more subject detail. You might omit information deliberately – or reveal it in another shot.
2. As you alter a shot's framing, you are repositioning line and tone within the picture, and modifying its audience impact.

All parts of the frame do not have equal pictorial value. The effect changes, depending on where you place the main subject.

How you frame a shot will not only alter composition balance, but can influence the viewer's interpretation of events. Framed in a certain way, a two-shot might lead him to expect someone is about to enter the room, or that an eavesdropper is outside a door.

Headroom changes proportionally with the length of shot; lessening as the shot tightens. But as there may be differing interpretations between

Fig. 5.4 part 1   Framing – frame positions
1. Center screen is generally the weakest area for holding the viewer's attention. Continual or sustained use of picture-center becomes monotonous.
2. Positions near frame edges seldom give good balance (particularly scenic lines running parallel with them). Frame corners exert an outward pull on subjects placed there. Subject strength and importance tends to increase higher in the frame and towards the right.

Fig. 5.4 part 2   Safety margins
As TV screen edges are usually masked off, avoid placing important action or titling near the frame edges. Some monitors and camera view-finders indicate the safe area (engraved, or from a special generator).

Fig. 5.4 part 3   Framing people
1. Avoid frame-cutting people at natural joints; as shown intermediate cutting–points appear more attractive. Similarly avoid framing so that they touch the screen edge as in 2.

Fig. 5.4 part 4   Relevant framing
Do not just frame the subject for an attractive effect, but to suit the program purpose.

Fig. 5.4 part 5   Tight framing
Close shots of people bring problems such as arm gestures, or explanatory items remaining unseen out of shot. Tight framing emphasizes the screen's confines. Head movements can pass out of frame, leaving it empty; thus requiring catch-up panning, which is a fidgety and obtrusive operation.

Fig. 5.4 part 6   Headroom
1. For good vertical balance, people should be framed with appropriate head-room (a). Avoid the cramping effect of insufficient headroom (b), or the bottom-heavy effect of excess (c).
2. Whether compositional elements become an incidental border, or oppressively overhang the action largely depends on how they are framed.

Fig. 5.4 part 7   Offset framing
For side or ¾ views, center-frame positions (a) provide an unattractive balance. Slight offsetting (b), sometimes referred to as 'looking room', is usually preferable; although this must not be overdone (c) unless you want to draw attention to that side of the frame, or imply isolation.
Horizontal framing can affect significance too. Notice when the door is included in the shot, someone's entry is expected (d).

cameramen, it as well for the director to check that comparable shots match.

Pictorial balance

For most purposes you will want *balanced* composition. Not the equal balance of formal symmetry, for that is uninteresting, but a picture with *equilibrium*.

Balance in a picture is affected by:

1. The *size* of a subject within the frame.
2. Its *tone*.
3. Its *position* within the frame.
4. The *interrelationship* of subjects in the shot.

Fig. 5.4 part 8   Reframing
As subjects leave or enter frame, the cameraman normally readjusts framing unobtrusively for the next situation. For dramatic purposes you may deliberately NOT reframe; the tension from the unbalance composition emphasizing the second subject's departure or absence.

Fig. 5.5 part 1   Adjusting balance
1. Balance pivots about the picture center.   2. Unbalanced shots are visually unstable and unattractive.   3. But formal *symmetrical* arrangements usually prove monotonous and uninteresting.   4. Certain compositional grouping has considerable stability, but must be correctly framed to appear balanced.   5. To reduce symmetry, you may *angle* subjects (avoiding head-on positions); (for balance can change with shape.   6. Or you can adjust relative *sizes* of subjects.   7. Altering the subjects relative *distances* from center-frame changes pictorial balance. (Try adjusting positions of cut-out card shapes.)   8. Isolation gives a subject weight. 9. By *grouping* individual subjects, they have greater collective 'weight'. (See unity.) 10. *Size and tone* combine to affect overall balance. Larger areas and darker tones should be framed carefully. Dark tones towards the top of the frame produce a strong downward thrust – top-heaviness, a depressed closed-in feeling. At the bottom of the frame, they provide a firm base for composition, lending it solidity.

Fig. 5.5 part 2   Changing balance
Balance and emphasis can be altered in several ways.   1. By changing the lens-angle (zooming) – size change.   2. By altering the camera-distance – proportions change.   3. Readjusting subject height.   4. Altering subject grouping. 5. Changing camera height.   6. Changing viewpoint – different tones, masses come into shot.   7. Lighting changes – altering tones or colors of areas.

Occasionally, the dynamic restlessness or tension of *deliberately unbalanced* arrangements is refreshing; but this should be used sparingly. Balance is not a fixed composition factor, and you can readjust it by moving a person, altering framing, etc., in order to redirect attention to another subject, or even alter the picture's import.

Pictorial balance is largely an instinctive choice, but we can detect useful guiding principles:

1. A center-frame position is satisfactory; safe but dull to watch.
2. As a subject moves from picture center, the shot feels progressively unbalanced.
3. This effect arises more strongly with bigger and/or darker objects; especially if high in the frame.
4. A subject or tonal mass to one side of the frame, usually requires compensatory counterbalancing in the remainder of the shot. This could be an equal opposite mass (symmetrical balance), or a series of smaller areas that together counter-balance the main offset region.
5. Tone influences visual *weight:* darker tone subjects look heavier and smaller than light-toned ones.
6. A small darker area slightly offset, can balance a larger light-toned one further from picture center.
7. Darker tones towards the top of the frame produce a strong downward thrust – top-heaviness, a depressed closed-in effect. At bottom frame they introduce stability and solidity.
8. Balance is more influenced by vertical elements than horizontals; although the overall horizontal effect determines the final balance.
9. Regularly shaped subjects have greater visual weight than irregular ones.
10. Warmer colors (red, orange) appear heavier than cooler ones (blue, green), bright (saturated) hues looking heavier than desaturated or darker ones.

■ *Unity (order)* Pictures must be unified to be effective. You should avoid randomness or scattering items around the frame. Instead, group them with real or imaginary composition lines to emphasize interrelationships. Similarly, between successive pictures in a scene there should be a unity of style, purpose, interest and mood. Where depth of

1   2   3

Fig. 5.6 Unity and order
Unity is cohesion, interrelationship of masses. 1. A picture can be balanced, yet not be unified, or (2) a group unified without overall balance. Real or imaginary compositional lines create visual unification. 3. Lines or tones that divide the screen disrupt unity.

Fig. 5.7   Visual rhythm
1. Pictorial arrangements can produce a monotonous repetitive effect, or interesting variety of emphasis in shape or tone; a visual rhythm.   2. While verticals and diagonals give an emphatic rhythm, horizontals and slow curves convey a restful rhythm.   3. Although identical repetition is dull, used as a progressive visual development, repetition can build and strengthen a theme.

field permits, you can compose *in depth*, unifying two or more planes of action in the foreground and distance.

■ *Visual rhythm*   In music and poetry the ear prefers a recognizable, but not too elementary, rhythmical beat; the eye also is attracted by a variety of pattern. *Visual rhythm* is a pattern term; a variation of visual emphasis, of outline. While a solemn quiet mood is suited by slow smooth flowing lines; a rapid spiky staccato would match an exciting dramatic situation.

Emotional influence of tone

The set designer and the lighting director use light and shade to create the picture's emotional key. Where light tones predominate, the effect is

Fig. 5.8 part 1   Tonal impressions
Sharply-defined tonal contrast (left) is used to isolate and define areas, suggest crispness, hardness, vitality, dynamism. *Graded tone* (right) blends areas together, guiding the eye from darker to lighter regions. It suggests softness, beauty, restfulness, vagueness, lack of vigor, mystery.

Fig. 5.8 part 2   Tonal emphasis
Tonal contrast emphasizes shape and mass. A small dark area becomes subjugated within a large white background, whereas a small light area stands prominently from a dark tone.

Fig. 5.8 part 3   Simultaneous contrast (spatial induction)
Adjacent tones interact. A light tone can make a nearby one look darker; while a dark area apparently lightens a light tone further. The same central tone here appears different as its background changes. The sharper the contrast and borders, the stronger this effect.

Fig. 5.9 Scale
The viewer judges scale subjectively; by how fully the subject fills the screen and by the presence of other objects of known size. If size-references are omitted (absent or obscured by viewpoint) accurate interpretation of scale may be impossible.

cheerful, delicate, airy, open, simple, and weak. Predominantly dark tones create a heavy, somber, sordid, forceful, dignified, or significant impact. When relieved by smaller distinct light areas, the effect tends to become mysterious, solemn, grave or dramatic.

A picture with an overabundance of dark tones does not televise well. Large areas of unrelieved dark or light values, that contain little tonal contrast, can be disappointingly dull and uninteresting. Large, well-marked areas of contrasting tone give a picture strength, vigor, significance. A light tone, relieved by small distinct areas, conveys liveliness and delicacy.

Scale

Scale is concerned with the apparent size relationships a picture conveys. An audience judges how large, how distant, how high, etc., by interpreting a series of visual clues:

1. By comparison of the surroundings with the subject's known real-life size.
2. By comparing the subject shown with adjacent subjects of known size.
3. According to how much of the picture frame is filled by the subject.
4. By relating to perspective clues in the shot.

Subject prominence

Inappropriately presented, a subject can lose strength, importance or vitality. It may even become overlooked or lost within its environment.

The subject's *surroundings* have a considerable influence on its

Fig. 5.10 Foreground and scale
Foregrounds influence our impression of scale and distance; particularly for isolated and remote subjects. Try to include foreground and perspective clues to define and unify depth; but avoid over-emphasized, stylized, and artificial relationships.

prominence, and on our attitude towards it. Consider the difference between a coin imposingly displayed on velvet . . . or heaped with others in a rusty junk box.

Subject isolation gives emphasis. Some of this emphasis stems from the subject's tone relative to its surroundings, or lighting treatment. But compositionally you can influence subject prominence in various ways: according to your camera height, shot size, framing, background form, differential focusing and spatial separation from other subjects.

Fig. 5.11 part 1   How subject strength is influenced by viewpoint
1. Unsuitably arranged, a subject's strength is diminished.   2. Low-angle shots emphasize subject strength and importance; while high-angle shots suggest weakness, unimportance.   3. Subject-strength grows as the shot gets closer.

Fig. 5.11 part 2   Subject strength – frame position
Set higher in the frame, the subject gains strength.

Fig. 5.11 part 3   Subject strength – size proportions
Relative proportions of subject size and surroundings will affect the subject's 'power'.

Fig. 5.11 part 4   Surroundings influence subject strength
1. A supported subject appears weaker than an unsupported one.   2. A subject can be dominated by dynamic scenic lines, or by other stronger subjects. 3. Background line and tone can strengthen or weaken the subject.

Subject attitude

A performer's associative attitudes can modify his effective strength, whether he looks forceful, cowed, submissive.

His general *posture* is significant, too. *Weak attitudes* include side or rear views, lying down, looking down, bowed, stooping, clasped hands, and slow movements. *Strong attitudes* include frontal view, uptilted head, hands clenched, stamping feet, and fast movement.

Camera treatment can have a considerable influence on our reactions to a subject. Shooting a ranting dictator in a high-angle long shot would make his gestures appear futile, weak, and ineffective. However, a low-angle mid-shot would give them a powerfully dramatic force.

Where you use a strong camera treatment for weak performance attitudes, you strengthen them; so that an old woman making weak submissive gestures could seem to have a dignity, and an inner strength against adversity when shot from a depressed viewpoint.

Picture shape

A picture's shape can affect the viewer's feelings towards the scene. A *horizontal* format can give it stability, restfulness, extent . . . A *vertical* format can imply height, balance, hope . . .

The original motion picture screen shape (aspect ratio) had 4:3 (1.33:1) proportions. But subsequently, to enhance big-screen presentation, several others were developed (1.65 to 2.55:1). Television adopted the original 4:3 format; and while this cannot be intrinsically altered, you can change its *effective shape* by introducing mattes (wipes), masks, scenic restriction or by lighting restriction.

Fig. 5.12   Picture shape
The effective picture shape can be modified by (1) electronic wipes, camera mattes (vignettes); or (2) by using a scenic opening as a border; or (3) by restricted lighting.

Unifying interest

You should normally arrange a picture so that the eye can find satisfaction within the frame; concentrating on certain features, while the rest become a subordinate background. Avoid three-ring circus techniques, with several things happening simultaneously. They divide attention, creating ambiguity and confusion. One picture – one focal point.

Unifying the center of interest does not prevent you moving it around freely. This continual flow, linking together parts of the picture, is often termed *transition* or *continuity*. The eye moves naturally from one area to the next.

Speed of composition lines

The eye scans some shapes at a leisurely rate (gently curved lines), while others are appreciated quickly (straight lines, zig-zags). Through suitable selection, you can adjust the picture's vitality and the speed with which the eye examines it. Faster lines move attention quickly and would allow fast intercutting.

Simple lines and shapes direct attention more readily than complex or disjointed ones. Interest is strongly attracted by clear-cut geometrical shapes, particularly when they seem to arise accidentally. An excess of simple line soon palls though, and leads to a stark unsympathetic atmosphere.

Fig. 5.13   Split interest
Aim to localize interest. Avoid split centers of attention, except for dramatic purposes.

Continuity of centers of interest

Although our eyes continually move around the picture, we usually find that interest is localized at any given moment to about one-twelfth of the screen area. You can divide the 4 by 3 frame into twelve equal segments.

Where successive centers of interest are widely spaced, the viewer's concentration must be disrupted to some extent while he seeks each new spot. Fast interlinking composition lines help here. This situation particularly arises, of course, whenever you cut to another shot. If the new picture presents an entirely different interest location, the audience becomes overaware of the transition; so the points should be reasonably matched.

Poorly matched transitions, especially between numerous brief duration shots, can accelerate mild audience resentment into marked hostility. This situation arises all too regularly where editors demonstrate their prowess by rapid cutting to the beat of fast music. Even if synchronism is perfect, inept matching of centers of interest (often with too little time to examine each shot) becomes totally frustrating.

Composition continuity in multicamera production

A regular problem in multicamera production, is that a composition set-up that looks great from one viewpoint, may be quite disappointing from

Fig. 5.14   Speed of compositional lines
1. A pattern or direction-of-line over which the eye lingers is termed 'slow'. Predominating curved lines suggest leisure, beauty, deliberation.   2. 'Fast' lines are usually straight or angular, creating an impression of speed and vitality. 3. Unbroken lines are faster than broken ones.   4. Direction of movement will affect 'speed'; the first three directions being generally faster than the remaining four directions.

another. Various weaknesses can arise: the new picture may lack cohesion, unity or balance. It may remain attractively composed but inept; laying wrong emphasis, perhaps.

Although these difficulties may only be slight where the set-ups are simple or haphazard, for more elaborate situations some anticipation is necessary.

There are several ways of coping with this situation:

1. You might dwell on the compositionally effective shot; accepting the weakness of others.

Fig. 5.15   Related shots
The compositional arrangements and action can move the eye about the picture. On cutting to another shot, a new center of interest presents itself. If the centers are too dissimilar, as in the first pair of illustrations, the viewer becomes over-aware of the change. But where reasonably matched, the transition may be almost unnoticed.

Fig. 5.16   Movement of interest
Good visual continuity between shots does not necessitate static arrangements. Composition and action can introduce unlimited interest-movement, providing successive shots match at the transition.

Fig. 5.17   Cross-cut shots
1. If successive pictures are matched accurately, some visual confusion can arise when inter-switching between cameras.   2. Where alternative foci are continually being intercut, it may be less disturbing to space (offset) centers of interest.

2. In *discontinuous* shooting you could rearrange (*cheat*) people's positions, set dressing, lighting, for each new camera set-up. This is time consuming and can cause continuity errors, but provides optimum results.
3. You may arrange the subjects so that they suit all the required angles (as in interviews).
4. Performers can be repositioned at the moment of transition to a new camera; e.g. having delivered a line, the actor turns away . . . on the cut.
5. You can recompose the first shot shortly before the transition, to suit the next shot's composition.

Fig. 5.18   Care in grouping
Cameras shooting actuality, have to select from available grouping. But by attention to people's positions a wider range of shots becomes possible. 1. People must normally work closer together than in everyday life, to avoid widely spaced shots. 2. Where close spacing is inappropriate, cross-shooting groups them. 3. Although parallel face-to-face conversation may seem more natural, slight angling improves shot-opportunity.   4. Similarly, closed groups are better opened up.

Fig. 5.19 part 1   Continuity of composition – two shot
The subject can be arranged to provide appropriate composition from several viewpoints.

Color and picture

Most of us take color for granted. We accept that a surface is a particular shade of green, for example. But in fact, what we are interpreting as 'green' can vary considerably: with the color of the light falling on the surface, its angle, any other nearby color, and various other factors.

■ *Surface effects*   The color of a smooth surface generally looks 'purer' (more saturated) than a rough-textured one of identical color; its brightness too, will change more noticeably with the light direction. The color of a surface can seem to vary with the quality of the incidental light, appearing

Fig. 5.19 part 2   Continuity of composition – three shot
Although composition continuity becomes more difficult with larger groups, a variety of shots is available with careful grouping.

Fig. 5.20   The influence of viewpoint
The viewer's feelings about the subjects, their environment and their relationship to it, can be modified according to the viewpoint selected for the camera.

brighter and more saturated under hard light, than under diffused lighting. A color surface may reflect light onto a nearby subject – so the face of a person wearing a yellow sweater may be tinged yellow by its reflected light.

■ *Fine color detail*   Our eyes cannot readily detect fine detail in color. Where a scene contains tiny areas of color (whether small patterns or distant subjects), these will seem to get paler as they grow smaller. The actual color of fine detail can become difficult to identify. Yellow, for instance, tends to become indistinguishable from light gray, and blue detail can become confused with dark gray. Similarly, bright areas of green, blue-green and blue appear identical when very small. Eventually as detail size diminishes, even strong reds and blue-greens become indistinguishable, so that you can only detect differences in brightness between them.

■ *Warm and cold colors*   When looking at colors, you will often find yourself unconsciously attributing 'temperature' and 'distance' to particular hues. Red, yellow and brown seem 'warm', and areas of these colors tend to look bigger and nearer than the 'cool' hues such as blue and green. You will find too, that darker and more saturated colors seem nearer than lighter or desaturated ones.

Subjectively, the pictorial 'weight' of a color is often affected by its 'warmth': warmer tones seem heavier than cooler ones, saturated colors look heavier than duller desaturated ones. For these reasons, it is desirable when composing masses in a picture, to keep areas of saturated color small, for they can easily balance much larger ones of desaturated color.

■ *Simultaneous color contrast (lateral color adaptation)*   The appearance of any color can be considerably affected by the background against which it appears; an effect known as *simultaneous contrast*. A green dress against gray drapes will not only look greener than normal, but the gray background itself may tend to take on the complementary hue (magenta) and appear 'warmer'. If you place a white object in white surroundings, and illuminate it with both

Fig. 5.21   Representing movement
Symbols can represent many different dynamic situations – the subjects, their direction, and their path within the TV frame.

white and magenta light, its shadow appears to be green! Clearly, the eye and the brain can play strange tricks!

The same turquoise object may look lighter, darker, bluer, greener, according to its background colors. When a strong color appears against a pale version of the same hue, the background seems grayer. A strong color will appear more vibrant when backed by white, than against black. Conversely, a darker color is more pronounced against a black background. Any color will look brightest and strongest against its complementary color.

Even *neutral tonal values* (white, grays, black) are modified by their background. The darker the background, the lighter will the subject tones appear to be (and vice versa). Light tonal areas look larger. Darker tones look heavier. All these factors can strongly influence our impressions of size, distance and pictorial balance.

■ *Separation of color*   Although color surfaces may in reality be some distance away from each other, they can appear adjacent when seen together within the shot. So there is a mutual interaction between them.

Fig. 5.22   Gravity
There is a tendency to interpret movement within the picture as if gravity were always involved. So in these illustrations movement is seen as: 1. Normal progress. 2. Moving uphill; climbing.   3. Moving downhill; descending.   4. Rising. 5. Falling. Such movement is regarded as difficult, easy, forceful, weak, etc.

■ *Bright colors* Bright colors hold the attention – particularly scarlets, bright yellows and orange. But their prominence can become embarrassing when they are defocused, for the eye turns to them, yet cannot see detail there. Pastel (desaturated) hues do not pose this problem – but they on the other hand can lack vigor and visual appeal if widely used.

Where there are reasonably equal areas of strong color, a disharmonious tension can develop between them, particularly where they are not complementary. So it is preferable to have one or more of them desaturated (i.e. grayed-off, less vivid).

■ *Approximate color constancy* This illusory effect continually influences our evaluation of color. We experience it when looking at a picture containing a familiar subject of known color – a mailbox, perhaps. Having fixed on this item, we go on to judge other colors in the picture accordingly. Even where the reproduced color of this subject is considerably different from that of the real thing, the brain adjusts its interpretation, so that we are pre-disposed to see it as 'correct'; perhaps regarding others nearby as inaccurate, although they are actually satisfactory.

All interpretation is subjective. We regularly misinterpret as 'white', areas that in reality are quite blue or yellow. Blue puddles on the sidewalk may look unnatural, although they truly reflect a blue sky. A 'black' object in bright sunlight may actually be reflecting more light than a dimly illuminated 'white' – although our brain, making a comparative judgement, refuses to believe this.

■ *After images* After looking at a color for some time, you will often experience a brief color 'hang-over' on switching to the next shot.

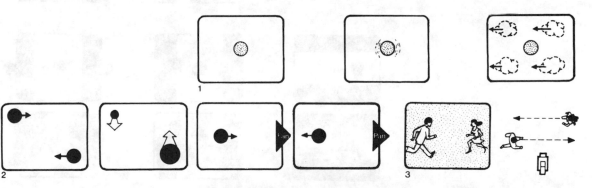

Fig, 5.23   The impression of movement
1. The interpretation largely depends on framing, and the apparent speed of other subjects and background. Firmly framed against a plain background, there is no sense of movement. If the subject's position wavers and it is known to be moving, the movement is assumed to be so fast as to be difficult to follow. Add signs of a background racing past (e.g. aircraft in clouds) and the sense of movement and speed grows considerably.   2. To this there can be added four general axioms. Movement across the screen tends to appear exaggeratedly fast. Movement to or from the lens seems slower for narrow-angle, faster for wide-angle lenses. Camera movement in the direction of subject movement reduces its speed. Camera and subject moving in opposite directions increase their mutual speed and impact. 3. The flat screen can cause the viewer to misinterpret spatial movements. On camera the people seem to be running to meet – but the plan view shows otherwise!

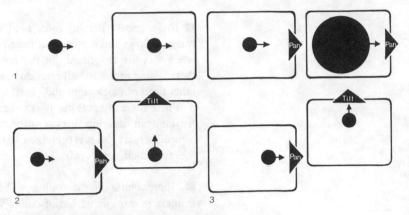

Fig. 5.24   Restriction of movement by the frame
1. Movement in free space is interpreted as having unrestricted freedom. But once a frame is placed around the subject, freedom is relative to these limits. There is potential restriction. Where the moving subject is held near center-frame, this restriction is not excessive. But close shots must always be cramped.   2. Restriction becomes less when the subject is kept near the lagging edge of the frame. 3. Restriction is emphasized when kept near the leading edge.

Fig. 5.25   Restriction of movement by masses
The shape and position of masses (moving or still) in the picture can alter the interpretation of events.   1. The mass in the path of the moving subject suggests imminent impact or arrest.   2. Converging, encircling, crushing, as when a crowd presses in on a central figure.   3. Expansion, new freedom, isolation, as when using an iris-out wipe. Even complicated situations can be arranged to emerge quite naturally.   4. The restricted feeling aroused by the traveler moving at dusk between darkened sky and ground.   5. The compression effect as the camera pans left (following the pursuer), and the wall moving frame-right create a pincers compression movement towards the distant victim.   6. As the camera dollies down the alley, the distant light area grows – creating an expansive effect.

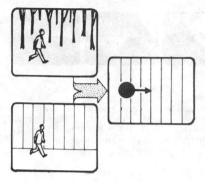

Fig. 5.26   Background patterns
As subjects move past them, background patterns can exert strong effects upon picture impact.

Fig. 5.27   Background and subject movement
Where movement is in the direction of background pattern, the movement will appear unimpeded if slightly restricted. The line emphasizes direction. Where the subject moves across (against) the pattern, effort is emphasized; movement appears stronger. Subject shape may modify these effects.

Fig. 5.28   Moving background and subject 'strength'
Against a plain background, the effect of this low-angle shot remains constant as the subject walks and the camera dollies back. But if a series of horizontals move downwards (crossboards in a ceiling) during the move, it is considerably strengthened.

Following exposure to red, you will see a blue-green (cyan) ghostly after-image on a black screen. After orange, a peacock-blue after-image follows. Yellow gives blue; green gives purple (magenta); while after blue an orange-yellow image is seen.

Bearing this in mind, you would expect some interaction between a succession of colors. Such *successive contrast* causes white to appear bluish-green after looking at a red screen. Similarly, yellow appears bright green; blue appears more intense and greenish; while repeated red has a grayed appearance.

Admittedly, these are extreme situations, but color distortion on quick cuts and the visual fatigue that follows overexposure to a strong color are not to be disregarded.

■ *Color associations*   Color and emotion are inextricably inter-linked. Color associations are legion. For example:

Red – with warmth, anger, crudity, excitement, power, strength.
Green – with spring, macabre, freshness.
Yellow – with sunlight, the Orient, treachery, brilliance.
White – with snow, delicacy, purity, cold.

Dynamic composition

Where you have static or semi-static shots, long-established composition principles clearly apply. But television and film are *dynamic media*. Therefore, it is essential that the distinctions between the still and the moving picture are understood; a study that may be termed *dynamic composition*.

Potentials of the still picture

The *still picture* has the particular advantage that we can study its details at leisure; concentrating on the aspects that attract our interest. A moving picture allows us only a limited time to examine the picture (the shot duration), before another shot replaces it.

Paradoxically, a frozen-action shot may have a stronger more sustained impact than the movement seen in real time, e.g. a boxer falling from a knock-out punch. Realizing this, some directors have introduced brief *freeze frames* or slow-motion sequences during powerful action, to savor and emphasize the dynamics.

This indefinable feeling of 'suspended animation about to recommence' is the underlying appeal of many great paintings and sculptures. A composition balance that is so forceful in a still version, would often be impossible to maintain or even ineffectual in a moving form.

Action that is intriguing when seen in a fragmentary glimpse, can appear commonplace when carried to its natural conclusion. Hence the production techniques of cutting between brief shots of uncompleted

Fig. 5.29   Background and direction
1. When the subject moves across a static patterned background, the viewer feels an undertow of movement. Where the subject is held in frame and the background passes the direction of this undertow changes.   2. As the subject moves over the upward-sweeping background, an upward force seems to be exerted on the subject. In addition, background tones modify its apparent size and importance.

action, or fading before a sequence has logically concluded are often used. This method is normally employed at a climax, where a continuing shot would result in an anticlimax.

A shot that is well composed while it is *still*, may become less pleasing when movement rearranges its component parts.

Potentials of the moving picture

The moving (or movable) picture has certain properties that the static shot lacks. It can depict *change*. You can modify the picture as the audience watches; altering subject prominence, redirecting attention, introducing or removing information, modifying the mood. You can convey directly the dynamics of movement, variation, growth, development, etc.

The moving picture offers *continued interest*; unlike the still picture whose attraction usually diminishes quite quickly. Movement attracts. It gives the director the opportunity to maintain interest in the subject aspects *he* intends, by presenting continually changing stimuli.

However, you must not forget that while the still picture allows the viewer freedom to scrutinize and assess, the moving picture often gives him time only to grasp essentials; particularly if action is fast or brief. You have to take care not to build resentment as you snatch one shot away and replace it with the next. Much will depend on the pace and complexity of information; and a sophisticated or informed audience can actually welcome brief segmentized dynamics.

Fig. 5.30   Speed
The subject's shape can affect its apparent speed. 1. Although moving at the same speed the 'tall' object appears to be moving faster than 'flat' object.   2. The apparent speed is also increased as the background becomes more detailed. Shot-size will modify how much of the background is visible and hence effective speed-impact.

Fig. 5.31   Rhythm
Visual rhythm from the passing background will seldom be as regular as these examples, although quite strong rhythmical patterns can be built up naturally from passing flags, trees, palings, etc.

A theory of dynamic composition

We evaluate movement in everyday life, by making a series of comparative assessments. We judge a subject's rate of progress relative to its surroundings and to other subjects. We interpret evaluate relative displacements. This happens when we watch pictures too, but the confining frame and the two-dimensional images impose further influences on our judgment.

Whether we see movement *directly* (the subject traveling within a static scene), or deduce it through secondary effects (passing background, light or shadows passing over it) our interpretation is at best very subjective and conditioned by previous experience.

Our impressions of picture dynamics are influenced by a number of often irrelevant factors:

1. We compare the apparent *relative speeds* of subjects within the picture.

Fig. 5.32 part 1   Patterns of movement
Some movement patterns have widely accepted associative feelings.   1. Continuity.   2. Vigor; excitement, indecision.   3. Beauty, charm.   4. Expansion. 5. Contraction, collapse. *Smooth* action suggests control, evenness, simplicity; while *jerky* irregular motion suggests the clumsy, erratic, uncontrollable.

Fig. 5.32 part 2   Patterns of movement
In massed dance and marching, the viewer sees simple pattern formations from group movement, and individual movements.

Fig. 5.33 The dynamic effect of tone
The effective strength of static and moving masses varies with tone. 1. When a dark subject moves through converging dark areas, the mutual impact is powerful. 2. The 'crushing' effect is lightweight against a heavy substantial subject. 3. The *apparently* larger but lightweight subject suggests less resistance to approaching forces. There is a hint of destruction. 4. Both subject and approaching forces are lightweight, so the effect is less dynamic than in the first example. 5. Dynamic pursuit. 6. Ineffectual pursuit of strong subject. 7. Annihilation of vulnerable subject. 8. Undramatic. Following rather than pursuing.

2. The amount of *border* (space) round a moving subject alters our impression of speed.

3. Where there are several movements in the picture, we often associate the movement pattern with *compression* (impact, collision), or *expansion* (parting, stretching, strain).

4. We judge a movement's *strength* or *speed* according to the apparent size, power, or force, that seems to be involved.

5. We subconsciously relate the position and movement of a subject within the frame to *gravity effects*, even where there are no actual gravitational relationships.

6. The visual impact of movement can depend on where we happen to fix our attention in the shot. Looking skyward, we see moving clouds and static buildings – or static clouds and toppling buildings.

7. The sounds accompanying a picture often influence our interpretations of speed.

8. The impact of movement may be greater in slow motion than at normal speed.

Accepted maxims

You see the principles of dynamic composition applied daily; and from experience, some excellent widely accepted working axioms have emerged.

■ *Direction of movement* Like vertical lines, vertical movement is stronger than horizontal, which is the least arresting.

A left-right move is stronger than a right-left action.

A rising action is stronger than a downward one. Hence a rise from a

Fig. 5.34   Changing visual significance
The visual significance or strength of a subject can be modified by altering its
appearance (e.g. by lighting), position or size in frame, or its background.   1. The
upward movement and higher position strengthens the left-hand person.   2. Striped
object is approaching. At first it is insignificant, but with increasing size, its
importance and interest exceed that of the static subject.   3. As the subject passes
from the dark background to the light one, there is an emotional uplift.   4. Passing
from a region of restrictive verticals to a plain background produces a sense of
freedom, and an effective speed change (fast to slow).   5. As the shot cants off the
horizontal, pictorial balance becomes unstable.   6. The camera tilts upwards, and
the verticals in this background converge into diagonals.

Fig. 5.35   Dynamic effects between pictures
Seeing a rapid succession of shots (still or moving), the viewer subconsciously compares or contrasts them.   1. Cutting between scenes with similar movement-form or shape, emphasizes this effect.   2. The vigorous verticals of one scene contrasts effectively with the restful horizontals of the next.   3. The successive size differences here produce expansive jumps.

seated position has greater attraction than a downward sitting movement.
An upward move generally looks faster than a horizontal one.

■ *Diagonal movement*   Like diagonal lines, this is the most dynamic movement direction.

■ *Movement towards the camera*   All forward gestures or movements are more powerful than recessive action away from the camera: a glance, a turned head, a pointing hand. Similarly, a shot moving towards a subject (dolly/zoom in) arouses greater interest than one withdrawing from it (dolly back/zoom out).

Fig. 5.36   Area of interest
1. Sloping to the right, the eye tends to favor the distance and so run out of frame.   2. With the reverse slope, the eye tends to favor the foreground.

Fig. 5.37   Concentration of interest
1. Placed on the left, the window is just part of the scene; the foreground person dominates. When on the right, the viewer anticipates important action through the window; the person becomes less important.   2. The viewer is very conscious of the watcher on the right, but only half-aware of his victims. Placed on the left, the watcher is nearly overlooked, attention focusing on his victims.

Table 5.1   Lateral reversal effects

Pictorial balance	Subjects tend to look heavier (affecting balance more markedly) on frame *right*. So frame left can support more weight (i.e. greater density or mass) than right. A predominant mass on frame right can make the picture unbalanced or lopsided. The space between subject and left frame may appear excessive where masses predominate on frame right.
Pictorial stability	The picture may look more stable one way round than another; dormant in one version – but dynamic when reversed.
Apparent proportions	Large dark foreground areas on frame right may produce a crowded, shut-in, or heavy feeling; while the reverse gives a more open impression.
Subject strength	A composition element that seems unimportant when located on the left, can become obtrusive on frame right (although the reverse seldom holds). A subject overlooked on left frame may become compositionally or dramatically significant on the right.
Area of interest	Our reaction to diagonal lines can vary with their slope direction. So our attention center can be directed in depth within the scene.
Concentration of interest	The eye tends to wander towards frame right (even with a predominant frame left subject). Where strong subjects are positioned frame right, left-hand subject may go almost unregarded.
Picture significance	Part of the scene may take on an implied significance in a mirrored version.
Visual interpretation	Our interpretation of what is happening or what the picture depicts, may be modified by left-right disposition.
Direction of slope	A down-slope to the right tends to be interpreted as downhill; and an up-slope as uphill. This influences how difficult or forceful lateral movements along such slopes appear to be as they move in an 'uphill' or 'downhill' version. Similarly, a vertical object leaning or falling to the right tends to 'fall forward,' rather than backward.

Where someone moves in front of another person (or scenery) they attract more attention than when moving behind them. Avoid such cross-moves in shots closer than mid-shot.

■ *Continuity of movement* While a moving subject attracts attention more readily than a static one, continuous movement at constant speed does not maintain maximum interest. Where action is momentarily interrupted or changes direction, the impact is greater than one carried straight through. Converging movements are usually more forceful than expanding ones.

Mirror images

If you look at any collection of photographs direct and then in a mirror, you invariably find a difference in the appeal of the two versions. Differences may be great or slight; but they do modify the picture's impact.

Fig. 5.38   Direction of slope
Direction of the slope can alter a picture's attractiveness, there being a tendency for version 1 to seem more dynamic than 2.

Fig. 5.39   Examples of combined effects
Several aspects of right-handedness can appear simultaneously.

The various effects that arise regularly through 'right-handedness' in composition treatment can influence which way round you arrange your picture to suit any particular purpose.

6 Editing

In television production you will meet editing in three forms:

1. Real-time video switching (vision mixing).
2. Post-production videotape editing (Chapter 12).
3. Film editing (Chapter 11).

Although these processes are quite different, the *artistic effects* of editing in each can be identical.

The nature of editing

In purely *mechanical* terms, editing is concerned with:

1. The *moment* you choose to change from one shot to another (the *cutting point*).
2. *How* you make that change (*cut, mix,* etc.), and the *speed* of this transition.
3. The *order of shots* (*sequence*), and their *duration* (*cutting rhythm*).
4. Maintaining good picture and audio *continuity*. Combining action that was shot at different times and places, perhaps by a single camera.

At a purely *practical* level, editing allows you to create a smooth-flowing picture development. You can omit moments that are irrelevant, or distracting, or contain errors. You can shorten or lengthen the duration of action.

Editing overcomes mechanical problems. If a subject is just about to move out of shot . . . you can cut to a new viewpoint, and show the action continuing, apparently uninterrupted. Editing can bridge space and time.

Artistically, the potentials of editing are far-reaching. Editing decisions have a direct influence on how your audience responds to the program material; their interpretation, their emotional reactions.

Even where it is possible to shoot action in one continuous unbroken take, it is often preferable to introduce changes in camera position, shot coverage, composition, or to interrupt action. By doing so, you can influence audience response, change dramatic impact.

1. Editing can shift the centre of interest, redirect attention to another aspect of the subject or the scene.
2. Editing can emphasize, or hold back information.
3. Editing is selective. The order and duration of shots can affect how an audience interprets and reacts to them.
4. Editing can give an audience a sense of freedom: of being able to move rapidly in space and time. It can juxtapose events occurring at quite different times and places.

107

5. Editing can create interrelationships – that may or may not have existed.
6. Editing can change the entire significance of an action in an instant – to create tension, humor, horror . . .

Editing and the TV director

In *film making*, a specialist editor and his assistants are responsible for the mechanics and techniques of the editing process; submitting the product for the director's critical appraisal in review. From the rough-cut, the final fine-cut version is developed.

In most TV shows, the director does his own editing – either making spontaneous decisions, or working to a detailed script. He may operate the *production switcher* (*vision mixer*) himself. But usually a *technical director* or specialist *switcher* (*vision mixer*) operates the equipment under his instruction. For multi-camera productions, most of the inter-shot switching is completed 'on the hoof' during the original recording.

Post-production VT editing mainly involves: joining separate 'takes', inserting corrections, cutting overmatter. During VT editing, video effects may also be added, and audio sweetening carried out.

Whether a director works from a marked-up camera script showing all his planned intershot transitions; arranges editing during rehearsal; or makes spontaneous decisions during taping, largely depends on the type of program.

Watching the preview picture monitors continuously showing his various video sources, the director selects at the required moment, switching the chosen sources onto line (transmission, main channel, studio output). The shots may have been planned precisely, approximately, or offered up by the cameramen and modified as necessary. Prerecorded film or videotape contributions are either totally inserted on cue, or excerpted from pre-arranged sections.

Each preview monitor *continually* displays all the pictures from its particular source. Not only the shots that have been set up ready to be switched to line (transmission), but the endless random pictures. So a bank of monitors will show off-shot cameras moving into position, film channels running up to their next cue, graphics being set up, lighting adjustments, VT shuttling through . . . With this background, the director is busy concentrating on the sources of the moment, guiding the production team, instructing, correcting, selecting, coordinating their work. All this is in addition to checking performance, keeping on schedule, and coping with various contingencies. It is little wonder that under these conditions, 'editing' can degenerate into mechanical switching!

Television editing techniques

As videotape recording developed, various production methods became possible that were quite impracticable during *live* transmissions. The elaboration of these techniques depends largely upon the sophistication of the videotape editing facilities available. Several production processes are widely used:

■ *Live on tape* The program is recorded continuously in its entirety, as if it were a live transmission. The videotape is used here as a straightforward recording medium to provide more convenient scheduling of facilities and transmission, repeat transmissions, later analysis, etc. All editing is carried out on the studio production switcher during performance, and the show is ready for transmission at the conclusion of the recording session.

■ *Basic retakes* Here the production is recorded continuously as for transmission, but any errors (performers, production, technical) are re-recorded and the corrected sections substituted. *Duration trimming* may require some editing cuts – often covered by introducing *cutaways/nod shots/reaction shots*. As most programs can be improved by such editing, this method is widely used.

■ *Discontinuous recording* The show may be taped in a series of sequences or scenes, each retaken as necessary to correct or improve. These *takes* can be shortened, action removed, or their order changed. Sometimes several versions are shot; the preferred one being selected later. The production switcher is used for most intershot transitions.
   During later videotape editing, sections (containing their own intrinsic editing) are dubbed off in their final order to form an edited composite tape. Further audio treatment (audio sweetening) can be added at this stage (background music, audio effects) from unsynchronized audio disc or tape. Various video effects may be introduced during postproduction editing (wipes, multi-images, color synthesizer treatment, detail insertions, etc.).

■ *Single-source recording* Here each camera's output is separately recorded on its own dedicated videotape recorder (VTR). No production switcher is used during recording; all transitions and selections being made during a postproduction dubbing session to form a composite tape.
   Videotape editing is carried out using complex computer-controlled facilities incorporating digital editing techniques, storage (cart, or video disc), all guided by time-code shot identification. As a one-hour program may involve 300–400 individual edits, the operation clearly requires systematic organization of sophisticated postproduction facilities.

Types of editing

Three types of editing are widely used that rely on the audience interpreting the interrelationship of successive shots: continuity cutting, relational cutting, and dynamic cutting.

Continuity cutting

In *film editing*, the editor may spend considerable time and thought in deciding on the final shot order, the exact cutting points, cutting rhythm, etc. Although this is possible with more sophisticated VT editing systems, time usually precludes this precision.

In most TV productions editing is simplistic, serving the practical purpose of interrelating viewpoints, creating a feeling of consecutiveness and order, interlinking dialogue and action. At best, the technique provides a clear straightforward narrative, a smooth pictorial flow, and unobtrusive transitions. At worst, such *continuity cutting* becomes a purely functional routine.

Example:
Mr. Brown speaks – cut to CU of Brown.
Mr. Smith speaks – cut to CU of Smith.
Anchorman speaks – cut to three-shot of group.

Relational cutting

Here through intercutting, shots that have no direct connection in reality, are deliberately given an implied relationship.

Examples:
Woman seen walking up to house, *cut* to woman in a room. We assume she entered house, and is now in a room there. (Actually shot with different women in similar costume, at different locations.)
Shot of aircraft in flight, cut to pilot at controls. (A library model shot has been intercut with a studio mock-up. Neither is real).
Man approaches foot of stairs, *cut* to him coming upstairs. (Action may have been shot on different occasions.)

In *parallel cutting* (*parallel action*), shots from two different locations or action groups are repeatedly intercut; usually as a dramatic development to heighten tension, e.g. fast intercutting between fugitive and pursuers. *Cross-cutting*, on the other hand, intercuts between different viewpoints of the same subject, usually for visual variety.

Whenever you join two shots together by a *cut*, you immediately establish a relationship between them. This juxtaposition is both *physical* and *intellectual*.

Physically, the viewer's eyes become aware of the change, and begin tracing a fresh interest pattern in the new picture.

Intellectually, the viewer has to interpret the new picture. (Where are we now? What is this? What is happening?).

These responses are, of course, interrelated. Where the shots are compositionally matched (matched cuts) and the significance of the second shot obvious, it will be a *smooth cut*.

Where shots are pictorially unmatched (jump cut, mismatched cut) the effect can be very disturbing, as the audience has to search around for the subject in the new shot. Similarly, their attention is disrupted if they do not instantly realize how the second shot relates to the first, or what it is all about.

Dynamic cutting

Sophisticated intercutting can create dramatic emphasis, convey moods or abstract ideas that are not readily expressed in more direct terms. The ideas themselves may not be implicit in the component shots. Cause-effect relationships are often interpreted.

Examples:
Shot of broken window, *cut* to small boy crying. (A lost ball? Punished after breaking the window?)
Intercut shots symbolically suggesting 'Spring', 'Progress', 'Terror', etc.

The cut

Fig. 6.1 The cut
The mechanics of picture transitions can be shown graphically. Here the *cut* (straight cut, flat cut) is shown – from one shot or scene to another.

The cut is the simplest transition. It is dynamic, instantly associating two situations. Sudden change has a more powerful audience impact than a gradual one, and here lies the cut's strength.

Cutting, like all production treatment, should be purposeful. An unmotivated cut interrupts continuity and can create false relationships between shots. Cutting is not akin to repositioning the eyes as we glance around a scene, for we move our eyes with a full knowledge of our surroundings and always remain correctly orientated. On the screen, we know only what the camera shows us; although guesses or previous knowledge may fill out the environment in our minds.

Cutting jumps attention between new viewpoints or locations, so the viewer has continually to relocate and interpret each new shot. This is a problem during fast intercutting between different locations.

Where quite dissimilar shots are intercut, your audience may have

Fig. 6.2 Intercut shots of the same subject
1. Avoid cutting between similar or near-similar shots. 2. Extreme changes in shot size (e.g. over 5:1) are distracting, unless explained by dialogue or story-line (See Fig. 15.1). 3. Viewpoint angle cuts of less than 20° or over 60° can be visually disturbing.

Fig. 6.3   Visual continuity
1. The viewer can lose sense of direction where there are dissimilar backgrounds.   2. This is unlikely to happen where there is background continuity, or (3) compositional links between pictures.

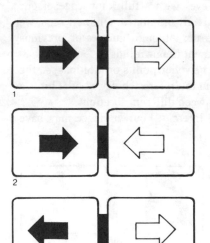

Fig. 6.4   Cutting between moving pictures
Cuts during movement create strong subjective effects.   1. *Directional* cuts between subjects moving in the same direction, suggests continuity of action or direction, pursuit, similar purpose.   2. *Reverse cuts* between opposite directions can suggest converging forces, impending meeting or collision, or (3) diverging forces, parting, expansion.

some difficulty in appreciating continuity or relationships. But you can establish an immediate connection through:

1. *Dialogue* – introducing or implying the next shot's substance.
2. *Action* – establishing a cause–effect relationship.
3. *Common reference points* (a person) in both shots.
4. *Audio continuity*.

Occasionally, and *only* occasionally, you may want to mislead the viewer's continuity deliberately for a comic or dramatic purpose.

Where a quick viewpoint change seems obtrusive, it has usually not been clearly *related*, and has not fulfilled the *purposes* outlined earlier. It is a change that the viewer has no reason to want or expect. Unmotivated changes rarely satisfy.

It is generally inadvisable to intercut between shots of widely differing size (LS to BCU), or over a wide angle unless the attention is tightly localized.

■ *The movement for the cut*   Cuts should preferably be made on an *action* or *reaction* – turning head, gasp of astonishment, a rise. However, there are two philosophies about the moment to make the cut. Some editors contend that the cutting moment should be *just before* or *after* an action. A transition during a movement can disrupt it and create a spurious cutting rhythm. Others maintain that by cutting *during* a movement you avoid the illusion of its being jerked into action or suddenly halted (from an in-motion shot, to a static one). Where the aim is to transfer attention rather than create a visual shock, the cut can be hidden within action, as the audience is preoccupied with the movement itself.

■ *The delayed cut*   A *late* cut is frustrating. Badly timed, it has missed the optimum moment for change. But the *delayed cut* has exciting possibilities. It deliberately withholds the new shot until after the expected moment – in order to create audience suspense, interest, and anticipation. Example:

1. *Cutting on a reaction:*
   Knock at door. Writer looks up –
   CUT – Door opens. Woman enters. 'May I come in?'
2. *Delaying the cut:*
   Knock at door. Writer looks up. Door heard opening.
   Woman's voice, 'May I come in?'
   CUT – To woman at door, who enters.

■ *Cutting between moving pictures*   When moving shots are intercut, you invariably create spatial interactions between them, even where none exists. Intercutting such shots suggests:

1. Moving together (meeting, collision).
2. Moving apart (parting, expansion).
3. Moving in the same direction (following, chasing, similar destination).

To avoid these effects, cutaway shots or intermediate movement directions (to or from camera) can be introduced. Where the viewer is watching a single moving subject, any direction changes should be obvious or deducible. Otherwise he will see distracting direction-jumps or may lose orientation.

■ *Cutting between static and moving pictures* Cutting from a static scene to a moving one, suddenly accelerates audience interest. The new shot springs into action; its speed, energy or violence being accentuated by its sudden appearance.

Cutting from a moving scene to a static shot, causes a sudden collapse in tension; which, if unsatisfied, can lead to a rapid fall-off in interest. Or it can produce a highly dramatic interruption. For example panning with a searcher around an empty room . . . and then CUT − to a static shot of someone watching his actions.

■ *Cut to begin or end action* These devices must be used with caution. They can too easily look like operational errors!

The cut in: a shock introduction to vigorous action, catastrophy, chaos.

The cut out: a severe, definite conclusive action as you cut to a blank screen at the end of a shot. An emphatic gesture or comment, of finality.

The fade

■ *The fade in* This provides a quiet introduction to action. A slow fade-in suggests the forming of an idea. A fast fade-in has rather less vitality and shock value than the cut.

■ *The fade out* A quick fade-out has rather less finality and suspense than the cut-out. A slow fade-out is a peaceful cessation of action.

■ *The fade out-in* Linking two sequences, the fade out-in introduces a pause in the flow of action. Mood and pace vary with their relative speeds and the pause time between them. You can use this transition to connect slow-tempo sequences, where a change in time or place is involved. Between two fast-moving scenes it may act as a momentary pause, emphasizing the activity of the second shot.

Fig. 6.5   Avoiding directional reversal
Where a subject appears in successive shots showing movement in opposite directions, you can avoid accidental subjective effects by introducing an intermediate buffer shot showing a head-on view (perhaps including the actual change in direction).

Fig. 6.6 part 1   Matched and mismatched cutting
Mismatching on cutting can take several forms, but in each case results in visual disruption.   1. Height changes – mismatched lens-heights (for no dramatic purpose).   2. Headroom changes – mismatched headroom.   3. Size jumps – instantaneous growth or shrinkage occurs if subject size changes only slightly on the cut (e.g. a–b, or b–c). A difference of at least a–c (4:3 previous size) is desirable.   4. Transformations – if too closely matched, the viewer may see 'magical transformations' on the cut!

Fig. 6.6 part 2   Matched and mismatched cutting
1. Jump cuts – if the same subject is included in successive shots, it may jump frame-position on the cut – a common dilemma in table shots.   2. It can arise also in group shots. Cameras A–B or A–C intercut, but not B–C.   3. Twists – a slight difference in the viewpoint, can produce a turn or twist on cutting. Hopefully, the disruption may be disguised by 'motivating' the change (e.g. a singer turns to face the new camera), or by a slow dissolve.   4. Continuity matching – when shooting *discontinuously*, you must match shot detail and action for each cut, during editing; e.g. the moment of turning a knob, opening a door, lifting a glass. Otherwise continuity is disrupted.

Fig. 6.7   Rediscovery on a cut
Camera 1 pans, following the action. The black pillar passes out of shot (frame left).
Cut to Camera 2 (to prevent shooting off) and the pillar is rediscovered on frame right
again! A similar situation arises when someone who has just entered a shot is seen,
after a cut, to re-enter the next.

A cut-out/cut-in with a pause between shots is valueless. It always looks
like a lost shot – or a mistake.

The mix (dissolve, lap dissolve)

The *mix* is produced by fading out one picture, while fading in the next.
The two images are momentarily superimposed; the first gradually
disappears being replaced by the second.

Mixing between shots provides a smooth restful transition, with
minimum interruption of the visual flow (except when a confusing
intermixture is used).

A *quick-mix* usually implies that their action is concurrent (parallel
action).

A *slow-mix* suggests differences in time or place.

Mixes are generally comparative:

1. Pointing similarities or differences.
2. Comparing time (especially time passing).
3. Comparing space or position (mixing a series of shots showing
   progress).
4. Helping to relate areas visually (when transferring attention from the
   whole subject to a localized part)

Mixes are widely used as 'softened-off' cuts, to provide an unobtrusive
transition for slow-tempo occasions where the violence of a cut would be
disruptive. Unfortunately, they are used also to hide an absence of
motivation when changing to a new shot!

Fig. 6.8 part 1   The cut-in   **Fig. 6.8 part 2   The cut-out**

Fig. 6.9   The fade-in and fade-out
1. Fast fade-in.   2. Slow fade-in.   3. Fast fade-out.   4. Slow fade-out. The fade-out and fade-in may be combined in permutation (slow-out, fast-in etc.) to link two shots producing a fade out-in.

A very slow mix produces sustained intermingled images that can be tediously confusing. Between different viewpoints of the same subject, they result in twin images.

■ *Matched dissolves*   By mixing between carefully matched shots with similarly framed subjects, you can obtain a transformation effect. Its main applications are to suggest time changes (boy to man, seasonal change), or *flashbacks* (reversed time), or magical changes (pumpkin to Cinderella's coach).

■ *Mixes on movement*   Mixes during movement are usually only completely satisfactory when their relative directions are similar. Mixing opposite directions can arouse feelings of confusion, impact or expansion, without necessarily indicating that these subjects are involved. But it is a transition to be used cautiously.

■ *Defocus dissolve*   The first camera gradually defocuses, while you mix to a second completely defocused shot which then sharpens. Normally used for *flashbacks*, but sometimes introduced for transformation effects, or decorative interscene transitions.

Fig. 6.10   Combinations of fade and cut
1. The cut/fade-in results in a surge, a visual crescendo, strongly introducing the new shot.   2. The fade-out/cut-in produces a visual punch; used between a succession of static shots (e.g. of captions, paintings), provides a dynamic introduction to each.

Fig. 6.11   The mix
The mix usually compares successive shots.   1. Fast mix   2. Slow mix.

■ *Ripple dissolve*   Here the first shot becomes increasingly broken up by horizontal rippling (weave), during which you mix to a second rippling shot . . . which steadies to a normal image. Generally introduced for flashback effects.

The wipe *(Fig. 6.12)*

The wipe is a visual effect, mainly used for decorative transitions. It can be produced by several methods, but most production switchers include electronic wipe facilities. It had a particular vogue in early movies, and is now widely used in trailers and commercials. There the visual impact of the wipes tends to disguise the raw edges of compositionally unrelated fragments.

The effect of the wipe is to uncover, reveal, conceal, fragment; according to how it is applied. In all forms it draws attention to the flat nature of the screen, destroying any three-dimensional illusion.

The wipe direction can aid or oppose the subject's movement, modifying its vigor accordingly. The edge may be sharp (hard-edged/hard wipe) or diffused (soft-edged/soft wipe), the latter being much less distracting. Broad soft-edged versions can have the unobtrusiveness of a mix.

Wipes take many geometric forms with a variety of applications. A circular (*iris*) wipe, for example, may be used as a transition between close-up detail (a soloist musician) and a wider viewpoint (the full orchestra).

■ *The split screen*   If a *wipe* is stopped during its travel, the screen remains divided; showing part of both shots. In this way you can produce a localized *inset*, showing a small part of a second shot, or where the proportions are more comparable, a *split screen*.

The split screen can show us simultaneously:

1. Concurrent events
2. The interaction of events in separate locations (phone conversations).
3. A comparison of appearance, behavior, etc., of two or more subjects,
4. A comparison of before and after (developments, growth, etc.).
5. A comparison of different versions (comparing a relief map with its aerial photograph).

Fig. 6.12 part 1   Uncover wipe
Second image is progressively uncovered.

Fig. 6.12 part 2   Pushover wipe
Second image pushes over, displacing original one. (Push-off/pull-off/push-on wipe).

Fig 6.12 part 3   Common wipe patterns
1. Horizontal wipe/line-split. (When static, this provides a split-screen.) 2. Downwards vertical wipe. 3. Iris/circle wipe (out or in, expanding or contracting). 4. Corner wipe – top right. (When static, this provides a *corner inset*). 5. Barndoors/line bar/horizontal split wipe (expanding or converging). 6. Vertical split wipe/field bar (wipes out or in). 7. Diagonal (top right). 8. Fan wipe (in or out). 9. Diamond wipe-in. 10. Box wipe-out. 11. Rotary/clock wipe.

Fig. 6.12 part 4   Multiple and complex wipes
1. Multiple iris (out). 2. Blind wipe (out). 3. Cross wipe. 4. Explosion.
5. Multiple wipe with ripple (only the wipe-pattern ripples, not the pictures involved).
6. Hard-edge wipe. 7. Soft-edge wipe.

Fig. 6.13   Split screen
The screen is split into two or more segments, showing a series of pictures or respective portions of these components.

Superimpositions (half-lap dissolves, supers)

In film, superimposition necessitates exposing each frame twice or more (double exposure) in the camera, or more usually in the laboratory's optical printer. In television, you simply fade up two or more picture channels simultaneously.

Because the tones of superimposed pictures are additive, the light areas of any picture generally break through the darker tones of other shots with which it is superimposed.

Whether superimposed subjects appear solid or transparent will, therefore, depend on relative picture tones. Where a lighter-toned subject is superimposed on a *black background*, it will appear solid. On lighter-toned backgrounds, it will be proportionately diluted. Superimposed over multitones, the result appears 'transparent'.

But you must always guard against messy confused images, particularly where multicolored or multitone shots are combined (color mixtures and lightness variations result). You should also avoid any movements (or zooms) of superimposed cameras where supers are being used to provide subject inserts, unless you want growth, shrinkage or side-slip effects.

Superimposition can be used productionally, to convey several ideas:

1. *Spatial montage:* suggesting that two or more events are occurring concurrently in different places.
2. *Comparison:* showing the similarity or difference between the subjects juxtaposed. (Bringing together action, events, locale, having parallel significance.)
3. *Development:* displaying stages in a process. (A half-built house with architectural sketches superimposed.)
4. *Relationship:* showing subjects' interrelationships, how components are positioned. (A mechanism superimposed on a faint image of the entire machine.)
5. *Thoughts:* a close shot of a person, with images of his thoughts superimposed.

Superimposition has a number of practical mechanical applications:

1. To obtain transparent-looking images (ghosts).
2. To achieve larger or smaller proportions (giants, dwarfs), by 'solid' superimposition.
3. To permit appearances and disappearances.
4. To combine titling with another picture.
5. To insert subjects (solid or transparent) into a separate background shot.
6. To add 'surface texture' (e.g. canvas), or a decorative border.
7. To emphasize or identify detail (map route, selected area pointer).

Fig. 6.14   Superimposition
Two or more pictures faded up at the same time; their relative strengths being controlled by video faders.

■ *Montage sequences*   These can take two forms:

1. *A rapid succession of shots* that together imply some total, often abstract, concept (progress, age).

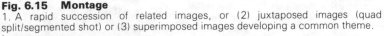

Fig. 6.15   Montage
1. A rapid succession of related images, or (2) juxtaposed images (quad split/segmented shot) or (3) superimposed images developing a common theme.

2. A *multi-image presentation* (superimposed, quad-split, multi-split) showing a series of related situations; for example combining different shots of the same scene, similar subjects, or similar action.

Order of shots

It is a characteristic of the human mind that we continually seek meaningful relationships in what we see and hear – even where none exists. In any rapid succession of shots, we subconsciously try to establish a connection between them (slow mixes between them reduce this effect).

We can interpret a succession of shots in several ways:

1. Shot A may cause (or lead to) Shot B's situation.
2. Shot A may be explained by Shot B.
3. Shots A and B together may give rise to Shot C.
4. Shots A and B together may be explained by Shot C.
5. Shot A juxtaposed with Shot B may imply an idea 'X' that is not implicit in either A or B alone.

In various circumstances you may find that the order in which you present a series of shots will influence your audience's interpretation of them.

Even a simple example shows the nuances that easily arise. *A burning building – a violent explosion – men running towards an automobile.*

Altering the order of these shots, can modify what seems to be happening:

1. Fire – automobile – explosion
   Men killed while trying to escape from fire.
2. Fire – explosion – automobile
   Running from fire, men escaped despite explosion.
3. Automobile – explosion – fire
   Running men caused explosion, firing the building.

Not only is the imagination stimulated more effectively by *implication* rather than direct statements, but indirect techniques overcome many practical difficulties.

Supposing you join two shots: *A boy looking upward . . . tree falling toward camera.* One's impression is that a boy is watching a tree being felled. Reverse the shots and the viewer could assume that the tree is falling towards the boy, who sensing danger looks up. The actual pictures might be totally unrelated; a couple of library shots.

■ *Cause–effect relationships*   Sometimes pictures convey practically the same idea, whichever way they are combined: *woman screaming* and *lion leaping.* But there is usually some distinction, especially where any cause–effect relationship is suggestible.

Cause–effect or effect–cause relationships are a common link between successive shots. Someone turns his head – the director cuts to show the reason. The viewer has become accustomed to this concept. Occasionally, you may deliberately show an unexpected outcome:

1. A bore and his victim are walking along a street.
2. Close-up of bore . . . who eventually turns to his companion.
3. *Cut to* shot of companion far behind, window gazing.

The result here is an amusingly sardonic comment.

But sometimes the viewer expects an outcome that does not develop and he feels frustrated or mystified, having jumped to wrong conclusions:

1. A lecturer in long-shot beside a wall-map.
2. *Cut to* a close-up of map.
3. Lecturer now in an entirely different setting.

The director used the map-shot to relocate the speaker for the next sequence, but the viewer expected to find the lecturer beside the map, and became disorientated.

Even more disturbing, are situations where there is no visual continuity, although action has implied one:

1. Hearing a knock at the door, the girl turns . . .
2. *Cut to* a shot of a train speeding through the night.

The director thought that he would create tension by withholding who was outside the door, but he inadvertently created a false relationship instead. Even where dialogue or action explains the second shot, this is an unsuitable transition. A mix or fade out/in would have prevented misunderstandings.

Quite often, in an attempt to shorten scene duration and to create filmic time, directors cut from one shot to another in which the same person appears in different costume at a different time and place. Whether the technique is acceptable or confusing, is challengeable.

Duration of shots

If a shot is too brief, the viewer will have insufficient time to appreciate its intended information. Held too long and attention wanders. Thoughts

Fig. 6.16   Response to cuts
1. The viewer's response to a cut is not instantaneous. When the cut is made, the audience-impact is slightly delayed; building to a peak and dying away gradually.
2. A series of cuts may achieve individual impacts; there being sufficient time for each reaction to subside.   3. Faster cutting may produce a cumulative build-up.
4. Through repetition, surprise may diminish with each cut, resulting in declining tension.

dwell on the sound, eventually giving way to rumination – or channel switching! The limit for most subjects is probably around 15–30 seconds; and for a static shot, much less. For a mute shot, it could be as little as 5–10 seconds. The belief that a close shot can sustain interest longer, is arguable.

The 'correct' duration for a shot depends on its purpose. We may show a hand holding a coin for half a minute as its features are described by a lecturer; whereas in a drama, a one-second shot would tell us that the thief has successfully stolen it from the owner's pocket. Given the right occasion, even a single subliminal frame (1/30 or 1/25 second) can be seen and responded to!

Fig. 6.17   Sequential inter-cutting
Each subject accuses the other of treachery, tension is rising. The camera dollies closer and closer, shots became larger and larger, and of increasingly shorter duration.

Many factors influence how long you can usefully hold a shot:

1. The amount of information you want the viewer to assimilate (general impression, minute detail).
2. How obvious and easily discerned the information is.
3. Subject familiarity (its appearance, viewpoint, associations, etc.).
4. How much action, change or movement the shot contains.
5. Picture quality (marked contrast, detail, strong composition, all hold most interest).

Audience attention is normally keyed to production pace. A short flash of information during a slow-tempo sequence may pass unnoticed, while in a fast-moving sequence it would have been fully comprehended.

Cutting rate

The frequency with which you can cut within a series of shots depends initially on successful shot matching, continuity, whether the transitions are motivated, and their purpose. Cuts may be used relatively unobtrusively; or used as deliberate interruptions to shock, surprise, emphasize, accentuate. With the latter, you have to judge carefully the borderline between pleasurable shock and distracting annoyance.

Where the picture contains fast action, the cutting rate can be high; whereas in a slow-moving scene, fast cutting would usually be intrusive – unless, perhaps, the accompanying sound has a rapid tempo.

Although some production switchers provide an ultrarapid interswitching facility, such an effect soon becomes visually disturbing, so that its use is quite limited. Even using more orthodox techniques, unless we are intercutting similar pictures, fast switching between video sources soon exhausts shots available.

A fast average cutting rate during continuous action imposes considerable strain on the entire TV production crew, as the switcher cuts to cue and cameras rapidly compose their next shots. Unless the production treatment is straightforward, camera moves limited, and action reliable; operation standards are liable to deteriorate. Typical live telecasts have contained some 200 shot changes in a half-hour show; but statistics as such reveal little without details of the operational complexities involved.

Videotape recording, like filming, permits any cutting rate we may choose. But clearly the less editing carried out on the switcher and the briefer the shots to be inserted into the program tape the more exacting and time consuming will be the VT editing.

Cutting rhythm

Within a picture sequence, we can become aware of certain intrinsic rhythms:

1. Subject movement – rhythm of moving machinery.

2. Composition changes – the dynamic effects of passing backgrounds (a line of trees).

3. Superimposed movement – regularly flashing street sign.

If you take two pictures (each with its own internal rhythms) and intercut them, a comparative effect results.

A *cutting rhythm* can be set up according to the durations of successive shots. Shot duration might, for example, be progressively shortened as tension rises – an increasing cutting rate. Long and short durations might be contrasted to compare leisurely and urgent paces. Similarly, you can use cutting rhythm to emphasize audio rhythm, or vice versa.

The production switcher

At first sight, the *production switcher* (*video switching panel, vision mixer*) can be extremely daunting. This is not helped by the variety of layouts and designs available. If you divide the panel into its separate parts though, the operation becomes much clearer.

Fig. 6.18 part 1   The production switcher – principles of the A–B switcher
There are two identical rows of push buttons called *buses* or *banks:* labelled A and B (or BUS-1, BUS-2). Each pair of A and B buttons selects a particular video source (typically 6 to 20 sources per Bus: cameras, film VTR, slide scanner, etc.). The *BUS fader lever(s)* position determines which bus is in use.

1. A single fader may be fitted (mixing or superimposing between A and B buses).

2. If twin faders are included, they may be operated together, or 'split' to fade A and B buses separately.
With the fader moved to the top, A-bus is active.
Switching buttons on A-BUS, cuts the chosen source (e.g. Cam 1) to the studio's line output (main channel; on-air). (B-bus switching produces no visible result, unless connected to a preview monitor; when it becomes a preparatory bus.)

Fig. 6.18 part 2   The production switcher – basic operations
1. MIX (DISSOLVE) between Cams 2 and 3. Select 2 on A-bus. It is now on line (on-air) as the bus fader is at A. Prepare for a Mix, by pressing 3 on B-bus.
Push down bus fader(s) from A to B, and output mixes from Cam 2 to 3. Move fader to A-bus: output mixes back from Cam 3 to 2.

2. SUPER CAMERAS 2 and 3: Either as for a Mix; stopping when superimposition strength is as required. Or split faders, moving appropriate lever towards the bus to be added.

3. FADE OUT CAM 2 (to black screen). Either split faders, pushing A-bus lever to OUT (B-bus is already faded out); or where the system would lose chroma using this method, select special *black-level* button in the other bus, and mix to black.

CAM 2 – On-Air
CAM 3 – Prepared for Mix

Fig. 6.18 part 1

1   MIX 2·3

2   SUPER 2·3

3   FADE OUT CAM 2 (to Blank Screen)

Fig. 6.18 part 2

Fig. 6.18 part 3   The 'A-B-C' switcher
A separate program bus is used only for *cutting* (switching to line). The A/B buses are used for setting up *mixes and effects* (supers, split-screen, wipes, chroma-key, inserts). The A/B fader lever can be used in either of two ways: (a) *Mix mode*, to provide mixes/dissolves/superimpositions between buses. (b) *Mask key mode*, in which it fades in a keying signal, or makes a pattern *transition*, or operates a wipe-pattern *movement*. A *take* button or bar may interswitch between A and B buses. Preview buttons switch chosen channels onto preview monitor for checking before use. (Do not affect output to line.)

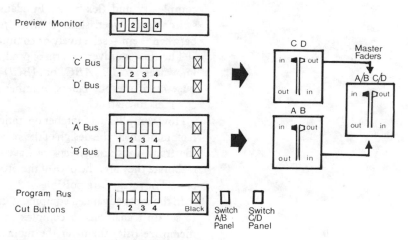

Fig. 6.18 part 4   The 'A-B-C-D' switcher
An elaboration, providing two duplicate pairs of buses – A/B and C/D. Now a pre-arranged combination of cameras can be set up on one pair of buses (e.g. for titling or effects), while the other pair is used for cuts and/or mixes. Master fader levers select the entire A/B and/or C/D combinations as required. A pair of buses (A/B or C/D) is called a MIX/EFFECTS (M/E) BANK.

The production switcher includes:

1. Arrangements for enabling you to *switch* or *mix* between selected video sources (inputs), presenting your choice to *line* for videotaping or transmission.
2. A bank of buttons for simply switching sources to *preview monitors*. This does not affect the output to line. It is just a means of checking combined picture arrangements, special effects, source availability, etc.
3. A special *video effects system* (wipes, pattern, key and matte electronic

insertion); enabling you to manipulate and combine shots in various ways.

Where productions use extensive digital video effects (see Chapter 19), these are often carried out on a separate *effects unit*; operated perhaps by a second person.

4. Perhaps *remote control* of slide scanner, film, VTR channels (remote start/stop, change).
5. Facilities for *title insertion, synthesized color*, etc
6. *Indicators* showing which channels are selected, and illuminating camera and picture monitor tally lights (cue lights).

Basic production switcher functions

The main production switcher enables you to:
1. Cut (switch); fade up/down; mix (dissolve); superimpose any sources.
2. Add/subtract from *superimposed* (*mixed*) sources by switching/fading.
3. Cutting (switching) between *combinations* of sources.

Switchers (vision mixers) are available with various degrees of complexity and flexibility. Fundamentally, *cut buttons* provide inter-switching between sources; while *fader levers* enable you to fade/mix between them – selectively or combining outputs.

The almost universal form of production switcher uses an arrangement known as an *AB*, *ABC*, or *ABCD* format with duplicated switching buses and interbus faders. Another design approach uses a 'fader-per-channel' format.

How complicated switcher operation becomes depends on a number of factors, such as: the design of the switcher unit; whether you can rehearse the transitions and effects, or have to make them spontaneously; how elaborate they are; the pace of the production; whether the action is 'live-on-air' or retakes are possible.

In the most advanced equipment, microprocessors enable the operator to set up transitions or complex multi-source effects at any time, and memorize (file) them for the moment they are required. These inter-source changes can then be selected and introduced simply by pushing a *take bar*.

Fig. 6.18 part 5   The fader-per-channel mixer
This European switcher (also known as 'knob-a-channel mixer') includes two identical independent banks (A and B), in which each video channel has its own individual fader and cut-button. So any group of sources can be chosen and mixed together in any proportions, on either bank. The central master control panel can select either bank as a prearranged group, or combine the two banks. The flexibility of this system makes it particularly useful when creating complex video effects.

Table 6.1   Production switcher terms *(see also Table 19.3)*

Audio-follow-video	Facility providing mike-channel switching to correspond with video switching (e.g. intercutting between both ends of a phone conversation).
Auto-switching	Provides automatic interchannel switching at an adjustable rate.
Black input/black buttons	On some switchers, one simply fades out the channel or line fader, to obtain a black screen. On others, this would result in a loss of color (chroma) during the fade out*, so a 'black-level' channel button is selected to fade to. (*Caused by loss of 'color-burst' when fading out a composite video signal.)
Border generator	A narrow line (tone or color) of adjustable width and sharpness, around a picture segment or lettering.
Bus/bank	A series of selector cut buttons (one for each source) associated with a particular function.
Cascading re-entry	An arrangement in which a composite picture (e.g. a quad-split screen derived from several sources) can be further treated (e.g. title insert), by reentering it at a later point in the switcher routing/chain.
Composite/coded signal	The combined NTSC (PAL or SECAM) signal including picture and sync pulses.
Cut buttons	Pushbuttons used to intercut sources (*Program bus*).
Decoded signal	The individual red, green, blue video signals of the total TV picture.
Double-take/double-cut	Switching the foreground subject shot, and the background scene shot simultaneously, in a combined picture.
Downstream keyer	Switching arrangement that enables graphics/titling to be inserted over the main program output from the main switcher unit, without involving a mix/effects system (so leaving that section available for wipes or chromakey use).
Effects bus/mix-effects bus	A bus used for intersource mixes (dissolves), or for combined-source effects.
Flip-flop controls	A circuit that interswitches the line output between a channel selected on the *program bus*, and a channel selected on the *preview (pre-set) bus*. On operating the flip-flop switch, the previewed channel is transferred to program bus and put on-air. Simultaneously, the channel that was on-air switches away to the preview bus and its monitor. This arrangement provides an automatic preview display of each upcoming shot (on a single-*line preview monitor*) before transferring it to line.
Channel fader	Individual video fader for each picture source.
Group fader	Fader controlling a group of sources (e.g. a bus/bank).
Inputs	Switches routing selected video sources to each channel on the switcher.
Joystick	A vertical stick (or roll-ball) controlling the movement, position, direction of wipes, mattes, etc., around the screen.
Knob-a-channel mixer	A vision mixer favored in some European studios, in which each video channel has its own independent fader. A switch bus facilitates cutting. Its simplicity eases operation for many types of program; particularly when mixing/dissolving fully-modulated pictures.
Lock-out	With some switchers, a 'lock-out' situation can develop when you arrange a succession of picture treatments (series insertion; cascade). no intermediate stage can be altered, without disrupting the entire composite. (For instance having combined mattes, titles, chroma key, colorized background, you cannot then decide to put borders around titling).

Table 6.1 (cont.)

Mix-effects (M/E)	A switcher arrangement in which a sub-fader enables sources on two separate buses to be combined (super, inset, wipe), then selected simultaneously in this form by the master fader.
Non-composite signal	A composite video signal with sync pulses removed (station syncs being re-added after processing).
Preview bus/preset bus	Switch buttons enabling any picture source(s) to be selected on a single preview monitor (to check effects, supers, split-screen, insertions, etc.).
Program bus	Cut buttons interswitching program sources. The result is seen on the line output (studio output, transmission).
Sync/non-sync mode	Adjusts switcher to accept video-sources that are *in-sync* or *out-of-sync* with local synchronizing pulses.
Take-bar	A facility in some switches that enables you to record a program's transitions (cut/mix/wipe, etc.) and composite effects in a memory/file/store and play them out to line as required, simply by pressing a *take-bar*. (Similarly *AUTO-TAKE, AUTO-DISSOLVE, AUTO-WIPE.*)

7 Lighting

Looking around the solid three-dimensional world, stereoscopic vision enables you to interpret space with considerable accuracy. Moreover, you are free to move your viewpoint and to choose where you want to concentrate your attention.

The TV screen's flat image, on the other hand, conveys only a limited two-dimensional impression of the scene. The picture's viewpoint is selected by the director, and changes frequently. All this can make it difficult to interpret correctly; to distinguish between different planes, to assess size, shape and distance.

If a subject is hidden, or is in shadow or unlit, it is invisible to the viewer. Unless given clues, he may not even realize it is there! Similarly, he is normally unaware of the presence or absence of anything that is out of shot. One surface can easily appear to merge with another far behind it. Even its shape may not be obvious. Sometimes you may deliberately lay false clues or create such ambiguities for dramatic effect, or as a staging technique.

Influence of lighting

Lighting directly influences the viewer's interpretation and reactions to the flat picture. It can modify his ideas about size, shape and distance; quite apart from the pictorial and environmental impact.

The lighting may enhance form, or suppress it. Lighting may draw attention to texture, or hide its existence. An environment lit in an unfamiliar way may appear excitingly mysterious, or boringly dull and characterless. So lighting not only enables the camera to see, but is a major contributory factor to your audience's responses.

Why is lighting necessary?

■ *The technical reasons* The TV camera can only handle relatively *limited tonal contrasts*, and requires carefully *controlled exposure* to produce the highest picture quality. So you need to adjust the contrast and intensity of the illumination for optimum results, and to minimize various video defects. If you want to select a lens *f*-stop to give a particular depth of field (shallow focus, deep focus), the light intensity or *level* must be adjusted to provide the correct exposure.

On location, you may need to augment or replace *natural lighting* that does not meet your requirements. For example, the intensity or direction of the available light may be unsuitable, causing high contrast or unwanted shadows. It may be too diffuse, so that pictures lack sparkle. The light's color quality might be unsatisfactory. Quite often, though,

129

the location lighting proves acceptable provided that you position the subject and camera to suit prevailing conditions.

■ *The artistic reasons* Lighting helps us to create a three-dimensional illusion – enhancing the impressions of distance, space, solidity and structural form. It can build up a particular atmospheric effect, mood or style. Lighting can simulate or imitate a certain environment; even suggesting the time of day, or weather conditions. You can use light selectively, to emphasize some aspects of the scene, while subduing others; avoiding or reducing distracting features. Light can enhance pictorial beauty, or deliberately create an unattractive sordid atmosphere.

Light quality – dispersion

For effective treatment you need a suitable blend of *hard* directional light and *soft* diffused light. Usually the hard light reveals the subject's contours and texture, while the soft reduces undue contrast or harshness and makes shadow detail visible. You may deliberately emphasize contour and texture; or equally deliberately minimize them (suppressing wrinkles and bumps – whether in backcloths or faces).

Table 7.1 Light dispersion

Soft light	This is diffused, shadowless illumination and is obtained from large area soft-light sources, broadly reflected light, or overcast sky.
	Advantages: Provides delicate half-tone values, subtle gradations, and gradual ('slow') shading. Avoids emphasis of modeling and texture. Can illuminate shadows without casting additional shadows.
	Disadvantages: Light spreads overall and is not readily restricted. Can create flat unmodeled illumination, suppressing textural beauty and form. Light intensity falls off rapidly with distance and approximately follows an inverse square law', i.e. the level at 2 meters is 0.25 (¼) that at 1 meter; at 4 meters = 0.06 ($^1/_{16}$); at 8 meters = 0.016($^1/_{64}$).
Hard light	This is highly directional illumination casting pronounced shadows; it is obtained from spotlights and direct sunlight.
	Advantages: Clear-cut vigorous effect, bold and well defined. Readily localized to specific areas. Shading (brightness fall-off) on surfaces is abrupt ('fast'). Light intensity is maintained over some distance (because the light rays are parallel).
	Disadvantages: Can overemphasize texture and surface modeling. Can produce harsh, crude, high-contrast illumination. Can create unattractive or spurious shadows. Multiple shadows arise when subject is lit by more than one hard source.

Fig. 7.1   Light quality
1. *Hard light* casts shadows, emphasizes surface modeling (texture, contours). It is emitted by many natural and artificial sources. The smaller the source, the harder its light quality (Brightness does not affect light quality.)
2. *Soft light* is diffused and produces shadowless lighting from scattered illumination. Only large-area sources produce really diffuse light.

Direction of the light *(Fig. 7.2)*

The effects of lighting changes with the angle at which it strikes the subject, relative to the camera's viewpoint. The light's direction will not only determine which parts of the subject are illuminated and which are thrown in shadow, but also how surface contour and texture is reproduced. The lighting direction will emphasize or subdue surface markings and undulations that characterize that particular subject. If you change the light direction or camera viewpoint, these features may become more or less apparent in the picture.

Fig. 7.2   Light direction
1. From a fixed viewpoint, the effect of the lighting changes as *the source* moves round the subject (shading develops on the side opposite the illumination).
2. Using a fixed lamp, appearance alters as *our viewpoint* changes.

Table 7.2 Light direction

Direct-frontal (from camera position)	*Effect:* Direct frontal lighting along the *lens axis*, reduces texture and modeling to minimum. Valuable for disguising wrinkles or avoiding confusing shadows.
Edge lighting (side lighting)	Light skimming along a surface (from above, side or beneath) emphasizes texture and surface contours. Ideal for revealing shallow relief such as in coins, embossing, wood grain, fabric and stonework. Produces poor portraiture on full-face shots (ugly facial contouring).
Back lighting	Light directly behind the subject and along the camera lens axis, is largely ineffectual unless the subject is translucent or has edge-detail (fur, hair feathers). Slightly offset back light illuminates the subject's outline, modeling its borders and helping to distinguish it tonally from its background.

Light intensity

The amount of light needed to suitably illuminate a subject, is partly a technical and partly an artistic decision.

Camera tubes are usually quoted as having a particular sensitivity – requiring a certain light level (intensity) for a given *f*-stop. But this is only a general guide. Much depends on the lightness of surroundings (a dark paneled room requires more illumination than another with white walls); on the color, tone, finish, and complexity of surfaces (whether plain or strongly contoured); and the type and direction of illumination. So ultimately, the light intensity from various directions must be adjusted to suit the subject and the required atmospheric effect (high or low key, environmental effects, etc.). This is the *lighting balance*.

Pictorial quality

Our impressions of pictorial quality are strongly influenced by the tones present. The highest quality normally comes from a full tonal range – from clean whites to deep blacks. Burned-out whites and muddy, detailless gray shadows are unattractive in most pictures.

A picture without darker tones can look 'thin', lacking body (an ethereal effect, perhaps). A picture without lighter tones can look dull and lack 'snap', vigor or sparkle (but may be suitable to simulate a misty locale). A picture with only a few mid-tones normally looks harsh and crude, but may be excellent for highly dramatic or sordid scenes.

Color quality of light

Although our brain can adapt remarkably to wide variations in illumination and still regard it as *white light*, color systems cannot do this. If they detect a different spectral balance from the one to which they are adjusted, the resultant pictures will show a strong color cast. Hence the orange-yellow results if we use 'daylight-balanced' film under tungsten lighting without filtering; or the overblue results when using 'tungsten-balanced' film for exteriors.

The color quality of white light (its *color temperature*) is measured in

Kelvins (K). Light of a warm yellowish-red quality (candles, dimmed tungsten lamps) is of a *low* color temperature; while cold bluish light sources (north sky light, carbon arcs) have a *high* color temperature.

Unlike color film stock, which is designed to be used with a certain luminant color (daylight – 6000 K; artificial light – 3200 to 3400 K), a color TV system can be readjusted easily, by altering RGB proportions to suit any balance as required.

In film or TV, a compensatory color filter can be used over the lens or over the light source, to adapt a system to another color temperature. As prevailing conditions can range from *clear sky* (10 000–20 000 K) to tungsten lighting (3000 K), appropriate compensation is essential for good color fidelity. In TV studios, the color quality is standardized around 2850–3000 K to improve lamp life (by being slightly underrun). Variations of 200 K due to dimming, generally result in unnoticed color changes; but even 50–100 K differences may be detectable in critical applications such as a series of lamps lighting a white cyclorama.

Lighting flat surfaces

Even a simple flat surface requires appropriate lighting. *Hard light* enables you to localize illumination and thus prevent spill onto nearby areas. But it can emphasize surface irregularities such as bumps, wrinkles and creases. It may also not be even overall (fall-off, shading). By using two opposing 45° sources such variations can normally be eliminated. Soft *light* is less liable to produce such spurious effects, but the wide light-spread can spill around uncontrollably.

Lighting an object

Most solid subjects require three basic light-source directions – referred to as *three-point lighting*. The exact angles depend on the subject and the aspects you want to emphasize.

Fig. 7.3   Lighting a flat surface
1. Light from a frontal position near the camera (B), may reflect to produce hotspots, flares. Offset at (A) will overcome reflections, but may cause uneven illumination.
2. For critical work, dual lighting from either side (30-45° offset) is preferable. Soft light sources reduce spurious surface texture or irregularities (blisters, wrinkles).
3. Shadowless lighting (along the lens axis) is necessary for multi-layer graphics (Pepper's ghost).

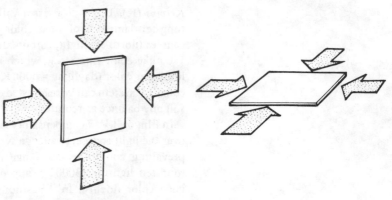

Fig. 7.4   Edge-lighting
Whatever the position of a surface, if light skims along it at an acute angle, any
texture or unevenness will be emphasized.

■ *Key light* This is a predominant hard light, normally in a cross-frontal position – for example up to around 45° vertical, 45° horizontal from the lens axis. This lamp creates the principal shadows; reveals form, surface formation and texture; and largely determines the exposure. Only one key light should normally be used for a subject.

■ *Fill light (fill-in, filler)* This soft shadowless illumination reduces tonal contrast between highlights and shadows, revealing shadow detail. It should not modify the exposure nor create additional shadows or modeling. The fill light is usually located 0–30° from the lens axis and on the opposite side from the key light.

Fig. 7.5   Lighting an object
Effective lighting treatment usually involves four basic lighting functions:
Key light – Usually one lamp (spotlight) in a cross-frontal position.
Fill light – Usually a soft light source illuminating shadows and reducing lighting contrast. But may not be required, or alternatively a reflected hard light is used (rarely a direct spotlight).
Back light – Usually a spotlight (or two) behind the subject, pointing towards the camera. (Occasionally soft light is used).
Background (setting) light – Backgrounds are preferably lit by specific lighting, but they may be illuminated by the key or fill-light spill.

Table 7.3   Additional lighting functions

Base light or foundation light	Diffuse light flooding the entire setting uniformly – used to prevent underexposure of shadows or excessive contrast.
Rim light or rimming	Illumination of subject edges by backlight.
Modeling light or accent light	Loose term for any hard light revealing texture and form.
Cross light, counter key or balance light	An occasional second frontal key – positioned 30–60° horizontally from lens axis.
Kicker, cross-back or ¾ back light	Back light some 30° off lens axis.
Effects light	Light producing specific highlight areas on backgrounds – e.g. around a light fitting.
Bounce light	Diffuse illumination obtained by reflection from a strongly-lit surface such as a ceiling or a *reflector board*.
Set light or background light	Light illuminating the background alone.
Eye light or catch light	Eye reflection (preferably one only) of a light source, giving lively expression. Sometimes from a low-powered camera light.
Camera light, basher, headlamp, camera fill light or spot bar	Small light source mounted on camera to reduce contrast for closer shots, improve/correct modeling, and for localized illumination (e.g. title card).
Hair light	Lamp localized to reveal hair detail.
Clothes light	Hard light revealing texture and form in clothing.
Top light	Vertical overhead lighting (edge lighting from above). Undesirable for portraiture.
Under lighting	Lamp below lens axis used to illuminate, relieve or disguise downward shadows. Also used to create uncanny effects.
Side light	Light located at right-angles to the lens axis. Reveals subject's contours. Creates ugly portraiture for full-face shots, but effective for profiles.
Contrast control light	Soft fill light from camera position illuminating shadows and reducing lighting contrast.
Edge light	Light skimming along a surface, revealing its texture and contours.

■ *Back light* This is a hard rimming light behind the subject, separating it from the background. It helps reveal edge contours, transparency and tracery. A single lamp or two spaced back lights may be used.

There is nothing mandatory about these arrangements. The key light is positioned to suit the object's particular features. If a single *side key* is sufficient, neither back light nor fill light may be needed. If the object is transparent or translucent you may only back light it, or even rest it on an illuminated panel for the best effect (e.g. engraved glass).

Fig. 7.6   Surface brightness
1. Apparent surface brightness depends on both surface tone and incident light intensity. Each of these examples would appear equally bright. The surface texture and finish, affect how brightness changes with light direction and the viewing angle.
2. complete absorption (e.g. black velvet). Little or no reflection. Surface appears dark from all viewpoints.
3. Diffuse reflection (rough irregular surface). Light scatters in all directions, fairly bright from all viewpoints.
4. Spread reflection (glossy surface). Fairly dark at a; fairly bright at b; bright at c.
5. Specular reflection (shiny surface). Fairly dark at a, b. Very bright at c.

Lighting people

Although facial details vary between individuals, the basic head formation remains similar enough, so that the unattractive effects produced by poor lighting are much the same for most people.

■ *General maxims*   There are a number of generally accepted principles when lighting people:

1. Place the key light within about 10–30° of a person's nose direction.
2. Have them look *toward* rather than away from the key light, if reangling their position.
3. Avoid *steep* lighting (above 40–45°) or oblique angles.
4. Avoid a very wide horizontal or vertical angle between the fill light and the key light.
5. Do not have more than one key light for each viewpoint.
6. Use properly placed soft light to fill shadows.
7. Avoid side light on full-face shots.
8. For profiles it is generally best to place the key light on the far side of the face (upstage). This gives improved solidity and avoids casting shadows of the sound boom.

■ *Lighting groups of people*   Check the direction in which each person is looking, and arrange their key/back/fill lights to fit (Fig. 7.10). One appropriate lamp may suit a whole group, but problems can arise if there are big differences in the relative tones of their costumes, skin and hair. Light intensity may be too strong for one; too weak for another. Then

Fig. 7.7   The effects of surface tones
1. A subject's tones affect its prominence (relative to background and other adjacent tones), its apparent size, and its apparent distance. Lighter tones generally appear more prominent, larger, and more distant than darker ones.
2. While our eye stops at the black openings, the white ones suggest space beyond.
3. Progressively lighter planes recede. Progressively darker ones advance.
4. Tonal gradation (shading) affects our impression of form. If a flat plain area is shaded, it appears to have shape.
5. Pictorial perspective conveys an impression of space, which is enhanced by appropriate tonal change – and largely destroyed by unsuitable treatment.

Fig. 7.8   Pitfalls in portrait lighting
Various unattractive effects can arise from unsuitable portrait lighting.
1. *Steep frontal key light:* Black eyes, harsh modeling, long nose shadow.
2. *Two frontal keys:* Twin nose-shadows and shoulder shadows (latter can also arise from two backlights).
3. *Steep backlight:* Hot head-top; bright nose-tip, and eartips; long bib-shadow on chest.
4. *Oblique frontal key:* Talking profile seen on shoulder. Bisected face.
5. *Side key:* In full face bisects the face. Half of it crudely edge-lit, half unlit.
6. *Dual side-keys:* Create central 'badger' shadow effect, and coarse modeling.

Table 7.4   Lamp positions and portrait lighting

	Front light	*Back light*
Lamp's vertical angle too steep	Harsh modeling which gives a haggard and ageing appearance. Gives black eyes, black neck and long vertical nose shadow. *Emphasizes:* forehead size, baldness and deep eyes. Figure appears busty. Casts hair shadows on to forehead. Hat brims and spectacles produce large shadows.	Nose becomes lit while face in shadow ('white nose'). Effect most marked when head tilted back. 'Hot top' to forehead and shoulders.
Lamp's vertical angle too shallow	Picture flat and subject lacks modeling. Produces shadows on background.	Lens flares or lamp actually in shot.
Underlighting	Inverted facial modeling. Shadows of movement beneath head level (e.g. of hands) appear on faces. Shadows may be cast up over background. 'Mysterious' atmosphere when underlighting used alone. Useful to soften harsh modeling from steep lighting. Reduces age lines in face and neck.	Largely ineffectual but can be used for back lighting women's hair. Shadows from ears and shoulders cast on face.
Light too far off camera axis	In full face, long nose shadow across opposite cheek. An asymmetric face can be further unbalanced if lit on wider side. One ear lighter than the other.	Ear and hair shadows are cast on cheek. One side of nose is 'hot'. Eye on same side as back light appears black – being left in shadow while temple is lit.

Note: All lamp positions are relative to camera viewpoint.

localized reduction with diffusers, or shading off light with a barndoor or flag may be the solution.

Where subjects are close, or you have few lamps, one light may have to serve two different purposes – e.g. as a key for one, and a back light for someone else (Fig. 7.11).

Where there are groups of people (audience, orchestra) you can either light them as a whole or in subdivided sections, still using three-point lighting principles and keeping overlaps to a minimum.

Table 7.5   Lighting balance

	Too bright	*Too dim*
Frontal light	Back light less effective. Skin tones are high and facial modeling lost. Lightest tones tend to be overexposed. Gives a harsh pictorial effect.	Back light predominates and often becomes excessive. Darker tones are underexposed. Can lead to muddy, lifeless pictorial effect.
Back light	Excessive rim light. Hot shoulders and top of heads. Exposing for areas lit by excess back light causes frontal light to appear inadequate.	Two-dimensional picture which lacks solidity. Subject and background tend to merge. Picture appears undynamic.
Filler	Modeling from key light reduced and flattened.	Produces excessive contrast and subject too harshly modeled.

Fig. 7.9   Lighting angles
1. The lighting angle chosen depends on the particular features you want to emphasize or suppress.
2. Using two imaginary clock faces, lamps' positions are easily designated. The camera is always shown as at 3 o'clock V (3V), 6 o'clock H (6H). (Hours are 30° steps, minutes are 6° each.) Intermediate positions between hours are shown by + (clockwise) or – (anticlockwise) signs.

Lighting areas

It is best to avoid flooding areas with light; e.g. spreading high intensity soft *base* or *foundation light* and superimposing spotlights for modeling and intensity variations; unless you are seeking a really high-key effect. (This low-contrast technique was used with early camera tubes, to compensate for their high gamma, limited contrast range and various spurious effects).

Except for high-key pictures, the visual appeal of intense soft light is limited – although it does make key light positioning less critical, as ugly modeling is strongly diluted (*lit out*). Such treatments flatten modeling and produce overlit backgrounds.

Dynamic lighting requires appropriately positioned spotlights, relieved by suitably placed and carefully controlled fill light. (The amount of fill light due to random reflections from floor and scenery, is usually minimal.)

The most attractive picture quality usually comes from analyzing the

Fig. 7.10   Lighting a single person
The plans and elevations show typical range of lighting angles within which good
portraiture is achieved.   1. Full face.   2. Offset head (¾ front, 45° turn).
3. Profile.   4. Vertical angles for each are shown.

Table 7.6   Basic lighting approach

Camera sensitivity	Check typical light levels required at your *f*-stop. For example 1600–2700 lux/150–250 fc at 3000 K, aperture *f*4–8
Subject	Scrutinize the subject and consider the particular features you want to emphasize or suppress.
	How critical will the shots be? (Revealingly close or the background predominating?)
	Is the subject static or moving/moved around?
	Is it being shot from several angles? (Which?)
	Any shadowing problems? Shadows falling onto subject, subject's shadows onto background.
Background	Normally light the subjects (people) before dealing with their background.
	Will subject lighting suitably illuminate the background also?
	Does the background require separate specific lighting?
	Will subject and background lighting mutually interfere (e.g. set lighting spuriously illuminating people)?

Facilities	What facilities are available? (Types and numbers of lamps, sufficient cabling and power?)
	Check methods of lamp suspension available (including safety considerations).
	Work within the available facilities, simplifying treatment if necessary.
Key light	Arrange an offset key light, suitable for camera position, subject direction, and movement.
	Does the key light cover more than one subject? (Check coverage, angle and intensity suitability.)
	Must this key light satisfy more than one subject or camera angle? (Compromise the angle or include a second lamp?)
	Check/adjust key light intensity. (Are diffusers needed?)
	Does light coverage need restricting – unwanted spill onto other areas? (Barndoors, flag.)
	Is key light likely to cause boom or camera shadows, ugly background shadows or hot spots?
	Will key light dazzle performer or prevent their reading prompter? Is key light too steep? (Long nose/neck shadows, dark eyes?) Is key light too offset? (Head profile on shoulder; half-lit face).
Fill light	Position to illuminate shadows, not adding to key light.
	Avoid steep or widely angled filler.
	Fill light must be diffused (place diffuser over sources if necessary). *Exceptionally*, use dim diffused spotlight (despite the extra shadow it casts) to provide localized filler in dark surroundings.
	Check that fill light does not overilluminate other subjects or background.
	Avoid excess fill light (little or none required for very frontal keys). Intensity typically half key light level.
Back light	Is backlight desirable? Not needed for some subjects, or where edge lit.
	Avoid steep back light because it becomes ugly top light – flattening head, hitting nose tip.
	Avoid very shallow back light because lamps may come into shot and lens flares may arise.
	Check that back light for one camera is not providing ugly side light from another viewpoint. Avoid excess back light. (Unnatural hot borders to subjects.) Intensity typically 1–1½ key light level.
Background lighting (set light)	When flat background lighting is appropriate, avoid spurious shadows, patches or hot spots, or emphasizing creases or undulations.
	For interiors, relate lighting to natural environmental effects (windows, light fittings).
	Generally shade off walls to about shoulder height.
	Avoid bright areas near top of shot. Avoid distracting contrasts.
	Avoid light scraping along walls (emphasizing surface blemishes, causing long shadows).

performance area into a series of *locating points* (by the table, at the door, looking out the window) and tailoring the three-point lighting at each to suit the action. One lighting arrangement will often suit other shots or action in that area (perhaps with slight lighting rebalance).

Given sufficient lighting facilities (enough lamps, dimmers, etc.) and adequate time to readjust lamps, you could light to suit each individual shot. But such elaboration is not normally feasible.

Fig. 7.11   Lighting two people
1. Several arrangements are effective (each has particular advantages) with keys at A and B, C and D, A and D, or C and B.
2. The lamps here may be shared, as Key A/back B, and Key B/back A. Or used specifically as keys, with extra backlights.

Fig. 7.12   Lighting areas
Where action is localized, the three-point lighting technique (1) can be applied at specific positions throughout the setting (2). One lamp may be used for several positions. Overall three-point treatment can be used for general action (3) or the area can be sectionalized (4).   5. For cross-shooting cameras, lamps over the set's side-walls can be used as key/backlights, with suitable positioned soft fill-light.

Where action is more general or widespread, you must cover the area in a systematic pattern of lamps.

Pictorial treatment

There are three broad styles of pictorial lighting style, through which we can depict the three-dimensional world on a flat screen *notan*, *silhouette* and *chiaroscuro*.

■ *Notan* Emphasis is on surface detail, outline and surface tones.

Table 7.7   Approaches to pictorial treatment

Illumination – overall (flat)	*Method* Main consideration is visibility. Lighting is almost entirely frontal and flat. Tends to *notan*. At its best, subjects distinguishable from each other, and from their background. At worst: flat, characterless pictures; ambiguously merging planes; low pictorial appeal.
Illumination – solid	By a careful balance of frontal and back light, subjects are made to appear solid. This and clarity are the principal considerations of this chiaroscuro approach. The lighting suggests no particular atmosphere.
Realism – direct imitation	*Direct* imitation of effect seen in real life. e.g. sunlight through a window imitated by a lamp shining through it at a similar angle.
Realism – indirect imitation	Imitation of a natural effect, but achieved by a *contrived* method. e.g. simulating sunlight by lighting a backing beyond a window and projecting a window shadow on to an adjacent wall, from a more convenient position.
Realism – simulated realism	An imitation of a natural effect, where there is no direct justification for it from within the visible scene. e.g. a window shadow on a far wall, that comes from an unseen (probably non-existent) window. (This may be a projected slide, cast from a cut-out stencil, or a real off-stage window.)
Atmospheric – 'natural'	A lighting treatment in which natural effects are not accurately reproduced, but *suggested* by discreet lighting. A pattern of light that highlights and suppresses pictorial detail selectively, to create an appealing effect. Suggesting realism in most instances, but seldom permitting dogmatic justification for each light source and direction. A typical motion picture approach.
Atmospheric – decorative	Associative light patterns. e.g. of leafy branches on a plain background.
Atmospheric – abstract	Light patterns that have no direct imitative associations, but create a visual appeal. e.g. a silhouetted unknown person, lit only by a rectangular slit of light across his eyes. A flickerwheel pattern cast over an exciting dance sequence.

Pattern rather than form predominates. The impression is flat (two-dimensional). Notan effects come from high-key, low-contrast treatments, an absence of modeling light, reduced back light and widespread diffused light.

■ *Chiaroscuro*   In this approach, light and shade conjure a remarkable illusion of solidity, depth and space. The style is so familiar that we are liable to overlook that it is actually contrived. When well handled, this treatment possesses arresting, vital qualities, as the Dutch Master painters found and depicted so convincingly.

Where subjects are set up before a totally black background (cameo), or a white background (limbo), the pictorial effect is more strictly a scenic design treatment than a lighting style, although commonly referred to as such. In *cameo* situations side light usually predominates (for maximum modeling); while *limbo* situations are often a notan treatment, avoiding shadows on a white background.

Unfortunately, terminology has too often become confused, so that *limbo* becomes used to indicate 'neutral backgrounds' of any tone. Similarly, for some people 'Rembrandt lighting' defines selectively localized lighting treatment, while for others it implies strongly modeled portraiture.

■ *Silhouette*   Here we concentrate on subject outline, suppressing all surface details. Apart from true silhouettes (black against a light background) used for dramatic, mysterious and decorative effects; *semi-silhouettes* arise in contre-jour (against the sun) shots where back light predominates and frontal light levels are low.

Light sources (luminants)

Several kinds of luminant are used in TV lighting: regular tungsten lamps, tungsten-halogen lamps ('quartz lamps'), gas discharge lamps (metal halide, HMI, CSI, linear light sources), and fluorescent tubes. Carbon arcs are now only used on some remotes (OBs) and location filming – to a decreasing extent.

Fig. 7.13   Internal reflector lamp (sealed beam)
Available in regular tungsten and quartz (tungsten halogen) forms. Used individually in clamps or grouped (Fig. 7.14 parts 1 and 3). The glass front may be clear, ribbed or frosted, to give a wide, medium or spot beam, *hard* or 'softened' quality. A color compensating filter (integrated, or attached) matches the luminant to daylight. Widely used *PAR lights* incorporate a parabolic aluminized reflector (650 watts, 3200 K).

■ *Regular tungsten lamps* Confusingly also called 'incandescent' (which *all* TV luminants inherently are!) or 'tungsten' (used in quartz lamps too!). Still extensively used, the regular tungsten filament lamp is relatively cheap, has a reasonably long life, exists in a wide range of intensities (power ratings), is generally reliable, and can be mounted in many types of fittings.

Against this, tungsten lamps waste much electrical energy as heat. Their relatively large filaments prevent them being true point sources and providing crisp, clear-cut shadows. Their color temperature is normally relatively low and decreases as they get older. The light output also decreases due to the bulb (globe) envelope blackening.

■ *Overrun lamps* These tungsten lamps are deliberately designed for a supply voltage that slightly exceeds the filament's normal rating. By this means, you achieve a much greater light output and a higher color temperature – but at the expense of a considerably shortened life. *Photoflood* and *Nitraphot* are widely used versions.

Such lamps can be used in *practical fittings* (wall brackets, table lamps) on sets, or location interiors.

Portable lightweight systems make use of overrun lamps in traditional tungsten or quartz form. For example, a *Colortran* unit using only 3 kW of power, can provide the light output of a regular 10 kW tungsten rig. So too, *Sunguns* run from belt-batteries can offer intense hand-held illumination on location.

■ *Tungsten-halogen (quartz lamps, halogen lamps, quartz iodine)* Here the tungsten filament is enclosed within a quartz or silica envelope filled with a halogen gas. This restricts the normal filament evaporation and bulb blackening, so providing a longer lamp life and/or a higher, more constant light output of increased color temperature (e.g. 3200 K), that is ideal for color television.

The bulb must not be handled since body acid attacks the surface, and the lamp becomes brittle and extemely hot in use. Tubular strip and compact designs are available, making lighter and much smaller fittings possible. Twin-filament lamps are produced which provide three intensities of similar color temperature by switching.

Fig. 7.14 part 1   Soft-light sources – open-lamp types
1. *Scoop* (1–1½ kW) has spun aluminum bowl of diameter 0.3–0.46 m (1–1½ ft).
Emergent light is not particularly soft (or controllable) where an open lamp is used
(tungsten or quartz). Spun-glass scrim fits into supports, aiding diffusion. The lamp is
obtainable in fixed-focus and adjustable (ring-focus) forms; the latter has adjustable
light-spread. (Versions with lamp-shields are available to prevent direct light
emergence.)   2. *Small broad* (½–1 kW) is a tubular quartz light. Flaps or barndoors
restrict light. Fairly hard source. (Lamp-shield versions available.)   3. *Floodlight
bank* (*cluster, nest*) consists of groups of internal reflector lamps (650 watt) that
create soft-light through multi-source light overlap. Its sections may be switchable
and adjustable (e.g. 3×3 to 3×5 lamp complement).   4. *Fluorescent bank* is a
group of fluorescent tubes providing diffuse illumination.

Fig. 7.14 part 2   Soft-light sources – internal reflection types
1. Internal reflection from shielded tubular quartz-lights, produces diffused high-
intensity illumination.   2. *Large broad* (1–6 kW typical) has a reflected internal lamp
(tubular quartz or fluorescent). A diffuser may also be attached.

Fig. 7.14 part 3   Soft-light sources – cyclorama lighting
1. *Ground-row* (*trough*) containing tubular quartz units (625 W–1500 W).
2. *Strip-light* (*border light*) consists of a row of internal-reflector lamps.
3. *Suspended cyc light* is a single or multi-unit fitting (for color mixing) with strip
quartz-lights.

CID compact iodide daylight
CSI compact source iodide
HMI hydrargyrum medium arc-
      length iodide

■ *Gas discharge lamps* These lamps are compact, extremely efficient sources, using a mercury arc ignited within argon gas. Special 'rare-earth additives' result in near-daylight illumination (5600–6000 K). Luminants of this type are found in CSI, CID and HMI lamps, and increasingly used for effects/pattern projectors, follow spotlights, high-intensity interior and exterior lighting.

Discharge lamps necessarily require auxiliary circuitry (ignitors and ballast units), and there is usually a 1½–3 minutes build-up time from switch-on (striking) to full light. Dimming methods are restricted and a lamp cannot usually be restruck quickly after switch-off. Film shot with

Fig. 7.15   Hard-light sources
1. *Fresnel spotlight* (100 W–10 kW, 8–38 cm/3–15 in lens diameter). Sliding the lamp assembly to/from fresnel lens adjusts light-spread – spot to flood. Adjusted by hand crank (crank or sweep lever), by pole (loop, ring, or T-fitting), or remote electronics. *Controls:* Focus, tilt, pan, filament-switch (where dual-filament lamps used). Barndoor may be permanently attached. Color-frame, French flags, etc., can be attached.
2. *Ellipsoidal spotlight* (profile spot) provides precisely-shaped hard-edged beams which are controlled by shutters, iris diaphragm, or metal plates (profiling blades). Shadow patterns can be projected using metal stencils (masks), wire mesh, etc.

an HMI light source may exhibit flicker problems (visible beat, dark-frame).

■ *Fluorescent tubes* The ubiquitous fluorescent tube has been used in TV lighting as a soft light source for base light, cycloramas, etc. Economical but bulky and fragile, this low-density non-directional source has some use in small installations, but its applications in color TV are limited.

Types of lamp housing – luminaires

Four basic lighting units are used in TV:

■ *Soft light fittings* These include *scoops*, *broads*, internal-reflector fittings, multilamp assemblies and strip lights. They are used for fill light (usually slung), and for lighting broad backgrounds (back-drops, cycloramas) from slung, stand and floor positions.

Fig. 7.16   Portable lighting
Typical portable lighting units include; 1. Small broad (600–1000 W).   2. Internal reflector lamp on plate (gaffer taped to wall, hung, hooked on bar) or fitted into clip-light.   3. Sun-gun (250 W) hand-held or clamped (gaffer-grip, or alligator clip). Powered from utility supply, or 30-volt battery belt (4).   5. External reflector spotlight, lensless spot, in lightweight stand.

■ *Spotlights/Fresnel spots* Focused spotlights with Fresnel lens and internal reflector are used as key lights, back lights, background/set lighting and for effects (sunlight, broad decorative patterns, dapples). Types relying on a mirror-reflector alone are less readily adjusted or controlled (peripheral spill-light, uneven beam).

■ *Effects/pattern projectors* These include effects spots, projection spotlights, profile spots, elipsoidal spotlights and pattern projectors. They are used to project precisely shaped areas of light (soft or sharp-edged cut-off) for localized effects lighting, or to project patterns of stencils or slides (windows, tracery, leafy branches, decorative motifs).

■ *Follow spots* Used for isolating static subjects or following moving performers (singers, skaters, dancers) in a confined pool of light. These large spotlights (e.g. 5 kW) are carefully balanced for continuous accurate

Fig. 7.17 Lamp supports
Studio lighting is mainly suspended (from a pipe-grid in this example).
1. Clamped directly to the grid (with a C-clamp fitting).
2. Lowered from an extendable hanger (sliding rod, drop-arm).
3. A movable trolley holding a vertically adjustable spring counter-balanced pantograph (extension 0.05–3.6 m/2–12 ft).
4. Telescopic hanger (skyhook, telescope, monopole).
5. In confined space, a spring-loaded support bar (barricuda, polecat) wedged between walls or floor/ceiling.
6. Telescopic floor stand (0.45–2.7 m/1½–9 ft).
7. Clip-lamp (spring clamp) attached to scenic flat.
8. Scenic bracket screws to top of flat.
9. Camera light (headlamp, basher). Low-power lamp for eye-light or local illumination. Safety bonds (wire or chain) are fitted to all hung fittings and accessories.

handling and are usually stand or scaffolding mounted. The beam intensity is often shutter-controlled, and its circular spot area (hard- or soft-edged) is adjustable to suit the subject.

Lamp supports

Several methods have become standardized for supporting lamps.

■ *Ground lamps* Lamp fittings may rest on the ground for certain purposes. *Ground rows, cyc lights, strip lights, troughs,* are used to light backgrounds; *spotlights* can provide underlighting effects or be used to reach otherwise inaccessible areas.

■ *Floor stands* Floor lights are mounted on telescopic three-castered stands. They have the disadvantages of occupying valuable floor space (perhaps impeding camera or sound-boom movement), casting shadows onto backgrounds, having trailing cables and being vulnerable. But they do permit easily adjusted precision lighting.

In fact, most TV lighting is suspended, to leave floor space uncluttered by lamps or cables.

Fig. 7.18 Lamp accessories
Various attachments control the light.
1. *Diffuser* consists of a translucent material (wire mesh, frosted plastic or spun-glass sheet). Diffuses light (overall or locally) and reduces intensity.
2. *Barndoor* has independently adjustable flaps (2 or 4) on rotatable frame; cuts off light beam selectively.
3. *Flag* is a small metal sheet (gobo) preventing light spill or cutting off light beam.
4. *Cookie* (*cucaloris, cuke*) is a perforated opaque or transparent sheet that creates dappling, shadows, light break-up, patterns.
5. *Reflector* is a flat sheet (white or silver surface) reflecting light to re-direct or diffuse it.

■ *Pipe grids*   Smaller studios frequently use a pipework lattice or ladder beams fixed below the ceiling. This piping (37–50 mm/1½–2 in diameter, at 1.2–1.8 m/4–6 ft apart) enables lamps to be clamped or suspended as required. Catwalks may allow overgrid access.

■ *Battens/barrels/bars*   These are arranged in a regular parallel pattern over the staging area and individual battens may be height-adjusted (counterbalanced by wall weights or motor-winched) to allow lamps to be rigged, or related to staging requirements.

■ *Ceiling tracks*   Crossbars that can be slid along parallel ceiling tracks offer flexibility in lamp-rigging density. Power rails in single or dual-track forms may support telescopic hangers or pantographs for individual or twin-lamp arrangements.

■ *Lamp adjustment*   When working from treads (stepladder) lamp adjustments are precise but time consuming. So many lamps are now designed with loop or 'T' controls to be operated from below by a long entendable pole. Lamp adjustments by remote electronic control are quite practicable (focus, pan, tilt, barndoors) and invaluable for isolated lamp positions, but add to expense and maintenance complications.

Light control

To achieve a pleasing lighting balance, you must control the relative brightness of your lamps. You can do this in several ways:

1. By the type and power of lamp you choose.
2. By adjusting the lamp to subject distance.
3. By introducing diffusers (wire mesh, spun glass, polyester).
4. By altering light concentration (flooding/spotting).
5. By selective switching in multilamp fittings.
6. By using a *dimmer* to control light intensity.

Even without dimmers, very effective lighting treatment is possible for simpler productions. But for maximum technical and artistic effect you need comprehensive light-control facilities to adjust exposure, balance, cuing and atmospheric treatment.

Lighting control equipment

Earlier methods of light control used several types of electrical dimming, including resistances, transformers, reactance dimmers, and magnetic amplifiers. But these have mostly been replaced by solid-state *SCR (silicon-controlled rectifier) dimmer/thyristor* devices. This system is extremely adaptable, and equally suitable for portable and complex computerized equipment. Control levers (faders) and channel switchers are grouped on a *lighting board* (*console*), remotely controlling the actual

Fig. 7.19 part 1   Patching and control – basic patching
Lamp on Bar 22 has been plugged into nearby batten outlet connecting it to the patchboard. There a similarly numbered patch cord can be plugged (patched) into any numbered power-circuit outlet (channel), incorporating its own control dimmer/switch (circuit 6 in this case). Similarly, Bar 23 is fed from power Channel 7. They can be dimmed/switched independently. (Avoid exceeding power loading limit e.g. 2 kW. Switch off circuit before patching.) Some installations use patch cords; others have miniature peg-boards, automatically switched or permanent connections.

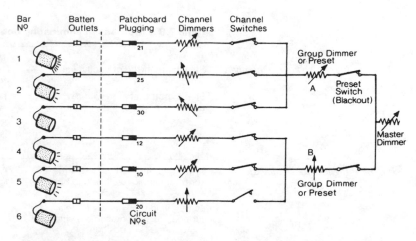

Fig. 7.19 part 2   Patching and control – group presets
A series of individually adjusted circuits can be grouped, to be dimmed/switched communally e.g. fading cyclorama lighting up/down. Typical situation is shown here: *Preset A* (fully faded up). Lamp 1 – Switched on, fully faded up (bright). Lamp 2 – On, faded down (dim). Lamp 3 – On, but faded out (out). *Preset B* Faded down, reducing supply to all group. Lamps 4 and 5 – On, individually faded up (but dim due to preset dimmer.) Lamp 6 – Channel switched off.

dimmer units. Intensity adjustment is smooth, and proportional over their range, even for varying loads (consumption).

The SCR dimmer is a semi-conductor device, which controls lamp current according to the timing of a series of electrical 'gating pulses' applied to it. Earlier problems causing 'lamp sing' (filament vibrating at audible rates) or audio injection (mike cables picking up interference) can now be overcome by suitable suppression.

■ *Dimmer board design* Basically, you want to switch lamps (on/off) singly or in groups, and to adjust lamp intensities individually and/or in groups (to a chosen or variable level). Dimmers (faders) are usually scaled (10 = full, 0 = out) and normally worked around '7', to extend lamp life and permit 'above normal' intensities when needed.

Smaller dimmer boards are usually transportable – often as wheeled installations on the studio floor. These include facilities for combining lamps in *preset* groups for communal control.

Larger sophisticated consoles use digital techniques and can store (file) any pattern of information, including relative intensities and lamp switching. This data can then be recalled at the press of a button, from computer memory, floppy disks, or cassette storage.

TV lighting problems

Lighting treatment affects and is affected by the work of most other studio activities. Consequently the lighting director needs to cooperate closely with others to achieve maximum pictorial standards and

Table 7.8   Methods of eliminating boom shadows

	Method	Result
By removing the shadow altogether	Switching off the offending light.	This interferes with lighting treatment.
	Shading off that area with a barndoor of gobo	Normally satisfactory, providing the subject remains lit.
		Shading walls above shoulder height is customary, to provide better prominence to subject.
By throwing the shadow out of shot	By placing the key light at a large horizontal angle relative to the boom arm.	A good working principle in all set lighting.
	By throwing the shadow on to a surface not seen on camera when the microphone is in position.	The normal lighting procedure.
By hiding the shadow	Arranging for it to coincide with a dark, broken up, or unseen angle of background.	Effective where possible, to augment other methods.
	By keeping the shadow still, and hoping that it will be overlooked.	Only suitable when inconspicuous, and when sound source is static.
By diluting the shadow with more light		Liable to overlight the surface, reduce surface modeling, or create multi-shadows. Inadvisable.
By using soft light instead of hard in that area of setting		Occasionally successful, but liable to lead to flat, characterless lighting
By using floor stand lamps instead of suspended lamps		Light creeps under the boom arm, avoiding shadows. But floor lamps occupy floor space; can impede camera and boom movements; can cast shadows of performers flat-on to walls.
By altering the position of the sound boom relative to the lighting treatment		May interfere with continuous sound pick-up or impede camera moves.
By changing method of sound pick-up	By using a low fishpole, hand-held rifle mike, slung, concealed, personal mikes, prerecording, etc.	These solutions may result in less flexible sound pick-up.

minimum mutual frustration. So let us now take a look in some detail at the main problem areas.

Electronic problems

The technical needs of the camera tube can frustrate your artistic aims. If a situation requires us to switch all lights off, or to provide very dim illumination, or to shoot against a very bright background, or have a scene lit by a single (usually unsuitable) source such as a candle, the camera would normally respond by producing inferior picture quality. So instead, the lighting treatment must necessarily be a compromise; a 'cheated treatment' aided by sympathetic video-controlled adjustment (Chapter 21). (In film-making a similar subterfuge is used when labs adjust processing and the printer light, for exposure and color balance control.)

Sound boom shadows

Shot anticipation and coordination are necessary to prevent boom shadows falling across people and backgrounds. The normal trick is to throw the inevitable shadow out of shot by careful key-light positioning. Obviously, difficulties arise when this lamp position is artistically incompatible.

Fig. 7.20 Sound boom shadows
1. From Camera 1, mike shadow is out of shot and lamp provides backlight, but from Camera 2 lamp is now frontal throwing shadow on background behind performer.
2. Mike shadow (a) is caused by frontal key light being in line with boom-arm at A, whilst by placing frontal key at B, at a wide horizontal angle to the boom-arm, shadow (b) is thrown out of shot.   3. Floor lighting avoids mike shadows unless the boom-arm dips into the lamp's beam.   4. Boom shadows can arise when the boom-arm is parallel with a wall, (5) when the boom operator cannot see his boom shadows, and (6) when the performer is playing away from the boom. Where two booms pick up near and far action, the latter can shadow the closer source.

How settings affect lighting treatment

The layout, shape and finish of settings necessarily affect how you can light them.

■ *Size* Usually, the larger the setting, the broader will be the production treatment. Size alone is not significant since a series of small sets often require more lamps than one large set. Also, there are difficulties in providing precision lighting (e.g. for close-ups) over a wide area, without overlaps.

■ *Height of settings* Low-angle shooting usually necessitates higher sets (studio height permitting). This involves higher, steeper, back and side lighting to ensure that lamps do not come into shot.

■ *Overhangs* Appropriate lighting can be difficult for people or scenery underneath any overhanging feature such as ceilings, canopies, beams, branches and chandeliers. This is particularly true when using slung lighting.

■ *Shapes of settings* Deep narrow sets (e.g. corridors) and wide shallow sets restrict lighting angles, and can therefore frustrate good overall coverage.

■ *Surface tones* Very dark backgrounds and furniture easily lose modeling on camera, causing foreground faces to appear unduly light. Extra lighting may improve reproduced tones, but can spill onto performers. Overlight surfaces appear glaringly hot on camera, often making faces look unduly dark. You can try to keep light off them, but even the illumination from distant soft light sources may leave them overbright. Darkening by spraying down with a lower tone (impractical over large areas) can inadvertently cause patchiness, ageing or dirtying.

The illusion of depth requires good subject/background tonal separation. Contrast ratios of 1½:1 to 2:1 are typical. Backgrounds should rarely exceed 1½ times face brightness.

Shiny surfaces facing the camera can be particularly embarrassing, as lamps reflect in window glass, pictures, glossy walls, etc.

Overbright surfaces are a regular problem. Newspapers, scripts, table tops, light costume, always require care; often having to be sprayed down (water-soluble color), dipped, or dulled down (wax dulling spray; anti-flare) to prevent excessive light bounce. A 'hot' back light can aggravate the situation. Shiny glossy surfaces inevitably produce bright specular reflections or glare, and each problem has to be treated as it arises (dull down, reangle, cover-up, relight).

Other factors affecting lighting

■ *Studio facilities* The elaborateness of lighting is directly affected by the time and labor available, the number and type of lamps, as well as

Fig. 7.21   Performer's positions
1. Mutual shadowing is often more easily remedied by repositioning people than by re-lighting.   2. Where people work too close to backgrounds, good backlight is impracticable. Side lighting or top-lighting (as shown) should be avoided,   3. Where action is in restricted or over-hung positions, lighting can be a compromise – or even impracticable.

suspension methods, light control and the power/patching arrangements. Where many lamps are prerigged (*blanket rig*) for immediate selection, time is saved; particularly with fast turnrounds between productions. Clearly, problems become more acute as the number of sets, changes, cues and diversity of camera angles are increased.

■ *Space limitations*   Most staging representing interiors has to be built in reasonably naturalistic proportions. So the working space available *within* the set for cameras, sound booms, and lamps remains pretty restricted. When action or treatment is complicated or continuous, lighting treatment becomes that much more of a compromise. Further lighting difficulties develop when, to conserve space, staging is located near a cyclorama (spurious shadows on cyclorama), or backings are positioned too close to windows for appropriate lighting.

■ *Multi-camera production*   Multi-camera   shooting   does   not necessarily frustrate good lighting. Much depends on shot duration, shot variations and duration of takes. Often one set-up can light several viewpoints successfully. Otherwise you will have to introduce lighting changes (unobtrusive or direct) to solve the difficulties.

Lighting for color

Color adds another artistic dimension to the TV picture, enabling you to distinguish between planes more easily (for now there is *hue* in addition to *tone*), and to perceive visual effects that are totally lost in monochrome.

■ *Lighting methods and color reproduction*   Many people associate color systems with 'flat lighting' and the extensive use of colored light. Neither is true. Flat overall lighting is as undesirable in color as it is with black-and-white systems. But reasonably *even* lighting is important for controlled results – with neither *hot spots* (paling out and desaturating colors), nor *underlit* (insufficiently illuminated) areas darkening and emphasizing hues. Remember too, that under soft light, colors tend to appear paler; while under hard light, they can look brighter and purer (more saturated).

■ *Exposure and color* Exposure and lighting balance are more critical in color. If you stop the lens down to correct the exposure of a brightly lit subject, its surroundings will reproduce darker as a result. Conversely, if you open up to expose an insufficiently lit subject correctly, other parts of the picture will look much brighter. So exposure compensations for unbalanced lighting can lead to brightness and saturation changes when pictures are intercut.

Face tones and color can become considerably modified by changes in exposure or color temperature variations of the light. Caucasian faces look pallid or ruddy when over- or underexposed respectively. Brown skin-tones tend to become yellowish when overlit, and brown-black or terracotta in shadow. So a high lighting contrast (key-to-fill ratio) can create color bisection effects. This situation is further exaggerated when lamps are being run at high and low color temperatures. In color too, you become more aware of the blocked-off white highlights from skin shine, or perspiration.

■ *Colored light* In fantasy or highly decorative situations, anything goes. Faces may be lit with outrageous color mixtures in the most startling combinations. But for most productions colored lighting (if any) is confined to backgrounds.

Sometimes even the subtlest changes of color temperature will be sufficient to tint light; for instance, low color temperature simulating an oil-lamp or candle-lit atmosphere. Otherwise, you can use plastic color-media sheets in front of selected lamps, or occasionally modify the camera channel's color balance. Certain color treatments, such as the blue used to suggest 'moonlight', or red-orange for fire, have become stylized to the point of cliché.

Colored light also enables you to ring changes on neutrally toned scenery and cycloramas. When combined with projected patterns, impressive effects can be obtained quite economically. However, take care that white lighting (from key lights or fill lights) does not dilute the treatment. Typical color media for lamps include sheets of acetate, polyester, mylar, acrylic sheets (rarely brittle gelatine) fitted into 'gel frames', which clip into light fittings.

Atmospheric lighting

Persuasive lighting treatment, can considerably change the appearance and mood of a scene:

1. Concentrating attention – Emphasizing particular features.
2. Revealing facts – Showing form, texture, surface design, etc.
3. Concealing facts – Preventing our discerning an object or plane; or seeing form, texture, detail, design, etc.

Fig. 7.22 Light measurement Light measurements avoid gross over or under exposure. Basic methods: 1. Incident light falling on subject. 2. Average light reflected from scene at camera. 3. Measuring surface brightnesses (tonal values and contrast).

Fig. 7.23 part 1 Water ripple-tray A spotlight shines through a water-filled glass tray, the rippling light being reflected on to the scene.

Fig. 7.23 part 2 Water ripple-trough Light reflects from mirror fragments in water-filled trough.

Table 7.9   Methods of light measurement

Incident light method	*Reflected light method*	*Surface brightness method*
Meter positioned beside the subject, pointing at light sources.	*Meter positioned* beside the camera, pointing at subject.	*Meter positioned* beside the camera, pointing at the subject.
Measures light intensity falling upon subject from each lamp direction in turn.	*Measures* average amount of light reflected from scene and received at camera lens.	*Measures* brightness of surface at which the instrument is directed.
Providing for (average) subjects of fairly restricted tonal range, typical incident light intensities and balance suitable to camera can be assessed. Base light, key light, fill light, and back light measured in turn.	*Providing* average reflected light levels suitable to cameras sensitivity. Measure lightest and (darkest tones separately, and use midway reading for guide exposure.)	*Provides* readings by measuring surfaces of known reflectance (skin, 'standard' white, black). You can then deduce the suitability of light intensities falling upon them. *Also* allows scenic tonal contrasts to be measured to prevent over-contrasty lighting, over-lit highlights, under lit shadows.
Ease of operation: method is simple and consistent. Does not require experienced interpolation. Widely used in motion picture lighting.	*Ease of operation:* readings vary with meter angling, and experience is needed to make allowance for subject tones, and contrast. Large dark areas cause readings to be falsely low, encouraging overexposure of highlights. Large light areas give high readings, which may cause underexposed shadows.	*Ease of operation:* method requires some experience in judging the *importance* of individual surfaces' brightness relative to overall exposure.
Advantages: when a show is to be repeated original levels can be duplicated readily. Balance between various light directions readily checked.	*Advantages:* method provides a quick rough check of average light levels. Can facilitate evenness of lighting.	*Advantages:* method is capable of assessing surface brightness and contrast very accurately.
Disadvantages: arbitrary allowance has to be made for subject tones.\n\nThe amount of light required depends upon the subject — which this method cannot assess.\n\nMethod only directly useful for 'average' subject-tones.\n\nDoes not take into account tonal values, proportion of tones and tonal contrast.	*Disadvantages:* meter readings are only of an 'average' nature; which varies considerably with tonal values and proportions.\nMethod does not indicate contrast range of subject or lighting.\n\nMeter's 'angle-of-view' seldom identical with the camera-lens'.\n\nWhere a single surface (e.g. a face), is to be equally exposed in a variety of settings, measured exposure *should* be constant; but will vary as adjacent tones change.	*Disadvantages:* several separate readings are necessary to check evenness of lighting, and contrast.\n\nMethod measures scenic tones, but does not distinguish their relative importance; and hence the desired exposure.\nTonal contrast measurements may not signify:\nIf the tones measured do not appear together in picture;\nif their proportions are small and unimportant;\nif they *may* be acceptably 'crushed out' without injuring pictorial quality.

Note: Where meter is held close to subject, measuring individual surface brightness, method becomes as for surface brightness method.

4. Associations of light — By light direction, intensity, distribution, recalling a particular atmosphere (firelight, sunset).
5. Associations of shade — Shadow formations recalling certain subjects, environment, or mood (tree branches, prison-cell bars).

Mood lighting comes from selectively emphasizing and subduing. It is not enough to just imitate natural lighting, for under the camera's

Fig. 7.24 part 1   Shadow size, sharpness and intensity
Shadow size is always larger than the subject increasing as lamp distance lessens.
Close lamps give greater size changes, and exaggerated proportions. Shadow size
increases with subject/background distance. *Shadow sharpness* decreases with
increased light source area, the lamp's closeness to subject, the subject's distance
from background. *Shadow intensity* depends on background tones and finish, and
spill-light diluting shadow.

Fig. 7.24 part 2   Shadow distortion
Distortion arises when camera and lamp are not aligned, and not at right angles to
background. Tilting background or angling lamp also creates distortion.

scrutiny true environmental illumination often produces ineffectual or ugly results; primarily hot tops, black eyes, half-lit faces and steep harsh modeling. Instead, we must stimulate the imagination with light and shade – intriguing, hinting, evocative effects.

■ *Animated lighting*   You can introduce life and action into a scene by lighting. The movement of light may be used as a dominating effect, or as part of an environmental illusion. You will often meet examples of this technique:

Rain running down a skylight throws streaking shadows into the room below.
Fluctuating light and shade patterning the interior of a moving automobile.
A room lit by a rhythmically flashing street sign.

Lighting has the particular merit of *flexibility*, for you can change mood or significance in an instant, or imperceptibly alter contrast and balance. For example:

A prowler is suddenly illuminated by a passing automobile . . . and we see that it is not the person we expected.
During a brawl, the room is broken . . . tension rises, as we no longer know who is winning.

Fig. 7.24 part 3   Multiple shadow effects
These are produced when several lamps combine to light the same subject (particularly successful in color). If they rotate, the multi-shadows weave from side to side.

Fig. 7.24 part 4   Passing shadows
A rotating framework fitted over a lamp, and hung with a stencil cut-out, branches, etc., to create passing shadows. Patterns must not be obviously repetitive.

Fig. 7.24 part 5   To lose background shadows
This is achieved by displacing the subject from its background (e.g. on a glass panel), or by using a translucent illuminated panel.

Fig. 7.25   Reflected shapes
1. Reflective material (metal foil, plastic mirror-sheet) held in a sharply-focused light-beam, projects its image on to nearby surfaces. Bending the reflector distorts the reflected shape.
2. Spotlight focused onto *mirror-drum* faced with plastic mirror, produces 'passing-lights' effect for vehicle interior shots.

Fig. 7.26   Fire flicker
Narrow strips of rag attached to a stick are gently waved in front of a lamp to simulate firelight flicker.

Opening a window blind, the room's appearance is transformed by sunshine.
A happy atmosphere . . . becomes sinister . . . and finally horrific.
The high key lighting gradually becomes contrasty . . . until finally underlighting predominates.

Lighting effects

■ *Reflected shapes*   Light can be reflected from metal foil sheeting or silvered plastic to throw decorative patterns. As the surface is moved or flexed, the pattern shapes and position change. Even stenciled symbols or lettering can be reflected to animate or distort titles.

Countless visual effects can be produced in this way (including nebulae, abstract and magical illusions), reflected directly onto backgrounds, front or rear projection screens, or superimposed.

■ *Firelight*   To simulate firelight, move a stick with close linen strips gently before a floor lamp. Smoke or gas jets are generally less convenient and most automatic devices provide mechanical-looking results.

8 Scenery

Television settings – known variously as staging, sets, scenery – have to satisfy several requirements:

1. *Artistically*, settings must be appropriate to the occasion – the subject and the production's purpose.
2. *Staging mechanics* must be practical for the studio – its dimensions, facilities and the production budget.
3. *Design* should provide suitable shot opportunities – operation freedom for sound, cameras, lighting, etc.
4. *The TV camera's characteristics* will influence the tones, colors, contrasts, and finish of settings.

Basic organization

Staging begins with the demands of the script and the aspirations of the director. Much depends on how effectively these can be related to the facilities, time and budget available. As with all craftsmanship in television, optimum results come from a blend of imaginative perception and down-to-earth practical planning. TV set designers achieve minor miracles in making ingenious use and reuse of materials.

Planning begins with discussions between the director and the set designer. Using sketches, scale plans and elevations, production concepts are transformed into the practicalities of man hours, costing, materials . . . For larger productions, there is close collaboration with various specialists, who consider:

Shot opportunities for cameras, performer action and moves, the various considerations of lighting, audio pick-up, camera treatment, costumes, make-up and technical requirements.

In such an interdependent venture, teamwork is essential.

■ *The studio plan* The basis for much of the organization is the standard printed *studio plan*, showing the studio's permanent staging area with such features and facilities as exits, technical supplies, cycloramas, service and storage areas, etc. A typical metric scale of 1:50, i.e. 2 cm = 1 m, is replacing the widely used ¼ in = 1 ft scale.

■ *The staging plan (floor plan, ground plan, setting plan)* A rough plan of the staging layout usually begins with drawing potential scale outlines of settings, including their main features – windows, doors, stairways. By moving small tracing overlays around the studio plan, you can make best use of available space, while ensuring maximum opportunities for cameras, sound booms and lighting.

Standardized symbols representing scenic units, furniture, etc., are added until you have a mutually accepted 'bird's-eye view' of the entire staging area. Copies of a final plot are distributed to the production director, technical and lighting directors, scenic construction workshops, and anyone else who needs one.

■ *Camera plan (production plan)* The importance of the staging plan becomes clearer, when you bear in mind that in a closely planned complex production, it is used by the director to evaluate or calculate his shots and devise a *camera plan* showing principal camera positions (Chapter 16).

Fig. 8.1 part 1   Staging – studio plan

■ *Lighting plot* The lighting director overlays his *studio lighting transparency* (showing battens/barrels, lighting suspension points, lighting grid, rails, supply points, etc), onto the staging plan. He then assesses the arrangements and types of lamps required for the effects he is seeking, bearing in mind the various production mechanics (Chapter 7).

■ *Furniture/props plot* A series of larger-scale plans may show the disposition of all *set-dressing* (furniture, drapes, etc.) and the main *props* listed on a props list.

■ *Elevations* Devised concurrently with the staging plan and to the same scale, *elevations* provide a scale side-view of surface detail, treatment and dimensions of all vertical scenic planes (walls, doors, windows, pillars, etc.). These not only guide construction and decoration, but help us to imagine the three-dimensional staging in the studio.

If cut out from thin card, these elevations can be attached to a staging plan to create a simple *scale model*. This is particularly useful in complicated situations, to aid visualization of the final scene (for director, performers, specialists, staging crew). A miniature viewfinder will even show shots obtainable from particular camera positions.

Fig. 8.1 part 2   Staging – staging plan

Fig. 8.1 part 3   Staging – elevations

Basic scenic forms

Staging is styled to suit each production's particular needs: *Neutral settings* offer the simplest and most economical backgrounds. Non-associative, they concentrate the audience's attention on the subjects and the action. An open cyclorama or an arrangement of flats is generally used; simply decorated perhaps with surface designs, graphics, or lighting treatment.

Realistic settings may represent a certain type of location (atmospheric realism), an actual place (replica), or through selected details conjure up a naturalistic impression (symbolic realism).

Decorative staging takes several stylized forms, including abstraction, silhouette, limbo, cameo, in which design is predominantly arranged to delight the eye and stimulate the imagination.

Most studio settings are built from an assembly of prefabricated scenic units. Carefully positioned to the staging plan (using wall/ceiling/floor 'footage' marks), they are fastened together and supported where necessary and subsequently dressed or decorated to create the total scenic effect.

Sectionalized units make transport, *setting-up* (erection), *striking* (dismantling) and storage much easier. Moreover, most of the component parts have been designed to be redecorated and reused over again, in different combinations, for many productions – as *stock units*.

Fig. 8.2   Flat construction
1. Top rail.
2. Corner block.
3. Lash cleat.
4. Stop cleat (to align flats).
5. Brace cleat (brace eye).
6. Stile.
7. Frame (1 × 3 in pine).
8. Lash eye.
9. Diagonal brace (corner brace).
10. Keystone.
11. Toggle (stretcher).
12. Bottom rail.

The flat

Most scenic flats are made from fireproof burlap (hessian), plywood or prepared boarding (fiberboard, hardboard) on wooden frames. Although canvas flats are lightweight, they are flimsy and lack rigidity. While 3.0–3.6 m (10–12 ft) high units are universal in larger studios, 2.5–3.0 m (8–10 ft) are more convenient in smaller studios where the camera is less likely to *shoot off* (*overshoot*) in longer shots. Widths from 0.15–3.6 m (6 in–12 ft) are used, the commonest being 0.6–1.8 m (2–6 ft).

Flattage can rise above 3.6 m (12 ft) but handling and safety problems increase. Tall flats are avoided where possible, for as lamps are forced upward to keep them out of shot, their steeper angles cause coarser portraiture.

Surface treatments are legion. Cheapest are distemper or casein prepared paints. Wall coverings (paper, vinyl) provide an extensive selection of patterns, tones, and textures. Finally, you can attach such materials as fabric or carpeting; or build up surfaces in relief with stuck-on forms or thin plastic-sheet mouldings.

Most flats are single sided (*single-clad*), but are made *double-clad* when you need to shoot them from either side. Curved flats are used for some applications.

Fig. 8.3 part 1 Setting flats — methods of joining
1. Scenic flats lashed together by line (sash cord). 2. Adjustable cramp/clamp butts firmly together. 3. Pin hinge. 4. L-plate clip. 5. Securing nut (wing-nut).

Fig. 8.3 part 2 Setting flats — supports
1. The flat can be supported by extendable stage-brace (held firm with a stage-weight or sandbag), or braced to studio wall plate. 2. A triangular wooden jack can be hinged or hooked onto flat rail (preferably bottom weighted). 3. Top bracing struts may secure unsupported settings. Suspension lines or bottom weighting are alternative arrangements.

Fig. 8.3 part 3 Setting flats — disguising joins
1. When flats are set edge-to-edge, their joins show. Joins may be covered with pasted-on paper or fabric (stripping); although this prevents later re-angling. Joins still remain visible in plain light surfaces.
2. Where possible breaks or returns are introduced, disguising joins, providing a more interesting effect, and improving acoustics.

Fig. 8.4 Architectural units
Stock architectural features can be combined.   1. Contoured flat or frame (an example of a single-sided unit — viewable on one face only).   2. Door plug.   3. Fireplace plug.   4. Window unit (an example of a double-clad unit — viewable on both faces).

Set pieces — (built pieces/solid pieces/rigid units)

■ *Architectural units* Although one can construct scenery complete with features such as doors, fireplaces, niches, the resulting units tend to be heavy, bulky, and less adaptable. So instead, it is often more practicable to use profile flats (frames), into which these details, made in the form of plugs (shells), can be bolted (Fig. 8.4). Where features such as room doors, closet/cupboard doors are non-practical (i.e. unused), they can even be made in dummy form, and simply attached to the surface of a standard flat.

Fig. 8.5   Solid pieces/built pieces
1. Pillars: cylinders or half-shells of 0.15–0.6 m (0.5–2 ft) diameter and up to 4.5 m (15 ft) high.   2. Staircases (stair units): groups of two or more treads, usually 0.15 m (6 in) risers, matching heights of stock parallels (rostra).   3. Parallels (platforms, rostra) which are variously shaped level platforms on folding/dismantling frames with boarded-in sides.   4. Ramp: sloping plane surfaces.   5. Arch. 6. Drape frame: light framework in single or hinged units carrying draperies (otherwise suspended from batten or bar).   7. Cove: shallow sloping surface used to merge horizontal/vertical planes and hide cyc units.   8. Step-box (riser block): wooden shells from e.g. 0.15 m (6 in) to 0.6 m (2 ft) square. All-purpose unit that provides half-steps, display tables, for raising furniture, etc.

■ *Free-standing units* A second, more extensive group of solid pieces provides not only such architectural features as stairways and arches, but structures for general production applications such as *parallels* (*rostra*) to create platforms or raised areas.

Profile pieces — (cut-outs)

These vertical profiles of plywood, prepared board, etc., may be arranged either free-standing, or attached to stock flats to modify their outline. Typical applications include:

1. Isolated decorative pieces – Flat cut-out representations.
2. Wings – Masking off the edges of an acting area.
3. Ground rows – Concealing background-to-floor joins.
4. Scenic planes – Representing a skyline, and the intermediate terrain.

Profile pieces can provide cheap, very effective substitutes for elaborate scenic arrangements; for as the camera moves, parallactic movement between these planes can create a surprisingly convincing three-dimensional effect.

Although they may not deceive the camera in closer shots, profile units can appear very realistic at a distance – especially if cut from photo blow-ups. When shot from an angle, though, their flatness may become obvious – although this seldom matters with decorative units.

Fig. 8.6 Profile pieces/cut-outs
1. Profiled flats painted in perspective, create a spatial illustion. 2. Profiled ground-rows suggest progressive planes. 3. Profiled flat supporting plastic-shell rock-face.

Fig. 8.7   Decorative screens
1. Decorated screens of expanded metal, wire mesh, perforated board. 2. Contoured flats of plastic shell or attached forms.   3. Woven screens. 4. Open screens of stretched wire or cord, poles, slats, etc., supporting motifs or profiles.   5. Curved flats, small solid cycs.   6. Flexible screens.

Cyclorama

Even the smallest studio makes full use of the cyclorama as a general-purpose background. The *cyc* (pronounced 'sike') is a suspended plain cloth; usually stretched taut by weights, battens or tubular piping along its bottom edge where a totally wrinkle-free surface is required.

■ *Cyc track*   The cyc is sometimes hung on straight or curved battens or scaffold tubing. But the most adaptable method is by gliders (runners) affixed to a permanent *cyc-track* (*cyc-rail*) round the staging area. Using this, the cyc can be repositioned, changed, and drawn back when not required. Sometimes a range of cyc tones is available for selection on parallel tracks.

■ *Materials*   Various materials are used – including duck, canvas, filled gauze, sharks-tooth scrim, and occasionally velours. Usual colors and tones include 'white' (60% reflectance), black, light gray, mid gray, light blue, dark blue, and chroma key blue. Although permanent (*board*) cycloramas are now seldom used, as they restrict staging areas and cause sound coloration, small shallow C-curved flats sometimes provide backings for windows.

■ *Adaptability*   The plain light-toned cyc is extremely adaptable, for its smooth unbroken appearance can be considerably modified by lighting treatment. Its brightness and color can be changed; it can be shaded, or patterned, with projected shadows. With care, you can even attach very lightweight motifs to the cyc (double-sided adhesive tape, or pinned).

Backgrounds

Strictly speaking, any surface seen behind a subject is its *background*. Some people use the term *backing* synonymously, but that really refers to the planes beyond windows and other voids in the setting. These

Fig. 8.8   Cyclorama
1. The cyc can be blended into the floor plane by (2) merging cove/ground cove. 3. Cyc lamps may be hidden to illuminate the lower cyc.

Fig. 8.9   Drapes
Drapes may be: 1. Suspended from bars (battens).   2. Attached to a flat or line across a flat.   3. Hung on tubular drape-frame.   4. Hung from timber arm (gallows arm) hinged to edge of flat.

backings imply space and distance and prevent cameras from shooting off the set.

■ *Neutral backgrounds*   Neutral backgrounds are used wherever you want non-specific environments e.g. for talks, *public (current) affairs* programs.

Neutrality does not necessarily involve plainness; although to avoid distraction, any decoration is usually restrained. Surface texturing, uneven lighting (shading, dappling), decorative screens, all have applications. Any drapes should avoid distinct patterning, for it easily becomes obtrusive and too recognizable for re-use.

Limbo (white) or *cameo* (black) backgrounds provide neutrality. Sustained viewing of either can be tiring, and similar subject or costume tones can inadvertently merge with them. The resultant effect easily vacillates between naturalism, fantasy and abstraction. Essential furnishings, props and set pieces (doorways, windows) can be set up in front of the background – either symbolically or to form 'open settings'.

The somber gloom of black backgrounds can be inappropriate for certain subjects; and on many TV receivers may reproduce as gray. Foreground subjects may look overlight against these tones. On the other hand, white backgrounds can appear ethereal and infinite; although subject tones may appear darkened.

■ *Pictorial backgrounds*   Because it is difficult to distinguish in the two-dimensional TV picture between distant objects that are flat and those that are solid, you can stimulate three-dimensional effects convincingly using a flat pictorial background. Ideally, it would need to be free from blemishes, evenly lit, and show no spurious shadows; its perspective, proportions, tones, etc., should match the foreground scene; and it should be shot straight-on. In practice, surprising deviations from the ideal will still work very well.

Painted cloths (*backdrops, backcloths, scenic cloths, canvas drops*). Ranging from pure vaudeville to near-photographic masterpieces of scenic art, these large painted sheets are used primarily as window backings. Of canvas or twill, painted cloths are normally hung on battens or pipes, or on wooden frames. In storage, a cloth may be rolled around the pole that weights its lower edge, or *flown* (hung high above the ground).

When used as backings, you may reduce a 'painted look' and suggest distance (the detail-loss of *aerial perspective*) by introducing a light overall spatter or spray. Alternatively, you can stretch a black or white scrim over windows to soften the effect.

Photographic enlargements (*photomurals, photo blow-ups*). Although expensive, enlarged photographs represent the ultimate realism obtainable from studio pictorial backgrounds. Enlargements are made on sections of photosensitized paper stuck onto a flat, or a canvas support. color is normally underplayed, dye-retouched monochrome versions being much cheaper and more convincing than even high-quality color photographs.

1   2   3

Fig. 8.10   Skeletal staging
1. May use isolated realistic scenic elements.   2. Decorative symbolism.
3. Abstract pattern.

Photoenlargements can be adapted and reused by retouching, stick-over alterations, or simply obscuring too recognizable details (by a strategically positioned bush or pillar).

Photoenlargements can be used too, as pictorial or decorative panels standing or hung within a setting.

Projected backgrounds. Two systems are used. *Rear projection* (*back projection* – BP) in which a still or moving background picture is projected onto the rear of a translucent screen situated behind the action. *Reflex* or *front projection* in which the image is projected along the lens axis, onto a special beaded screen (see Chapter 19).

Electronically inserted backgrounds. (Chroma-key, CSO). By special electronic switching circuits, foreground subjects can be inserted into the background picture from any other video source (photograph, drawing, miniature, TV camera, etc.). (See Chapter 19.)

Surface detail and contouring

■ *Painted detail*   Because you can suggest solidity by suitable drawing and shading, it is possible to create an illusion of brickwork, paneling, molding, etc., by brush alone. Realism depends on the scenic artist's skill, how closely the camera sees the effect, and whether oblique viewpoints or cast shadows reveal the true contours.

■ *Wallpapers*   Various photographic wallpapers of brickwork, stonework, wood graining, are easily struck to flattage – retouched or sprayed over where necessary.

■ *Molded pieces*   Ingenious lightweight imitations now exist for a diversity of subjects. Statuary, architectural features (beams, moldings), tree trunks, brickworks, roofing tiles, cobbled paving . . . are recreated with such conviction that they bear scrutiny – even up to fingernail-scratching distance.

Earlier techniques with papier mâché and plaster, or canvas on wire mesh have been largely superseded by glass fiber, molded rubber and plastic forms. Solid items such as statues and rocks may be hand-carved

Table 8.1 Surface finish

	Method	Purpose
Flat lay-in	Even-toned surface painting.	Textureless finish.
Dry-brush work	Overpainting a flat tone with a nearly dry brush. Sparse brush marks aross the ground color.	Suggests metal, wood, stone, fabric.
Stippling	Series of small close dots of color on a different ground tone; using coarse brush, sponge cloth, wrinkled paper.	Suggests stone, cement, earth
Puddling	Wet colors flowed together, intermixed for random variations.	Suggests ageing plaster, earth.
Daubing	Dabs of color with rolled rag, patted irregularly over a surface.	Varying density of tone.
Scumbling	Translucent coating, usually of darker tone over a lighter one.	Suggests surface undulations.
Glaze	Transparent dry brush application of lighter tone.	Suggests highlight sheen.
Scuffing (Dragging)	Skimming surface with brush, leaving textural depressions untouched.	Texturing a plain surface.
Wash	Thin coating of lighter or darker tone over background body color.	Suggests highlights or shadows.
Roughcast	Sprinkling material (sawdust, sand) irregularly onto freshly painted surface.	Random changes in tone or texture.
Spattering (Dottling)	Mottling with random brush-thrown splashes.	Textural effect.
Stenciling	Applications of decorative motifs by stencils or rollers.	Decoration.

by hot-wire cutters from lightweight styrofoam (expanded polystyrene foam blocks).

Most outstanding of all, are the molded surfaces of thin plastic sheets (PVC). These are vacuum formed, up to about $2.5 \times 1.25 \, m$ ($8 \times 4 \, ft$) to produce realistic contouring shells depicting carved panels, rock-face, stonework, brickwork, tiling, mullioned windows, as well as various wall-furnishings (escutcheons, pistols, fish). These versatile panels are simply cut out, stapled onto stock scenic units, and painted. They have the merits of being low-cost, featherweight, adaptable. But they must be handled with care, to avoid compression damage.

Floor treatment

The studio floor's matte mid-tone surface serves as a neutral ground for most productions. But it can also provide some interesting staging opportunities.

Fig. 8.11   Floor treatment
1. The studio floor may be treated decoratively (painted, stenciled, stuck-on designs).   2. Painting simulates surfaces economically, leaving them flat for camera moves. a, crazy paving; b, paving slabs; c, pavé bricks; d, cobbles.   3. The floor surface can be covered by: a, sawdust; b, scattered peat; c, dead leaves; d, sheets of rubber/plastic cobbles, brickwork, etc; e, grass matting (surface contours changed by f, sawdust sacks, or g, sack-filled platforms).

■ *Painting*   Temporary floor treatment can be applied, using special water-soluble paints, either to change the overall tone or decorate the floor with realistic effects (floorboards, paving) or ornamental designs. Whether stenciled, hand-painted, or roller-printed, the treatment can be washed off after use. This means strictly avoiding spilled liquids, for they destroy the treatment and make it treacherously slippery and sticky. Temporary adhesive floor tapes can simplify or augment painted designs.

Fig. 8.12   Ceilings
1. Complete ceilings over settings are feasible, providing appropriate lighting can be introduced (through windows, doors, lamps behind furniture, false returns, etc.). Translucent ceilings can help but light may be hot or patchy.   2. Partial ceilings in corners or (3) localized areas may prevent shoot-off.   4. Cutting pieces suggesting beams, vaulting; and suspended lamps (chandeliers) suggest a ceiling.   5. A scenic background (cloth, photo, chroma-key insert) may contain a ceiling.   6. A foreground camera matte simulates a ceiling on the studio setting (Chapter 19).

Fig. 8.13   The staging area
Locations are normally described in relation to a given camera's viewpoint.

Painted floors do not frustrate dolly movements as carpets and floor cloths can; but they are liable to become dirtied. Black floors all too readily show wheel and foot marks.

Where facilities allow, lighting may provide projected floor patterns; but these are very easily diluted by other lighting treatment.

■ *Scattering*   Scattering innocuous materials such as peat, sawdust, leaves, cork chips, bark, transforms a surface rapidly for naturalistic effects. However, material tends to stray around the studio (particularly when using wind machines) and must be confined. Avoid salt or sand — they foul up equipment!

■ *Floor coverings*   The floor can be decorated by covering it with a *floor cloth* made of heavy duck, canvas, or tarpaulin (plain or prepainted); photographic or patterned papers; or panels of prepared board. Thin materials may tear or ruck-up under action or camera movements. Bulky materials such as turf or carpets can impede cameras.

Ceilings

Ceilings are introduced both to prevent cameras from shooting over sets into the studio beyond, and to create environmental effects. However, unless carefully confined, a ceiling can frustrate the lighting treatment and produce boxy sound quality. Usually, the viewer simply assumes the ceiling, just as he does the non-existent fourth wall of a setting. Where ceilings are essential (in very low or long shots) and where high walls or a void (black drapes) would be unrealistic, various subterfuges are used.

Size and shape of sets

Space and budget restrictions usually prevent you from building sets much larger than they need be. Instead, you can *suggest* space by scenic treatment. Where spacious effects are required, wide-angle lenses can exaggerate distance, so that even quite sawn-off versions appear impressive on camera. The kind and extent of action anticipated will influence set sizes. The smaller the setting the more restricted will the camera and lighting treatments normally be.

Shooting off (overshoot)

Wherever you inadvertently shoot past the confines of the setting, the solution is self-evident: readjust the shot, or add *masking* (intermediate planes, a screen, border, wall-extension, drapes, etc.). Anticipation during planning can prevent needless last-minute rearrangements.

Shoot-off (overshoot) mostly arises when:

1. Cross-shooting on a shallow set.
2. Shooting downstage from an upstage viewpoint.

Fig. 8.14   Typical sizes of settings
1. Two-fold set.   2. Three-fold set.

3. Windows or doors are inadequately backed.

4. Reverse-shooting into a set through a window or door.

5. Using low-angle shots.

6. Offstage areas seen in mirrors/reflective surfaces.

7. Seeing through communicating openings (windows, arches) into adjacent sets.

Height and depth in floors

Vari-height platforms (parallels, rostra) are used where you need elevated floor areas. Any irregularities are built up with blocks, additional framework, tightly packed sawdust or sandbags.

To create 'holes in the ground' (graves, bomb craters, trapdoors, wells)

Fig. 8.15 part 1   Proportions of settings — flat backgrounds
On flat backgrounds cross shots shoot-off easily.   1. The set lacks depth and solidity, but occupies little room (can be piled or nested).   2. Slightly improved, but setting looks disproportionately wide in cross-shots.   3. Very satisfactory proportions for general use.

Fig. 8.15 part 2   Proportions of settings — walls
1. Walls may be splayed slightly to improve camera access.   2. Right angled walls may restrict camera movement, but prevent exaggerated room-size in cross-shots, 3, 4. As sets narrow, little deviation from straight-on shooting is possible. Sound pickup may be 'boxy' and lighting tends to be steep.

Fig. 8.15 part 3   Proportions of settings — staging height
The height necessary for staging depends on the longest shot to be taken (A), the lowest camera height (B), and the height of the subject (e.g. action on a staircase). A 3 m (10 ft) high flat is adequate for general use, a 3.6 m (12 ft) one being needed for larger settings. High backgrounds should be avoided to prevent steep lighting.

Fig. 8.16   Shooting off
1. Cameras can easily shoot past the edges of a set, and see the studio beyond. Solutions include (2) modifying the shot; (3) extending the set; (4) introducing appropriate masking pieces to prevent shoot-off (e.g. screen, wall, drapes).

it is best to build up the overall floor level and leave the required 'hole'. This flooring must be suitably reinforced, and where heavy loads of scenery, people or equipment are involved, tubular scaffold structures are essential. Where cameras are to move around on the elevated areas, surfaces must be level, flat and non-skid.

To prevent unnaturally resonant flooring, platforms are best surfaced with felt, flexible urethane foam (foam-plastic sheeting), carpeting or similar sound absorbants, plus internal packing where necessary.

Space economies

In the small studio space is at a premium, and you may find that there is insufficient room for all the sets you need for a production. You can overcome such problems by discontinuous recording (altering or striking sets during recording breaks), by using prerecorded inserts (on film or videotape), use chroma-key insertion processes, or introduce versatile staging techniques.

Multiplane techniques

Our impressions of *scenic depth* are comparative. They come from our relating the appearance of progressively distant planes, overlapping, scale, and a series of similar visual clues. The more planes visible between our viewpoint and the horizon, the stronger is the illusion of depth. When there are few spatial clues in a shot (e.g. an open stage), the picture seldom conveys a convincing three-dimensional effect.

These impressions of depth derive primarily from the foreground and middle distance. So you can arrange your staging techniques accordingly. Foreground pieces particularly enhance the feeling of depth and dimension. These can be such diverse objects as tree branches, furniture,

Fig. 8.17   Height and depth in floors
Covered platforms (parallels, rostra) can be used to build up floor levels where height or depth are required.

Fig. 8.18   Space economies
1. Where congestion is acute, flats may be moved aside for camera access (hinged folds, wheeled, man-handled, or hung).   2. Settings' appearance may be changed by re-vamping (retain structure, alter dressing), rearranging scenery, and changing lighting.   3. Nesting sets, where the inner unit is used and struck to give access to the second set.   4. Part of a setting can be built on a low wheeled platform (stage wagon, truck, float) and moved aside for access. Combined with chroma-key backgrounds (Chapter 19), considerable flexibility is possible.

Fig. 8.19   Scale changes
1. Where the set is built with everything proportionately scaled down, people assume gigantic proportions.   2. If everything is scaled up, people are dwarfed.

Fig. 8.20   False perspective
The background can deliberately convey a false impression of space.   1. A flat background (photographic, painting, chroma-key) may contain an illusion of depth. But give-away shadows, wrong scale, or wrong foreground-background perspective can destroy the effect.   2. The whole setting may be built in false perspective (exaggerated size-reduction with distance), but then action must be kept downstage.   3. By deliberately arranging to have large objects in the foreground and progressively smaller items further from the camera, perspective can be cheated.

tracery screens and columns; all used to provide progressive scenic planes.

When carefully organized, foreground planes come into shot quite naturally as the camera moves around. But the effect can appear contrived, particularly when the viewpoint is unfamiliar. Overdone, this technique could leave cameras continually weaving amongst foreground obstacles, with the viewer failing to get a clear view of the action.

The illusion of four walls

It is not necessary to have *four* walls to an 'interior' setting to convey a convincing impression of completeness. Even a single background plane may suffice; the rest being imagined by our audience. You can even build a room in *separate sections*, and by careful intercutting imply that they are part of a whole.

An actual four-walled room can be very restrictive to shoot, for the camera has difficulty in getting far enough away from subjects to provide

Fig. 8.21   Multiplane techniques
Foreground planes enhance the impression of depth.   1. They may arise naturally from the camera viewpoint.   2. Items can be deliberately positioned in the foreground.   3. Even a localized foreground piece can be effective.

Fig. 8.22   The illusion of four walls
1. The fourth wall is usually assumed to be at the camera's position. Where the foreground wall must be seen, a mobile scenic piece (door, window) is often used. Designed as a *break-through piece* if camera dollies 'through' it.   2. Cameras can shoot over a low four-walled set for group discussions. (Beware of reverse cuts!)

Fig. 8.23   Partial settings
An environment can be implied by building a complete but abbreviated section.

wider (longer) shots. This occurs even when using wide-angle lenses or shooting in through doors or windows. Also, where several cameras are being used, they are liable to get in each other's shots if space is very restricted. On location, you just have to make the best of circumstances.

Where four walls are essential in a studio setting, you may use intermittent videotaping to move in, or strike walls to shoot each viewpoint. Or you can actually build a complete four-walled set; arranging to raise, hinge, slide *wild walls* out when needed to give access to cameras and booms. In these situations lighting may become a compromise.

It may be simpler to provide peepholes for cameras – through doors, windows, fireplaces; *camera traps* as hinged wall flaps, e.g. behind pictures or camera-concealing drapes. When shooting a four-walled set, you must particularly guard against *frame jumps* or disorientation by inadvertently cutting over the imaginary (*action*) *line*.

Partial settings

Why build more than the camera needs to see? Although some

Fig. 8.24   Multiple use of units
Individual scenic units can be transformed.   1. Two glazed doors become a long window, or a ceiling light.   2. A low window can be turned into a throne.   3. An arch becomes book-shelves.

Fig. 8.25   Visual detail
1. Excessive scenic detail is distracting, confusing, fussy.   2. If all but essentials are excluded, the result can be meager, cheap, empty; although suitably applied it becomes open, expensive.   3. Coordinated shape and line produce a stimulating arresting effect.

production situations require a total overall viewpoint or extensive construction, many shots need only a sectional view – a *partial setting.* Two deliberately restricted staging approaches are widely used. The first implies the whole by showing a *complete but localized part* – the doorway shot suggesting that the rest of the building is there – if we could see it. Audio effects help to create the illusion. The second method creates an impression by *judiciously placed foreground pieces* suggesting that the staging is more extensive than it really is, e.g. shooting through a foreground bookshelf, you imagine an entire library.

Admittedly such restrictions may not allow the director much latitude to change his mind, but the economies achieved in cost, space and materials are considerable. The resultant effect can be totally convincing for short, relatively static scenes, and provide greater elaboration and scenic variety than would otherwise be practicable. Although, when unskillfully used it can lead to a cramped, restricted quality in the staging.

Realism of settings

The artificiality of theatrical scenery is generally unacceptable in television wherever realism is intended. Yet paradoxically, where artificiality creates a genuine-looking effect, deception can go to any lengths. You may successfully use a fishline-activated curtain to suggest billowing winds, or have a leafy branch shadow indicate a nearby tree. Yet a genuine tapestry may look less realistic than a dye-painted canvas replica.

Realism can derive from quite subtle touches. A living room set must look lived-in. Too tidy, too pristine, and it loses conviction. Surreptitious *dirtying-up* (*antiquing, blowing down*) with a fine film of dark water paint can suggest wear, grubbiness and discoloration around switches and door handles. Hand-sprays are useful for rapid localized treatment; although for large-scale effects (a slummy tenement) broad spray gun work becomes necessary.

Deception must be discreet. You must not expect photobackgrounds with foaming breakers that never move, to fool anyone. Occasionally still backgrounds containing motionless trees, even static people will be acceptable, but sooner or later they look suspiciously inert; particularly when accompanied by sounds of associated movement.

Sometimes the most convincing results come from using the real thing (e.g. real turf, tall grasses) while at others, grass matting (suitably discolored), plastic flowers, and foliage, would be preferable to natural growth wilting under hot lights. Real water pools may be no more realistic on camera, than clear plastic sheeting.

Scrim (scenic gauze)

Scrim or *gauzes* consist of thin cotton or synthetic net with a mesh of around 1.5–3 mm (1/16–1/8 in) diameter, in white, light gray or black. Although it can be used in draped form, the material is generally stretched taut without visible seams or wrinkles. It needs to be of sufficiently open weave to prevent excessive light absorption or obscuring subjects beyond, yet robust enough to stand handling and stretching.

Fig. 8.26   Scrims/gauzes
Lit from the front alone (1), the scrim appears a solid plane. Surface painting or decoration shows up brightly against a plain white or black background. Unlit subjects behind the scrim are invisible. By reducing brightness of front illumination (1) and lighting the subject (2) (behind scrim), the subject and setting are revealed with outlines and contrast softened, surface painting having almost disappeared. A third lamp (3) added to rear-light the scrim, increases the mistiness over the scene, while silhouetting details on the surface of the scrim.

Stretched before a light-toned cyclorama, a scrim diffuses and obscures irregularities, and enhances the impression of spaciousness. Over a scenic background, a scrim reduces contrast and artificiality. The material may be used as a glass substitute in scenery; it is safer, lighter, and gives no reflection problems. Lettering or decorative shapes can be attached to 'window panes' of scrim.

By adjusting its lighting, you can alter the appearance of the scrim in several ways. When frontally lit, the scrim will look like a flat 'solid' surface. Lit from the rear, it becomes translucent with surface details silhouetted on it. Unlit, the scrim appears transparent, softening the distant scene.

Mobile scenic units

■ *Mobile vehicles*   To create a convincing illusion that a studio vehicle is

Fig. 8.27 Movable units
1. The movements of a vehicle can be imitated by mounting it on a sprung platform or truck.   2. Using movable scenic sections, the large staircase splits to leave the soloist isolated, 3.

moving, you need to introduce a variety of 'clues': moving passing backgrounds; parts of the vehicle shaking; people being swayed or jogged; lights or shadows passing over them; perhaps wind, or dust clouds; sounds of progress (engine noise, hoof beats, wheel noises, etc); and the sounds of other passing subjects.

You have to interrelate these various features carefully, and above all ensure that there is compatible action between the subject and its background scene. If the vehicle stops, the background must stop too! This requires close coordination. Where moving film or videotape backgrounds are used (rear projection or chroma key) their timing and duration should be anticipated to prevent run-out or incompatibility.

A *sprung platform* when suitable handled, can provide realistic movements for a variety of applications – from rowboats, buggies, hansom cabs, to automobiles.

For a large structure such as a ship, you may need to imitate movement by gently tilting the camera, introducing moving light (e.g. a key light rising and falling), and even having people sway in unison.

■ *Movable scenic sections* When you want to move around a subject and space is restricted, or to reposition staging to form new composition arrangements, you can often do this by using movable scenic sections. These may be flats or solid units on wheels, low wheeled trucks, (floats, stage wagons), turntables, and similarly adaptable staging.

Set dressing

Dressing is the process of furnishing and decorating the built setting . . . the arrangement of furniture, ornaments, drapes. This is the treatment that personalizes an environment.

These properties (props) are of several categories:

1. *Dressing props* used solely as decorative features.
2. *Action props* used in the course of plot action; e.g. a newspaper or telephone.
3. *Personal props* used or worn by specific performers; eyeglasses, wallet.

Where the item is *non-practical* it is not functional, for instance a revolver that cannot fire or is simply not loaded. A *fully practical* article is completely working – the revolver is loaded, and used in the course of the action.

A setting soon acquires a filled-up look, cluttered with bric-a-brac that never registers on camera. So appropriate selection rather than profusion is the aim (Fig. 8.25).

Where foreground space has been left clear for performers and cameras, you may need to introduce (*set-in*) extra props or furniture there for longer shots, removing (*striking*) them for camera moves. Although camera cranes can extend over foreground furniture to some degree, even slight obstacles impede pedestal dollies.

Furniture should not only be environmentally suitable, but physically practical. Deep well-sprung armchairs, for instance, can encourage people to slouch, to look leggy when sitting, and to have difficulty in rising. Cushions may help where unsuitable design in unavoidable. So too, seats that allow guests to swivel round, or that perch them uncomfortably, are best avoided.

If there can be said to be any specific tool for set-dressing, it must surely be the *staple-hammer* or the *staple-gun*, which can shoot wire staples through prepared board and soft wood up to 3 mm (⅛ in) thick. These versatile tools can attach pictures, drapes, posters, foliage, wall coverings, plastic moldings to flats; felting to flooring . . . A close runner-up is *double-sided adhesive tape*, which prevents articles from slipping or being moved out of position, attaches decorative motifs, holds arranged drapes in place, and fixes graphics. Adhesive gray *gaffer tape* too, is a tough many-purpose plasticized cloth, sticking firmly to many surfaces, yet removed without marking them. Its main purpose is to attach lightweight lamp fittings or cables to walls on location.

Electronic and lighting considerations

Production treatment and the camera's idiosyncracies place a number of restrictions on set design. Occasionally you can disregard them – but only occasionally.

■ *The final effect*   It is important to remember that the audience only sees what the camera *shows*. Many a delightful skeletal setting has resolved itself into just a series of 'pole-through-the-head' shots as the director has concentrated on close viewpoints. Many a setting has looked fine in an establishing long shot, but been quite ineffectual in closer shots, or from other camera positions.

Color and tonal proportions in the picture can vary considerably with the shots selected. There may be only one small area of bright red in the set; but this could totally dominate and distract in a close-up.

Various hues are quite distinct in color, yet may merge indecipherably in monochrome; and for graphics (titles, graphs, maps) this can be a real embarrassment.

■ *Tonal values*   Marked tonal contrasts give a long-shot a more definite emphasis than subtle pastel shades. But when you pan in closer shots over sharply contrasting background tones, or intercut between them, pictorial quality and visual continuity can be badly upset.

Conversely, if subject tones are too similar to their backgrounds the overall effect is unsatisfyingly flat or confused. So the tonal contributions of the setting, lighting, costume and make-up need to be coordinated for optimum results.

To ensure good tonal reproduction, it is best to work within a fairly restricted scenic contrast range for most purposes – around 10:1 to 15:1 (40–60 per cent reflectance) is sometimes quoted. Unless lighting is diffused, it will usually extend this effective contrast to the system's limits.

■ *Surface detail* Plain surfaces, unbroken by detail or modeling, have limited pictorial appeal, but they can be considerably enhanced by lighting (shading, dappling, color variations).

Bold details such as a strong pattern or elaborate motif, are attractive as long as they do not draw attention from the action. They are most likely to do this if isolated within a plain background, or appearing unexpectedly in isolated shots.

Very small detail easily becomes lost in longer shots, or defocused where depth of field is restricted. So an attractive pattern that is quite clear in closer shots, may dilute to an unexciting overall gray background at a distance. Consequently, where action moves to and from such a background, we find pattern prominence altering as the focused plane changes.

Very close vertical or horizontal stripes are best avoided at all times – whether they derive from distant coarse patterns or close fine ones – for they can produce violent line beating (strobing).

■ *Surface brightness* Bright surfaces leave the TV camera at a disadvantage where a full tonal range is to be reproduced. Even if no technical defects arise, the effect is generally distracting. So it is a good working principle to avoid overlight or shiny surfaces, unless for a specific effect.

Whereas in a *monochrome* system excessive highlights simply reproduce as white areas within grays, in *color* TV they block-off to become white blotches on colored surfaces – and are therefore more prominent.

Highly reflective materials such as decorative aluminium foil or shiny plastic are notorious for causing troublesome hot spots, flares or trailing. Providing any defects are not obtrusive, their attractive sheen can introduce vitality to a shot. But the borderline between pictorially attractive effects and disturbingly eye-catching blobs can be very slight.

■ *'First-aid treatment'* Exposure is normally adjusted to achieve the most realistic *face* tones. If there are any disproportionally brighter surfaces in the shot, they will block-off to a detailless white. The result may be quite unobtrusive. But if it is unacceptable, the only solutions, are to modify the lighting, remove the offending subject, or apply 'first-aid treatment'.

Although there are times when excessive lighting has aggravated the situation (as when strong back light burns out the shoulders of light-toned garments), such problems are more often due to high-reflectance or smooth surface textures.

The obvious way to improve any over-bright surface is to reduce or cut off the light falling onto it. But this may be impractical, especially where it robs adjacent areas of light. Flares or strong reflections (speculars) from a shiny surface can usually be cured by reangling or tilting it, or changing the camera position slightly, or even by masking it with another subject.

Various aids can be applied to reduce such reflections (on automobiles, glossy paint, plastics), including dulling spray/anti-flare (wax-spray), water paste, latex spray, putty and modeling clay. Spurious reflections in glass or clear plastic can be similarly treated, although we may well obscure the surface by doing so.

Sometimes the only way to reduce overbright surface tones, is to spray or spatter the surface lightly with black water-soluble paint or dye. Overdone though, this can produce a dirty lifeless result, and destroy surface pattern.

Overdark surfaces may be improved similarly by light-toned treatment, picking out (edge-painting) molding or detail, or perhaps by increased localized lighting.

Care is needed too, in avoiding white or near-white set dressings; clothing, drapes, table coverings, papers, bed sheets, etc. You may substitute cream or light gray materials, or lightly dye them, or have them strategically sprayed or powdered down. Carefully done, the results on camera are well-modeled light-toned surfaces, reproducing as white.

Fig. 8.28   Costume problems
1. Avoid costume tones merging with the background.   2. Beware detailed or fussy patterns in both costume and background.   3. Close stripes and checks in costume flicker (strobe) at certain distances.   4. Low necklines appear topless in close shots.

Overdone, though, you may finish up with people in dirty shirts reading gray newspapers!

Although modern camera-tubes can handle wider tonal variations, it is best to avoid tonal extremes as far as possible.

Staging for color

Staging for color TV tends to fall into two broad categories:

1. Situations in which the excitement, vigor, and persuasive potentials of color can be fully exploited (singers, music groups, dance).
2. Situations in which color, unless carefully controlled, can inadvertently create false associations, appear tawdry, overglamorize, or provide an inappropriately vivid background to action (talks, newscasts, demonstrations).

In excess, color defeats its purpose and becomes visually tiring. Too subdued, and the picture lacks vigor.

For various psychological and physiological reasons, the TV screen can often exaggerate – even caricature – reproduced color. Certainly the general practice is to underplay color, rather than have color emphasis.

As a good working principle, it is best to choose the surrounding décor to match the unalterable objects in the scene. Strong color is easily achieved; but subtle, sensitive color staging without simply resorting to gray-scale neutrals, requires interpretive skill. Somber, slummy, drab surroundings can be particularly difficult to stage realistically in color.

Large areas of even, unrelieved color are best avoided, preferably being broken up with lighting, scenic elements, or set dressing.

Emphasis is generally achieved through the use of color in costumes, key props, and furnishings, rather than in the set walls or drapes. Strong background hues easily dominate.

Costume (wardrobe)

Costume effectiveness is strongly influenced by its background. In larger TV organizations, performers' clothing (costume, wardrobe) is the responsibility of a specialist. But for many productions people wear their own clothing, and diplomatic guidance may be necessary to ensure that unsuitable attire is avoided.

You need to be sensitive to talents' feelings and taste when suggesting changes; particularly when you want them to wear an item from stock (off-white shirt, or a different necktie) to replace their own. Experienced talent may bring along alternative garments for selection on camera.

A costume that looks attractive full-length, may be less successful when seen as a head-and-shoulders behind a desk. Color matching looks good to the eye, can reproduce quite differently; for example 'reds' that differ due to their having dissimilar brown or blue proportions. Colors that have a strong bold appeal in leg shots, can seem harshly crude in closer views.

Table 8.2   Costume problems

White shirts, blouses, etc.	Details and modeling lost where surfaces block-off to white.
Glossy materials — satin, etc.	High sheen. especially from shoulders, blocks-off to white or reflects color of incident light.
Light tones	These emphasize size, but if loosely cut, light garments can appear formless.
Dark tones	These minimize size, but modeling is easily lost in reproduction; particularly with dark velvets.
Strong, vibrant colors	Usually appear oversaturated and reflect onto neck and chin.
Fine stripes, checks, or herringbone patterns on clothing	Pattern strobes causing localized flicker, or produce blue-colored fringes (cross color), or creates color break-up. Color detail is liable to be unsharp and lost in longer shots.
Shiny, sequinned or metallic finishes	Blocked-off highlights. Reflects onto nearby surfaces.
'Noisy' jewelry or ornamentation — e.g., multi-string bead	With a personal mike these cause extraneous clinks, rattles, or rustles.
Rhinestones and other highly reflective jewelry	Reflects bright spots of light onto chin, neck, face; and flashes obtrusively, especially when using star filters.
Very low necklines	In close shots, can create a topless look.
Color fidelity	Certain colors can become emphasized or distorted (blues, magentas, deep reds) due to deficiencies in electronic or film processing.

9 Make-up

Types of make-up

Television make-up treatment follows three general forms: *straight*; *corrective*; and *character* make-up.

Straight make-up

Straight make-up is a basic compensatory treatment, affecting the performer's appearance to a minimum extent.

■ *Skin-tone adjustment* This provides a good tonal balance in the picture: darkening pale faces and lightening swarthy complexions.

■ *Routine improvements* These subdue blotchy skin tones, shiny foreheads; strengthen lips and eyebrows; remove beard line (blue chin); darken overlight ears; lighten deep-set eyes; and lighten bags under eyes.

For many TV productions, performers require little or no make-up, with minimum correction and brief last-minute improvements often being sufficient. Regular performers may do their own.

Fig. 9.1 Make-up chart
Outline chart is used to record detailed notes of make-up treatment, materials, hairwork, etc.

Corrective make-up

Corrective make-up seeks to reduce less pleasing facial characteristics, while enhancing more attractive points. Actual treatment can range from slight modifications of lips, eyes and nose; to strapping sagging skin or outstanding ears, or concealing baldness.

The general aim is to treat the person without their appearing 'made-up'. Skin blemishes and unattractive natural color must normally be covered; preferably by using several thin applications of increased pigmentation, rather than trying to obscure with heavy mask-like

187

Fig. 9.2   Corrective make-up
Make-up can improve or disguise various effects that may appear emphasized on camera.   1. Shiny bald head; untidy hair; scalp showing through thin hair; hair too light, dark, dense, to show well.   2. Perspiration shine.   3. Deep eye sockets; eyes appear too prominent or small; eyes lack definition.   4. Shiny nose; nose coloration prominent.   5. Beard-line prominent (blue chin).   6. Neck scrawny.   7. Lips need definition or shaping; normal lipstick too dark or light on camera.   8. Age-lines; wrinkles over-prominent.   9. Ears too prominent; different color from adjacent skin.   10. Eyebrows barely discernible, over-prominent, untidy.

coatings. Arms, hands, necks, ears may need blending to an even tone (body make-up).

A person's skin quality will modify the make-up materials used. While coarser skin textures provide more definite modeling, finer complexions tend to reveal veining or blotches that the camera may accentuate. In color, ears can appear reddish and translucent. Complexions become flushed with exposure to heat (or hospitality). Make-up can become disturbed in the course of action (e.g. lip colors 'eaten off'). Also, bleached hair can exhibit alarmingly greenish shading, while blue-tinted white hair can look startlingly overcolored, only improved by corrective rinses.

Character make-up

Here, emphasis is upon the specific character or type that the actor is playing. By facial reshaping, remodeling, changes in hair, etc., the subject may even be totally transformed; for example Frankenstein's monster. But most character make-up involves less spectacular, subtle changes. Theatrical make-up treatments appear rather too broad and crude under the camera's scrutiny, except for such stylized characters as clowns, ballet, pierrot.

Conditions of television make-up

The principles and practices of television make-up are almost identical with those of motion pictures, except that in television the tempo and continuous performance usually prevent the elaboration or shot-by-shot changes that are possible in film.

A long shot ideally requires more defined, prominent treatment than a close-up. A similar situation, in fact, to that found in lighting techniques. But such refinements are seldom possible under typical conditions. You may not even be able to do anything about such distractions as perspiration, or disheveled hair, when the actor is on-camera for long periods – except to correct them for any retakes, where time permits.

For the very exacting demands of television drama, careful planning and presentation are essential. At a preliminary meeting with the program's director, the supervisory make-up artist will discuss such details as character interpretation, hair styling, special treatments, and any transformations during the program (ageing, etc.). Actors who need fitted wigs, or trial make-up, are then contacted.

■ *Camera rehearsal*   For camera rehearsal, either of two approaches is common. In the first, the performers are made-up beforehand as experience suggests. When seen on camera, this treatment enables the make-up artist to judge more exactly the eventual detail work and tones needed. It also allows the lighting director and video control operator to assess tonal balance, contrast, and exposure.

While watching camera rehearsals on a picture monitor, the

supervisory make-up artist notes any changes that seem desirable, to guide the individual make-up artists handling the performers. The other make-up approach (especially for straight or corrective forms) is to see performers on the screen first, treating them as time and facilities allow.

■ *Make-up treatment* Generally speaking, a straight make-up for men may take around 3 to 10 minutes; women require 6 to 20 minutes on average. Elaborate needs can double or even treble these times.

After a few hours, cosmetics tend to become partly absorbed or dispersed through body heat and perspiration. Surface finish, texture and tones will have lost their original definition, and fresh make-up or refurbishing becomes necessary. Apart from on-the-spot retouching and freshening (mopping off and applying astringents), performers are normally treated in make-up rooms near the studio. Miracles of makeshift quick-changes have been achieved on the studio floor amidst the turmoil of production. But unless time limits or body position necessitates this (as with wounds), a more leisurely procedure is preferable.

There will always be problem occasions. Some performers cannot have make-up, owing to allergy or temperament. There are times when make-up has to be done immediately before air time, without any opportunity to see the performer on camera beforehand – a situation that the wise director avoids.

■ *Varying conditions* Apart from artistic considerations, many technical factors affect make-up treatment:

1. Lighting – intensity, balance, direction, etc.
2. Scenery – relative face/background contrasts (simultaneous contrast effects).
3. Video adjustment (picture control) - exposure, gamma, black level, color balance.
4. Costume – relative to face/costume tonal contrast.

Such variations help to explain why the same performer's treatment may need to alter from one show to the next. Sometimes an astringent and light powdering may suffice, while at others more particular make-up becomes necessary.

Principles of make-up

The broad aims of facial make-up and lighting are complementary. Make-up can sometimes compensate for lighting problems, lightening eye sockets to anticipate shadowing cast by steep lamps. But, whereas the effect of lighting changes as the subject moves, that of make-up remains constant. This distinction is important when we consider corrective treatment:

1. Large area tonal changes – making the entire face lighter.
2. Small area tonal changes – darkening part of the forehead.

3. Broad shading – blending one tonal area into another.
4. Localized shading – pronounced shading to simulate a jawline.
5. Drawing – accurately lineated lines and outlines.
6. Contour changes – built-up surfaces.
7. Hair work – moustaches, wigs, etc.

Localized highlighting by slight color accents will increase the apparent size and prominence of an area, while darkening reduces its effective size and causes it to recede. By selective highlighting and shading, therefore, you can vary the impression of surface relief and proportions considerably. But you must take particular care to prevent shading looking like grime!

You can reduce or emphasize existing modeling, or suggest modeling where none exists; remembering though, that the deceit may not stand close scrutiny.

A base or foundation tone covers any blotchiness in the natural skin coloring, blemishes, beard shadows, etc. This can be extended, where necessary, to block-out the normal lips, eyebrows, or hairline, before drawing in another different formation.

Selected regions can be treated with media a few tones lighter or darker than the main foundation, and worked into adjacent areas with fingertips, brush or sponge. After this highlighting and shading, any detailed drawing is done using special wax lining pencils and lining brushes.

Make-up materials

The make-up media used in television and motion pictures include:

1. A dry matt cake of compressed powder (Pancake).
2. A non-greasy base of creamy consistency, in small stick-containers (Pan-Stik) or jars.
3. A greasepaint foundation, contained in tubes.
4. Powder and liquid base.

Before applying a foundation (base), the skin is first prepared by thoroughly working it over with a cleansing cream or lotion (or cold cream) to remove any traces of existing cosmetics. Wiping this off with paper tissues, an astringent (e.g. eau de cologne) is patted on, to close skin pores, reduce absorption and perspiration, and generally freshen. Following an after-transmission clean-off, the skin is cleansed with special removers and washed with soap and water.

Which of the various make-up media is used, depends on the effect required, the degree and nature of the treatment and personal preferences. Each material has its particular features.

■ *The cake foundation* This base is worked up with watermoist sponge, and applied thinly over the whole face. Its covering power (ability to overlay other tones, blemishes, etc.) is excellent. Its finish is predominantly matt. When too thickly applied, it can produce a mask-like appearance, flattening out facial modeling. Highlights and shading

Fig. 9.3 part 1   Basic make-up techniques — general treatment
1. Hard hairline, forehead lowered by shading, face width reduced cheeks depressed.   2. Softened-off hairline, forehead width reduced by shading, deep-set eyes lightened, cheek and chin modeling increased.   3. Hairline reshaped and extended, forehead height reduced, chin made to recede, 'apple-cheeks' highlighted.

Fig. 9.3 part 2   Basic make-up techniques — nose treatment
Variations in nose shape achieved by shading (side shading, ridge highlighting).

Fig. 9.3 part 3   Basic make-up techniques — eye make-up
1. Untouched.   2. Area above eye protrudes as a result of lightening, eyebrows raised and thinned, making eye seem smaller.   3. Eyebrows thickened and lowered, and area above eye shaded. This opens up the eye and make it appear larger. 4. Method of lengthening eyes.   5. Method of broadening eyes.   6. Distance between eyes reduced by shading.   7. Distance between eyes increased by shortening brows.   8. Detailed example of eye treatment: base of top lashes underlined thinly from center to just beyond outer corner, end being upturned. A short upturned line is occasionally drawn under lower lashes, but this tends to reduce the eye size. Eye shadow light towards the inner corners, slightly heavier at outer corners. A white penciled line along inside edge of lower lid.

can be introduced with a sponge edge, using shades two or four tones different from the foundation color.

■ *Cream base* This is dabbed on to small areas, and worked by fingertips evenly over the regions being treated. Localized high-lighting and shading with different tones is pat-blended or merged with flat-topped sable brushes. Surface finish depends upon any subsequent powdering to set the foundation. Unpowdered, the skin has a soft sheen. Powdering reduces shine leaving a smooth, satin finish. The cream has reasonable covering power and may be retouched easily. Leaving the skin's natural texture visible, it permits lighting to reveal more subtle half-tone modeling.

■ *Greasepaint* This is similarly spread from small dabs. Although it has little covering power and may need refurbishing sooner than a heavier foundation, it is easily worked and retouched (by brush or fingertips). Powdering modifies its distinct shine to a silky gloss.

Such after-powdering, when applied to any completed make-up, softens contrasts and binds the materials. Any excess can be removed with a powder brush. A *beardstick* using a grease base can reduce a prominent beard line.

■ *Powder bases* These are supplied in compacts and resemble reinforced face powder. Applied with a puff, their covering power is moderate. They have general use for broad shading and tonal improvement, emergency repairs, shiny foreheads, and the like. Most liquid-type media have poor covering power, and tend to become streaky and patchy.

Any powdering, whether to 'set' a foundation, reduce shine, or to absorb perspiration, must be applied judiciously. This is because the powder often tends to change color in use, or obscure base coloring.

Several accessory preparations are common to the beauty salon and the make-up room alike, e.g. mascara, eye shadow, and false eyelashes. A few, like rouge, have a less value on-camera and are better stimulated by other means; while materials such as tooth enamel (to blacken or whiten teeth), artificial blood capsules, are more suitable to the television and film studios.

The make-up artist's tools range from brushes (for modeling, lining, applying lip color, etc.), sponges, wax pencils, to palette knives. But for many workers, their fingertips are their most-used aid, with which they blend foundation media into a homogeneously molded complexion.

Surface modeling (prosthetics)

Manipulation of the subject's own skin or by sticking on new formations can change the physical contours of the flesh.

■ *Manipulation* To produce scars, ridges, etc., *non-flexible collodion* may be brushed on to the skin. This mixture of proxylin, alcohol and ether, contracts the flesh; the painless contraction increasing with successive layers. Although readily removed, collodion can irritate sensitive skins. In such cases, quick-drying, liquid-plastic sealers may be preferable.

Fish skin can be used to contort the flesh within limits. The selected area of flesh is drawn into its new position, and the fish skin spirit-gummed to hold it in place. Apart from imparting an oriental slant to eyes, this material is mostly used to emphasize or flatten out folds of superfluous flesh.

■ *Surface contours* Surface contours such as warts, eye-bags, wounds, nose modeling can be built up by several methods. Wax nose putty, mortician's wax, and modeling clay (Plasticine), can all be moulded into shape and stuck on. A latex rubber-base solution, *flexible* collodion (resin, caster oil, ether, alcohol), or various plastic equivalents, can be coated over a selected area until it is sufficiently extended. For larger protruberances, pads of absorbent cotton wool or sponge can be attached first by spirit gum. Surfacing is then carried out over this substructure. Because normal foundation media do not take to these surfaces, plastic sealers are finally brushed over to key them on and prevent any interaction.

For more drastic changes, partial or complete latex masks are molded and attached. They provide us with anything from double chins to grotesques. The advantage here is not only that more extensive alterations are possible, but that they can be prepared beforehand, and the fitting/removal process is quicker and easier. All prosthetics are best camera tested to ensure color and textural suitability.

Hair

Hair may be treated and arranged by the make-up artist, or by a separate specialist. Such hair work includes: alterations to the performer's own hair: the addition of supplementary hair pieces; and complete wigs covering existing hair.

■ *Hair alterations* In television, a certain amount of restyling, resetting or waving, may be carried out on the performer's own hair, but where extensive alterations such as cutting or shaving are needed, complete wigs are more popular. Hair color is readily changed by sprays, rinses or bleaches. Hair whitener suffices for both localized and overall graying. Overlight hair can be darkened to provide better modeling on-camera, while dark hair may need gold or silver dust, or brilliantine, to give it life.

■ *Supplementary hair pieces* Where the performer's natural hair is unsuitable for treatment, hair pieces or full toupees can be attached to the scalp, and unified with existing hair. Where staining of the scalp with masque cannot hide baldness, these made-up hair pieces may be necessary. For women, postiche work (pinned-on-hair) may provide flowing tresses, buns, ringlets, etc., augmenting a short coiffure.

Beards, mustaches, side-burns (side-boards), stubble and the like, may be 'home-grown', preformed by using prepared hair goods, or built up from cut hair lengths. Prepared hair goods are, undoubtedly, most popular. These are obtained pre-fabricated by wig specialists. Here, hair has been tied strand-by-strand to a fine nylon silk or nylon netting (lace), and can be dressed to suit beforehand. This method is less demanding of the time and skill of the make-up artist.

On the other hand, treatment built up from cut hair is a lengthy and skilled business, but more versatile. Human and yak hair are the most-used materials. (Crepe hair has limited application.) Such hair may be laid in spirit-gummed sections, until the required area has been covered. The result is trimmed, waved, and fixed (laquer sprayed), as necessary.

■ *Wigs* They cover the performer's own hair entirely and are again formed from hair tied to a shaped foundation net. The front and sides of this net may be stuck to the forehead and temples and, where necessary, hidden by overlaying it with the base medium.

10 Audio

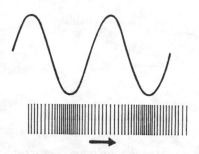

Fig. 10.1 Sound wave
When any material vibrates, its movement creates compressions and rarefactions in the surrounding air. In its simplest form, the air-pressure fluctuates at a sinusoidal rate. Sound in this pure form (*sine wave*, tone) is emitted by certain sources.

It is easy to take TV sound pick-up for granted. A desk stand, a tie clip mike, or the ubiquitous baton microphone seem to meet most needs. We adjust audio amplification so that the reproduction is loud enough. Where is the problem? We can hear what people are saying.

The trouble with casual sound pick-up is that we often cannot. The audio quality alters so much; it does not sound like the original. It becomes amazingly sibilant, muffled, distorted, volume varies, we hear random noise and distracting background sounds. The scale or proportions of the audio do not match the picture (close-up sound for a distant shot). Voices can become inaudible or confusingly jumbled together. The result is unrealistic and tiring to listen to. Little wonder that the professional audio man takes so much trouble to achieve the 'obvious'.

Sound quality

The simplest sound vibrates regularly in a sinusoidal fashion. Its oscillatory motion traces a *sine wave* of a certain frequency. Some sources

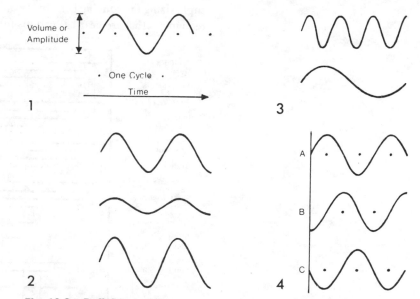

Fig. 10.2 Defining sound
1. *Audio frequency*: The number of complete vibrations (cycles) made per second in hertz. The distance the wave travels while completing a cycle, is its *wavelength*. Its amplitude (strength) is measured in deciblels (dBs) or phons.   2. *Loudness*: Quiet sounds produce slight fluctuations, loud sounds, strong fluctuations.   3. *Pitch*: As the number of vibrations increases, the sound's pitch rises — from low to high frequency.   4. *Phase*: The relative time displacement between two sounds (in degrees, one cycle = 360°).

195

Fig. 10.3   Audibility
The ear's coverage of the audio range varies with sound volume. Highest and lowest extremes are less audible for soft sounds.

(tuning forks, flutes, oscillators) can produce such pure tones. But most emit more complex sounds comprising a main note (the *fundamental*) accompanied by a mixture of multiple tones (*harmonics, overtones*). Their proportions alter with the source; e.g. the type of instrument, its design, how it is played. Sometimes, as with the oboe, these harmonics may even be louder than the fundamental note. Transient sounds on the other hand (clicks, crashes, bangs) contain a broad random mixture of frequencies.

We come to recognize the characteristic ratios of fundamental and harmonics from various sources as their particular *quality*. Ideally we want to reproduce the original proportions exactly – but that is only possible within limits. Most audio systems modify quality due to their emphasizing or reducing parts of the audio spectrum, or adding spurious frequencies that are heard as various forms of *distortion*.

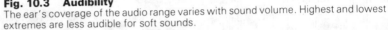

Fig. 10.4   Frequency range
Here the audible frequency range of various sources are compared.

Paradoxically, while our brain is astonishingly tolerant and can interpret even wild travesties as substitutes for the original sound (as small radios continually demonstrate!), yet we remain quite critical of certain distortions – sibilance, overload distortion, severe loss of higher notes (top loss), strong resonances.

Reproduced sound

TV audio is predominantly *monaural* or *'mono'* (one-eared), and like a two-dimensional picture, lacks the ability to convey spatial information directly (although this is possible in stereophonic and quadraphonic systems). Mono sounds can only be segregated by volume, pitch and quality differences.

■ *Monaural problems* Our ears demand a wider frequency range for mono-sound reproduction, than is necessary to achieve similar fidelity in stereo. Also, we become more aware of (and confused by) reverberation in monaural reproduction.

The mono microphone can give equal prominence to any sounds in its pick-up range. So careful microphone positioning is often necessary to avoid one sound masking another, or sources merging in reproduction, or our overhearing extraneous noises.

■ *The audio system* The *dynamic range* (volume range) that any audio system can handle is limited. When too loud, sounds will cause *overload distortion*, producing spurious discordant overtones. If too quiet, wanted sounds will become merged with background noise of comparable level (volume), such as: tape noise, hum and ventilation.

So to avoid exceeding these limits it is essential that you do not overload the microphone itself (too near a loud source), or over-amplify the signal (overmodulation, 'overmod'). Conversely, you must prevent the audio signal from becoming too weak (undermodulation, 'undermod') by placing the microphone close enough and using sufficient amplification. But at the same time, as you will see later, you must not destroy an impression of the dynamics of the original sound source.

Acoustics

Although acoustic design is the concern of the specialist, we are interested as users of the studio in how acoustic characteristics can affect audio quality, studio operations and audio-visual matching.

■ *Reverberant studios* A *live*, highly reflective studio would emphasize all sounds – wanted (speech, music) or unwanted (camera moves, cable drag, footsteps, ventilation, scenery movement). Even using close directional microphones, extraneous sounds would intrude; particularly during quiet scenes.

No staging depicting exterior scenes or small rooms, can hope to be

—————— Direct Sound
- - - - - - Reflected Sound

Fig. 10.5   Studio acoustics
As sound strikes surfaces a proportion is absorbed (frequency-selectively), or reinforced by structural resonance. The reflected sound, now modified, adds to the original (augmenting or partially masking it). Some coloration is artistically desirable. The time taken for the sound to die away (decay time; reverberation period) largely depends on room volume, surface materials, shape, and can range from less than 1 second up to about 6 seconds.

convincing if accompanied by echoing sound! It is always possible to *add* simulated reverberation to any sound, but not normally practicable to remove it to deaden the effect.

Strong acoustic reflections can mask the original sound, reducing intelligibility. And, due to quality changes caused by frequency-selective absorption, the overall effect may become hollow, hard, boomy, 'woofy'.

■ *Dead studios* We can only avoid reflected sounds completely in free space, or in special highly absorbent, multi-surfaced *anechoic chambers*. But by using carefully-positioned sound absorbing materials, we can suppress most acoustic reflections, and produce *dead* (non-reverberant) surroundings. Such conditions reduce the pick-up of extraneous noise, and make 'exterior' sets in studios sound more convincing. However, because sound waves do not carry well in such surroundings (reflections help to reinforce sound strength), they can be very tiring to perform in (especially for singers, musicians), and mikes need to be positioned closer as sounds seem weaker.

■ *Practical acoustics* A certain amount of reverberation enriches and strengthens sounds, conveying an impression of vitality and spaciousness. Therefore, most studios have quite carefully chosen acoustics; neither too live, not too dead.

In practice, quality and sound absorption become modified by staging, equipment, audience, etc. Local acoustics within a setting can introduce considerable quality changes (sound becoming harsh, hollow, boxy), especially if there is a ceiling.

On location, the audio engineer has to contend with a wide variety of acoustic conditions and encroaching environmental noise, and must rely heavily on selective microphones and careful positioning to obtain optimum audio quality.

Microphone characteristics

The main thing you want to know before using a microphone concern:

1. Physical features.
2. Audio quality.
3. Sensitivity and directional properties.
4. Installation suitability.

Which aspects are most important to you, depends largely on the type of sound pick-up involved and operating conditions. For example, ruggedness may be at the expense of fidelity.

■ *Physical features* While *size* may be unimportant for a slung microphone, it can matter where the microphone is to appear in shot or to be handled. *Appearance* then counts too. *Ruggedness* is a consideration where rough or inexperienced usage is likely. *Handling noise* too can be a distraction, for some sensitive microphones. *Stability and reliability* are

Fig. 10.6 part 1   Lavalier (lanyard, neck)
This microphone is slung on a neck cord 15 cm (6 in) below chin.

Fig. 10.6 part 2   Miniature capsule mike (electret or dynamic)
This is clipped to necktie, lapel, or shirt, in single or dual-redundancy form (with standby mike). Presence filters may improve quality. Plastic foam windshields reduce wind-noise.

features that only time and experience reveal, and most high-grade microphones can be relied on if given careful treatment.

■ *Audio quality Ideally* a microphone should cover the entire audio spectrum evenly. Its *transient response* to brief sharp sounds (from musical triangle to jingling keys) should be impeccable. Audio should be accurately reproduced without coloration or distortion. Fortunately, such parameters are less critical in practice!

■ *Sensitivity and directionality* A microphone's *sensitivity* determines how large an audio signal it produces for a given sound volume. Although audio amplifiers can compensate for even the least sensitive microphones, excessive amplification adds spurious hiss and hum to the audio signal.

Any microphone will normally have to work closer to quiet sounds than louder ones, but less sensitive mikes must be positioned that much closer. However, they are less liable to be overloaded or damaged by loud sounds, so that in certain applications (percussion) they may be preferable.

A sound-boom microphone needs to be pretty sensitive, or it would have to work too close to sources (casting shadows); and yet it must not suffer from *rumble* (when racking the boom arm in and out), or wind noise (as it moves through the air). So condenser or dynamic mikes are generally used.

The *directional properties* of the microphone (*polar diagram*) are simply its sensitivity pattern in space. Sometimes you will need an *omnidirectional* response, that hears equally well in all directions. At others you require a very *directional* response, able to pick out a selected sound source and ignore or suppress others nearby. Certain microphones have adjustable directionality.

■ *Installation suitability* When you connect together various pieces of audio equipment interfacing problems can arise. Inter-unit cable plugs are not standardized, and you must use the appropriate connectors or adapters. (Types include: Mini, phono, RCA, Din, Cannon.) As with all audio equipment the electrical *impedance* of your microphone must match the line or amplifier into which it connects. Although a low impedance unit may sound fine in a higher impedance input, the reverse is less likely. Low impedance mikes (50–600 ohms) are most versatile for you can use longer cable lengths without top-loss; unlike high impedance mikes (2000–10 000 ohms) which are also susceptible to hum/electrical interference pickup.

In European designs the amplifier input should be at least five times the mike's rated impedance (typically 200 ohms) to avoid high frequency distortion.

■ *Choice of microphone* All audio men have prejudices about the right mike for the job and exactly where to place it; for no two situations are *identical*. Listening to a piano performance, we find the instrument's tone varies considerably with its manufacturer, tuning, performer; and even changes with temperature, humidity and acoustics. While most specialists would agree to use a condenser or ribbon microphone, its positioning is influenced by many subtle factors.

While there is no 'universal' microphone type, one design may fulfil several different purposes. A certain condenser mike may well serve for a boom, floor stand, hung, or desk stand. But it would be unsuitable beside a boisterous drummer or as a hand mike at a remote, due to its susceptibility to overload.

Personal microphones

One widely used method of audio pick-up employs a personal microphone attached to the speaker. Audio quality is generally good, even under fairly noisy conditions. The main disadvantages are that: the mike can be muffled by clothing; loud noises can occur from contact with clothing (especially personal ornaments), or objects being demonstrated, or from handling; quality and volume vary as the wearer's head turns; and the mike may overhear other nearby sources.

Small windshields should be fitted for use outside the studio. And remember, leads and connections are particularly vulnerable and should be thoroughly checked.

Although a lavalier or a clip-on mike is itself unobtrusive enough, its cable (visible, or unseen beneath clothing) usually connects the wearer via an audio plug, to a long umbilical audio cable stretching away to a distant outlet. If a guest is seated, you will have to link him up once he is in position. If he moves around he has to drag the cable along behind. Some people quickly accept the idea, others feel tethered, others foul up their cable on obstacles . . . In any case, this cable must be unplugged after program contribution, before the guest can depart.

■ *Wireless (radio) microphone*   This is simply a miniature mike operating into a small pocket or belt transmitter. Its signal is picked up by the nearby antenna (aerial) of a sensitive FM (frequency-modulated) receiver, and fed into the audio mixer. Although modern units are now reliable, transmission pick-up is not entirely predictable. Radio black-out (dead spots; dropout), fading, distortion or interference can arise from multi-path reception or screening due to metal structures or equipment. Diversity reception using multi-antennae arrangements can improve reliability. The system's range is often limited to around 400 m (440 yd) and the transmitter's battery should be regularly checked (life about 4 to 6 hours).

Each microphone needs its own transmitter/receiver system (at its own frequency), and there may be interaction. For long distance reception, a more sensitive antenna array may be essential. A preliminary site survey is generally desirable.

■ *Hearing-aid earpiece*   A technique that is being increasingly used, it to

Fig. 10.7   Hand microphone
The baton microphone is widely used for interviews. Directional response (cardioid) reduces extraneous noise pick-up. *Techniques:* 1. Held just below shoulder height. Pointing at speaker improves quality but can be daunting, and mike may then be too close. Avoid omnidirectional mike, which needs closer use (23 cm/9 in). 2. Avoid low mike position (it picks up background noises). If visible microphone is unacceptable then use personal, fishpole, or rifle mike.

fit experienced commentators or presenters with a *hearing-aid earpiece* (*deaf-aid*). This may be fed by a trailing cable or a small pocket receiver. A combination of wireless mike and earpiece can provide the wearer with considerable freedom of movement, while enabling him to have continuous contact with production staff for instructions, up-to-date information, editorial guidance, or prompting.

His earpiece can be fed with private line information, intercom (talkback), program audio, or remote sources (distant interviewees). This arrangement is known variously as *interrupted feedback* (*IFB*), *program interrupt, switched talkback* (*STB*).

Fig. 10.8   Lip microphone
Used under high-noise conditions; the bar is held against upper lip to maintain constant mouth-distance. All noise-canceling mikes are susceptible to breath noises, and mike-to-mouth distance can be critical.

Fig. 10.9   Stand microphone
Floor stands are height-adjustable and may be fitted with angled extensions. Microphone clips into quick-release head. Heavy base prevents instability.

Hand microphone (baton mike, stick mike)

The hand microphone, which is usually of the omnidirectional type, must be rugged, permit free handling, and have an efficient *windshield* (*wind gag, blast filter, pop filter*). This cloth or foam-plastic shield suppresses the rumbles and thumps from wind noise or close explosive sounds.

Quality is usually satisfactory, but unless users are reasonably competent results can be unpredictable, and there is always the risk of misuse or careless handling. Although most hand mikes use a trailing lead, the cordless *wireless microphone* incorporates a tiny radio transmitter – perhaps with a brief 'hanging tail' antenna.

Many hand microphones are fitted with a *spherical ball mesh*. This permits very close positioning when used outdoors in noisy environments (to exclude extraneous sounds), or to avoid *howl-round* (*audio feedback*) where the mike feeds a PA system (public address, studio address loudspeaker) for a studio audience. It is a safeguard, too, where singers traditionally '*mug the mike*', holding it close to the mouth to add presence to their performance. A close directional mike exaggerates bass, so often needs filtering.

■ *Lip mike/noise canceling microphone*   This specially designed hand-held mike is invaluable for off-camera commentaries in noisy surroundings. Its mouthguard is held against the upper lip.

Equalized for close speech (attenuating its normal bass excess), the environmental noise becomes inaudible. Because it obscures the user's face, the lip mike is seldom used in shot.

Stand microphone

Made in various sizes and of adjustable height (0.3 to 1.5 m/1 to 5 ft) the stand microphone is used for soloists/speakers and for instrumental pick-up in orchestras, groups, etc. Various offset tubes (swan-necks) permit precision positioning and small slim fittings prevent the stand from being obtrusive. A quick-release top-clip enables the mike to be removed and hand-held where necessary.

The main disadvantages of the stand microphone are that the

performer (talent) may kick it causing loud resonant noises, or displace it, and its cable can prove a hazard (floor tape it if necessary). Remember too, that it is essentially a *static* pick-up arrangement and people may easily move off-mike.

Desk microphone

Microphones can be clamped into small supports to enable them to stand on tables or desks. Formerly used to give an 'authoritative air' to a broadcaster, today the mike is small and unobrusive, or sometimes hidden. A foam-plastic pad may prevent table-thump pick-up. Some audio engineers prefer to use stand mikes, hidden by a false table-front or through table-top holes, to circumvent this noise (Fig. 10.10).

When audio pick-up is difficult, a desk mike is sometimes used in drama productions to augment other microphones – hidden at a vantage point within staging, furniture props.

Fig. 10.10   Desk microphone
1. For desk discussions, mikes in small fittings are often used.   2. Careful positioning is essential for good sound pickup; typical distances D = 0.9–1.2 m (3–4 ft) and d = 0.3–0.6 m (–2 ft).   3. Desk-top mikes may be vulnerable (desk thumps, displacement).   4. Alternatively the mike may be isolated on a floor-stand, either using holes in desk-top or behind false desk front.

■ *Desk discussions*   Although personal mikes can be used for this situation, desk microphones offer better quality and are preferable. Microphones should be positioned in the direction of head movement. Directional mikes reduce unwanted pick-up of acoustic and environmental noise or audience loudspeakers, but placement may be more critical. Do not intermix different types of microphone because quality will be inconsistent. Cables should be concealed, tidied and taped (to desk and floor). Never run them alongside power cables and only cross them at right angles.

Fig. 10.11   Slung microphone
Suitable for area pickup or nearby sounds. Problems arise when people move, or are at different distances, or are seated.

Prerehearsal checking includes: connections, microphone routing to the audio control board (scratch mikes, never blow on them when identifying) and *phasing* (connections). If mikes are not all similarly connected, the quality will change when their outputs are mixed together (bass loss).

Slung microphone (hung, hanging mike)

Where space is restricted or orthodox mountings cannot be used, you can suspend a microphone over the performance area. Slung microphones should not be used for well-balanced pick-up of individuals in a seated group especially for close-ups. Although they are useful for such broad group sounds as orchestral sections or an audience. If the slung mike is to be kept out of long shots, its positioning can become a compromise.

In a limited-access area (e.g. a narrow hallway), a slung microphone may be effective providing the performers play to the mike and there are not excessive reflections from nearby walls. Sometimes the microphone can be disguised as a light fitting.

If a *directional* microphone is used, you can reduce pick-up of acoustic reflections and environmental noise, but run the risk of people moving 'off-mike'. A non-directional (omni) pattern is less restrictive but needs to be closer to avoid reflected sound.

A slung microphone must be rigged securely with safety lines and placed to avoid distracting shadows or overheating by nearby lamps.

Fishpole (fishing rod)

Here a microphone is attached via a rumble-insulating cradle, to the end of an aluminum or bamboo pole (2–2.5 m, 6–9 ft long). The mike angle is fixed. Suitable for short-duration use under difficult conditions or to save a sound boom, the device is extremely flexible but tiring to operate. The fishpole, like the shotgun (rifle) mike, is very widely used for fieldwork.

Fig. 10.12   Fishpole operation
The fishpole is fitted with the mike (preferably in shock-proof cradle) at one end, and a counter-balancing audio cable connector-box (intercom to operator, audio to console) at the other. The fishpole can be held well-balanced above head or tucked under arm. 'Pole-in-belt' methods are unbalanced, particularly tiring, and hazardous.

Fig. 10.13   Small studio boom
The pre-adjusted telescopic arm (counterweighted) is pivoted on a column of adjustable height in a swivel-castered tripod stand. The boom arm can be tilted and panned, the stand wheeled around, and the microphone can usually be turned and tilted. Boom stretch is typically 3–4.5 m (10–15 ft).

Sound booms

■ *Small sound boom (small giraffe, lazy arm)* Extensively used in smaller studios, this lightweight supplementary sound boom is used for static pick-up or limited movement over a smooth floor. Due to its fixed (preadjusted) arm length, the mounting must be pushed around to follow action; an operation that can be cumbersome and preoccupying.

As its central column height is raised the assembly becomes increasingly top-heavy and less stable (particularly during moves), so you normally tilt the boom arm for higher mike positions, keeping the column low. The boom's closeness to the subject makes it correspondingly more difficult to keep out of shot.

Cable guards on wheels prevent accidental cable overrun. Pushing over floor cables can be hazardous. The microphone's cable is laid along the floor away from cameras and lamp cables. The boom operator often plugs his headset into a nearby camera's auxiliary outlets for program and intercom.

■ *Large sound boom (big boom)* Operationally, the large boom provides the most flexible method of audio pick-up, for you can easily follow movement and favor selected sources. This ensures optimum sound quality while keeping just out of shot and avoiding boom shadows.

Fig. 10.14 part 1   Fisher boom
1. Three-wheeled base (1.1 × 1.6 m/3 ft 9 in × 5 ft 3 in).   2. Brake and gear change.   3. Control to hydraulically raise/lower platform (moves with column), max column height 2.4 m (7 ft 10 in), pump handle to recharge cylinder. Operator's seat for standby periods.   4. Pan and tilt lock screws (pans over 360°).   5. Right-handed crank (max mike height 4.5 m/15 ft).   6. Script board.   7. Left hand-grip (squeeze for mike tilt, turn for mike turn).

Fig. 10.14 part 2   Typical boom operations
1. *Microphone position* is adjusted to suit shot, remaining just outside frame limits. Boom arm is raised/retracted as shot widens. Operator must anticipate cuts to longer shots.   2. Head-turn: Either a swing and mike turn (slight arm-length change), or a static compromise position with mike turn.   3. Reverse turn: Extend and swing arm, with mike turn. Aim to avoid over-reaching subjects and turning mike back (any face shadows cannot be seen by operator).   4. Ascending: Boom arm tilts up and extends, mike tipping down during walk.   5. Split sound: Boom can accommodate separate sources up to about 2 m (7 ft) apart, by turning mike and/or swinging boom. Otherwise sources must move closer together, or use a second mike.

The boom's microphone is held in a swiveling cradle at the end of its long telescoping tubular arm. This counterweighted arm is pivoted on the central vertical column of the wheeled boom perambulator (pram).

With his left hand the standing operator controls mike tilt and direction (gripping and turning respectively) and swings the boom arm, while extending/retracting the boom with his right (hand crank). The platform's operational height is adjustable – useful for seeing action past cameras. The microphone cable may be suspended or run along the floor to a wall outlet.

The large boom's main disadvantage for the smaller studio lies in its size. Also, unless the operator descends and moves his boom around, a second person is needed to reposition it. Boom tracking (moving the pram while in use) is only normally necessary for large-area working, to follow widespread action, to move aside for cameras, or for fast relocation.

Omnidirectional characteristics

This microphone design provides pick-up of equal sensitivity and quality in all directions. So it cannot discriminate between wanted and unwanted

Fig. 10.15   Omni-directional resonse
Equally sensitive in all directions. Rugged, generally less susceptible to breath pops, or impact shock.

sounds. It responds to nearby speech, acoustic reflections, and environmental noises equally well! It is useful for groups or where subject moves are unpredictable.

Unidirectional characteristics

The directional response (polar diagram – directional or directivity patterns) of a microphone is determined by its type and design. Its behavior may not be constant throughout the audio range. If it is more directional at higher frequencies, sources in line with the microphone axis will reproduce well. But as they move to one side, or the mike turns, the audio loses *definition* (brilliance, highs) as the high frequency response deteriorates.

The unidirectional microphone is sensitive over a particular angle and relatively deaf in other directions. This characteristic helps you to concentrate on certain pick-up areas and suppress background sounds, or to favor quieter sounds (weak voices) against louder ones. The exact response-angle needed, depends on its intended application. A unidirectional mike is invariably used in a sound boom, so that it can

Fig. 10.16   Cardioid response
A broad heart-shaped pickup pattern, insensitive on its rear side.

DEAD AREA

Fig. 10.17   Hypercardioid response
A modified cardioid response — more directional with a prominent rear sensitivity lobe.

work further away without extraneous pick-up. Certain mikes can be switched to different coverage patterns, and frequency response to suit the occasion.

■ *Cardioid* This broad heart-shaped unidirectional pattern covers some 160°. Used for general purpose sound pick-up, it readily, accepts spaced sources, unlike a half-eight pattern which is more restrictive at close distances. Rear pick-up is limited; although some designs are more *omni*directional at lower frequencies.

■ *Hypercardioid (supercardioid, 'cottage loaf')* A modified cardioid response with a narrower frontal *lobe* (pick-up pattern), and a weaker rear pattern. Generally considered as providing the best balance between incident and ambient sound.

■ *Bidirectional* Both faces of the microphone are live, providing a two-directional figure-of-eight pick-up patterns of about 100° each. To either side are two dead (deaf) areas. A typical traditional ribbon-microphone characteristic, this pattern is occasionally used for musical set-ups.

■ *Highly directional microphones* These are used wherever you want extremely selective pick-up, to avoid environmental noise or for distant sources.

Table 10.1   Checking out the sound boom

Microphone	Speak to the audio engineer to identify mike and check audio quality. *Phase* the microphone if necessary, with others.
	Check mike connector is secure (waggle cable end).
	Check mike cradle — suspension OK? Free movement?
	Turn and tip mike. Operating strings taut and free moving?
Boom arm	Extend/retract boom arm (*racking* in/out). Any rumble? Controls and movement smooth? Is arm balanced throughout movement? (Adjust weights to suit mike weight.)
	Lock off the arm's pan and tilt.
Pram (perambulator)	Raise/lower platform (hand crank or hydraulic pump).
	Check wheel brake, lock and steering.
	If steering mode is adjustable (steer/crab) check action.
	Tires OK? (Not over-inflated, no stuck-on floor tape?) Check the seat.
Cable	Check plug into wall outlet.
	Is cable routing satisfactory? *Slung cable* — avoiding lamps, anticipating moves. *Floor cable* — not obstructing, sufficient available, free for boom moves.
Additional	Check intercom/talkback and private line (reverse talkback) to audio engineer.
	Check script board is secure and script available.
	Check picture monitor being used by boom operator (fixed to boom, or slung).
	If a loudspeaker is attached to boom (for *foldback* of effects, music, talkback instructions, etc.), check cables, connections, and reproducing levels.

Table 10.2   Sound boom operation

Preliminaries

Check the boom is in the planned floor position relative to lighting treatment, and angle it to provide maximum use.

Check platform height to give good viewpoint over cameras, but avoid hanging lamps when operating.

Check boom arm at max/min reach relative to area coverage, obstructions, accommodating possible action spread.

Note key-light positions, look for potential shadow problems.

Operation

Mike position	Positioning depends on several factors: microphone sensitivity, and directivity, acoustics, ambient noise, source loudness and shot size. Closeness varies with the ambience required; a close mike minimizes studio acoustics, provides deader sound and has better presence. It also avoids extraneous sounds. Very close mike positions coarsen sound quality, reveal breath noises, etc. Close microphones come into shot and cast shadows. A more distant mike may provide inappropriate sound quality.
A steady boom	For a stationary situation, hold the boom arm still and the mike location steady towards the speaker. Avoid overhead positions — except when an omnidirectional mike covers random groups.
Swiveling the mike	A directional boom mike may be turned successively to favor each person speaking (gunning the mike), but someone can inadvertently be left *off-mike* unless the show is scripted. Benefits with closely positioned people are arguable.
Anticipate action	Lead rather than follow talent as they move around. Do not rely on script memory, or instructions alone, but watch people for preliminary signs (e.g. before they rise or sit).
Locking off	Beware locking off the boom arm (tilt and pan) except for a static subject, or when leaving or moving the boom. People may unexpectedly move away, get up or sit!
Fully extended	Despite counterweighting, the boom arm becomes less manageable when extended. Swinging (arc) and raising the arm is less controllable, particularly when done quickly. By retracting during wide swings, it is easier to move and avoids causing shadows.

Divide your attention between:

Performers	What performers are doing — are going to do.
Headset	The audio is 'split' on your earphones — one ear has *program sound*, the other has *intercom* from director and audio engineer. You can only judge audio quality and balance approximately, so be guided.
Shots	Be aware of picture monitors showing line (transmission) picture; check shot size. Camera tally lights show which is switched on-air. Monitors are usually too distant to detect whether your mike is appearing in shot. If in doubt, during rehearsal carefully dip it into shot; and when told of the shot limits remember these for subsequent mike positions.
Boom shadows	Watch for mike shadows on people or backgrounds. Move the mike and check if sound quality is still acceptable. If not, indicate that it cannot be cleared. (Changes in the volume, shot, or lighting may be necessary.) During transmission (or a 'take'), hold the shadow still, or creep it out stealthily, or slowly raise the boom, or try to hide it, or wait until off-shot before repositioning.
Repositioning the boom	Boom moves to a new floor position may require a separate operator's aid (*tracker*) under instruction. Coordinate boom moves with cameras; watch for cable or boom arm catching in lamps. Take care when running over cables (damage, noise, instability).
Script or show format	Keep up to date on deleted or extra shots, or moves. Mark *take-over points* where action is to be covered by another boom.

Fig. 10.18   Bidirectional response
Sensitive on either face, but deaf to sound pickup at the sides.

Fig. 10.19   Line microphones
A form of highly-directional microphone. The popular shotgun (rifle) form is shown here with and without its windscreen (windshield). Usually hand-held, it can be affixed to a camera, or used (without shield) in a sound boom.

Fig. 10.20   Parabolic reflector
Extremely directional and sensitive, sound is focused by the reflector into the central microphone.

Line microphones use a slotted interference tube(s) with an attached electrostatic mike. The smallest version (0.54 m, 22 in long), the *shotgun* or *rifle* mike (50° coverage), can be hand-held in the studio to isolate people within an audience; and in the field, hand-held or attached to the top of a camera. For exteriors, a foam-plastic windscreen/windshield is fitted.

The largest *machine-gun* versions (2.5 m, 8 ft long) use combined tubes of varying lengths and are tripod-mounted. Although rather cumbersome and producing inferior quality (particularly off-axis), the device is useful for isolating individuals in a distant group. Because directivity worsens below 2000 Hz, a bass cut is often introduced to reduce noise pick-up.

Parabolic reflectors provide a sensitive highly directional system (10–40°) in which a parabolic-shaped metal reflector (0.6–0.9 m, 2–3 ft diameter) focuses sound into a central cardioid microphone. Ineffective below about 300 Hz, the reflector is bulky and liable to wind rock unless firmly mounted. Whereas the *line microphone's* directionality is achieved by rejecting sounds outside its pick-up angle, the *parabolic reflector* actually concentrates sounds by acoustical reflection, and so has increased sensitivity.

Dynamic (moving coil) microphone

A very robust design, the dynamic mike is not sensitive to handling and has a wide range of applications: baton, fishpole, small boom, desk or stand, slung, and field (location) use. It is often used for less critical sound quality (close singer) or close loud sources (e.g. drums). Small versions are used as lavaliere and clip-on personal microphones.

The microphone tends to be unidirectional to higher frequencies, but non-directional to low frequencies. Consequently there is a top fall-off as subjects move off-axis (center line). This feature is useful with sources that are shrill, toppy or sibilant; when one deliberately positions them off-axis.

This type of microphone works by sound wave pressure variations vibrating a diaphragm which has a small coil of wire attached. Coil movement within a magnetic field generates audio currents. A typical frequency range is 40–16 000 Hz.

Condenser (electrostatic) microphone

The condenser microphone produces the highest audio quality (typically 20–18 000 Hz), and has an excellent response to transient sounds. It is used for high grade pick-up (moving or static), especially when some distance from source (e.g. slung over an orchestra). It can be fitted to a boom, stand, fishpole, or slung.

The condenser mike has the disadvantages that it is relatively large, and being highly sensitive, it is liable to input overload distortion by very loud nearby sources. In addition, the unit requires a polarizing voltage supply and an adjacent preamplifier.

In the condenser microphone a light flexible metallic membrane is stretched close to a flat metal plate and a polarizing potential (e.g. 60 V DC) is applied between them. Sound wave pressure fluctuations alter the intervening space and hence their intercapacity. Varying current continually taken to recharge this changing capacitance constitutes the audio signal.

■ *Electret capsule* The electret capsule is very extensively used as a personal or a concealed mike, providing good quality pick-up. This relatively cheap miniature microphone incorporates a plastic film diaphragm with an inbuilt 'permanent' electrostatic charge; thus eliminating the need for an applied polarizing voltage. A tiny associated amplifier (battery powered) is enclosed in the mike housing.

Performance deteriorates with ageing, resulting in a loss of higher frequencies (top, highs), reduced sensitivity, and increased background noise. Deterioration can be accelerated by high humidity, moisture, heat and dust. Rapid unexpected failure is not uncommon.

A *pressure-zone microphone* (*PZM*) is an unobtrusive low-profile, plate-mounted electret capsule with a hemispherical or a semi-cardioid pickup pattern. Attached to e.g. floor, table or wall surfaces near the sound source, the rugged PZM combines sensitivity and high-quality output, with considerable freedom from contact noise, or audio overload. It is, however, liable to emphasize ambient reflected noise from surroundings. (See Glossary – *Pressure-zone microphone*).

Ribbon (velocity, pressure-gradient) microphone

This microphone is suitable for static pick-up of speech and music, and for stand and slung applications. It has an excellent transient response and produces the highest audio quality. The ribbon microphone has an even frequency response (e.g. 30–18 000 Hz) over its pick-up field – although there is some top-loss for pick-up oblique to its ribbon. Bass notes are emphasized when the source is very close. Its normal figure-of-eight directional response is often made unidirectional (asymmetrical) by internal design.

On the debit side, the ribbon mike is not generally robust or compact. It is not normally suitable for mobile boom use (or hand use), being susceptible to wind rumble and wind damage. Also it is subject to overload from close loud sounds.

In the ribbon microphone, a thin corrugated foil strip held between magnet poles vibrates with air pressure differences on either face, so generating an electric audio current in the foil.

Crystal microphone

Although very cheap, highly sensitive and of small size, the crystal mike is fragile and its audio quality is restricted. Only adequate for less exacting use (field interviews), it is very suited to *contact* applications (electric guitar).

When sound strikes its diaphragm, a small bimorph (two-sliced) crystal is twisted, and piezo-electric effect produces a corresponding voltage, the audio signal.

Audio control

Located at his *audio control console* (board, desk, mixer panel) the *audio control engineer* (*sound mixer, sound supervisor*) selects and blends the various program sound sources.

His attention is divided variously between:

1. Selecting and controlling the outputs of various audio sources (mikes, discs, tape, film, VT).

212

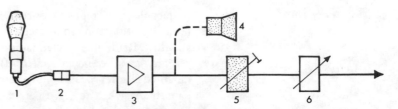

Fig. 10.21 part 1   Basic audio control
1. *Microphone plugs* into (2) studio wall outlet and (3) the audio is amplified.   4. A side-chain *audition/pre-hear circuit* provides check-point before further processing. 5. A pre-set *attenuator/pad* adjusts channel amplification (*gain*) and (6) a *channel fader* (slide, quadrant, or knob) controls it overall.

Fig. 10.21 part 2   Audio console
Pre-set gain. Adjusts audio channel gain (amplification) to compensate for variations in levels from sources.

Group selector. Switches a sound channel to a group fader (A or B).

Echo. Adjusts the amount of artificial echo added to an individual audio channel.

Equalizer. Adjustable tone filters altering sound quality by boosting/reducing/cutting high or low notes, or part of audio spectrum.

Channel fader. The main control adjusted to suit the volume of an individual source (e.g. quiet voice, loud instrument).

Audition/cue/pre-hear. A switch enabling the audio engineer to check-listen (earphones or loudspeaker) to a channel that is faded out; so not audible on the main audio output.

Group fader/group master/sub-master. All sources switched to that group (here labelled A or B) will be faded in/out simultaneously. The audio signal's strength (amplitude) is monitored by a local indicator.

Master fader. The outputs of the group faders are routed to this master control, which adjusts the overall program level, as shown on the master volume indicator.

Audio-control desks are made as completely integrated units, or in modular form as above (plug-in sub-units).
Additional facilities include: audio limiter/compressor; audio batons; echo devices; program monitoring level adjustment; control of audience address/foldback/playback system.

INDIVIDUAL AUDIO CHANNELS

Preset Gain

Group Selector

Echo

Equalizer

A Group

B Group

Channel Fader

Audition (Pre Hear)

Group Volume Indicator

GROUP FADERS

A Group

B Group

Group Fader

Master Volume Indicator

MASTER FADER

Audio Output

2. Keeping the volume indicator within system limits by adjusting appropriate channel faders (amplifier gains).
3. Following the program audio and pictures (script, breakdown sheet), and the director's intercom (talkback) information.
4. Checking audio quality on high-grade loudspeakers.

5. Scrutinizing picture monitors showing line and preview shots, to check sound perspective, warn against mikes coming into shot, and boom shadows.
6. Guiding (and cueing) audio operators on booms, studio floor, audio disc and tape repro.
7. Perhaps operating audio disc/tape equipment.
8. Liaison with other production team members.

Before rehearsal, the audio engineer selects the circuits of all required audio sources (local and remote) on a *patch panel*, and plugs them into the channels of the audio control console where *input/channel switches* select the sources as required.

The outputs of audio equipment vary from a few millivolts (requiring a *low-level/microphone level* input system), to higher signals from audio tape or cartridge machines, film and VT channels. Having already been amplified to e.g. 1 volt, these are fed into *high-level/line-level inputs*. Each audio channel includes a *pre-amplifier* (*pre-amp*) to boost weaker sources and/or *attenuators* (*pads*) to reduce strong audio signals. Comparisons of average volume are made during rehearsal (*level tests*) to match their relative levels (volumes).

The gain (amplification) of the *program/channel amplifier* for each source is adjusted with a channel fader or 'pot' (potentiometer). This may be a rotating knob, or slider/quadrant control. (The latter has the advantages that several can be operated simultaneously with one hand, and their relative positions are obvious.) These channel faders can be used to fade individual sources in/out ('pot in/out') as well as control their average level. On some consoles, you can switch to a pre-set pot setting (*keying in*); but there is always the danger of clipping the start of the incoming sound through a *late cut* (*upcutting*).

Having adjusted their relative strengths with individual *balance* faders, these sources (e.g. several choir mikes) can be linked to a single *group fader*, and are controlled simultaneously. The outputs of all group faders are controlled by a *master pot* (*line/main-channel control*). *VU meters* show the signal strength at control points, enabling audio to be maintained within system limits. (See Glossary – *Volume indicators*.)

Dynamic range control

We need to control the system's amplification (gain) to keep the audio signal within its volume limits (*dynamic range*). This is done both manually and by automatic limiter/compressor circuits.

■ *Manual control* Although our ears are tolerant of a wide volume range, tensing to very loud sounds and relaxing to receive quiet ones, straight audio systems do not have this property. If you keep audio amplification down to prevent peak overloads, quietest sounds will be inaudible. Increase amplification to hear these and even fairly loud sounds now reach upper system limits and distort.

You can overcome this dilemma by imperceptibly altering the audio

Fig. 10.22   Volume indicator
1. *Volume Meter* (*VU Meter*): The upper scale, marked in decibels (dBs), is for calibration and line-up purposes (using steady tone). The lower scale shows percentage modulation, where 100% is system's max limit.
2. *Peak Program Meter* (*European*): Designed specifically to indicate sound volume *peaks*. Has fast-rise/slow-return characteristics, so its needle fluctuates less than VU meter. Its easily read seven section logarithmic scale is akin to ear's loudness response (unlike VU meter).

gain manually, to compensate for these volume peaks and troughs. Some sound sources need little or no control, while others (symphony orchestras) require continual sensitive readjustments. The trick is to anticipate, and to make any changes gradually, so that the listener is unaware of the subterfuge. You must not 'snatch back' peaks, or boost quiet passages, destroying dynamics completely through overcontrol (riding the gain).

VU meters and PPMs show the audio signal's strength relative to the system's available range (Fig. 10.22). (See Glossary – *Volume indicators*.)

■ *Audio processors* Automatic circuits can be used to adjust audio amplification; restricting the volume range, controlling unanticipated peaks or wildly varying sound levels. They can substitute for manual judgement – but electronics make no artistic evaluation and can create unnaturally strangled crescendos, or inappropriately boost quiet sounds. Most audio engineers regard such equipment as a useful safety facility for the unexpected moment, rather than an artistically viable control method (compressors; limiters).

While both variable gain systems prevent peak overloads above a selected volume, the compressor also increases amplification of quieter passages, and can be used to compensate for unwanted volume variations, e.g. fading as a vocalist's hand-mike position changes. In radio, DJs deliberately use (misuse?) such facilities to make quiet background music surge in whenever they stop speaking. Similarly, the surging beat of *peak-limiting* is used as an audio effect. (See Glossary – *Ducker*.)

Sound balance

When you *balance* various sound sources, you are adjusting their relative volumes, clarity, quality, scale, perspective, and the ambience of direct to indirect sound. The audio engineer is concerned in practice with two forms of program balance, that we can consider as *continuity balance* and *internal balance*.

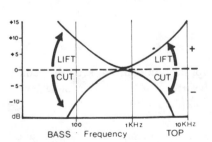

Fig. 10.23 part 1   Equalizers, audio filters, response selection amplifiers (RSA)
Filters for compensatory or dramatic effect. Progressive accentuation or reduction of top or bass. Bass and top roll-off are widely used, e.g. to remedy boomy reproduction, reduce air-conditioner noise, wind, traffic noise.

■ *Continuity balance* Here he controls a succession of sources; ensures that one person is not disproportionately louder or quieter than another; that the background music or effects are proportional to the dialogue; that other audio sources (film) match with studio sound. (Preliminary *level tests/voice levels* assess typical audio control settings needed.)

■ *Internal balance* Internal balance involves combining and blending a group of sound sources; e.g. arranging a microphone set-up for a musical group, an orchestra or a choir. Actual techniques vary with personal preferences, the sound sources, acoustics, and the final effect required.

A *single microphone balance* places a single highly sensitive (often non-directional) mike at an optimum point for communal pick-up. At best this method avoids the phase distortion created when several microphones pick up and blend a particular instrument, and blur its

Fig. 10.23 part 2   High and low pass filters
Suppress rumble, hum, or high-pitched noises respectively.

Fig. 10.23 part 3   Audio baton, octave filter, shaping filter, graphic equalizer
A series of slider controls boost or reduce chosen frequency segments in the audio spectrum. Slider positions show effective response.

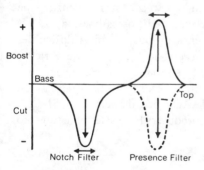

Fig. 10.23 part 4   Notch filter, presence circuits
Notch filter puts very steep localized dip into audio spectrum to diminish interference (e.g. hum) without substantially affecting overall quality. *Presence circuits* (*mid-lift*) provide boost or cut (up to 6 dB) around selectable frequencies (2 to 6 kHz) to improve clarity and audio separation, improve sibilants lost with distance, or bring sounds 'forward' (presence) from others.

attack. It avoids the variations in perspective and proportion we get when giving varying emphasis to selected instruments, while backgrounding others. But its effectiveness depends upon acoustics, layout and suitable positioning.

A *multimicrophone balance* uses a series of pick-up points. It is seldom possible in imperfect acoustic conditions to find one good mike position to suit a variety of instruments having different quality and attack. Distant pick-up of soloists when using one communal microphone can sound rather thin. The blending of a multimicrophone set-up offers better balance flexibility when rehearsal time is short.

Close balance techniques now widely used for musical group recordings are virtually a 'sound processing' operation. Each instrument's (or sub-group's) output is recorded on a separate track of a multitrack audio tape (16, 24, 32 parallel tracks on a 2 in. wide tape; 4, 8 tracks on 1 in. tape). Instrumentalists or singers (using earphones) may perform together, or to prerecorded tracks. Individual tracks can be *lifted-off*, replaced, treated selectively (adjusting volume, quality, reverberation, pitch), synchronized and blended with the others to achieve exactly the required combined sound. This complex *track-laying* or *mixdown* process can be computer assisted in the *dub-down* to a final track!

Sound perspective

At first sight it seems self-evident that the sound's proportions should match its associated picture. Close-up sound for a close-up shot; more distant sound for a long shot. This is a good working maxim. But there are exceptions where it is preferable to cheat this relationship and deliberately introduce nearer or more constant perspective than the actual shot suggests.

For example: the scene intercuts between shots of a bedroom where an old lady is dying, and shots of a street parade showing her long-lost soldier son's band returning from overseas. Audio cuts from the quiet death bed, to the blaring military band. Should we avoid the rapid volume jumps that would actually take place – and either reduce the differences, or spread the same sound over both scenes? The optimum treatment is a matter of taste, the effect you want to achieve, and the need to avoid ambiguity.

If a singer wanders around a spacious set, moving from close to long shots, do we really want the volume to vary? Can the mike maintain a constant relationship to the singer? It may be necessary to prerecord the song and have the performance mimed on camera to its playback.

We normally adjust sound perspective within a scene by altering the mike distance to suit the shot size by boom movement or intermicrophone mixing. As closer sounds tend to seem louder, with stronger bass and top than more distant pick-up, *presence filters* (*dialogue equalizers*) may be introduced to simulate or emphasize differences between close and remote sound quality.

Sound quality

Although high fidelity is our normal aim, there are good technical and artistic arguments for using audio filters to modify the system's frequency response when necessary:

1. Cutting low bass to reduce boom rumble, hum, improve speech clarity, improve the hollow or boomy quality in boxy scenery; reduce background noise/atmosphere (e.g. ventilation).
2. Cutting upper parts of the audio spectrum to reduce sibilant speech or S-blasting, quieten studio noise, reduce disc or tape noise.
3. Cut bass and top to enhance the illusion of exterior settings.
4. Slightly accentuate bass to increase the impression of size and grandeur of vast interiors.
5. Effects filters to simulate telephone (300–3000 Hz) intercom, public announcements. Phone filters (*distort*) are often controlled by the video switcher equipment, to provide automatic *audio-follow-video* switching as the picture intercuts between the two ends of a phone conversation.
6. By matching different types of mikes' frequency responses, we can reduce audible quality differences.
7. Quality matching between different sound sources (e.g. studio and film) can be improved.

Filtering can provide better audio continuity, and helps you to remedy such defects. Where the director is using *electronically inserted backgrounds* (e.g. by chroma-key), or studio settings have inappropriate acoustics (e.g. a 'cave' constructed of timber and plastics), the audio quality can be made much more convincing by audio filtering and reverberation treatment.

■ *Equalization* When disc or audio tape recordings are made, the frequency spectrum is automatically modified (top is boosted, bass is reduced). This anticipates or overcomes various technical difficulties such as background noise. There are several 'standards' in use. Strictly, therefore, a disc or tape should always be reproduced with compensatory equalization matching the standard used for recording (*Audio tape:* NAB, NARTB, CCIR, IEC, DIN. *Disc:* RIAA, Standard Spectra, ANSI, BSI, DIN, IEC, ISO, NAB, etc.). Some reproducers have selectable filters to suit a variety of standards.

Audio tape – recording and replay

Operationally, audio magnetic tape recording is simplicity itself. You have only to avoid over- or undermodulation, and many recorders have automatic recording-level controls.

■ *Audio tape* There are several types of audio recording tape: ferric, chrome (and 'pseudo-chrome', i.e. cobalt-treated ferric), ferrichrome, metal. For minimum background noise, least distortion, and best top

Fig. 10.24 part 1   Typical layout of a reel-to-reel tape recorder
1. Supply spool.   2. Erase head.   3. Record head.   4. Replay head.   5. Capstan
roller.   6. Pressure idler roller.   7. Take-up spool.

response the appropriate bias setting and equalization should be switched
in on the recorder/reproducer, to suit the type of tape used. Longer-play
tapes are thinner, less rugged, and liable to print-through between
adjacent layers (echo; pre-echo).

■ *Recording*   Before recording, the tape must be magnetically
neutralized (wiped, erased). This can be done initially by a bulk
electromagnetic eraser (bulked), but is usually a regular part of the
recording process. In the recording mode, the tape first passes an *erase
head* where strong ultrasonic currents eliminate any previous recording.
The result when played would be a barely audible rustling – *tape noise*.
This *clean* tape passes against the *record head*, which is fed with the audio
signal you wish to record. As each particle of the tape contacts the head's
gap, it becomes magnetized in proportion to the audio at that instant.
The modulated magnetic pattern is invisible. To assist this recording
process the record head is also fed with an ultrasonic *bias current*, which
substantially reduces distortion and background noise.

■ *Replay*   The tape can be replayed (monitored) during recording and
subsequently reproduced (and/or recorded on) several hundred times. To
reproduce the tape, it is passed over a *replay head* (playback, reproducer);
the tape's magnetic pattern inducing weak electric currents in the head,
corresponding with the original audio. An interlock mechanism usually
prevents your activating the recording circuit accidentally and wiping the
tape during replay.

Fig. 10.24 part 2   Splicing audio tape
After marking edit point at replay head gap, the tape is cut at 45° on splicer groove.
The tape is then butted together and adhesive jointing tape is attached to the *back* of
the splice.

■ *Tape speed* The tape must be reproduced at the recording speed, or you will get a marked pitch change; fine for chipmunk effects, but otherwise to be avoided. Higher tape speeds provide a better high-frequency response, lower background noise, less obvious *drop-out* (momentarily silent gaps due to tape surface irregularities or damage), easier audio editing (the audio pattern is more spread out), but it uses more tape per minute.

■ *Editing* You can edit magnetic tape by physically cutting (45° diagonally, with an unmagnetized razor blade) and joining sections with an adhesive patch on the back of the tape. This quick flexible process produces a silent joint but disrupts the original recording, particularly if it contains several different tracks. Instead, you can rerecord (*dub, dub-off*) sections onto a new tape; but this can result in cumulative distortion, hum, background noise, etc. Colored non-magnetic tape is often interspliced as lace-up *leader*, or as mute *blanking* between sequences for identification.

■ *Production use of audio tape*

1. Providing a premixed track of music, effects, background, to simplify handling during the show.
2. Bringing back sounds from location shooting, to provide audio background to studio action.
3. To suggest that there is an unseen speaker (e.g. at the other end of a phone, outside a door).
4. Providing taped commentary while a lecturer moves to another exhibit, or is out of microphone range.
5. Providing total prerecorded commentary to film or videotape voice over, voices off, VO; sound over vision, SOV).
6. Preselected effects or music dubbed from disc for cuing or treatment.
7. Recording atmospheric sounds (*room tone*), or other non-synchronized sound (*wild track*) for use when laying audio tracks during subsequent videotape editing. To provide overlays (bridging sound) between scenes.
8. Checking what was said during impromptu discussion (to guide editing).

Audio contributions

Most TV programs contain not only speech, but a proportion of music and effects also. These vary with the type of program. While a chat show is only likely to have music at the start and end, to 'top and tail' the production, and give it a 'packaged' feel, a dramatic presentation may well be strewn with a variety of carefully selected atmospheric effects, and musical passages (bridges, stings, mood music).

In Chapter 18, we shall discuss the *artistic* potentials of sound, but meanwhile, let us look at the very *practical* approaches to the preparation of program audio. Program audio is of several kinds:

1. Dialogue   direct pickup of people in shot.
2. Voices off – Someone out of shot (e.g. at the other end of a phone; in the next room).
3. Voice over – Commentator or announcer, explaining or making observations.
4. Spot effects – Effects made on-the-spot, such as door knocks, phone bells, car siren, baby cries, dog barks. Some can be made to order, while others may not happen when you need them (e.g. a parrot's comment).
5. Background effects – General atmospheric sounds (e.g. wind, seawash, birdsong, traffic).
6. Foreground music – Someone playing (or miming) an instrument.
7. Background music – Mood music, nearby source (a radio playing, the music at a ball).
8. Special effects – Treated sounds (that may in fact be used in roles 3 to 7) to simulate robots, prehistoric animals, ray guns, phantoms . . .

Operationally, you can approach program audio in several ways. The direct method is often the easiest. You can simply produce the sound in the studio during taping; in front of a mike, or by playing and mixing in discs and tapes as needed.

Direct sounds (spot effects) in the studio are often pretty unconvincing, and a disc or tape recording may sound much more realistic (e.g. a battering ram on a castle door, an explosion, an angry mob).

You can simplify operations on the recording day by preparing music and effects beforehand, and maybe mix down several tracks/discs onto one audio tape (e.g. seagulls, sea, wind, thunder . . .). Then you have only to cue up and play this at the crucial moment, instead of going to and fro between various sources. This is a particularly useful idea when your playback resources are limited.

Whichever method you choose, music and effects are played-in during rehearsal and the taping session, to form a completed program.

The main drawback of this direct approach is that it provides a *composite soundtrack* (*married track*), so that if you do any VT editing afterwards, you will disturb its continuity. If you decide, for example, that the action in a scene is taking too long, and cut out some boring 'business', the background music will suddenly jump where you have made this tape edit cut! So where you anticipate detailed post-production editing, it may not be a good idea to add all music and effects during studio taping.

Instead there are advantages in leaving the addition of all music and effects until the videotape has been edited; then at a dubbing session you can add these to the final speech/dialogue track. This does give increased flexibility, but takes time, and further delays the completion of the program, after VT editing. If you are single-camera shooting of course, you have no option but to build the program in this way.

Finally, one can always modify/supplement the program audio during the VT editing session itself, and in a small or simple production, this may be quite practicable (e.g. adding title music). But most VT editing sessions are costly in hire charges and time, so that anything delaying actual picture editing is undesirable.

This process of working on the program sound after studio production is called *audio sweetening*. In broad terms, we can say that it is concerned with:

1. *Correction* – Adjusting relative sound levels, filtering (e.g. hum, rumble).
2. *Enhancement* – Changing sound quality to improve realism, or for dramatic effect (e.g. adding reverberation, equalization.)
3. *Blending* – Selecting, arranging, and balancing, the various sources being intermixed (e.g. relative strengths of dialogue, effects, music).
4. *Continuity* – Ensuring that the sound levels, balance, and the sources heard, are consistent from one shot to the next.

When intercutting a series of shots taken at different times, or introducing cutaways, inserts, etc., we must make sure that the sound appears continuous; that there is a match in dialogue continuity, background effects (wild track), atmosphere (e.g. air conditioner noise), and music. Level jumps and quality changes arise all too easily! A regular technique here is to use a common *overlay track* throughout a sequence (e.g. the same traffic-noise track runs continuously behind all the different car-interior shots). The sounds are uninterrupted, and their volume can be adjusted to suit the situation. They stay in the background while people are chatting, but rise (grow louder) as the driver sees he is about to get stuck in a traffic snarl-up.

There are occasions when VT editing involves intercutting between 'shots with soundtrack' and *mute* shots; yet we want program sound to be continuous throughout.

This situation is common in TV and film interviews, shot on just one camera. The camera concentrates on the guest throughout (picture with sound), later taking a few separate silent 'nod shots' (reaction shots) of the interviewer 'showing interest'. (Sometimes the director will also take after-shots of the guest 'reacting silently', followed by shots of the interviewer repeating the questions on-camera.)

To build the final soundtrack, make a separate synchronized audio recording during the take, or a dubbing from the original VT audio. Then you can run this speech as a continuous track throughout. Or dub off and insert appropriate sections of this track into the edited VT version, wherever a mute cut-in is introduced (*lift-off/layback*). The result appears quite natural, even where parts of the original speech have been edited out.

Playback (foldback)

By reproducing sound effects or music over studio floor loud-speakers (*playback, foldback*) performers can relate or synchronize their cues or action. However, this reproduced sound becomes colored by studio acoustics, and if picked up by the action microphones it often has a falsely hollow quality.

Fig. 10.25 part 1   Echo room
Sound to be treated is reproduced over loudspeaker in echoing room (hard walls, baffle) — reverberant sound being picked up by microphone and mixed with direct original sound. Largely superseded by space-saving electronic methods.

■ *Miming and postsynchronizing* Good sound pickup may not be possible where the action is very energetic, too distant, or taking place in very noisy surroundings. There are several solutions, although these may have varying success. You can prerecord the appropriate sound, and have someone synchronize their performance to its playback (*prescoring*). Or you can shoot despite poor sound quality, and have the performer (or someone else!) record the required song, dialogue, later in the studio, in time with the reproduced pictures (*postsyncing*); a technique widely used in film-making. With either method, it can be extremely difficult to sustain *lip-sync*; any mismatch becoming distracting, even ridiculous. Really accurate synchronism is only possible by postsyncing short repetitive loops of a brief section, as when dubbing foreign language films (*dialogue looping*), or by using *time-compression* techniques (see Glossary).

The simplest and cheapest solution, where it is possible, is to avoid shots that show clear mouth movements. Use more distant shots, point-of-view (POV) or over-shoulder shots, and reaction shots, which do not reveal any lip-sync errors, and add a separate voice-over track recording to the picture later!

Music and effects (M & E track)

As television has spread throughout the world, it has become increasingly profitable when taping productions to anticipate foreign-language markets. Arrangements are now often made to supply videotape or film programs without speech, but with a *music and effects track* (M & E) which includes all atmospheric sounds, effects and music. The purchasing organization then adds its required language commentary or dialogue, based on the original scripting.

Audio effects

You can modify audio quality in various ways to create or enhance a particular impact; for dramatic, environmental, or novelty effect.

Fig. 10.25 part 2   Magnetic tape delay
Time lag as audio tape travels from record to replay head can be used to produce a delayed reproduction of original — an echo when mixed with incoming sound. If this delayed reproduction is fed back into recorder input, *flutter echo* develops. The multi-replay head system shown here produces a succession of delays, which can be mixed with original sound or fed to series of studio loud-speakers to modify effective acoustics (ambiophony). The tape loop or magnetic disc records continuously, erasing each revolution.

■ *Filtering* As we saw earlier, audio filters (equalizers) enable you to emphasize or reduce parts of the audio spectrum to any degree – either correctively or to modify quality. So you can make sounds seem shrill, edgy, thin, tubby, hollow, harsh, brittle, etc.

■ *Distortion* To simulate the audio distortion from shortwave radio pick-up, public address systems, or intercom, you can hold a microphone near an earphone or earpiece, or small loudspeaker. You can alter tonal quality further by placing the assembly in a box, jug or pipe.

■ *Acoustic feedback* When a microphone's amplified output is fed to a nearby loudspeaker, and then overheard by the same microphone reamplified, a loud oscillatory howlround (acoustic feedback) can build

Fig. 10.25 part 3   Mechanical spring delays
The original audio signal causes transducer head to vibrate the spring(s). The mechanical resonances detected by pickup transducer head have a reverberant coloration and are converted into corresponding audio signal. The inherent coloration of spring systems ('twang') has been considerably improved to provide most realistic effects.

up. This situation is a hazard when using public address/sound reinforcement systems. The cure is to reduce the loudspeaker output, move the mike or loudspeaker, use a more directional mike or loudspeakers; or even use digital processing, which moves successive repetitions away from the original frequency. As an *effect*, you may deliberately introduce controlled acoustic feedback to produce a hollow, echoing sound quality.

■ *Reverberation* Artificial reververation can be produced in several ways, and mixed with the direct, untreated ('dry') sound in appropriate proportions for the effect required. The *reverb* or *audio delay* units most commonly used are spring types, plate types, and increasingly, analogue/digital methods (see Fig. 10.25, and Glossary – *Audio enhancement*).

Audio effects using tape

Audio tape provides a valuable range of sound treatment opportunities.

■ *Feedback* During recording, the tape output is controllably fed back to mix the replay sound with the input. The result can be varied from a drawn-out hangover effect, to distinct echo, or stutter effects (rapid multi-echoes – flutter echo).

■ *Speed change* Replaying at *slower* speeds than the original recording lowers pitch and tempo, increasing reverberation. Most sounds take on a deliberate, sinister character. Xylophones, bells, thunder, gongs, become strikingly powerful. Other are totally transformed (e.g. slow-speed wind or water) and can be used for 'synthetic' or atmospheric effects.
Reproduction at a faster than recording speed raises pitch and tempo. About one-and-a-half to two times, sounds become 'miniaturized', appearing perky and comic – the audioland of singing mice, insects, household utensils, etc., of cartoon. Reproducers with special rotating multihead turrets can provide pitch changes at normal tape speeds, or correct the pitch for tapes reproduced at the wrong speed.

Fig. 10.25 part 4   Reverberation plate
A similar principle to part 3, using a suspended steel sheet as the vibrating medium. Adjusting the closeness of a parallel sheet of porous material modifies the reverberation time (1½–5 sec). Although effects are very realistic, temperature changes can affect performance.

■ *Reversal sound* Tape reproduced backward (a normal recording fed in tail first) can modify the character of sounds. Sustained sounds tend not to change, but percussive or transient ones have a characteristic 'indrawn-breath' quality.

■ *Time compression and expansion* (see Glossary).

■ *Repeated sound* A tape loop enables you to repeat a sound over and over again, for example to heighten tension, imply hysteria or mental derangement.

■ *Fading* Slightly misguiding a tape during replay can simulate fading and top loss. Alternatively, two identical discs played slightly out of step produces fading and distortion.

Table 10.3   Disc and tape reproduction

	Disc	*Tape*
Advantages	Lightweight, easily stored (vertically) and occupies little space. Even brief sections are quickly selected from a disc, particularly if recorded in a series of *cuts/bands* (multi-cut/multi-band). Extensive library sources available. Two pick-ups can play one disc (for continuous repetition, echo effects, simultaneous play of different sections). Speed adjustment permits pitch change (for effects). Two turntables provide continuous playing, mixing, crossfades. Only two basic disc formats; 33⅓ rpm, 45 rpm (plus obsolete 78 rpm format).	With moderate care, not easily damaged (but rapid stop-starts can cause tape snarl-up!) High audio quality, consistent throughout tape; permitting many replays. High reliability and durability. Tape length can be chosen to suit duration required. Recording can be revised, edited. Audio tape can be erased and reused. Background noise remains generally low. Tape recording is a simple reliable process. Process can be automated.
Disadvantages	Surface noise (static attracts dust, fingermarks) worsens with use. Playing life limited (lightweight pick-ups are not robust, vulnerable), distortion and defects increase with use. Quality deteriorates towards disc center (waveform compression). Disc is easily damaged (scratches, blemishes, warping). Pick-up stylus is easily damaged; can ruin recording. Equipment may have speed instability (wow, flutter); and rumble. Unwanted sections cannot be removed. Disc recording involves precision processing (results vary); or *direct recording* onto lacquer/acetate discs (short life).	Larger reels are bulky and pose storage problems. Recording is damaged by magnetic fields, heat, humidity. Tape is susceptible to damage. Tape *drop-out* can disrupt the recording. Tape is not rapidly excerpted. *Unwanted* passages necessitate play-thro, fast run-thro, editing out, or dubbing on to another recorder. Tape has to be rewound before reproduction. Various incompatible tape formats. Recorder heads must be demagnetized with small electromagnet to obviate background noise build-up.
Cuing	Requires skill (monitor output at an audition/prefader/prehear point with channel faded out). *Methods:* 1. *Monitor.* Play silent up to cue point, then fade in channel. 2. *Back-cuing.* With a rapid-start turntable (0.2 sec to full speed). Play to cue point. Switch off turntable with stylus in groove. Hand-reverse disc to cue point, then back a further e.g. ½ revolution (to provide run-up time at switch-on). When disc is required, switch on (microswitch on fader, or push-button start) and fade up. 3. *Slip-cue.* Use felt *slip mat* under disc. Find cue point as in 2, but do not reverse. Pinch-hold the mat, switch on turntable — disc remains still, turntable revolves. On cue, release mat and fade up.	Precision cuing is simple. (Check on monitoring system.) Equipment provides immediate start at any required points. *Methods:* 1. Play to cue point. Stop. Wind back by hand to exact cue point. (Rear mark tape at replay point for future cuing.) 2. Wind tape to footage indicator and check precise cue point. Cue point seeking can be automated: metallic cue tag; photostop (wipe off magnetic coating with solvent — clear backing-gap stops tape); microprocessor memory. Identifying color leader can be spliced in. Tape carts may use *cue-tones* (1 kHz) on an auxiliary track; to switch channels, fast run, or start the next cart in a stack.

Synthetic sound

There are many fascinating program opportunities for synthesized sounds including abstract background noises, voices for the inarticulate or mute, newly created sounds for monsters and science fiction (see Glossary – *Audio enhancement*).

■ *Treated sounds* You can use one audio signal to control another, modulating its volume or pitch by using voltage controlled amplifiers, ring modulators, hybrid coils, etc. So you can articulate sound effects; a locomotive whistle cries 'All aboard', or an organ sings its own lyrics.

Taking fragments from existing recordings, you can modify their quality by juxtaposing them in any order (reversing, modulating or repeating) to produce sounds quite dissociated from their origins. The resultant *musique concrète* may have a musical character (for jingles, title music) or provide imitative or humorous noises.

■ *Dissociated sounds* Many sounds lose their identity when divorced from their original context. Some are unfamiliar anyway (straining pack-ice, roaring gas flames, insect noises). You can often transpose sounds for dramatic effect – jet engine noise to accompany typhoon scenes. Some take on an entirely new significance – a crushed matchbox simulating a collapsing barn.

Musical instruments can be used to produce a fantastic range of sound effects – disembodied waverings from a musical saw; squeaks, grunts, whines and creaks from a violin. These noises can in turn be treated and modified. Such devices are more than audio stunts. They enable you to stimulate the imagination, often improve on available sounds, and to materialize the unknown or the impossible.

■ *Synthesized sounds* Entirely synthetic sounds can be created electronically by an *audio synthesizer*, which enables a keyboard or interconnected control circuits to manipulate specially generated and processed sounds. Oscillations of various shapes, frequency, repetition rate, can be selected and treated; volume can be varied (*vibrato, crescendo, diminuendo*); build-up and die-away adjustments can be used (attack and decay times); quality can be modified (selective filtering) and so on. The resultant synthesized sounds may deliberately simulate recognizable sources, or provide a new audio impression. Even quite modest home computers can now produce a wide range of sound effects that can be used (or further treated) for program applications.

Noise reduction

As we saw in *Reproduced sound* (page 197), the audio engineer has to control the strength of the audio signal, to prevent its exceeding the system's limits. (A loud sound can overload and create unpleasant distortion. A very quiet sound can be lost amongst background noise.) This control of the volume range flattens the sound's dynamics.

Particularly where a sound is re-recorded several times in the course of preparing a program, relative dynamic ranges can be noticeably reduced.

The simplest method of reducing high-pitched background noise is to boost the upper part of the audio spectrum during recording (*pre-*

Table 10.4   Audio tape and disc formats

Reel-to-reel tape

The supply spool is manually threaded through the tape path, to the take-up spool. The tape is easily edited, fitted with inter-section color leader tape, and self-stop tape (foil or photostop).

Tape width	¼ in (6.35 mm) is universal. (½ in/12.7 mm, 1 in/25 mm, 2 in/50 mm, specialist versions are also used.)
Spool diameters and capacity (standard tape)	3 in (75 mm) with 175 ft; 4 in (100 mm) with 300 ft; 5 in (125 mm) with 600 ft; 5¾ in (145 mm) with 900 ft; 7 in (175 mm) with 1200 ft; 8¼ in (210 mm) cine with 1800 ft; 10½ in (265 mm) NAB with 2400 ft; 11½ in (290 mm) European with 3250 ft.
Tape speeds per second	$^{15}/_{16}$ in (2.35 cm); 1$^7/_8$ in (4.75 cm); 3¾ in (9.5 cm); 7½ in (19 cm); 15 in (38 cm); 30 in (76 cm).
Tape thicknes	Standard play — 0.002 in (0.05 mm); Long play — 0.0015 in (0.04 mm). Double play — 0.001 in (0.025 mm); Triple play — 0.00075 in (0.02 mm). Quadruple play — 0.0005 in (0.013 mm).
Tracks	1 (full tape width); 2 (half-track); 4 (quarter-track) formats.
Running time (at 7½ in/19 cm per second)	1200 ft = 32 minutes; 1 minute = 38 ft (11.6 m); 30 minutes = 1125 ft (342 m). Other lengths and speeds in this ratio. For other tape thicknesses multiply duration by: Long × 1.5; Double play × 2; Triple play × 3; Quad play × 4.

Cassette

A small enclosed two- or four-track reel-to-reel system. Self threading. Rapid loading and instant start (no wow or slur on run-up). End of track may not include auto-stop. Not readily edited.

Tape width 3.5 mm; speed 4.75 cm/second (1.7/8 ips). Cassette maximum durations: Mono — 30, 60, 90, 120 minutes (half-track, turning cassette over at end of first play through); Stereo — maximum 15, 30, 45, 60 minutes.

Cartridge (cart)

Its container houses a single enclosed spool, holding an *endless* tape loop; feeding from its inside, and winding onto its outside.

Tape width ¼ in (6.3 mm); speed 7½ ips (19 cms). Self-threading. Auto-rewind by running on at normal speed to beginning of recording. Rapid loading. Instant start. Eight mono tracks, or four stereo.

Three NAB standard sizes (durations at 19 cms): A & AA = few seconds to 10½ minutes; B & BB = up to 16 minutes maximum; C & CC up to 31 minutes maximum. (Short-duration versions used for identification announcements, brief inserts of music, speech, effects.)

Widely used for automatic replay of spot commercials in a *carousel* playing, say, 24 carts in succession. Other equipment can play several carts simultaneously. Earlier design shortcomings now largely overcome (wow, flutter, stereo phase errors).

Disc formats

78 rpm	Obsolete. Coarse-groove reproducing stylus. Mono only.
45 rpm	Modern fine-groove reproducing stylus (tip radius 0.0005–0.0007 in), in mono and stereo forms. For wide-hole discs, a special center adapter is needed.
33⅓ rpm	Similar fine-groove format. Available in mono, stereo, and experimental quad forms. Stereo discs can be played on fine-groove mono pick-up. Quad replays in stereo.
Digital audio disc	See Glossary — *Compact disc*.

emphasis) and reduce it correspondingly during replay (*de-emphasis*); but this is only partially successful.

A number of ingenious *noise reduction* (*NR*) circuits have evolved, which considerably reduce background noise, permit quieter sounds to be reproduced, and so extend the effective dynamic range. Unfortunately these systems are not mutually compatible, and it is as well to realize this, when reproducing a recording using a particular NR system.

Although designs differ, NR systems fundamentally aim to automatically compress the dynamic range during recording, and expand it (in a mirror image) during reproduction. The widest-used noise reduction processes include Dolby A, B, C, HX; the *dBx*, the *Telecom* system. (See Glossary – *Noise reduction*.)

11 Film

Although it can be difficult to discern on the screen whether a program originates from film or television cameras, there are very practical differences in the production mechanics of these media. Paradoxically, as the TV system becomes more flexible, the edges blur between these differing techniques.

Basic filming process

Film making involves a series of processes, each one hopefully taking into account later stages – the cameraman shooting in anticipation of the film editor's continuity problems, days or weeks later.

It is not possible to examine results while filming and you have to wait for proof prints (*dailies, rushes*) to show whether action, camerawork, lighting, etc., was successful. Occasionally, a small TV camera is fitted to the film camera (electronic viewfinder), providing an *approximate* monochrome check on a nearby TV monitor. Otherwise only the camera operator can know, for example, whether the mike dipped into shot – and he might have overlooked it while preoccupied with the action. As a result of retakes to correct faults or errors and selective editing, about $1/10$ to $1/20$ of the overall film exposed is finally used (a $10:1-20:1$ *shooting ratio*). To save processing costs faulty takes (NG) are not printed.

Synchronized audio may be recorded separately on a portable magnetic recorder; or in the sound film camera itself, on a magnetic stripe alongside the picture. Entire scenes are often shot with a *silent camera*, the eventual audio track being devised later in the dubbing suite.

Scripting

There are several approaches to shooting a film, ranging from the hopefully empirical to the meticulously planned.

In *unscripted* off-the-cuff shooting, the camera tends to record available events: perhaps working from a rough outline (*shooting plan*). Material is selected during editing and compiled into a program format with added commentary. This technique is often used when shooting documentaries and news stories.

Fully scripted productions on the other hand, are first broken down into their component shots or scenes, and the mechanics involved for each shot or group of shots are assessed. The staged action is then methodically shot out of story sequence (*shooting schedule/plan*) for maximum economy and efficiency. For example, if the story line requires a series of intercut shots between the heroine at the cliff-top and the hero

227

camera is often 'left behind' as he moves away – yet is at his destination as he arrives. Shots intercut from his viewpoint, to that of the person to whom he is speaking.

The overall effect here is smooth-flowing and provides a variety of viewpoints. To do the obvious and shoot this entire sequence as *continuous* action would have required several cameras, spread over an appreciable distance – an approach that might not be practical anyway. Usually it would not provide the same effect.

Filmed shots tend to be of briefer duration than those in continuous TV production. Watching a well-made film, we see that most shots (the period between picture transitions) last only a few seconds (typically 3–15 seconds). A good serial film unit may achieve as many as 120 shots a day (about 18 minutes running time), although this is untypical. A live TV production might last 25 minutes, and contain 100–200 shots, edited 'on the hoof'.

Production decisions

■ *Film making* In *film production*, the director works in very close proximity to his single-camera crew. He normally discusses shots, treatment, action, with the cameraman, who then interprets these instructions. The director will only see the results later, and must rely on his judgement and his crew. The brief action segment is rehearsed, shot; and then retaken if necessary. Additional cover shots (protection shots) may be taken, 'just in case'.

Positive prints are made of the good takes (checked as the *dailies/rushes*), which the film editor separates, examines, selects, relates and interconnects. He uses a script or brief, cue-sheet and *continuity-report* information (forms giving action detail, slate numbers, etc., identifying each *take*). So he forms the individual clips of film into a cohesive and appropriate continuity (the *cutting copy*). The editor evaluates processing and grading (print density and color quality). Having decided on shot relationships, cutting points and suitable transitions, the editor submits his *rough-cut* for the director's approval. Subsequently he may modify the precise cutting points, tightening scenes, making final revisions to produce the final *fine-cut*.

Later the processing labs match the stored master negatives to his cut version, using the edge-numbers printed along the original film edge to guide them. An optical print is then made, using the transitions he has wax pencil codemarked on his cutting copy.

The sound track is compiled (*laying tracks*) and the *dubbing mixer* skilfully blends dialogue, commentary, effects and music. A *rock-and-roll* facility enables picture and sound tracks to be run synchronously forward/backward for rapid correction during dubbing.

There are opportunities to examine and reconsider at each step (time permitting!), and to remedy or improve results. Each stage in this exacting process paradoxically leads to a product with seemingly absolute freedom in time and dimension.

■ *Television techniques* For the *TV camera* to achieve this degree of flexibility, it has to be used segmentally, in exactly the same way. It is not surprising, therefore, to find that many TV directors are aiming to do just that, now that more mobile facilities are available – despite the complexities of continuity and postproduction editing that consequently arise.

In practise, TV production approaches now range from the discontinuous 'near filmic' shooting alternative material for later postproduction decisions, to continuously performed multi-camera presentations that provide a completed product at the end of the taping session.

For the most part, tight studio scheduling means that the majority of production decisions have to be made by the time you are due to videotape the program. Most transitions (cuts, mixes) are introduced while taping. Retakes are essentially corrective rather than experimental. So scenes are seldom reshot with several variations of action or treatment, for subsequent selection in editing. Background sounds (music and effects) are mainly included during the take. The greater time pressure of TV studio production usually precludes the opportunity for polishing, precision and experiment, that film making offers. There is little use of postsyncing. The elaboration of postproduction editing/dubbing in television depends largely on available facilities.

Uses of film in TV

Film has always had a regular place in TV studio production. And although videotape is progressively used for similar purposes, it remains a convenient medium for many applications.

■ *As a total presentation* Studio talent introduces or provides commentary for a predominantly filmed presentation. Audio comes from studio and from the film's soundtrack.

■ *As illustrative material* Film is often used to illustrate lectures, demonstrations and talks. It may be specially shot for the program, or *library* (*stock*) *shots* may be used. The latter are obtained from organizational archives, or rented from specialist libraries. These short film clips of news events, locations, processes, personalities, etc., provide both historical records and sequences where it would be impractical or uneconomical to shoot new material.

The picture quality of library shots can be variable in color, blemishes and definition – they may not cut into studio shots unobtrusively. Also, available library shots can become too familiar, particularly when they are the only record of an event.

Where only monochrome shots are available and the program content is appropriate, these clips may be tinted (sepia, blue, red-orange). This is achieved by using a color synthesizer, by adjusting color balance, or using 'tarif' controls. Snow scenes and night shots may still prove convincing in black-and-white, although transmitted in a color system.

Varying Light/Weather

Extraneous Noise

Extras
Crowd Control
Accommodation, Liaison

Transport
Catering
Road Access
Parking, Travel time
Permits

Asst. Director

Cameraman

Scenery

Sound

Wardrobe

Props
Set Dressing

Actors

Continuity
Anticipating
Editing

DIRECTOR

Make-up

Power
Supplies

Lighting
Electrician

PRODUCER
Costing
Budget
Scheduling

Additional Labor
Material
Supplies
Equipment

Fig. 11.3   Location filming
The location film team needs to be self-sufficient, anticipatory, well organized and adaptable.

Library shots are often run mute (silent), and new effects or music substituted for any original soundtrack.

■ *To extend action*   By using a recorded insert, we can have a person leave an apartment (studio set) and walk into the street (on film). The technique is used regularly in TV drama productions. Continuity can be important both visually and for audio treatment (background sounds). Location wild-track may be used in the studio, or 'dropped into' the final videotape during dubbing/editing. However, the wise director keeps matching needs to a minimum.

■ *To extend settings*   Shooting a *partial setting* in the studio (e.g. a shop doorway); we cut to the complete street location in the film insert.

■ *Reducing the number of studio settings*   Where studio space is too limited for the required number of settings, additional scenes can be insert-filmed.

■ *Once-only action*   Prefilming or videotaping is essential where action might prove unsuccessful in the studio (for example involving animals); or take too much time during the videotaping period (an elaborate make-

Table 11.1   Typical equipment for small-unit filming

16 mm camera lens	Arriflex, Eclair, Auricon Cine-Voice, Bolex.
	Zoom e.g. focal length 12 mm–120 mm (hand-crank or rod-operated).
	'Normal' angle at 25 mm.
	Or turret lenses — 12, 16, 25, 50, 75, 100, 120 mm focal length.
Camera support	Body brace, shoulder brace, shoulder pad.
	Light tripod, with triangular spreader (spider).
	Sometimes a small lightweight dolly, for dollying (tracking) shots.
	Lens angles below 12°, i.e. focal length greater than 50 mm require a firmly supported camera.
Shooting duration	Maximum 11 minutes with 400 ft (122 m) magazine.
	Battery-powered camera runs typically 1½ hours (3000 ft of film).
Lighting equipment	Small portable lamps on camera or hand-held (e.g. Sun-gun, Frezzi). Lightweight lamps, Red-heads, Lowell-lites, Colortran quartz lights; quarts broads, Mini-brutes; Photofloods in small scoops; reflector boards.
	Lamp supports — hand-held, gaffer-tape attached, screw-clamps, gaffer-clamps (spring-jaw clamps), clip-lights, lightweight tripod stands, telescopic spring-loaded support poles (polecat, barricuda) fitted ceiling-to-floor or wall-to-wall.
Microphones	Lanyard, electret or baton personal mike (cable connected, or wireless mike).
	Sound men with fishpole or shotgun (rifle) mike.
Sound recorder	Lightweight portable synchronized magnetic audio recorder (e.g. Nagra), earphone monitored.
	Synchronous sound using a camera-to-recorder sync connection (cable or wireless), crystal lock or time code.

up change); or is too dangerous (fire); or is non-repeatable (an explosion); or is very critical (an accurately thrown knife).

■ *Visual effects*   To produce time-lapse effects, reversed action, transformations, etc.

■ *Animation sequences*   These may be cartoon or animated still-life.

■ *To include performers not otherwise available*   Filming persons who could not attend the taping session (e.g. overseas guests).

■ *Situations where effective studio staging is impractical*   Filming location exteriors, spectacle, etc., where studio replicas would be impractical or less effective.

Sound on film

■ *Double-system*   Using this method the picture and sound are recorded separately; so providing maximum editing flexibility. However, apart from general background sounds, close synchronization is normally

Fig. 11.4   Film sound
Optical track – combined (married) print.   1. Variable area track.   2. Variable
density track. *Magnetic track* – 3. Magnetic stripe. Balancing stripe facilitates flat
smooth roll wind.   4. Mute picture, separate 16 mm perforated magnetic film.

essential between the film camera and its associated audio tape recorder;
for speech we have to maintain exact *lip sync*.

To achieve precise synchronization, camera and recorder may be
connected by a special sync-pulse cable, but this is physically restrictive.
Instead, matched crystal controls, can be fitted to independently
maintain accurate motor speeds; or alternatively, wireless control
interlocks or an edge time code may be used.

As the start of each take, *an identifying head slate* is filmed, giving all
reference details to aid eventual editing. By matching up the sound and
picture at its small clapper-board closing (*sync marks*), we ensure that
film and soundtrack are in step for that take. Automatic slating facilities
are sometimes fitted – these 'flash' a frame and bleep the soundtrack
simultaneously. Alternatively, a *tail slate/end board* (upside down) is shot
at the end of a scene.

■ *Single system*   This method, frequently used for TV news filming,
records the audio beside the picture on a magnetic *track*. However, the
audio's 28 frame separation (in advance) from its corresponding picture
(about one second difference), means that editing the picture will cut the
audio too – but not at the same point.

An audio track may be recorded *optically* on film, using variable area or
variable density light modulation systems. This optical track is printed

Fig. 11.5   Film formats
1. 35 mm gauge.   2. 16 mm.   3. Super-8.

Fig. 11.6   Joining film
The two shots to be joined, are cut in the splicer and connected by: a *temporary splice* using translucent adhesive splicing tape (butt join), or a *permanent overlap weld* using film cement, (scraping off film emulsion for overlap join), or a *heat butt-welded splice* along frame-line (used for negative editing).

photographically along one edge of the released film, in a *combined* (*married*) *print*.

Many TV organizations keep picture and magnetically recorded sound separate throughout, and reproduce them in synchronism (*double-headed*) in the telecine equipment.

Most TV organizations use 16 mm film almost exclusively; a gauge that provides an optimum balance between running costs and good picture quality. Equipment is reasonably lightweight, especially when compared with costly, bulky 35 mm cameras. Editing, which becomes progressively difficult with smaller gauges, is still reasonably easy; although reliably unobtrusive splices require checkerboard (A–B roll) cutting.

In a search for further economy, a Super-8 format with magnetic stripe soundtrack is increasingly used; despite its inferior picture quality. To simplify editing, the film may be transferred to videotape; the stripe soundtrack being dubbed onto a separate magnetic (sep-mag) film.

Fig. 11.7   Checkerboard and A/B roll assemblies
When printing narrow-gauge film, material is usually distributed between two rolls A and B, interspaced by blanking (black leader). By inter-switching/dissolving between rolls, optical combinations (dissolve, wipe, etc.) and invisible splices (not intruding into picture area) become possible. The system avoids intermediate duplication stages for combined effects.   1. For *checkerboard assembly*, the output changes between A and B rolls at each cut; except where an overlap is required for a combined effect (dissolve, wipe, etc.).   2. *For A/B roll assembly*, shots are spliced consecutively on one roll, until an overlap is required for a combined effect. The output then remains with the other roll for successive shots until the next combination is required. These techniques are also used for rapid excerpting from complete programs (film and VT).

Transmitting negative film

After the *negative stock* used for most filming is processed, a *positive print* is made. The original negative itself is generally considered too precious to risk damage through continual handling and projection, for any blemishes or dust (reproducing as white 'sparkle') can irremediably deface the picture.

However, to save the cost and time involved in printing, the negative film (electronically reversed) may be transmitted, e.g. for urgent news stories. The important compensatory color and exposure corrections (*grading*) normally made during printing have instead to be introduced operationally when the film is reproduced (on sight, or using programmed electronic correction).

Negative film is sometimes used when dark or dense scenes are to be transmitted from a vidicon telecine system; this method overcomes lag (trailing) problems otherwise arising from low-light conditions.

Reversal film

Film emulsions designed for *reversal*, produce a normal positive image with natural colors and tones on the original camera film. There is no negative involved. No print is necessary, so processing is quicker.

The advantages of reversal film include higher available sensitivity (*speed*), finer grain, improved sharpness, and better color reproduction. Against this, the exposure range is very limited, which may produce crushed highlights and shadows. Also, there is less opportunity to correct exposure and color errors. Most important, the original film is itself projected and is vulnerable. So a print may be needed, anyway, to provide a cutting copy for editing in order to preserve the master film.

Mechanics of film reproduction

We use film in television production in several forms:

1. As a *reel* of 1 minute to greater than 2 hours duration.
2. As a series of brief-duration sections (*clips*) joined by opaque *blanking*, or *cue leaders*.
3. As closed *film loops*, joined tail-to-head to provide continuous repetition (mist, snow, rain), or repeated cyclic motion (e.g. to study machine movement) using a centreless spool or take-up pulleys.
4. As short *film strips* containing a series of different still frames.
5. As individual *film slides/transparencies* – televised by a transparency-projector (picked up by a TV camera), or a special slide scanner.

Telecine

The European television picture rate is 25 pps (50 Hz power supplies). If standard films (24 fps) are projected at this slightly higher rate (4 per cent) there is no discernible speed-up. However, film shot specifically for European TV is normally exposed at 25 fps instead of the motion picture standard.

■ *Camera-type telecines* This arrangement is extensively used in North America. On a *film island* installation, a standard TV camera faces a mirror or prism multiplexer system. Through this it can see selectively, the output of two film projectors or a 2×2 inches slide (transparency) projector.

A storage-type camera tube (vidicon, plumbicon) is used to produce the

Fig. 11.8   Multiplexed telecine
A mirror or prism system enables one TV camera to selectively shoot a slide projector or either of two film projectors. The assembly is mounted on a film island.

Fig. 11.9   Picture-rate conversion
To relate the standard film projection rate (24 frames per sec) to TV standards of 30 pictures (USA) per sec, several sampling methods are used (e.g. project one film frame 3 times, the next twice; fast film pulldown with light-source pulsing 5 times per film frame/4 times per TV picture).

Fig. 11.10   Color flying-spot scanner
A plain white raster traced on the cathode ray tube focused onto the moving film. This exploratory light spot is focused through color filters, into corresponding photo cells. Their outputs as each point is scanned, constituting red, green, blue video signals. To compensate for film movement, twin displaced rasters, twin-lens systems, or a rotating polygonal prism are used.

video signals, coupled with a film projector exposing each film frame for 2½ TV fields. This compensates for the discrepancy between the standard film projection rate of 24 frames per second, and the standard TV picture rate of 30 pps (related to 60 Hz power supply frequency) in USA and Canada.

The intermittent projector moves the film in rhythmic 'pull-and-hold' jerks, to freeze each frame momentarily as it passes the picture gate, so giving the TV camera time to discern successive pictures clearly. The resultant video signals are then adjusted and processed.

■ *Flying-spot scanners* are widely used, and are capable of the highest-quality film reproduction. The film travels at a constant speed (*continuous motion*) through the telecine equipment. On a special picture tube a constant-brightness raster is scanned. The focused image of this scanning light pattern explores the moving film. The resultant fluctuations, as the varying film densities interrupt the scanning light beam, are picked up by photocells. Their modulated electrical signal forms the telecine's video output.

■ *Digital telecine* systems use three full-line sensors (RGB) to scan the passing film. These charge-coupled devices (CCD) analyse its light variations. The resulting charges are held in a digital frame store to be read out as the video signal. This system provides flicker-free slow motion, jog and still frame pictures.

Video control for telecine

Film is capable of superb color reproduction, but it is not an entirely consistent material. We shall find some variations in color balance between different batches of the same film stock; and between different types of color film. Moreover when filming, exposure or color temperature may not have been accurate or consistent. Where film has aged, or is a copy of the original print (dupe), further changes arise. So in printing, film labs adjust the intensity and color balance of their printer lights to compensate empirically for discrepancies (grading).

However, when televising a film, such errors are more apparent than in theater viewing, where eye adaptation and subjective effects tend to compensate. Consequently, a film that may appear satisfactory when theater-reviewed beforehand, often requires further compensations when televised. Where the film has not been finely graded, these may be considerable.

By adjusting video gain, black level (sometimes gamma), color balance, and saturation, considerable improvements become possible. Color correction may also be introduced by *electronic masking circuits*, compensating for film dye deficiencies, and certain *analysis errors* arising when televising color film. Video gain and gamma adjustments to the RGB color channels. ('TARIF' operation) provide good correction for various errors. Similar correction can be applied to slide (transparency) scanners.

Exposure and color-correction adjustments may be made 'on the fly' by an operator during replay; either empirically, or to settings found during rehearsal. Some systems enable corrective settings to be filed, selected and activated; automatically, or by push-button.

Fig. 11.11   TV film sync leader
Several types of film leader are in use. In the American National Standard leader shown (35 and 16 mm motion-picture theatre, and TV studios), a *start identification frame* ensures exact picture sync with the sound-head. A series of numbers from 8 to 2 (seconds) appear (a black background then a dark wedge moving clockwise in series of 15° steps) provide a visual count-down.

Non-standard projection

Depending on design, telecine equipment may be able to provide several kinds of non-standard projection:

1. Hold a selected single frame (*still frame, hold frame, freeze frame*).
2. Dissolve slowly from one frame to the next (*inching*).
3. Run up from still frame to full speed (mute) without frame-roll or flicker.
4. Run at non-standard constant speeds (e.g. 16– 60 fps) – forward or backward.
5. Fast wind-on (run-on) and rewind.
6. *Remote manual cueing* (from the production switcher), or *automatic cueing* using attached metalized cue tags or tape strip, or by microprocessor selection.

Fig. 11.12   Changeover synchronizing
At the appearance of a white (or black) circular dot in the top right corner of the picture area, the second projector is started (motor cue). After 7 seconds, a similar dot cues the changeover switch-point. This mark is printed or punched in the print (during processing, or editing).

Cueing film

Telecine equipment cannot normally provide an instantaneous start for picture and audio. A brief run-up period is necessary for audio to stabilize. By attaching a time-scaled *sync leader* (e.g. SMPTE universal leader) to the head of a film, you can ensure that the first picture frame with fully stabilized audio will appear a predictable time after switch-on. The required picture sync marker is positioned in the projector's picture gate, the director giving an anticipatory run cue 4 (or 8) seconds before cutting to film channel output. This avoids inadvertently switching to a stationary or unstable channel. To ensure that the film reproduction is

Fig. 11.13   Wide-screen films
Wide screen motion pictures do not use the TV screen's aspect ratio (4 × 3 shape; i.e. 1.33:1). If the picture is fitted to frame side-edges, so seeing all of film, overall picture size is small and areas are wasted at top/bottom of TV screen. If the *top/bottom* of the frame is fitted to the TV screen, then the sides of the film picture are lost. Solutions to this problem include zooming to full height, panning left/right to follow main action (top-fit) as shown (A to B). These operations involve scanning circuit adjustments (on-air or pre-coded), or compensated film prints.

Fig. 11.14 part 1   Cutting combined prints — problem
In a combined print (optical or magnetic stripe) the sound is displaced ahead of its corresponding picture (to suit the picture-gate to sound-head separation distance). Physically cutting this combined print creates a dilemma; If the sound track is cut at a specific point (S), then over a second (26–28 picture frames) of unwanted picture is included in the selected film. When editing continuous speech, this can result in *lip-flap* before the wanted action, i.e. silent mouth movements left from the previous material, without any accompanying sound. In the above example, cutting at the end of the picture sequence (P), will spuriously introduce sound from the next shot; while cutting after the explosion sound (S) will lose the picture of the event. The problem can be overcome by intercutting a mute shot (e.g. cutaway), or re-laying the sound track.

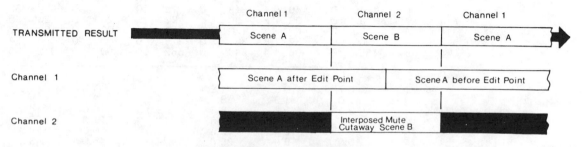

Fig. 11.14 part 2   Cutting combined prints — solution
A standard method uses a *double chain* or *A/B system*. A brief silent cutaway shot (reaction shot) is interposed to hide any lip-flap, jump-cut, etc., by strategically switching away.

neither clipped at its beginning, nor runs out immediately after action finishes, a few *buffer (safety) frames* of the scene are included at the head and tail of each section.

Where several film lengths are conjoined, you can:

1. Use timed lengths of blanking between them; leaving the machine running while cutting away to studio (*roll-through*).
2. Introduce a series of sync leaders; recuing each section.
3. Cue the film at any time, switching to it when it appears.

Having previously ascertained the exact 'timing' (duration), the *in-cue* (first words) and *out-cue* (last words), precision insertion into the program becomes practicable. Occasionally, the exact entry/exit points for a videotaped film – insert are determined during subsequent VT editing.

Recording color TV on film

Several methods have evolved for transferring video pictures to standard color film stock. Each has its particular advantages and limitations. At best, results are excellent. Film recordings have advantages in certain markets. They overcome incompatible TV standards that frustrate the world distribution of videotape recordings. Film prints permit large-screen projection, have wider educational and library applications, and are more convenient for certain field work.

Several major films have been shot with video cameras, and then transferred to film stock, for theatrical release. The main advantages here have included: the opportunity to monitor while shooting, immediate playback checks, more convenient and economical videotape editing.

Table 11.2 Film running times

		35 mm (16 fr per ft) 24 fps		35 mm (16 fr per ft) 25 fps		16 mm (40 fr per ft) 24 fps		16 mm (40 fr per ft) 25 fps		Super 8 mm (72 fr per ft) 24 fps		Super 8 mm (72 fr per ft) 25 fps	
		ft	fr	ft	fr	ft	fr	ft	fr	ft	fr	ft	fr
Seconds	1	1	8	1	9	0	24	0	25	0	24	0	25
	3	4	8	4	11	1	32	1	35	1	0	1	3
	5	7	8	7	13	3	0	3	5	1	48	1	53
	7	10	8	10	15	4	8	4	15	2	24	2	31
	10	15	0	15	10	6	0	6	10	3	24	3	24
	30	45	0	46	14	18	0	18	30	10	0	10	30
Minutes	1	90	0	93	12	36	0	37	20	20	0	20	60
	5	450	0	468	12	180	0	187	20	100	0	104	12
	10	900	0	937	8	360	0	375	0	200	0	208	24
	15	1350	0	1406	4	540	0	562	20	300	0	312	36

		Seconds					
Feet	1	0.7	0.6	1.8	1.6	3.0	2.9
	3	2.0	1.9	5.0	4.8	9.0	8.6
	5	3.3	3.2	8.3	8.0	15.0	14.4
	7	4.7	4.5	11.6	11.2	21.0	20.2
	10	6.6	6.4	16.6	16.0	30.0	28.8
	15	10.0	9.6	25.0	24.0	45.0	43.2
	20	13.2	12.8	33.3	32.0	1 min 0.0	57.6
	30	20.0	19.2	50.0	48.0	1 min 30.0	1 min 24.0
	50	33.2	32.0	1 min 23.0	1 min 20.0	2 min 30.0	2 min 24.0

Table 11.3   Displacement of picture and sound

	35 mm	*16 mm*	*Super 8 mm*
Magnetic track	28 frames behind pic.	28 ahead of pic.	18 ahead of pic.
Optical track	21 frames ahead.	26 ahead.	22 ahead.

And all this has become possible due to the high image-transfer quality now possible.

■ *Image transfer*   Several image-transfer methods are current:

1. A special film camera (using color film) shoots a color TV picture tube.
2. A similar set-up, filming a monochrome picture tube which displays in three successive runs, the red, blue, and green component images from a videotape. The three separate monochrome recording of the color information are combined to full color during laboratory printing.
3. *Laser beam* recording, in which three separate video-modulated lasers (RGB) combine optically on *color* film.
4. Electron beam recording (EBR) produces three separation negatives (RGB) on black-and-white film, scanned by electron beams akin to those in picture tubes. These records are combined during laboratory printing, using corresponding red, green, blue light sources.

12 Videotape

Videotape recording (VTR) is technically an extremely sophisticated process. But happily for the user, equipment has become increasingly simpler to operate, more compact, and reliable.

The filmed program

For many years, the only alternative to televising action *live*, 'as-it-happens' in front of the TV camera, was to transmit a *film record* of the subject, using a telecine system. This could be regular film that had been shot, processed, edited, in the normal way, or a specially prepared *kinescope recording* (*telerecording*) obtained by having a film camera shoot the TV picture on the face of high-intensity picture-tube (kinescope). Results of such off-tube recording ranged from surprisingly good (suitable for archives or re-transmission) to abysmal (useful only as program checks).

The coming of videotape

Various efforts made to record video on *magnetic tape* were finally successful in the 1950s, and the Ampex Corporation's *Quadruplex* ('Quad'; transverse) system became a broadcast standard that held its position for over two decades (see Glossary – *Quadruplex VTR*). This system is capable, in its developed forms, of recording/reproduction of color television pictures, that is virtually indistinguishable from the original program material. As we shall see, this was the forerunner of the various videorecording innovations that have given new freedoms to production techniques.

Fig. 12.1 Quadruplex system
The 2 in/50.8 mm wide magnetic tape passes over an *erase head* that demagnetizes (wipes) its full width. The four record/replay heads on the headwheel press against the tape, recording across it in a series of parallel transverse tracks, each covering a 16-line segment of the picture (20 lines in European 625-line system). Heads are switched successively to provide a continuous video signal, recording or replaying the tape. The video heads are upstream of the corresponding audio heads (by 23.5 cm/9.25 in). Recording is checked by replaying random selections (spot checks). The Quad II system uses the track format: audio 1, cue/code track, audio 2, video, control.

The advantages of VTR

Videotape recording has several important advantages for the program maker:

1. At best, the quality of the videotaped program is indistinguishable from the original video.
2. The recording can be replayed immediately, without any intermediate processing. Some equipment designs provide continuous off-tape monitoring (*confidence playback*) to check quality.
3. The videotape can be reproduced many times without deterioration.
4. The recording can be erased (*wiped*) totally or selectively, and new program material recorded in its place.
5. Videotape is easily edited, and faulty or unwanted sections can be replaced. The audience-impact of programs can be enhanced in various ways by selective editing. Performance can be improved by appropriate cuts (deletions), retakes. Long pauses, ineffectual material, or lagging pace can be corrected – usually by introducing cutaway shots to disguise editing-out. Censor cuts (*continuity acceptance*) can be made unobtrusively; and any distractions, redundant shots, ambiguities removed.
6. Videotaping aids scheduling. Programs can be recorded when convenient, and replayed when required. This is particularly valuable where multi-time zones are involved; to suit training schedules; to facilitate study.
7. Taping can compensate for limited camera facilities, and provide apparent viewpoint mobility as separate recordings are edited together.

Table 12.1   Videotape tracks

Video track	A pattern of narrow tracks across the magnetic tape, recording the video signal in FM (frequency modulated) form. (*helical* – slant tracks; *quad* – transverse tracks.)
Audio track	A regular audio recording on a track along the tape edge (edge track). Up to three such tracks may be available. Audio quality is unavoidably limited on these longitudinal tracks; particularly at low tape speeds, as the tape performance is optimized for slanting video tracks (oblique grain orientation). For *depth multiplex* systems, see Glossary – *Consumer video formats*.
Control track	An edge track recording special regular pulses, that accurately synchronize the tape movement and scanning rate, ensuring that the video heads re-scan the existing tracks correctly, and aid color frame identification.
Cue track	An edge track, recording a special *address code/time code* to identify each part of the program for electronic editing. Otherwise the track may carry audio (of lower grade) for productional information, commentary, or a second language; or record cue tones.
Erase head	An electromagnet head that completely saturates, then demagnetizes the magnetic tape (across total tape width, or a track), leaving it neutral, ready for recording. Erasing (wiping) is carried out immediately before recording head scans the tape.

8. Various problems in staging can be overcome (e.g. moving wild walls, refurbishing sets, re-lighting, etc.) by stop-start taping, as can changes in costume, makeup, etc.
9. Any video effects can be taped, and checked immediately. This recording can then be replayed, and further electronic treatment added if required.
10. Within broadcast organizations, motion pictures are regularly transferred to videotape (i.e. telecine-to-VTR copying) to add identifying sub-titles; for language translation; for optimum presentation of wide-screen prints; when adding music and effects to silent (mute) films; to preserve a valuable or damaged film print, or to edit Super-8 mm film records,
11. The director can make off-line editing judgments before the final post-production editing session.

Videotaping techniques

The director has the option of using videotape recording in several ways when shooting his production. Most involve post-production editing (i.e. working on the taped program afterwards in a VT recording room). This can become a rather time-consuming, expensive process. But it does allow one to correct and considerably improve the end product. Recording is usually done in duplicate, to provide a *back-up copy* (*backing, insurance copy*) in case technical faults develop in the original master recording.

The commonest ways of taping a production include:

1. *Continuously* – Making an uninterrupted record of events; 'live-on-tape'. This saves the time, effort and expense of a full editing session. A few minor corrections or revisions may be made during taping, or in a short post-production editing session.
2. *In sections* – Recording one complete sequence or scene at a time, retaking it if necessary, and continuing when satisfied.
3. *In segments* – Recording brief takes, or shot-by-shot. One can even shoot frame-by-frame (single-frame), for special effects, or for animation build-up.
4. *Changing time-scales* – Videotaping to provide fast, slow, reverse motion, stop action, freeze-frame, or time-lapse recording.

The development of VTR recording

Video recording systems have undergone a number of radical changes over the past decade, but a pattern of relative stability now seems to have emerged.

■ *Helical scanning systems* Although the quadruplex format provides very high-quality results, rising costs and competitive market opportunities encouraged manufacturers to seek cheaper methods of videotape recording. They turned instead to the development of more compact *helical scanning* systems, which offered tape economies, reduced tape storage space, required less power, and had extra facilities (e.g. still frame, vari-speed, picture during shuttle). They were generally easier to operate. Results were not immediately comparable with the established Quad standards, but videotape recording now became practicable for many commercial, industrial, educational, and other closed-circuit, in-house applications.

The Sony *U-matic* system which was originally of industrial standard (low-band) was pressed into service by broadcasters to provide 'lightweight' mobile videorecording facilities for news gathering, location shooting, economic local-station taping. Design improvements resulted in the hi-band U-Matic or *BVU* range. Various limitations in this recording method were reduced or minimized, so that pictures became generally acceptable for broadcast use – particularly where program urgency rather than highest picture quality was all-important.

■ *Picture defects* It is worth reminding ourselves here how very subjective this matter of picture quality really is. Many defects are normally overlooked by the uncritical eye: picture noise, reduced texture, artificial edges to subjects (ringing, reflections), color distortions, spurious moire-patterning effects (chroma-luminance interference), displaced color, edge jitter, crushing of highlights and shadows, flattened-out tonal gradations (cartooning), poor detail resolution . . .! These are all visible on close inspection of your home TV picture! However, when the subject is really interesting, such defects seem unimportant if we *do* happen to notice them. Only when they distract us, or prevent our seeing clearly, are we normally aware of them.

For the program-maker, though, these shortcomings must be reduced to a minimum, for they worsen considerably whenever the videotape is re-recorded (dubbed) in the course of editing or making further copies.

■ *VTR systems today* Towards the end of the 1970s, two major broadcast-quality helical-scan color VTR systems were introduced: the 'B' and the 'C' formats. These were accepted as world standards, and are in widespread professional use today.

In the domestic market, the *Betamax* and *VHS* videotape recording systems have become universal, while others (e.g. Philips V2000) offer alternative formats.

Further important developments in the videorecording fields have led to the idea of an integrated video-camera/recorder assembly. These *combos/camcorders* combine a high-grade lightweight camera, with a broadcast standard video recorder using ½ inch or ¼ inch tape cassettes; particularly suitable for single-camera shooting/recording on location.

The next technological step forward lies in digital video recording, with all the advantages that it provides: e.g. high picture quality, stability, multi-generation copies with no image deterioration.

■ *Tape formats* Today's various incompatible VTR tape systems use three basic tape formats:

Table 12.2   Typical videotape formats
(See Glossary: *Videotape standards*)

Broadcast standards	*QUADRUPLEX (QUAD)* Tape width 2 in (open reel/reel-to-reel; cartridge; cassette). Quad 1: 38 cm/second. Quad 2: 19 cm/second. Super-high-band.
Open-reel, 1 in	*HELICAL SCAN* (various incompatible formats) *'B' format*. Segmented field. Current standard for broadcast use. *'C' format*. Non-segmented field. Current standard for broadcast use.
Cassette, ¾ in	*U-matic (U-format)*. Initially designed for industrial/commercial closed-circuit use; subsequently adapted to broadcast use (especially ENG/EFP).
	BVU-Matic. A high-band U-matic system designed for broadcast use. Widely used in ENG/EFP production. Incompatible with standard U-Matic format. Two cassette sizes: 'portable short-play' and 'playback/edit'.
Cassette, ½ in	*'M-format'*: 'VHS type' system running at high speed. Luminance and chrominance on separate adjacent tracks.
	'L-format': 'Beta type' system running at high speed. Separate luminance and chrominance tracks.
Domestic standard/consumer formats	*Betamax (Beta)*: ½ in cassette. Maximum duration 3 hrs 35 min. *VHS*: ½ in cassette. Maximum duration: 4hrs. *CVC/compact video cassette* (Funai system — Technicolor, Rank): ¼ in cassette. Maximum duration: 30 minutes.
	Domestic units include: *Compact video* — dual-purpose portable recorders (for home-camera/off-air/video films) in multi-unit combinations. *Transportable units* — a.c. outlet/battery powered. *Compact portable* — with separate or combined camera and VTR (e.g. Sony 'Video 8'). *PCM* (Pulse code modulation) of audio signals on domestic format VCRs, for high quality stereo sound.
Combination video camera and recorder (Combo; Camcorder; VRC)	Developing broadcast-quality systems, using cassettes (½ in and ¼ in tape). Several design variations, including: *Betacam* (Sony); *Hawkeye* (RCA); *QuarterCam/Lineplex* (Bosch); *ARC* (Ampex); *Recam* (Panasonic); *Camescope* (Thomson-CSF).

1. *Open reel* (*reel-to-reel*). Here the tape is unwound from a full supply spool, laced manually through the tape path/transport system, and secured to an empty take-up spool. The tape needs careful handling to avoid damage (creasing, scrape, edge crushing), or contamination (finger marks, grease, dust).
2. *Cartridge* (*cart*). Often misleadingly called a 'cassette', the cart is an enclosed plastic box in which tape is held on a single reel in an endless loop. This arrangement reduces the overall volume of the package. As tape is drawn off, it is re-wound onto the same reel. This format is often used for short-duration sequences (e.g. 6 min) – commercials, news inserts. In *carousel* equipment, a store of carts can be loaded and selected automatically, or by random access.
3. *Cassette*. A plastic box enclosing two spools (supply and take-up). Currently, cassettes may contain tape lasting from 5 min (ENG use of U-Matic), up to some 8 hours (domestic VCC system).

Where a cart or cassette is used, it is only necessary to plug it into the recorder, the equipment self-lacing the tape for recording or replay.

■ *Helical (slant-track) scanning*   This method of scanning the videotape has become universal. The tape travels from the supply reel, past a fixed erase head (wiping its entire width during recording), moving in a helical (spiral) path to wrap round a cylindrical *head-drum/scanning drum*. From the surface of this drum protrudes a video record/replay head(s). As the upper section of the drum (or an internal disc) rotates, the head(s) on it turns, rhythmically pressing against the passing tape (tip penetration) and scanning across it. Due to the tape's slanting path, the head records an oblique video track. Various helical systems designs have their particular inherent weaknesses, such as information loss at the end of each scan (which produces a *noise-bar*, picture disturbances, visual errors), that are arranged to fall outside the viewed 'safe-action' picture area.

Recorded along the upper and/or lower tape edges are the *audio track(s)*, a *control track*, and a *cue track* (or Audio 3); which may be selectively wiped.

The amount of picture information recorded on each video track on the tape depends on equipment design.

In the *non-segmented* or *continuous system*, a single video head records one *field* on each track. (Remember, it takes two interlaced fields, odd and even, to form one complete TV picture.) This method has certain technical advantages (simple freeze frame, vari-speed), but unfortunately it omits several picture lines from each field, and all information during the vertical interval.

In the *segmented system*, two video heads scan the tape in turn, each recording a succession of picture lines (e.g. 52 lines) on their respective tape tracks. Their outputs are interswitched to provide continuous, uninterrupted video output. Between them, the tracks record all picture and vertical interval information.

■ *The U-Matic standard* The *BVU* (high-band U-Matic) format provides a portable, robust, and relatively economical videotape recorder. Although developed from the original low-band industrial grade U-Matic, its upgraded extended form is not compatible with it. Standard U-Matic ¾ in tape cassettes (1½ hour duration) fit both older and later versions, but smaller cassettes are used in portable equipment.

There are several versions of the BVU format, including systems incorporating dynamic tracking, time-code, etc. Larger machines are intended for use at base as play-off or editing facilities.

Of course, all systems have their associated limitations. The U-Matic format (like domestic VTRs) uses a *color-under* recording process (see Glossary), and picture quality can deteriorate noticeably if a sequence is copied and this dubbing re-recorded in the course of editing (multi-dubs).

When used in a precision broadcast chain (e.g. for ENG), a *timebase corrector* (TBC) must be used to stabilize replay. Because the resulting video signal is non-phased (out of phase), it cannot be mixed with other video (although individual monitors may cope with the irregular sync signals).

The equipment needs careful handling if you are recording while moving, as severe speed variations (gyro errors) can arise (e.g. a 30 lines error); although this can usually be compensated for by digital time-base corrector circuits.

This type of recorder is rather slow in running-up to full speed from switch-on; a situation which could result in your losing a shot of unanticipated action during ENG. So a 'standby mode' is provided, in which the head-drum rotates at half-speed, while the tape waits wrapped round it, ready to be cued.

■ *Broadcast one-inch helical systems*   Two high-grade broadcast standards have become established for 1 inch helical-scan recording: the SMPTE *Type C (non-segmented)*, and the SMPTE *Type B (segmented) forms.*

SMPTE Type C standard (non-segmented). As each video track contains one complete *field*, it is possible to stop tape travel, and rotate the head-drum to continually re-read the same track. The *still-frame* this provides can be held for a while (tape wear develops). By adjusting the tape motion, you can reproduce a succession of complete pictures at various speeds: slow motion, fast motion, time-lapse (ultra-fast motion), and inching/jogging (frame-by-frame). Such facilities are invaluable for fast searching, selecting individual frames, analysis, etc., particularly when editing sequences. This format also permits continuous replay during recording (confidence playback), actually enabling you to monitor results *off tape* while recording. (Other methods only monitor the video signal within the equipment, but do not show whether it was successfully recorded.)

Fig. 12.2 part 1   Typical helical scanning arrangement
The tape is wrapped in a slanting path round a drum. Within the drum a disc head-wheel supporting recording (and erase) heads rotates, pressing heads against the tape at an acute angle as it slides past. (Designs include rotating upper drum, or slot scanner with narrow rotating center section.)

Fig. 12.2 part 2   SMPTE one-inch Type 'B' and Type 'C' standards
Left: Type 'B' standard (segmented field format). Each head-drum revolution records 5 video tracks per field (525 line/60 field system), or 6 tracks (625/50 system). Tape wraps 190° round drum (50 mm diameter, 150 revs/second). Tape speed is 24.3 cm/second (9.57 in/second). Head drum contains 2 video heads and control head. Three audio tracks along tape: 2 program, third for time-code or cue-track. Video is recorded as FM carrier (blanking level 7.9 MHz, peak-white 10 MHz, for 525/60 system; 7.4 to 8.9 MHz for 625/50 system).
Right: Type 'C' standard (continuous/non segmented field format). Each head-drum revolution *video track* records one field (2 fields of 262½/312½ lines comprise complete picture); from line 16 of one field to line 5 of following field. This video track contains all picture information (active lines), plus insertion signals in vertical-interval (VITS, VIRS). The *sync track* records remaining 10 lines of vertical interval, with a small overlap. Tape wraps 360° round head-drum (135 mm diameter, 60 revs/second). Tape speed is 24.4 cm/second (9.61 in/second). Head-drum has 6 *head-tip locations*, separate record and replay heads for video and for sync tracks; both have simultaneous playback check heads; optional automatic tracking control head. Three audio tracks along tape: 2 program; third for time-code, cue-track, or extra audio. All longitudinal recording heads are aligned and perpendicular to tape edge. Separate control track identifies odd and even fields, and alternate frames. Video is recorded using standard high-band FM technique.

Fig. 12.2 part 3   Tape paths
Several tape-path arrangements are used: omega, alpha, half-wrap forms.

However, this system does not normally record all the picture information, or data transmitted during the vertical blanking period.

SMPTE Type B standard (segmented). Because this system records e.g. 52 picture lines on each track, it needs to read 5 (6) tracks to reproduce one field. So it is not possible to obtain a still-frame simply by repeat-reading a single track. Instead, an electronic frame store/field store is necessary, to build up five track's worth of video (i.e. one field), which can be continuously read out from store. This can be done at a range of speeds, from slow-motion up to say, 12 times normal speed; to facilitate rapid picture selection during editing.

■ *Combination camera/VTR formats* (see Glossary – *Combination cameras)* The combination of a broadcast-quality video camera with its own inbuilt VTR, offers considerable production opportunities. Known variously as a *combo, VRC (video-recording camera), camcorder*, three new incompatible formats have emerged, to compete with B, C, and ¾ in systems. They are based on the VHS, Betamax, and CVC (compact video cassette) techniques used in the domestic recorders, but with important technical differences (recording luminance and chroma separately; *dual-track recording)*, their performance equalling or exceeding current ENG/EFP lightweight cameras.

■ *Consumer video formats/Domestic VTRs*   Narrow-format video recorders are used extensively in domestic, educational and commercial fields. The two main systems are the incompatible *Betamax (Beta)* and *VHS* formats. (Others such as the Philips Video 2000/VCC are less widely used.) Both helical-scan systems use half-inch wide (12.5 mm) tape cassettes. Picture quality is subjectively very acceptable for many purposes, although sound fidelity is normally limited due to the low tape speed. The systems will record direct video and sound (e.g. from a camera), or off-air (via an internal modulator unit), and replay through a TV receiver, or a video monitor. (See Glossary – *Consumer video formats*.)

Fig. 12.3   Magnetic video disc
The magnetic video disc continuously records a mute 30 (36) second segment of the program video, progressively erasing and re-recording over the earliest material. The disc can be started/stopped instantaneously. Having captured the required piece of action (e.g. a high-jump), you have instant replay on cue at normal speed, slow, fast, vari-speed, reverse, freeze-frame. The equipment contains one or two discs (16 in/0.46 m diameter) rotating at 60 revs/second (locked to vertical sync reference). The record/replay heads on either face, alternately move inwards (later retracing outwards) in steps, to form 450 concentric video tracks total. Each track contains one video field.

■ *Vari-speed replay*   In many types of program, one wants to replay action in slow motion, or as selected freeze-frames, to demonstrate movement, to analyze, or to provide an artistic effect. Both magnetic video discs and vari-speed VTRs are used for this purpose. But there is an unavoidable problem here.

To capture really sharp images of fast action, individual pictures of the event must be recorded at a comparable speed, and be of sufficiently brief duration (short exposure). A standard TV system shoots at 30 (25) pictures or frames a second, and this rate is not sufficiently rapid or brief to capture fast movements. A movie camera shooting at 24 fps has a similar problem (although its shutter opening may be reduced, light permitting, to reduce exposure and improve the sharpness to some extent). Reproduced at normal or fast rates, the eye does not usually notice this unsharp motion; but if we look at individual frames, we will see that faster movements appear quite blurred, while a transient such as a bursting balloon, may even fail to register at all!

If a *film camera* shoots at a faster frame-rate than normal (e.g. 64 frames/second), it records more separate versions of any movement (64 instead of 24), and correspondingly clearer images. But for really sharp individual frames of fast-moving subjects (hummingbirds' wings, bullets in flight), film cameras designed to shoot at e.g. 64–100 fps, up to 10 000, even 8 000 000 fps are used. Special video-recording equipment can achieve up to 2000 fps.

Further applications

Video disc and tape can also provide:

1. Still store – A recording of a series of individual stills, which can then be selected in sequence, or at random (see Glossary – *Electronic still store*).
2. Time-lapse effects – Events are shot at a slow regular rate (e.g. 1 frame per hour), and replayed at normal speed to give a speeded-up presentation. Used to demonstrate traffic flow, plant growth, cloud formation.
3. Time-controlled freeze frame – A system in which a still frame is held for a selected duration, during action replay.
4. Animated graphics – Creating animation of graphics by stop-start (stop-motion) recording; i.e. readjusting graphics between a series of very brief shots. Replaying the complete sequence at normal speed produces animation.

Reasons for videotape editing

You can sometimes shoot a flawless performance 'live-on-tape', making all inter-shot transitions on the switcher as you go, and produce a very satisfying program that is ready for immediate replay. It needs no editing of any kind. But most productions can usually be improved in various ways. Then you can either repeat and re-record the complete performance (often quite practicable for a short production), or retake the less-successful sections, and edit them into the original program.

A *film editor* always has to work from scratch; integrating material from many isolated brief takes, including several different versions of the action. This can pose continuity problems. He instructs processing labs on the transitions needed, by wax marks on the editing print.

A *videotape editor*, too, may need to piece together many separate shots, if the production has been shot on a single camera, or a dedicated VTR. How easily this can be done depends on how comprehensive and sophisticated the editing equipment is.

Most multi-camera studio productions use a production switcher to introduce all (or most) of the required transitions and effects during performance. Then the VT editor is mainly concerned with *corrective* work; removing faulty sections and inserting retakes, rearranging the

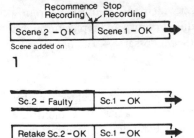

Fig. 12.4 part 1   Electronic editing — assemble mode
Program is built up either (1) A scene at a time or (2) shot continuously, retaking any faulty scene immediately from its opening point. Assembly involves switching from replay (of Scene 1) to *record mode* at a chosen cue point (manually or automatically). As assemble mode automatically lays down a fresh control-track for each take, sync pulses change at joins, thus disturbing replay.

Fig. 12.4 part 2 Electronic editing — insert mode
If new material is to be inserted precisely between existing wanted shots, the 'in' and 'out' points must coincide with original, unwanted scene to avoid wiping wanted program. The original control track is not erased during the insert process, so no sync disturbances occur at the electronic splice.

Fig. 12.4 part 3 A/B dubbing
Here duplicate copies of the program are used on VTRs A and B to permit quicker search for sections, than by shuttling a single tape to and fro for selection. A simple production switcher can be used to cut/mix/super during transfer to VTR-C.

sequence of scenes (e.g. from 'recording order' to 'program running order'), shortening introducing inserts (e.g. cutaway shots), censor cuts, etc.

Physical editing

With transverse Quad VTR systems, it was possible to make a clean edit in a program by physically cutting the tape, and splicing the sections together. However, all mechanical tape damage, including splices, causes *drop-out* (momentary signal loss), and can damage the recorder's heads. Physical editing is impracticable with helical-scan systems, because any transverse cut interrupts several video tracks, and at best produces a crude vertical picture 'wipe' at the join. The displacement of the audio and video tracks prevents their being cut simultaneously.

Electronic editing

There are really three basic editing situations: Editing in camera, Editing during replay, and Editing by copying.

1. Editing *in camera*. This technique is widely used in portable camera set-ups. The VTR can be controlled remotely, with a switch on the camera grip. Recording is stopped at the end of a shot, and restarted for the next, to give a noiseless cut at that point. On replay, the result can (with luck!) be a complete, continuous, edited program. If you have misjudged, you will have overlong shots, and clipped starts.

Fig. 12.4 part 4 Roll back and mix
Problem: Scene 1 has been recorded. You now wish to *mix* from Scene 1 to Scene 2 live in studio. Two VTRs available. *Solution:* Roll back Scene 1 on VTR 'A' to convenient cutting point before mix. Recording on VTR 'B', replay VTR 'A' tape, mixing to studio when required. VTR 'B' tape now incorporates mix. Result can be inserted within original VTR 'A' tape at the earlier butt-join.

2. *Editing during replay.* Here the program tape is replayed on a suitable editing VTR. When up to working speed and stable (locked up), the equipment is switched from 'play' to 'record' mode (*Edit* or *Mode-change button*), at the point where the next shot is to begin; either replacing faulty material, or introducing new. Results can be excellent, although the editing point is rather approximate. It is best to cut at a non-critical moment. (If you use this technique with a non-edit VTR, there will normally be severe picture breakup at the edit point.)

3. *Editing by copying (re-recording, dubbing).* In this approach you replay your program material on one or more machines, and re-record the output on another, to form a new compilation tape. This method is widely used in post-production editing.

Each approach has its advantages and limitations. Methods 1 and 2 result in *first generation* recordings. Method 3 produces copies that are *second generation* (or more), of a quality that is to some extent inferior to the original. Methods 2 and 3 can be carried out either while taping the production, or later in a separate editing session.

■ *Post production editing*   Here you record your program material in any convenient order, retaking any unsatisfactory sections as you go. Simply stop the recording, discuss the problem, cue action, and record the new attempt. You finish up with a tape(s) containing both wanted and rejected sequences.

Later, in a post-production editing session, you sort through the tape for the required takes, which are then selectively dubbed off. Editing equipment provides straight cuts between sections, but for mixes, supers, wipes, etc., a switcher is needed.

How complex this editing process becomes is influenced, of course, by the number of takes involved, their lengths, their order, how many NG (no good) takes there are, etc. But much depends too, on systematic note-taking while shooting, and on the editing facilities available.

Even routine post-production editing is very time-consuming. A typical finished half-hour program can involve some 150 to 200 cuts. You may find that you can make around 6–10 straight cut edits an hour; but combined-shot video effects can slow you to only 1–4. Even to run straight through a 1-hour tape on a ¾ in VTR can take about 12 min, so shuttling/searching for shots (especially with tape-changing), and arranging the edit points can be quite a lengthy process.

Because picture quality deteriorates noticeably when tape is copied (increased picture noise, definition loss, edge effects), most organizations try to avoid dubbing beyond a copy of a copy (i.e. 3rd generation). However, this stage is soon reached when creating special effects. Quality losses on *dubbing down* from larger tape formats (e.g. 1 in) to smaller ones (½ in) are less severe than when dubbing-up; or when dubbing between color-under systems.

A similar deterioration arises in film copying (*duping*), where copies of copies show color errors, increasing graininess, and definition loss, which cannot be remedied. This occurs when copying film library shots for program inserts.

Electronic splicing

Two forms of electronic splicing are widely used:

1. *Assemble* (*assembly*) *mode* New material is added consecutively to the *end* of existing shots, by recording new video, audio *and* reference control track pulses (that govern tape position and speed).
2. *Insert mode* A period of new material is slotted *within* an existing recorded sequence, replacing that section only. Video and audio are replaced, leaving the *original* reference control track pulses.

Because the erase (wipe) and record heads are physically displaced, there is a time lag as any part of the tape moves between the heads. In quad systems, this is electronically compensated during editing, by erasing just before the mode switches. In helical systems, the shallow slant track poses editing problems and a *flying erase head* is used to make the erase coincide with the seen edit point. Otherwise visible patterning arises (*edit moiré*) due to brief overrecording of the old material. Even so, the edit may cause some control track or audio interference.

It is worth getting to know the idiosyncracies of the equipment you are using. For example, when pressing 'Record' on some VTRs, they automatically backspace a few seconds, then run forwards, and when up to speed, begin recording. The unwary can find that the end of the last shot has now been lopped off! This does not happen if you play to the edit point, *pause* (i.e. tape stops, but head-drum continues turning), then press 'Record'. This can produce a clean cut.

■ *Laying a control track (helical)* When a helical scan videotape is recorded, internal circuits generate special, regular motor stabilizing pulses, which are continuously recorded on the *control track*; therefore ensuring a stable constant speed replay. If these pulses are interrupted, picture stability will be affected at that point.

However, if you *re*record on this master tape (as when assembly dubbing) the editing VTR would normally create its own fresh pulses for the new material. And because the act of editing usually involves stopping/starting the editing recorder, this will interrupt the exact positioning of these new pulses in the edited composite at each edit point. So on reproducing the new composite tape, you are liable to encounter frame-roll or line tearing at the edits.

To overcome this problem, it is common practice *before* a helical scan editing session (whether you actually want to fit in, or add on the new material), to record an entire continuous control track alone on the clean editing tape. Then the actual dubbings are made using the *insert mode* of the VTR; for this mode leaves the prepared control track pulses undisturbed. So you have an uninterrupted control track and optimum sync stability.

Edit controller

Here we come to the heart of the VT editing process; the *edit controller*. This unit is a computerized switching panel with a handwheel or joystick control. It remotely selects and controls the VTR equipment; activating it to play, record, rewind, etc. Designs vary considerably, but basically they follow similar principles.

Specialized microprocessors using programmed memory instructions, serve as 'intelligent interfaces' to automatically calculate and time various VT operations. They assess machine run-up time, synchronize switching, energize the appropriate functions in the correct sequence at the right instant.

The simplest controlled-editing set-up comprises two machine-to-machine VTR editors: one as source, the other as recorder. An *edit-controller* (counting the control-track pulses for indexing) remotely controls two machines: enabling you to view either the source tape or the edited-copy tape; to select edit points in both decks; to rehearse, then check-review edits. Some systems can also perform *split-edits*, in which the recorded audio can be treated separately from the video (layover/layback techniques). Audio mixing between a pair of sound tracks on the same tape may be possible.

More sophisticated multi-source editors provide a wide range of facilities: edit points can be marked while the tape is in motion or stationary; edit points can be moved with exact color framing; audio tracks can be built independently (music, effects); variable search and jog speeds give very accurate point location. A/B roll edits can be made (Fig. 12.4 part 3) with two sources feeding the recorder (through a switcher, or effects unit). Timecode can be used to remotely control an audio recorder, switcher, character generator, etc.

The equipment prepares a revisable *edit-decision list*, which in advanced control systems will check when you have accepted the workprint version of the editing, and automatically create a *final edited master tape* to match (see Glossary – *Automatic assembly*).

Where a *backtrack* feature is available, the first cut version of the program is used to activate subsequent editing.

Having located your edit point on the *replay VTR* (at slow speed) you need to set up the replay and recording machines so that they run up, stabilize and synchronize to make the edit at precisely that point on their respective tapes. The editing *controller* does all this 'housekeeping' for you automatically! It counts off the tape's recorded control-track pulses (and/or coded time signal) relative to your chosen edit point, and times operations accordingly. You can *simulate* the edit to check the effect, and the replay machine will automatically back to its pre-roll position, stop, restart and 'cut' at the chosen place. If you are satisfied, the controller will repeat operations and make a real edit. (The point is adjustable.) This simply operated system can be quite accurate but has the disadvantage that the edit point can become misplaced or lost during operations unlike the more expensive precision time-code methods.

Editing methods

If you want to edit a simple straightforward sequence (e.g. selecting and joining shots with uncritical heads/tails), you can often do this on the fly

Fig. 12.5 Time address code
Monitor display shows the precise time at which the recording was made — hours, mins, seconds, frames — to facilitate identification, cueing and editing. (For special applications such as time-lapse recording — day, month, year may be indicated.) Time-code may be seen *burned in* to the picture as above, or as a separate display. Many studios time-code to actual *clock time*, so that any notes made during production can be coded simply by glancing at an accurate clock nearby. Some organizations use *zero start* (*lapsed time*) coding, i.e. zero time at the beginning of each reel or session; using the hour digit position to denote the reel No.

(editing as you go, while viewing the replay), or *cue-marking* the running tapes, preparing it to produce a first-cut/rough-cut.

But for really accurate editing you need to start with hand-logged details listed during the production in a *take-sheet* or *edit log*. This information will include: Reel No.; Scene No.; Shot No.; subject description; in-point/out-point time-codes; segment duration; audio information; notes. This helps you to anticipate and select potential edit-points when off-line reviewing a time-coded copy of the program later.

The actual editing process begins at the controller, where you enter on a key-pad, the time code number or control track pulse count, to direct the system to specific places on the tape. You can examine the program material, by shuttling the tape forwards/backwards at vari-speeds (handwheel or joystick control). Having selected in/out points, you can *frame trim* (i.e. add or cut frames to get exactly the right cutting moment), check these edit points, and if necessary shift them.

The more sophisticated edit controllers allow you to make edits that are out of running order, and will then, using a *list management* facility, arrange the filed edits in a logical sequence. A keyboard-entered *edit decision list* (*EDL*) can be presented as a monitor-screen display, and/or as a hardcopy printout sheet. This provides you with both a current guide, and a record of how material was used. A list-cleaning program can automatically remove all irrelevant or cancelled data.

Editing using a time code

The most sophisticated electronic editing systems make use of a *time address code/digital frame address system*. Operationally, this is simply a continuous record of a real-time 24-hour digital clock, showing precisely when each fragment of the videotape was recorded. The information is

Fig. 12.6 part 1 Video tape leaders SMPTE standard
A video equivalent of the film leader, providing program identification details, technical alignment, and synchronizing information. The diagram shows the time sequence.

Fig. 12.6 part 2 Video tape leaders — typical British practice
Color bars and tone are recorded in prerecording line-up period. One-minute clock with seconds sweep-hand provides visual countdown. Retakes are identified by taped FM announcement (e.g. Retaking Shots 20–34, Take 1). Electronically generated numbered 'leader' counting down in seconds is used for some VT operations.

stored on the tape's *cue track* (in the LTC format) in binary digital code; as four sets of figures: hour, minutes, seconds, frame (0–29 SMPTE, 0–24 EBU) plus 32 user bits of information.

If necessary, the time code could be recorded on the tape simply as reference points, before or after program recording. But if it is laid down during production recording, it also offers you a real-time check of: when an event happened, its duration, available time left, and elapsed time. You can log clock time in anticipation of later editing; viz: 'We'll use the retake recorded at 15.25.30 not the one at 15.20.10.'

■ *Random access editing* Time code pulses form a unique address, even identifying individual frames within the total recording (although recordings made on different *days* could have similar coding). Selected code locations can be programmed into a memory system to instruct microprocessors controlling VTRs, giving rapid *random access* to any point in the recording: to preview, replay, cue, select edit point, etc. So the address code can be used as an identification and search aid, or form the basis of entirely automated dubbing according to prescribed editing instructions, producing a continuous, correctly assembled presentation.

Off-line editing techniques

One way of approaching production editing is to arrive at the videotape channel armed with notes made during the recording session, review the program, dubbing it progressively (with experimentation), until a new composite videotape is obtained – the 'edited master tape'. But this *on-line editing* technique uses costly facilities and personnel for considerable periods.

The regular solution is to make an identical copy of the program on a

Table 12.3 Videotape — before recording

Precautions	Regular equipment maintenance checks anticipate trouble before it happens.
	Always ensure that the tape heads, tape path (transport), and head-drum are clean (using suitable solvents), free from tape-dust clog, and regularly demagnetized (degaussed). After use, clean and cover equipment.
Tape care	Avoid touching the tape surface (skin oils). Also avoid smoking, dust, crumbs, etc., near the VTR as these all cause drop-out. Do not hand-stop tape because it causes stretching.
	Cut off damaged leader on open-reel tapes, to avoid head damage.
	Check tape for uneven or loose winding (cinching, edge-damage).
	Store tape upright in boxes and away from extreme heat, cold, dryness, humidity, magnetic fields.
	Allow tape and equipment to normalize after transit (e.g. from warm interior to cold exterior) to avoid condensation friction problems.
Pre-recording	Check audio and video levels are within limits. Check tracking and tension adjustments.
	Record and reproduce a test sequence at the start of tape (black level, audio tone, tonal step-wedge or sawtooth, and color bars) for alignment on replay.

portable VTR, during taping or by transfer afterwards. This *workprint* has a time-code/address code *burned-in* (i.e. visible in picture – Fig. 12.5), usually relating to clock-time during the recording period.

The director can scrutinize this copy 'at leisure', and referring to a *take-sheet* made during the production, use it to list the excerpting he requires, the exact edit points, transitions, etc. Later, at an editing session, the chosen address-coded edit points are used to guide the VT editor, or fed into VTR equipment processors for automated editing.

Table 12.4   Videotape-fault tracing

	Check replay with a known good tape program.
No video	Check all units are switched on; correctly operated (facility switches and routing); connections OK. Check video input is OK. Is correct tape-type or system being used (compatibility)?
General noise	Adjust *tracking control* for maximum signal and minimum noise. Is head-tip penetration insufficient? Is head clogged? Is the record current/video level too low? Any head damage (chipped)?
	Adjust playback (replay) equalization for sharp undistorted pictures with minimum noise.
Noise band over top section of picture	If not corrected by tracking control, this may be due to an incompatible recording (misaligned tape path).
Horizontal noise bars across screen	Tracking control or control-track phasing incorrectly set. Capstan servo off lock.
Small black flashes on picture	Drop-out due to tape condition. Insufficient head-tip penetration. Ineffective drop-out compensator.
Close vertical bars (high frequency, RF pattern)	Incorrect adjustment of demodulator balance or limiter (interdependent effects).
Coarse beat-pattern across picture	Clogged erase head. Faulty tracking.
Picture flicker on playback	On a two-headed machine, imbalance between head outputs.
Breakthrough of previous recording	Badly clogged or faulty erase head, or low erase oscillator output.
Rhythmical picture break-up	Faulty servo system (responsible for picture-timing, speed, and synchronism). Other servo faults include noise or disturbance over a few horizontal lines (switching line fault), localised color loss, and inaccurate or noisy edit-points. Audio speed variations (rapid flutter/slower wow).
Hooking (skew), verticals bending over at top of frame	Adjust tape tension (for minimum).
Edge scalloping	Regular horizontal displacement due to low-level video (undermodulation).
Audio playback low level (quiet, high background noise)	Tape recorded at low level. Clogged audio head. Bias too low.
Audio distortion	Damaged tape edge. Overrecorded (overmodulated). Poor head/tape contact. Bias level wrong.
Buzz on audio	Video tracks are audible (poor erasure). Carrier frequency drift.
Wow or flutter	Dirty capstan or roller. Servo off-lock. Spool warped.

■ *Time code problems* Where time code is recorded on an edge track (*longitudinal time code – LTC*), the tape must move past a replay head at over $\frac{1}{5}$ normal speed to be read reliably. On stopping the tape motion (for a still frame), code readout ceases altogether; although the video replay heads continue to scan, reading out the *picture information*. But during VT editing, tape motion varies considerably: fast search, slow motion, jogging (frame-by-frame). To overcome this dilemma, another time code format was introduced (*vertical interval time code – VITC*) in which the code is incorporated within the picture sync information period. (See Glossary – *Time code*.) Simpler editor systems often count control track pulses (deriving 'user bits') to aid frame identification during editing.

13 Graphics

Graphics (captions) are widely used in television and film production, taking a variety of forms: titling, decorative and pictorial illustration, explanatory charts, maps, graphs, diagrams, etc.

The purpose of titles

Opening titles establish the style and atmosphere of the production. The type face, its size, color, and its background, create a foretaste of the program itself.

Above all, titling must be appropriate. Good titling attracts, informs and excites interest. It should be neither confusingly decorative, nor severely characterless. Titling should be compact without being crowded; not spread out, to be lost beyond the frame edge.

Readability

Lettering is there to convey information, and if it cannot be read quickly and easily, it has failed to communicate effectively. The legibility of any graphic detail will depend on its size, elaboration, and background contrast. Lettering sizes below 1/10 to 1/25 of picture height are undesirable. Lettering should generally be bold and firm rather than slight. Thin outlines, serifs, fine striping or hatching, are best avoided. Such detail will either be lost or will strobe distractingly. Conversely, type faces that are too condensed will lose form, particularly if keyed into pictures or given edge enhancement.

Aim to keep titling information to a minimum, particularly if is

Fig. 13.1   Frame proportions
1. To fit the TV frame shape, graphics must have 4 by 3 proportions. The graph shows relative height-width proportions e.g. if a card is 12 units wide, it should be 9 units high.   2. To avoid edge cut-off on the receiver screen, graphic information should be confined to the *safe title area*.

combined with detailed background. A screen full of 'printed information' can be daunting to most viewers, and tiring to read. People are easily discouraged from reading rapid titles. Leave information on the screen long enough to allow it to be read aloud twice, so that the slowest reader can assimilate it. If, for any reason, an announcer is to read out text that is clearly displayed, ensure that the reading is *accurate*!

Backgrounds to titles

Whether plain backgrounds unobtrusively emphasize titling, or appear dull and uninteresting, really depends on the occasion. Ornamental backgrounds (texture, abstract design) may add visual appeal, or they can become fussy and distracting.

Lettering against a multihue or multitone background is invariably harder to read. If you insert titles over location shots (e.g. a street scene) the eye may have some difficulty in discerning information, and may also be tempted to wander around the background instead.

In most cases, by using larger type in light tones (white or yellow) with strong borders (black edged), legibility is considerably improved. But even plain titling can be unclear in certain color relationships (red on green, or red on gray); or in monochrome when gray-scale of lettering and background are similar.

As a general rule, avoid introducing lettering over backgrounds of similar tones or hues, or over printed matter (e.g. titles over a newspaper page). Obvious enough, but people do! Light lettering is usually more easily read than dark; and pastel or neutral backgrounds are preferable to saturated hues. Unless *superimposed* lettering has a black background (it

Table 13.1   Televising graphics using studio camera

	Advantages	Disadvantages
Graphics on stand or easel	Simple method. Camera can zoom, select any section, adjust framing. The original artwork can be used (avoids extra copying stages). Graphics can easily be modified or updated. Graphics can be animated.	Method ties up a studio camera. Graphics require an operator (opportunities for errors, wrong positioning, etc.). Graphics may shake during rapid operation or changes. If graphics sizes vary, camera may have to refocus and reframe. Positioning may vary, causing glare, specular reflections, or revealing surface unevenness.
Projected graphics Front-projected graphics	Camera can zoom, select frame. Slides provide rapid, predictable changes.	Graphics must be prepared in a standard format (e.g. 35 mm slides). Spill light on screen may spoil image. Color quality variations are not easily compensated for. Apparatus usually requires an operator.
Rear-projected graphics	As above	As above. Uneven illumination likely (central hotspot). Screen grain may be apparent in close shots.

then appears 'solid'), it is best keyed-in (electronically inserted) from white-on-black title cards or slides; or in film, by *burn-through* using masking or controlled overexposure. Black lettering cannot be superimposed on a white background.

If lettering on a title card proves to be too large, or needs to be offset, a larger black card placed behind it will enable the cameraman to take a longer shot or reframe without shooting off. Similarly, a chroma key title card (usually white lettering on a blue card) can be extended with a large blue backing sheet.

Transparent plastic overlay sheets (cels) may be used for titling, which is then laid over background graphics. But there is always the danger of light reflections from the surface of the cel.

Although cameras can shoot titling on a foreground glass panel, depth of field is usually too restricted to obtain a sharply focused background scene at the same time. Instead, you would have to pull focus from the titling to 'dissolve' to the action.

Forms of lettering

Although lettering is usually taken for granted, nothing looks more amateurish than ill-proportioned, badly spaced, or poorly laid-out titles. Nowadays there are many short cuts to efficient titling:

1. *Dry-transfer (rub-down, instant transfer) sheets* – with a wide variety of rub-off lettering.
2. *Hot-press lettering* – which hot stamps regular metal type through

Table 13.2   Televising graphics using special apparatus

	Advantages	Disadvantages
Telop	Multiplexing apparatus enabling one TV camera to continuously shoot several stills or transparencies. Lighting changes provide cuts, mixes, supers, all on one camera.	Equipment requires specially prepared graphics. All graphics sizes require a fixed format (100 × 127 mm 4 × 5 in). Size changes or reframing not possible. Some images reversed.
Caption scanners	Designs vary considerably: slide transport by carousel or vertical drums; tray/box carriers, discs. Slide selection in sequential, random, or programmed order. Flexible color correction facilities included in equipment control. Can be remotely controlled.	Slides must be shot and mounted in proportions and framing required — position and size cannot normally be adjusted. Slides are nor readily modified/ corrected, and may acquire blemishes, dirt Equipment reliability varies.
Rostrum camera	An adjustable overhead camera shooting horizontal artwork. Used to record a series of graphics (stills) on film or videotape; in order to simplify a rapid graphics sequence, to record a complex graphics presentation, or to animate a succession of shots. Sequence can be prerecorded, simplifying studio production.	Revision of individual segments requires editing or remake.

Fig. 13.2 Methods of televising graphics
1. Studio camera shoots graphic supported on easel or stand. 2. Caption projection unit; Slide is projected onto screen within box, via a mirror. Camera shooting via same mirror, sees and explores the picture. 3. Camera explores picture from rear-projected slides on translucent screen. Slides are usually transmitted using a multiplexed film-island projector (see fig. 11.8) or a flying-spot scanner (see fig. 11.10). Opaques may use similar systems.

pigment-faced plastic foil, to produce white, black, or color characters.
3. *Plastic lettering* – stuck or clipped onto a background (slotted feltboard, magnetic board).
4. *Constructed lettering* – arranged from toy bricks; formed in thumb tacks, toothpaste, rope; finger traced in sand or snow.
5. *Decorative lettering effects* – using shadows, silhouettes, reflections, stencils, etc.
6. *Handwritten lettering* – which is extremely difficult for the inexperienced (even using lettering aids), and best avoided. May be successful where unsophisticated effects are required (on walls, sidewalks, chalk boards).
7. *Video character-generators* – enabling electronically generated lettering to be 'typed into the picture', or presented as complete stored information.

Character generators (alpha-numeric generators)

Using programmed digital circuits, a range of lettering, numbers, and symbols can be electronically generated in selectable fonts and sizes; including such variants as Roman, Cyrillic, Japanese, Arabic.

Most titling and basic graphics are only required for a single TV program; so the rapidly produced low-cost display that the character generator provides, offers considerable advantages.

Fig. 13.3 Title positions
Titling is normally localized for maximum impact, avoiding important subject areas (e.g. face).

Fig. 13.4   Border Generators
1. White solid lettering.   2. black-
edge border.   3. drop shadow effect.
4. outline.

A standard typewriter/computer keyboard is used, and aided by a location cursor symbol indicating the next character position, the typed copy is prepared on a monitor screen display. Information could be inserted into the studio *line* (*master*) *picture* as it is being typed, but usually the prepared message is stored (magnetic floppy disc or tape, programmable microprocessors, or punched paper tape), recalled and inserted as required.

Lettering can be corrected or revised instantly, and moved around the frame for layout adjustment, or to create vertical roll or horizontal crawl titles. Lettering may be selectively flashed (blink). Refinements include autocentring and tabulation, varisize, and multipage storage.

Using a color synthesizer, the lettering and background (normally white-on-black) can be given push-button selected colors – sometimes colorizing individual words.

■ *Border generators*   To improve legibility or impact, lettering can be processed in various ways (whether from the character generator or other sources):

1. It can be given a black, white, or color edge *outline border*; all round, or at one edge.
2. A *dropped shadow* can be produced to create pseudo solidity.
3. An *edge outline* can be developed from the original solid character.

■ *Electronic keying/matting (inlay)*   Electronic insertion by keying or non-additive mixing, enables lettering to be 'punched solid' into an existing picture, so avoiding the interaction of hues and tones that arises when *superimposing* lettering. It is customary when adding titles to multitone color pictures, to use keyed-in black-edged characters for optimum clarity.

Table 13.3   Typical graphics sizes

Smallest size for convenient handling (smallest type size 24–36 pt)	30.5 × 23 cm (12 × 9 in)
Commonly used sizes shooting a 30.5 × 23 cm (12 × 9 in) area	43 × 35.6 cm (17 × 14 in) 40 × 30 cm (16 × 12 in)
Flip cards – copy area 23.5 × 18 cm (9.5 × 7 in)	35.6 × 28 cm (14 × 11 in)
Largest size for elaborate artwork	61 × 46 cm (24 × 18 in)
Thickness of support art board	2 mm (1/16 in) minimum

Forms of graphics

Pictorial and diagrammatic graphics can make a valuable contribution to all types of TV program, for they show information succinctly and unambiguously in a few seconds. You can demonstrate developments, proportions, relationships; make statistics attractively meaningful, thus simplifying complex data.

Graphics can be presented by any of the methods discussed in Tables 13.1 and 13.2. You can also introduce them as part of the studio setting: as display screens, desk charts, wall maps, and free-standing panels. However, you must ensure that they do not become obtrusive or distract attention – you can do this by keeping them out of shot, or obscuring them (sliding panels, revolving units, etc.) until required.

Although it is possible to show graphics on an in-shot picture monitor, a better scale image is generally obtained from a wall display screen. This enables you to present a succession of graphics, while relating them to a demonstrator. Either *rear-projected* slides, or electronically inserted graphics can be used (Chapter 19). He will be able to see and point out detail in inserted graphics, by using a nearby picture monitor for reference.

There is a special attraction in seeing someone draw upon or alter diagrammatic displays, particularly where information is to be built up progressively. Figure 13.10 shows several widely used methods of adding, removing or changing detail. Alternatively, graphics can be *animated* (usually out of shot) to introduce variations.

Three-dimensional graphics often make information more interesting, for example a giant ear showing all its component parts. Everyday objects such as coins or wooden blocks can be used to demonstrate principles. Elaboration may be ingenious, but it is often arguable whether a three-dimensional multilayer graphical model in styrofoam is any more informative than its humble flat counterpart. It is certainly more expensive!

Occasionally, you may introduce titling or pictorial graphics as 'natural features' of a scene: a book title on a shelf, wall poster, street sign, baggage label . . . even attached to people (a sweatshirt).

Computer graphics can be created by electronic equipment ranging from home computers, to complex specialist systems that enable the graphics artist to produce totally realistic, fully animated cartoons. Advanced computer graphics allow the artist to simulate on the video

Fig. 13.5   Graphics supports
1. *Caption stand* (tiltable shelf, adjustable height) suitable for title cards.   2. *Card-pulls* attached to edges make removal easier.   3. *Title card box* – Top card pulled out to reveal next title.   4. *Strap easel* used for larger graphics. Weighted webbing straps adjust to suit all sizes.   5. *Flat* displays various graphics of different sizes.

Fig. 13.6   Types of graph
Graphical presentation enables information to be assimilated and compared rapidly.
Several forms are available, having greater visual interest than a routine line-graph.
1. Multi-surface or strata graph.   2. Column graph.   3. Combined column graph.
4. Bar graph.   5. Sector, pie, or circle chart.   6. Volume chart, height chart, area
chart.   7. Pictogram pictorial chart.   8. Pictorial symbols.   9. Flow chart.

screen, in a wide selection of hues, saturation, and brightnesses, such
diverse media as pen, watercolor, pencil, air-brush, using freehand,
stored images, cut-and-paste modes (photo-derived images), simply by
'drawing' with an electronic stylus on a table.

Animated graphics

Movement brings a graphic alive. But if you are not careful, it awakens
interest only in the ingenuity of the animation!

The simplest methods of introducing movement into a graphic, are to
pan over it from one detail to another, to zoom in/out, or to intercut
between sections of it. Such techniques are used for illustrated children's
stories – an inexpensive method of continually redistributing attention.

Graphics can be built up in vision, progressively adding details or
sections (uncover wipes, lighting changes, superimpositions, etc.). Or
detail can change or disappear. Graphics have been made more arresting
by introducing such animation as falling snow, swirling mist (obscuring
one title, and clearing to reveal the next), falling rain, traveling light
patterns; and even by setting fire to them! Puppets have 'operated' them
or pointed out information. Ingenuity knows no bounds!

Fig. 13.7 Shooting graphics
Only when shot straight-on, will the image of a flat plane be undistorted. Shooting off-axis produces *keystone* distortion, e.g. when the viewpoint is too high or shot from the side. In geometrical subjects (music, print, diagrams) the effect may be pronounced.

Graphics with movement *(see pages 268–269)*

■ *Card pull/pull-out/pull title* One title card is slid aside to reveal another underneath. A series of edge-attached pull tags help to remove one at a time. The cards may be stacked on a caption stand (easel) or supported within a slotted box. During operation, a rapid smooth pull is preferable to a quick jerk. Take care that cards do not become displaced or upset.

Fig. 13.8 3-D graphics
Three-dimensional graphics have a considerable visual appeal and provide demonstrator-involvement. Examples shown are models (left) and a transparent graph (right).

Fig. 13.9 Exploring graphics
A graphic can be 'animated' by exploring it with the camera, so creating continual visual change, e.g. from shot A, zoom out to include B, then to the full picture C, zooming in to select frame D, then E.

■ *Flip* Easily operated, but susceptible to jamming or falling out of position. Ensure that card holes are of suitable size and undamaged.
Flip-in/drop-in title cards are top-hinged on a ring binder (or sometimes tape hinges).
Flip-out/drop-out versions are bottom hinged.
Flip-over or flip-round types rotate on a central rod, but require a black backing behind them to prevent shoot-off.

■ *Traveler/roller caption* This continuously moving *crawl title* enables a lot of printed information to be presented in an easily read form. Hot-press or photo-printed on a strip of stiff black paper, the *traveler* or *roller caption* is a convenient one-camera alternative to a series of brief title cards.

Fig. 13.10 Attached detail
Regular methods of attaching detail, labels, symbols, sections to graphics: *Flannelboard* – Both the rear-strip behind shape and the background have surface of felt, baize, flannelette, PVC (plastograph). *Teazlegraph* (Velcro) – Shape backed with small nylon multi-hook strip; background has multi-loop strip. *Adhesive strip* – Double-sided adhesive tape behind shape; smooth background. *Magnetic* – Magnetic plastic strip or small magnets, attached to steel-sheet background.

Table 13.4 Precautions with graphics design

Always work within 4:3 proportions.

Provide an adequate border for camera framing.

Use matt materials. Avoid spurious reflections from shiny or glossy lettering, paint, plastic tape, overlay sheets, pencil marks, etc.

Avoid buckling, wrinkles, and similar surface unevenness. Attach thin copy to heavy illustrated board, which can be reused.

A large graphic can look the same as a smaller one on the screen. But considerable size reduction will noticeably weaken thin lines; while magnification of small graphics coarsens detail.

Ensure that graphics are evenly lit, and shadows do not disrupt multiplane captions.

Coarse tonal variations, for example, five spaced gray scale steps between black and white, provide more dynamic reproduction than subtle half tones.

Always consider how colored graphics will appear in monochrome.

Color impact in titling and graphics is important. A vibrant hue (red, yellow) may be arresting, forceful, giving emphasis, or disturbing, brash, tasteless, or aesthetically inappropriate.

Simplification of detail, clear symbolism, and unambiguous approaches have maximum effect.

Keep information detail to a minimum for rapid assimilation.

Choose simple structural forms for diagrams, particularly for comparative graphics.

Maps should contain only relevant main features, with good tonal and color contrasts; water areas (sea, lakes, rivers) being shown in darker tones. Name labels may be provided by a plastic overlay, superimposition, keyed in, or manually attached.

Comparative information on a single graph is preferable to a succession of graphics.

The machine may be hand-operated, or motor driven at an even adjustable rate. A motorized machine can be timed, and then cued to synchronize with a program play-out for end-of-show credits. Either upward or right-left drive directions can be used, but lateral word movement is less easily read. You can also use either method to display

(*cont. on page 270*)

Fig. 13.11 Traveler/roller-caption
This continuous strip display may be rolled up, or rolled horizontally. Varying the frame position of titling produces a *crawl title*. It may also be used as a traveling path display.

Fig. 13.12 part 1   Animated graphics – flips
1. Title-cards in ring binders, flip into shot (drop-in); or bottom hinged flip-out (drop-out). Margin finger-grip tabs aid operation.   2. Flip-over – double-faced title-card horizontally pivoted.   3. Flip-round.   4. Rotating flip.

Fig. 13.12 part 2   Animated graphics – pull outs (reveals)
1. Top card is slid aside to reveal the next.   2. Black slide-out section in black card, reveals titling underneath.   3. As each black card is pulled, titling on the clear sheet beneath is revealed.   4. Slide provides push-over wipe effect.   5. Shutters slide aside to reveal new information below.   6. *Breakaway*, where top graphic splits (slides apart or hinges) to reveal another.

Fig. 13.12 part 3   Animated graphics – rotates
1. Turntable.   2. Flop-over or vertical slide.   3. Rotating box.   4. Rotating strips.

Fig. 13.12 part 4   Animated graphics – stencil and lighting methods
1. Stencil where pull-off tape (seen from rear) progressively uncovers rear-lit stenciled titling.   2. Animation by lighting – shadows grow, directing attention or creating atmospheric effect. Localized illumination can be used similarly.

Fig. 13.12 part 5   Animated graphics – drum titles
1. Large vertical drum.   2. Surface-lettered drum as part of a model shot.   3. Stand-up lettering.   4. Drum lettering appears to move around an object (superimposed or keyed-in).

13.12 part 6   Animated detail
1. Rotating and sliding sections.   2. Hinged or pivoted sections.   3. Pull-out reveals.   4. Rear illumination.

Table 13.5   Designing animated graphics

A number of ingenious techniques have been developed to create animation in graphics for cartoons, diagrams, etc. The cost is considerably lower than frame-by-frame film or videotape animation, and the action can be adjusted or timed to suit the production.

To add or remove information (names, details, parts, etc)	Change part of the graphic using pop-ins, pop-outs, reveals, pull-outs, breakaways, or multiplane treatment.
	Use electronic insertion (chroma key, CSO).
	Manually attach or detach detail. Superimpose detail.
	Drop transparent cel detail over caption.
To show movement (moving wheels, heart-beating	Have moving surfaces pivoted, hinged, or in runners; operated by tags, levers, strings, magnets, threads, or rubberband 'springs'.
	Intercut shots showing different stages of movement (e.g. hand up . . . hand down).
To show flow (liquid down a pipe)	Cut-out background areas requiring flow treatment. Simulate flow by turning patterns, pull-outs, roller-strip, interference patterns (e.g. a striped strip moving behind a striped transparent panel).
To show flow variation (pressure or density fluctuations)	Change density, tone or speed of flow pattern.
To show direction (aircraft track moving across a map).	Stenciled pull-out. Slide symbol on surface cel over background. Move lighting pattern. Use electronic insertion.
To direct attention to detail	Use indicator (ring, arrow, spotlight) superimposed or electronically inserted. Projected light. Rear-illuminated area.
To move detail about (a product along a conveyor belt)	Use rear magnets, surface cel, thread-operated animation, tags or wires in background slots. Superimpose or electronically insert detail, and pan/tilt its camera.
To show changes in size, volume, quantity	Build subject in a series of subdivided sections, animated simultaneously to change overall size. Intercut between captions showing progressive stages. Use superimposed or inserted detail, and zoom its camera in/out for size changes.
Removing surface to show subsurface detail or sectional views	Remove surfaces by pop-out/pop-in, or by detaching, unflapping, sliding apart.
To show enlarged portions of a subject	Use pop-in enlargement of detail. Electronically insert shot of detail.

continuous graphics – for example the development of a manufacturing process, or a series of illustrative stills. A more controllable method than trucking past long *pan cards*.

■ *Rotating titles*   *Rotating box, rotating strips, rotating turntable* – these devices turn to present new information on each face. *Drum titling* can be used to provide a crawl, or made to rotate round a central motif, or appear within a small display.

■ *Reveals*   These all *uncover* information in various ways:

1. *Breakaway* – The graphic slides apart to show new information.
2. *Shutters* – Sections slide under each other.
3. *Multiplane* – A sandwich of transparent planes with black cards between each. As the cards are moved, information is added progressively.

Table 13.6   Problems with graphics

Even quite simple graphics can reproduce badly on the TV screen, if they are not prepared, shot, and lit carefully.

Graphic size	*If too small* Close-up details appear coarsened (e.g. texture looks crude, lines rough-edged). When close shooting with a narrow-angle lens, to get big enough detail, any camera movement is exaggerated. No room to pan around (explore or re-frame) without shooting off. Camera may not be able to get large enough image due to limited minimum focused distance. Camera may shadow the graphic. *If too large* Camera may not be able to position far enough away to take in the entire graphic. If shot on a wide-angle lens, the graphic may appear distorted. Finer lines may be unclear or merge in a full shot.
Graphic shape	If a graphic is not roughly 4 by 3 horizontal format, it will not fit the TV screen shape. (See Fig. 13.14).
Surface	*Tones too light* Light tones block off. Flare. Loss of detail/gradation in lightest tones and/or darkest tones. *Tones too dark* Picture usually lacks contrast. Lower tones merge. Muddy appearance. *Black tones* Various 'black' surfaces may have such different reflectances (shades, textures), that when intermixed in a graphic e.g. black card, paint, ink, plastic tape), the picture cannot be set down to crush and unify black areas, without degrading other picture tones. *Texture* Shiny surfaces appear either strongly saturated (bright color), or reflect light as unwanted white patches. Surface details and lettering become lost in the glare. (Tilting the graphic, or altering camera height slightly, may clear the reflection.) *Distractions* Graphics are easily defaced by surface wrinkles, finger marks, scrapes, scratches, lettering faults, adhesive, etc., that the casual glance overlooks, but stand out plainly on the screen.
Lighting	*Uneven lighting* Brighter towards the top, or to one side. (Lamp too steep, or far off the lens axis.) *Central hotspot* Lamp spotted; too close; filament image; lamp too close to lens axis. *Multiplane shadows* One surface surface can shadow another under it. (Centralize and soften the light; use Pepper's ghost device.) *Camera shadows* If lighting is at too shallow angle; or the camera is too close to graphic. (Use narrower lens angle.) Optimize lighting.
Camera angle	*Distortion* If camera is not straight-on to graphic (trapezium distortion); too high, off-center. Wide-angle lens distortion (barrel/pincushion distortion). Graphic not correctly positioned on its support.

■ *Graphics treatment*   If you have a complicated graphics sequence, there are real advantages in taping it beforehand, particularly for a live show, to ensure that all that goes smoothly. You can enliven even simple graphics with *stop-start* (*stop-motion*) *animation*. Just by adding, moving, removing, blanking out detail between shots, items can be made to change or be given movement. This type of animation is best done with

Fig. 13.13   Animation table
The mirror reflects operations on the glass-topped table. Sections can be moved, removed, added, animated (in vision or single-frame recorded). It can be used for unseen writing.

move-around sections, or overlay cels, rather than actually altering the artwork, for if anything goes wrong, it will be easy enough to repeat the sequence!

■ *Stencils/cut-out cards*   These pierced graphics enable a background to be seen through a stenciled background. They can be used in several ways:

1. A rear adhesive strip is pulled off to reveal the pierced sections (a map route or lettering).
2. An animated surface is created by a rear moving-card pattern; or by sliding together sandwiches of fine wire-mesh, photo-engraving screens, or plastic sheet interference patterns.

■ *Animation by lighting*   Lighting treatment can create apparent movement or change by:

1. Selectively lighting details.
2. Creating shadow effects that reveal, conceal or decorate information.
3. Producing reflections and appearance changes as the lighting angle varies.
4. Selectively rear lighting detail (words, points on a map).

■ *Letter movement*   Individual words or letters can be made to move, using pull-strips, magnets, pop-in or slide-in sections.

Fig. 13.14   Picture shape
1. Only a graphic in 4 by 3 proportions will fit the TV screen.   2. A tall narrow graphic can be shot as a whole, with black-sided borders.   3. Or it can be shot in selected sections.

Unseen drawing

Seeing a drawing gradually form as we watch, has a persuasive fascination. It is a useful method of introducing complex information piecemeal, or making a little material go a long way. However, its extended use can become tedious.

Methods of obtaining unseen writing include:

1. Rear writing in white paint on a clear glass sheet backed by black drapes. The performer is totally dressed in black.
2. Rear writing with a felt-pen on a paper sheet; the camera shooting the bleed-through on the reverse.
3. Drawing on a surface of chroma key (CSO) hue (e.g. blue) for electron insertion.
4. Writing on an overhead projector cel.
5. Special electronic 'remote-writing' equipment.

14 The background of production

The TV director's job varies considerably with the organization, and the size and type of production.

■ *Combined functions* For a smaller show he may be both producer and director. He is responsible for the entire business and artistic arrangements: origination, interpretation, casting, staging and treatment, and subsequently directing studio operations.

■ *Separate functions* The director may concentrate on the program's interpretation, staging and direction; while his producer as business head is responsible for organization, finance and policy. Sometimes a producer serves as artistic and business coordinator for several directors.

Fig. 14.1 Production team
Studio production requires the services and skills of a large number of people. Their exact job functions and titles vary between organizations.

The director's role

In all organizations, the director is the key figure who unifies and guides the production team. With regular contributory productions, such as public affairs/current affairs, newscasts, magazine and talk programs, the director usually has a *presentation role*. Here he/she visualizes production treatment, and coordinates for a series of separate items (*stories*) that have been prepared by individuals in an editorial group (researchers/writers/editors).

In a *selective role*, the director heads a team of specialists (set design, lighting, audio, costume, make-up, graphics, etc.). After preliminary briefing/planning, they contribute their interpretations, which he subsequently appraises during rehearsal. Then, apart from indicating any alterations or preferences, he concentrates mainly on the dynamics of performance, camera treatment and switching (editing).

Occasionally the director, as *originator*, has written the script and initiated the staging. Then his specialist team aims to fulfil his ideas by organizing facilities, mechanics, labor and costing.

Production emphasis

The art of television is not *specific*. Emphasis changes considerably according to the type of production. While a drama production may benefit from painstaking shot-by-shot planning, a director of a live sports telecast relies on an almost clairvoyant ability to anticipate and switch shot opportunities from strategic camera positions.

In some shows (interviews), the staging and production treatment must provide an unobtrusive background to performance, while in others (spectaculars) these play a strong supporting role for action. Camera and audio treatment may aim at direct reportage or dramatically interpret mood.

While some productions have a relatively loose format, others require split-second timing with accurately cued inserts from live remotes, tape or film sources. Some types of production concentrate on action; others on *re*action. Dialogue may be all-important or incidental.

Away from the studio, the opportunities for coverage and treatment are invariably restricted. The considerable areas and distances often involved at remotes, the limitations of facilities, and the environmental problems, all influence production potentials. Lightweight cameras provide mobility, but various inherent problems (local acoustics, extraneous noise, weather, light variations, continuity, etc.) must affect treatment.

Production approaches

There is no 'standard correct way' of presenting subjects. Directors have tried most, over the years. But certainly, if we use an unsuitable approach our audience is quite likely to become confused, distracted, resentful . . . or simply lose interest.

Table 14.1   Production personnel

Producer	Organizational and administrative head of production group. May select program concepts, production personnel, and control budget.
Director	Responsible for staging the production, coordinating services, directing performers and crew; decides the final visual and audio treatment. May also operate video switcher.
Assistant producer/assistant director	Director's aide. May line up shots, prepare inserts, etc. Supervises pre-studio rehearsals. Advises director of up-coming cues.
Production assistant/script girl	Checks performance against script. Times program.
Producer's assistant	As script girl, with certain cue preparation duties.
Floor manager (FM)/stage manager (SM)	Director's representative and contact man on studio floor. Cues performers. Directs floormen. Responsible for general floor organization, safety, discipline. Assisted by AFM, who also ensures talent are present.
Technical director (TD)	Coordinates and supervises engineering facilities. Evaluates technical quality. May operate video switcher. May instruct operational crew during production.
Switcher/vision mixer	Specialist operating video switcher (and perhaps electronic effects).
Set designer/scenic designer	Conceives, designs, and organizes scenic treatment.
Make-up artist	Prepares and applies make-up treatment; aided by *make-up assistants* and *hair stylists*.
Costume designer	Designs/selects performers' costume (wardrobe). Assisted by *dressers/ wardrobe handlers*.
Graphics artist	Designs/prepares all graphics and visuals.
Lighting director	Designs, arranges and controls lighting treatment (technically and artistically).
Video operator/video control/ video engineer/shader	Controls picture quality by adjusting video equipment.
Audio engineer/audio control/ sound supervisor	Controls audio level, quality, balance; technical and artistic aspects of sound.
Camera crew	Cameramen, dolly operators, etc., responsible for camera operation.
Sound crew	Mike boom operators, audio personnel positioning microphones; operating audio tape and discs.
Floor men/stage hands/facilities men	Crew responsible for scenic changes, set dressing, properties, graphics operation, etc.
Electricians	Crew responsible for rigging and setting lamps, and electrical apparatus (including electrical props).
Special effects	Specialist designing and operating such mechanical illusions as fire, snow, explosions. Electronics effects specialist may devise/operate complex electronic insertion.
Announcer	Concerned with on/off announcements, commentary, continuity, etc.

■ *Appropriateness* What is *appropriate*! Well, this is largely a matter of custom, fashion, convention:

1. *Informal situations* are often provided in naturalistic surroundings – the craftsman in his workshop, the fireside chat, the country-walk interview.
2. *Formal situations* often follow a very stylized artificial format – carefully positioned chairs, desks, 'rules of procedure.'
3. *Display presentations* are generally unrealistic, with emphasis on decorative effects (singers and music groups).
4. *Simulated presentations* recreate a realistic environmental atmosphere, as in drama presentations; where any hint of the mechanics involved would destroy the effect.
5. *Actuality* has been emphasized (or imitated) by deliberately revealing mechanics. Somewhat unsteady hand-held cameras and microphones dipping into shot have supposedly added to the veracity of the occasion, as in 'vox pop' street interviews.

Routines

Some production techniques have become so familiar through convention or suitability, that it could seem strangely unorthodox if we presented them in any other way – e.g. a newscaster sitting in a lounge.

Certain approaches have become so stereotyped that they enter the realms of cliché; routine methods for routine situations. The sheer extent and repetition of TV productions has thrown up a number of such formats: newscasts: studio interviews, game shows, chat shows, etc. If we analyze such productions, we usually find that styles have evolved as the most effective, economic and reliable ways of handling their particular subjects.

If we regard such a packaging as 'a container for the goods,' then these routine treatments can free the audience to concentrate on the event. If however, we consider the presentation treatment as an opportunity to encourage interest and heighten enjoyment, then any 'routine' becomes unacceptable.

However, any dramatic or emphatic treatment would clearly be quite gratuitous for many types of TV production. Instead, it is best to aim for pictorial variety, coupled with clear unambiguous visual statements that direct and concentrate attention, rather than introduce any imposed 'style.'

Many non-dramatic subjects are *inherently* limited in their potential treatment. How many sensible meaningful shot variations can you take of people speaking to each other, or driving an automobile, or playing an instrument, or demonstrating an article – the range is small.

For certain subjects, the picture is virtually irrelevant. What a person has to *say* may be extremely important; while what he *looks* like, is immaterial to the message. It may even prove a distraction or create prejudicial bias. 'Talking heads' appear in most TV shows, but unless the speaker is particularly animated, the viewers' visual interest is seldom sustained. Changing viewpoint helps – but can appear fidgety.

Motion pictures inform us through continual illustration and commentary. Television's more economic but less enticing approach, is for people to tell us about matters instead. They sit in the studio with graphics or film clips, or stand at the scene of activities and talk directly to us, instead of using the camera itself to demonstrate. Here the difference in approach is not inherent in the medium, but the way it is being used.

Ambience

From the moment a show begins, we are influencing our audience's attitude to the production itself. Introductory music and titling style can immediately convey a serious or a jokey feeling towards what is to come.

We have only to recall how the hushed voice, quiet organ notes, slow visual pace, impart a reverential air to proceedings; or the difference between a regal and a 'show-biz' opening fanfare, to realize how our expectancy changes.

Surroundings can also directly affect how convincingly we convey information. Certain environments, for example, impart authority or scholarship: classroom, laboratory, museum, study. A plow shown at work on the farm will not only be more readily understood, but will carry a conviction that is lacking in the studio demonstration.

Selective tools

The camera and microphone do not behave like our eyes and ears, but substitute for them. Our eyes flick around with a knowledge of our surroundings, providing us with an impression of unrestricted stereoscopic vision; in fact, we can only detect detail and color over a tiny angle (about $1\frac{1}{2}°$), and our peripheral vision is monochromatic and quite blurred. Also, our ears provide us with selective biaural pick-up, quite unlike the TV audio system.

In daily life, we build up an impression of our environment by personally controlled sampling; concentrating on certain details while ignoring others. The camera and microphone on the other hand, provide us with only restricted segments. And the information provided in these segments is modified in various ways, as we have seen, by the characteristics of the medium (distorting space, proportions, scale, etc.).

Selective techniques

If you simply set up your camera and microphone overlooking the action, the viewer soon becomes overaware of the small restricted screen and limited detail. He is prevented from seeing whatever is outside the shot. Go closer for detail and he progressively loses the overall view. Show more of the scene and particular detail becomes indiscernible. In the choice of suitable viewpoint and shot size for a particular purpose, lies the concept of guided selection; the beginnings of techniques.

Good production techniques provide *variety*: of scale and proportion; of composition pattern; of centers of attention and changing subject influence. You achieve these things by variation in shot size and camera viewpoint, by moving the subject and/or the camera, or by altering the subject seen.

Although you may sometimes encourage the viewer to browse around a shot, more often you will want him to look at a particular feature, and follow a certain thought process. The screen can all too easily become 'moving wallpaper', with our audience seeing – but not looking, hearing – but not listening!

The screen transforms reality

The camera and microphone can only convey an *impression* of the subject and scene. Whatever the limitations or inaccuracies of these images, they are the only direct information our viewer has available. And, of course, his interpretation must vary with his own experience and foreknowledge.

Table 14.2   Typical reasons for production techniques

Artistically	To disguise the restrictions of the small flat TV screen and limited viewpoints.
	To guide and concentrate audience attention.
	To obtain visual variety and encourage continued interest.
	To emphasize, exaggerate, reduce or subdue information.
	To create a particular emotional impact (horror, tension).
	To beautify, glamorize, make more attractive (diffusion discs, soft focus, star filters).
	To expand/contract/distort space or form.
	To build up an illusion or effect purely by editing, viewpoint, camera-angle.
	To transform time and motion (time lapse, slow motion movement).
	To simulate an emotional or physical state (flying, drowning, unconsciousness).
	To achieve 'magical' effects (transformation, shrinkage, growth).
Technically	To disguise limited technical facilities (shooting on a single camera).
	To avoid visual discontinuity in time, place, position, angle, etc. (using cutaway shots to disguise time lapses, jump cuts, reverse cuts, etc.).
	To enable specific shots to be obtained (despite distance, terrain, confined space, etc.).
	To disguise or overcome spurious or intrusive factors.
	To permit editing cuts (shortening, correcting, covering lip-flap, etc.).
	To give time for moves (of performer, camera, boom).
	To provide space for moves.
	To overcome mechanical problems (prevent a camera appearing in shot).
	To overcome practical absurdities (shooting in the dark), or impracticalities (a succession of shots that would reveal the respective cameras if taken during continuous action).
	To create an illusion that would be impracticable or expensive if achieved directly.
	To provide picture (or sound) where none is strictly possible or available (see 'Visual padding').
	To analyze or synthesize (e.g. a study freeze-frame of action).

Whether you are aiming to convey an accurate account (newscast) or to conjure an illusion (drama) the screen will transform reality.

You could fill the screen with a shot of a huge aircraft, or with its diminutive model. The pictures would look very similar. Yet neither conveys the subjective essentials; i.e. how you *feel* standing beside the giant plane or handling the tiny model. Introducing a person into shot would establish scale, but it would still not include our characteristic responses to such a situation: the way we would ourselves be overawed by size, or intrigued by minute detail.

Use your camera to select detail from a painting or a photograph and your TV screen puts a frame around it, to make this isolated area into a new complete picture; an arrangement that did not exist in its own right within the original; an arrangement that if sustained in close-up can become detached and dissociated in the audience's minds, from the complete subject.

When you shoot solid sculpture, its three-dimensional form becomes reproduced as a flat pattern on the TV screen. Planes merge and interact as they cannot do when we ourselves examine the real sculpture. Only on the flat screen can a billiard ball become transformed into a flat disc under diffused lighting. In practice, you can continually make use of this falsification of reality. The very principles of scenic design rely on it. But it is as well to appreciate that the camera and microphone do inevitably modify the images they convey; and that these images are easily mistaken for truth.

Interpretative techniques

It is one of those production paradoxes, that although your camera can show what is happening, it will often fail to convey the atmosphere or spirit of the occasion. You can frequently achieve more convincing representative results by deliberately using selective techniques, than by direct reportage.

Straightforward shots of a mountain climb impart none of the thrills and hazards of the situation. But use low camera angles to emphasize the treacherous slope; show threatening overhangs, straining fingers, slipping feet, dislodged stones, laboring breath, slow ascending music . . . and the illusion grows. Even climbing a gentle slope can appear hazardous if strong interpretative techniques are used.

Sometimes the audience can be so strongly moved by this subjective treatment, that sympathetic bodily reactions set in when watching such scenes – dizziness, nausea. Even situations outside the viewer's personal experience (the elation of free fall, the horror of quicksands) can be conveyed to some degree by carefully chosen stimulii.

Making the contrived arise 'naturally'

You can introduce techniques *obtrusively* for dramatic effect, or so *unobtrusively* that the effect appears 'natural' and the viewer is quite unaware that the situation *is* contrived:

Obtrusive: The camera suddenly depresses from an eye-level shot to a low-angle viewpoint.

Unobtrusive: The camera shoots a seated actor at eye-level. He stands, and the camera tilts up with him. We now have a low-angle shot.

Where situations seem to occur accidentally or unobtrusively, they are invariably more effective. For example, as an intruder moves towards camera, he becomes menacingly underlit by a nearby table lamp.

Where an effect is blatantly contrived, it often appears to challenge our credulity and we tend to reject it: A sinister figure is reflected in the victim's sunglasses; the camera whip-pans to show him standing nearby.

As conventions become understood and accepted by our audience, even flagrant changes become permissible: *flash cut-ins* (lasting ½–2 seconds) to convey 'recognition' or 'recall'; extreme viewpoint changes, close sound on long shots; exaggerated filmic time. But a director who deliberately misuses an established convention, trying to give it a new significance, treads a thorny path.

Many techniques have become so familiar, that we now regard them as the normal and natural way of doing things. But they are really artifices that help us to convey particular concepts:

1. Chipmunk voices (high-pitched through tape speed-up) for small creatures.
2. Echo behind ghostly manifestations.
3. Rim light in 'totally dark' scenes.
4. Background music.
5. Wipes, supers, etc.

Gratuitous techniques

Skilful presentation blends a carefully selected combination of visual and audio techniques to attract and persuade. But you can too easily use techniques for their own sake.

1. Rapid cutting in time with music – that provides a disjointed dissatisfying jumble of images.
2. Video effects – that leave us preoccupied with how it was done.
3. 'Clever' camerawork – focusing on irrelevant foreground objects while main subjects remain unsharp; shooting into lamps or specular reflections.

Such contrived methods have their occasional purpose, but they can quickly degenerate into imposed gimmicks.

Production pressures

Preoccupation with the organization and coordination of production mechanics, leaves most directors little time to mediate on the medium's aesthetics. Rehearsal time is limited. The camera and sound crews are meeting the director's brainchild for the first time and need to be guided in his interpretation. If the treatment is elaborate and exacting, there is greater opportunity for problems that require immediate solution. If the production is shot out of sequence, it becomes that much more difficult to ensure that each segment is coherent, and will provide good continuity when edited together. In such circumstances, there is an understandable temptation to substitute effective known mechanics for creative experiment.

Also, when you are closely involved with a production, it can be quite difficult to estimate accurately the audience impact of pace, timing, tension, etc. Watching a film clip through *several* times, you will see how the stresses, emphasis, speed, and even its significance can change. A word or gesture can have more or less impact with repetition, while heavily pointed action may appear hackneyed or mannered.

15 Production practices

Over the years, various production practices have evolved. Some derive directly from the mechanics of the medium, while other result from established procedures.

Single-camera treatment

Most TV productions are shot with a multicamera set-up. But effective visual treatment does not necessarily involve such complexity. There are normally two situations in which a single camera is used:

1. In the first, we deliberately restrict camera treatment to a single mobile camera; often arranging action and staging to suit this technique.
2. In the second, due to limited resources, we have only one camera available to shoot action.

■ *Discontinuous shooting* Normal *filming* practice uses a single camera and breaks down all treatment into individually photographed shots; the action and camera set-up (sometimes staging) being arranged to suit each in turn. This technique requires care in maintaining *continuity* (of action, position, expression, etc.), and often involves repeating action (performance) to reshoot it from different viewpoints and so facilitate editing. Exactly the same technique can be followed with the TV camera – providing the extensive videotape editing is practical with available facilities.

■ *Restricted facilities* With careful organization, it is possible, even with a *single static camera* using a fixed lens angle, to shoot continuously

Fig. 15.1 part 1 Subject movement and the single camera – equidistant positions
Items can be arranged equidistant from the camera, to provide a series of similar shots as the talent moves around.

**Fig. 15.1 part 2   Subject movement and the camera –
movement in depth**
Where subjects of various sizes are involved, the largest can be located furthest
away; the smallest closest to the camera.

and yet introduce flexibility and shot variety. This is achieved by arranging action to provide mobility; moving people around the setting, transferring attention from one area to another.

You obtain variations in shot size by placing subjects at different distances from the camera. Larger items may be located furthest away, while small ones on a foreground table provide close-ups. A turntable helps the camera to see objects from various angles (mirrors are also useful). Occasionally, by pulling focus from one object to another, you can transfer attention.

■ *Variations*   If your single camera is mobile and fitted with a zoom lens, you have further opportunities. To change the camera's viewpoint unobtrusively, you might reposition it during action; for example, arcing round during a walk and perhaps incorporating slight zooming to reduce the amount of dolly movement. As a lecturer turns to point to a wall chart, the camera can zoom in to detail. When he lifts an object we have been studying in close-up, the camera zooms back to a mid-shot. Zooming here provides shot variety without becoming intrusive.

■ *Inserts*   Use of *insert material* such as slides, film, and videotape, can give opportunities to reposition the camera or change the shot. Inserts may show information not readily seen by the studio camera (hallmarks on silverware), or may provide supplementary illustrations. Take care, though, not to introduce visual discontinuity.

Multicamera treatment

Using two or more cameras you have the opportunity for continuous production: for instant visual change, intercutting different shot sizes and viewpoints of the same subject, or moving from one area to another.

So you can immediately provide fresh information, alter emphasis, point new detail, show reactions, shift audience attention, compare relationships, and introduce visual variety. Also you can combine

**Fig. 15.1 part 3   Subject
movement and the single
camera – repositioned camera**
Here the camera zooms out from a
close-up, and arcs round to a new
viewpoint as the talent moves to the
new subject.

Fig. 15.2   Relocation
During an insert shot, the talent has unexpectedly moved to a new location and is
discovered there; often disconcerting the viewer.

cameras – for supers, inserts, split screen or vignette effects. One camera
can be fitted with a visual effect (lens attachment) while others provide
normal pictures.

When using only one camera you might have to alter a shot for solely
mechanical reasons (e.g. widening it to accommodate an extra person).
Two or more cameras help us to overcome this problem.

Fig. 15.3   Continuity
When retaking shots, inattention to detail can lead to poor continuity during editing;
due to items having been consumed, moved, action or positions wrongly repeated,
etc.

Visual variety

Static shots easily become a bore. So audience interest is encouraged by
introducing movement and change. Although, if overdone the pictures
can become a strain to watch. Rapid cutting demands continual viewer
concentration ... that is not readily sustained. Ceaseless action and
camera moves, lead to pictures that fidget with movement. As always, the
aim is a well-balanced blend with variations in pace, tempo and
emphasis.

Cam1   Cam 2   Cam 1   Cam 2

Fig. 15.4   Two-camera treatment
Here shots are divided between two cameras. Cam 1 concentrates on long shots.
Cam 2 takes close-ups of maps and speaker.

Fig. 15.5   Maximum use of cameras
1. One camera to each set is unnecessarily restrictive.   2. Near the end of a two-camera scene. Cam 2 pans to the next area.   3. Cameras move away successively. Cam 2 moves first (A to B), then Cam 1 joins it.

■ *Performer movement* Most visual variety stems from action within the scene, as people alter positions and regroup. Quite often more meaningful changes are achieved by performer movement than by camera moves or editing.

In a close shot, the performer dominates. As he moves away from camera, the audience becomes more aware of his relationship to his surroundings. In long shots, these surroundings may dominate. So by changing the length of shot, you change emphasis and create visual variation.

These moves are motivated in various ways:

1. By *deliberately arranging* subjects (props, demonstration items) so that a performer is artificially 'motivated' to move to them in the course of the production.
2. By introducing a *gesture* (hand pointing) towards a subject – the camera pans over to see.
3. By a deliberate *turn* of the head or body – to initiate a pan, dolly or zoom to a subject.
4. By a *verbal reference* ('The machine over there') providing a direct introduction to a shot change.

■ *Changes by grouping* Where people are seated (panels, talk shows), you can achieve visual variety by *isolation*; selectively shooting individuals, two-shots, sub-groups.

When people are mobile, you can *regroup* them to provide freshly composed shots by introducing 'natural' moves (sitting, going over to pick up a book), or introduce visually motivated cuts (turning as a guest arrives). By varying emphasis and composition balance in this way, the movement attracts attention and conceals the deliberate shift of interest.

Fig. 15.6   Visual variety
Depending on how a picture is arranged, its centre of attention, emphasis, and even the audience's interpretation can change.

■ *Shooting static subjects* Visual variety can be introduced into your treatment of non-moving subjects (statuary, pottery, paintings, flowers) by the way you shoot and light them:

1. Camera movements alter the viewpoint.
2. You can selectively pan over the subject, interrelating its various parts.
3. Changing lighting can isolate or emphasize sections or alter the subject's appearance.
4. Small objects can be handled, turned to show different features, or turntable-displayed.

Fig. 15.7 part 1   Subject/camera relationship
1. Here subject and action have been arranged to suit the camera's static viewpoint (playing to the camera).   2. Here the camera moves, relating to the static subject and action.

■ *Variety by decor*   The presentation of certain subjects is necessarily restricted (piano playing, singers). They are relatively static and meaningful shot variations are limited. You can prevent sameness between productions by introducing variations in the decor – whether by scenic changes or lighting. The pictures *look* different, even if the shots and viewpoints follow a recognizable format.

■ *Variety by effects*   This is achieved by introducing various visual effects such as: combined shots, superimpositions, multi-images, split screens, decorative inserted backgrounds (using chroma key), and synthesized color.

Fig. 15.7 part 2   Subject/camera relationship
Subjects may be arranged to provide shot opportunities, while cameras are moved or intercut to explore these arrangements.

Fig. 15.8   Forming shots by isolation
By intercutting various shots of a group, you can introduce visual variety into a static situation.

Shot organization

It takes time to experiment, and production time is limited. So directors need a rational plan of campaign. You could distribute cameras around the scene and choose from shots the cameramen offered – but there would usually be little relationship between these pictures. Subject coverage would be patchy. There would probably be several near-identical shots of the pretty girl guest and none of the chairman! Perhaps several overall views or dramatic close-ups – but who could use them?

Shots have to be appropriately chosen and interrelated according to a coordinated plan, and only the *director* is in a position to do this.

Fig. 15.9   Forming shots by subject movement
By introducing 'natural' moves you can form new groupings. Here *C* sits, *B* turns to him. *A* turns and exits, camera tightens to shot *BC*. A series of compositional changes have moved attention between the people.

Fig. 15.10   Composition change altering significance
By a single change in the picture's composition, you can alter its significance. The girl confronts her father (her frame position gives her strength, even in a rear view). He rises – the strength of his upward move and new position now make him dominant.

■ *Planned viewpoints*   Using this technique, you begin with the action's mechanics (where people move, what they do there) and arrange strategic camera viewpoints from which to shoot it. Each camera position provides a series of shot opportunities and you select from these available shots as required.

At sports events and other large-scale public occasions, this is the only practical approach. Cameras are often widely dispersed, camera

Fig. 15.11 part 1   The imaginary line – intercut facing shots
Shots can be intercut (cross-cut) between cameras located on the same side of the imaginary line; i.e. between 1 and 2, or 3 and 4. But inter-switching between cameras on opposite sides of this line, causes jump cuts (1 and 3, 1 and 4, 2 and 3, 2 and 4).

Fig. 15.11 part 2   The imaginary line – reverse-angle shots
1. Direction is reversed on the cut, for cameras have crossed the line.   2. A common scenic unit (doorway, window) usually makes reverse-angle cuts acceptable, providing cameras remain on one side of the line.

Fig. 15.11 part 3   The imaginary line – forward-facing positions
Whenever someone faces the camera (walking, sitting, singing, demonstrating) it is all too easy to interswitch inadvertently across the line to region X, and reverse direction.

movement is restricted, and the director relies on cameramen to use their initiative to find appropriate shots. The director's knowledge of actual shot opportunities is mostly derived from what his cameras reveal and on-the-spot assistants. He guides selection, adjusts shot sizes, suggests desirable shots, and chooses from the available material.

You can use a similar strategy in *studio* production, for certain types of shows with a regular format. For example:

Camera 1 – taking wider, *cover shots* (mid to long shots).
Camera 2 – primarily close-up shots.
Camera 3 – supporting close-ups, close detail, title cards, graphics.

This approach can be particularly useful for unscripted, off-the-cuff situations. But it is also valuable for a demonstrator, who consequently knows which camera to play to for close-ups at any time. However, you should resist any temptation to apply such a routine where more exploratory camera treatment is possible.

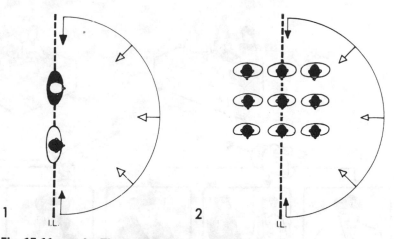

Fig. 15.11 part 4   The imaginary line – aligned positions
1. Where people are shoulder to shoulder (riding, walking) wide viewpoint changes are acceptable.   2. But for a larger gathering (audience, choir, parade) cameras should keep to one side of the front-rear axis when interswitching viewpoints.

Fig. 15.11 part 5   The imaginary line – curving path
Where action follows a curved path, only a head-on viewpoint is reliable if shooting is discontinuous. With continuous action viewpoint changes such as 1–2 are practicable.

Fig. 15.11 part 6   The imaginary line – three-way situations
If you assume that the direction of person A's look has established the axis AC, then you can intercut shots along the AC axis. Now, if he turns towards B, the axis is changed to AB (excluding C from shot) and shots can be intercut along the BC axis. Eyelines can be changed (even cheated) to permit inter-axis cutting.

Fig. 15.11 part 7   The imaginary line – exits and entrances
If during supposedly uninterrupted action a person exits beside camera-right 1, a straight cut showing action continuation should show him entering camera-right also 2.

■ *Storyboard approach* Where systematic planning is practical, a director may use a storyboard technique; sketching the required picture treatment for selected *key shots* or for scene-by-scene treatment. Here we are concerned with *shot significance*; ensuring that the shots have the appropriate dramatic value, attract attention to certain features, emphasize a particular point, and engender a mood.

Storyboard methods involve analyzing the script, deciding on composition arrangements, and then working out how to get them. You can use such planning as a general or specific guide. Accurate

Fig. 15.12 part 1   Visual treatment – planned viewpoints
Cameras are placed at vantage points, from which appropriate shots can be selected and intercut.

Table 15.1   Arranging the shot

	In arranging a shot, you should be able to answer such questions as:
Broad objectives	What is the *purpose* of the shot? What is it aiming to *show*?
	Is it to *emphasize* a particular point or feature?
	Which is the *main* subject?
	Are we *primarily concerned* with: the subject, its relationship to another, or to its background/environment?
The actual picture	Is the shot *too close or distant* for its purpose?
	Is the *attention* reasonably localized – or split or diffused?
	Is the *composition arrangement* appropriate?
	Is the subject suitably *framed*? (Headroom, offset, edge cut-off, overcrowded frame).
	Are subjects *clearly seen*? (Sharp, unobscured, good background contrast?)
	Is there any *ambiguity* or *distraction* in the shot?
The action	Are we aiming to show what a person is *doing* – clearly, forcefully, incidentally, not at all?
	Does action (movement gestures) *pass outside the frame*?
	Are any *important features* or action accidentally excluded?
More specific objectives	Is the presentation to be *straightforward* or *dramatic*?
	Do we want to indicate subject *strength* or *weakness*?
	Do we aim to *reveal, conceal, mislead, puzzle*?
	What *effect, mood, atmosphere* are we seeking? (Businesslike, clinical, romantic, sinister) . . .
	Does the shot *relate successfully* to previous and subsequent shots?

Fig. 15.12 part 2   Visual treatment – storyboard approach
Following script analysis, treatment is visualized and broken down into key shots, which are sketched to show required camera treatment.

prerehearsal planning can achieve the highest standards; but it must be *realistic*, taking into account how one set-up needs to be developed from another. Most directors dislike the commitment of such planning methods and prefer a more flexible empirical approach. Although, where complex special effects are involved the storyboard may become essential.

Program opening

Establishing shots introduce the scene and the action, setting the mood, influencing your audience's frame of mind towards what you have to say and show. There are several familiar openings:

1. *The formal start*   Beginning with a 'Good evening' or 'Hello', introduces the show and gets on with it. Whether the presenter appears casual, reverent, indifferent or enthusiastic, can create an ambience directly influencing the audience's attitude.
2. *The teaser*   Showing dramatic, provocative, intriguing high-lights from the production, before opening titles. Sometimes this inadvertently gives away the plot before the show even begins!
3. *The crash start*   Takes us straight into the program, which probably appears to have begun already. An automobile screams to a stop outside a store, a figure throws a bomb . . . which explodes, an alarm bell shrills, a police siren wails – the show has begun and titles roll over the chasing vehicles.
4. *The character introduction*   A rapid montage of symbols or shots of the hero in various predicaments, provides an introduction to the characters we are to meet.
5. *The eavesdropping start*   The camera peers through a house window, sees a group round a TV screen, and moves in to join them.

Table 15.2 Selecting camera treatment

	Mechanical purpose	*Artistic purpose*
Why pan or tilt	To follow action. To show a series of conjoined parts. To exclude unwanted subjects. To show an area that is too large to be contained in a static shot.	To join separate items. To show spatial relationships. To show cause/effect. To transfer attention. To build up anticipation or suspense. As an introductory move.
Why elevate? (ped up)	To see over foreground objects. To see overall action.	To reduce prominence of foreground. To look down onto objects. To reduce subject strength.
Why depress? (ped down)	To frame picture with foreground objects. To obscure distant action. To obtain level shots of low subjects.	To increase their prominence. To emphasize subject strength.
Why zoom?	*See Tables 4.1 and 4.2*	
Why dolly (track) in?	To see or emphasize detail or action. To exclude nearby subjects. To recompose shot after one of subjects has repositioned or exited. To change emphasis to another subject. To emphasize an advancing subject.	To underline an action or reaction. To emphasize subject importance. To localize attention. To reveal new information. To transfer attention. To follow a receding subject. To provide spatial awareness. To increase tension. To create a subjective effect.
Why dolly back?	To extend field of view. To include more of subject(s). To include widespread action. To reveal new information. To include entry of a new subject. To accommodate advancing action To withdraw from action.	To reduce emphasis. To show relationship or scale of previous shot, to the wider view (whole of subject, other subjects.) To increase tension, as more significance is gradually revealed. To create surprise (e.g. reveal unsuspected onlooker). To provide spatial awareness. To create a subjective effect.
Why truck (crab)?	To follow subject moving across the scene. To reveal the extent of a subject/scene, section by section. To examine a long subject or series of subjects.	To emphasize planes in depth (parallactic movement).
Why arc?	To see subject from another viewpoint. without transitions. To exclude/include a foreground/background subject. To realign or recompose subject(s) when it moves. To reveal new information or a new (extra) subject. To correct for inaccurate subject positions (actor off marks).	To change visual emphasis.
Why follow a moving subject?	In *close shots* – to keep it in frame, while showing reactions or detail information. In *long shots* – to show subject progress through an environment, or its relationship to other subjects.	To spatially interrelate subjects. To avoid transitions or viewpoint changes; maintaining continuity.

Fig. 15.13 part 1   The moving subject – direction of movement
1. A movement across the screen, quickly passes out of shot.   2. Diagonal moves are preferable, for they are visually more interesting.   3. Moves towards the camera from a distance are sustained longest, but can seem drawn-out.

6. *The coy welcome* The camera dollies in to someone who is supposedly preoccupied. Realizing that we have arrived, his welcome of 'Oh, there you are!' provides informality – or nauseating artifice.

7. *The slow build-up* The camera pans slowly round, arousing curiosity or suspense . . . until we reach a climax point (the bloodstained dagger). It is essential to avoid diminishing interest or anticlimax.

8. *The atmosphere introduction* A series of strongly associative symbols establish the place, period, mood or personality. On a mantleshelf: the brass telescope, ship in bottle, and well-worn uniform cap – the old sea captain is introduced long before we see him.

Fig. 15.13 part 2   The moving subject – widely spaced moves
Moves between widely-spaced points are best shot obliquely (Cam 1), rather than with a following pan (Cam 2).

Fig. 15.13 part 3   The moving subject – avoid decapitation
1. The cameraman must be warned of a 'rise' or 'sit', to avoid the bizarre effects of a delayed following tilt.   2. Equally ridiculous effects can arise if framing does not follow action.

Subjective and objective approaches

You can use the camera either:

Objectively – in which the viewer becomes an *observer*.

Subjectively – in which he finds himself a *participant* in the action.

In his *objective* role, the viewer becomes an onlooker, eavesdropper, an invited audience at a vantage point, or a casual bystander. He sees what is going on but is never addressed directly.

Subjective approaches are a regular part of TV, as performers speak straight to camera, using the screen as a communicating opening to our home. The *subjective* role can be an extremely powerful one, when the camera lens moves within the scene as our eyes – or those of a character. It goes up to see an object. It moves amongst a group of dancers. It follows a guide around a museum. The concept can be used forcefully, linking us closely with the action as the camera 'climbs stairs' or jumps out of a plane. Taken to extremes, it all becomes a visual stunt as we find ourselves punched, kissed, fired at, even drowned!

Fig. 15.14   The developing shot
Continuous camera movement may explore the scene where intercutting would disturb the sustained mood, yet you wish to change the focus of attention, reveal new information, show various reactions, etc.

In developing (development) shots, the camera moves from one viewpoint to another; helping us to build spatial impressions and to see varying aspects of the action. This requires carefully controlled camerawork, but it can be most effective in *slow-paced* scenes involving tension, expectancy, solemn or romantic occasions.

Providing the viewer realizes his intended relationship to the scene, you can change techniques between subjective and objective treatment. At times, the distinction may be very nominal.

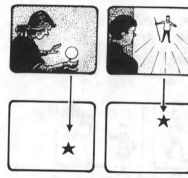

Fig. 15.15 The center of interest
You can attract attention to a specific place in the shot, by the way you arrange and present the subject.

Focusing audience attention

It is as well not to overrate how much effort the audience is willing to make to evaluate your picture. You can do a great deal to localize and hold their attention, by taking care how you arrange and present subjects.

Audience concentration easily lapses, so you need to continually direct and redirect their attention, to hold interest along particular lines. Such redirection implies *change*. But excess or uncontrolled change can lead to confusion or irritation. Pictorial change must be clearly motivated, to allow the viewer to readjust himself easily to each new situation.

■ *Varying concentration* You have to strike a balance between *sustained concentration* (where interest soon flags) and free association (where minds wander):

Fig. 15.16 Unifying interest
The eye should normally be led to (1) a single (2) unambiguous center of interest.

Fig. 15.17 Changing the center of interest
1. The eye-lines and attitudes of performers guide the viewer to a particular center of interest. If there are no visual clues, his attention is not readily transferred to another point. He must look around to see who is speaking. 2. By introducing eye-line and posture clues, the transference becomes obvious. 3. In moving interest around the picture, you must take care not to draw attention to a focal point where there is no real interest or create ambiguous centers. 4. Avoid leading attention out of the frame.

Fig. 15.18   How to focus visual attention
1. Avoiding spurious centers of interest, e.g. prominent lettering, tonal contrast, etc., in supporting subjects.   2. Compositional lines (real or implied).   3. Tonal gradation. The eye naturally follows gradation from dark to light areas.   4. By deliberate unbalance (tonal or linear), with the subject in the heaviest position. By isolating the main subject: (5) In depth, (6) Horizontally.   7. By body position. 8. By height.   9. Using a stronger part of the frame.   10. With lighting. 11, 12. By similarity between the subject and its surroundings, although too great a similarity can pall or (13, 14) lead to confusion.

1. In some shots you will aim to concentrate attention on a particular center of interest.
2. In others, you will encourage attention to move around, on ordered detectable lines.
3. While others of a more general nature, encourage free ruminative inspection; concentrating perhaps on the audio (commentary, dialogue, music).

Although you cannot expect to direct an entire audience's attention with any precision, you can do a great deal to lead them in their selection and influence their associated thoughts.

■ *Shifting visual interest*   It is just as necessary to be able to shift the viewer's concentration to another aspect of the picture, as it was to localize his attention originally. You can do this by readjusting any of the influences listed:

1. Having a person stand up within a seated group.
2. Give the first person weaker movements (turn away), strengthening those of the new subject (face the camera).

Table 15.3   Methods of focusing attention

Exclusion	Taking close shots. Excluding unwanted subjects. Using neutral backgrounds.
Visual indication	Indication with a finger, inserted or superimposed marker (arrow, circle).
Aural indication	A verbal clue or instruction – 'Look at the black box.'
Color	Using prominent contrasting hues against neutrals or muted (pastel) colors.
Camera control	Avoid weak viewpoints (side or rear) or weakening angles (high or long shots). Concentrate interest by differential focusing or camera movement.
Composition	Using convergent line or pattern, picture balance, isolation, prominence through scale.
Contrasting the subject with its surroundings	Through differences in relative size, shape, proportions, scale, type of line, movement, association (e.g. elaborate with plain), disposition (e.g. seated with standing), etc. The area of interest might have the lightest tones or maximum contrast in the picture.
By movement	Movement attracts according to its speed, strength, and direction. Change direction during motion, or interrupt and resume, rather than maintain sustained action.
	According to how it is introduced, a movement can attract attention to: *itself* (a moving hand), the *subject* (person whose hand it is), or the *purpose* of the movement (what the hand is pointing at). Remember, when the camera moves (or zooms) it can virtually create the illusion of subject movement, so drawing attention to it.
	Synchronizing a movement *with* dialogue, music, effects (especially the subject's own), gives it strength and draws attention to it. Having a person move on his own dialogue emphasizes both action and speech.
By subject attitude	Having performers use strong movements – upward or diagonal, stand up, play to camera, move in front of others or scenic elements.

3. Transfer the original emphasis (contrast, isolation, etc.) to the new subject.
4. Use linking action; first person looks to camera right . . . cut to new subject on screen right.
5. Weaken original subject, having him move to the new stronger subject.
6. Alter the shot size, camera height, etc.
7. Pull focus from old subject to the new.
8. Change the sound source; new person speaks instead.

Creating tension

Tension in a dramatic situation derives partly from the dialogue, story line, and interaction between characters; but it can also be considerably influenced by the way in which you present the subject:

1. Using progressively more powerful shots (intercutting closer and closer shots; lower viewpoints, gradual canting).
2. Using suspenseful music and effects.

Fig. 15.19   Hidden areas of interest
If an implied center of interest falls outside the frame, or is obscured, you may either intrigue or frustrate the audience. Subtly introduced, the technique may make a change of viewpoint welcome.

Fig. 15.20   Eyelines
Sometimes a more attractive convincing shot is obtained by having an actor cheat his eyeline. Instead of looking at the other person, he turns his eyes/head along an axis roughly bisecting the centerline and the lens axis (using a distant marker). Cheated eyelines may also be used to intercut across the imaginary line (see Fig. 15.11).

Fig. 15.21   Viewpoint and subject attitude
While frontal viewpoints can suggest alliance, over-shoulder reverse-angle shots can convey conflict.

3. Presenting ambiguous information – is the nocturnal shadow a bush . . . or a prowler?
4. Presenting insufficient information – the audience sees the figure in the doorway . . . is it the villain?
5. Withholding information – have the pursuers arrived yet?
6. The audience knows something a character does not – he runs to escape . . . we know the route is blocked.
7. A character is suddenly confronted with an insurmountable problem – the stairway collapses as he reaches it.
8. We anticipate what is going to happen – surely someone will burst in through that door.

The borderline between tension and bathos can be narrow. An intended climax too easily becomes an *anti*climax. So you have to take care not to emphasize the trivial, or unintentionally to permit an emotional let-down after an emotional peak.

Pace

We might define *pace* as the rate of emotional progression. While a *slow pace* suggests dignity, solemnity, contemplation, deep emotion; a *fast pace* conveys vigor, excitement, confusion, brashness, etc.

A well-balanced show continually readjusts its pace. A constant rapid tempo is exhausting; while a slow sustained one becomes dull. Pace comes from an accumulation of factors:

1. *The script* – Scene length, speech durations, phrasing, word lengths. Sharp snappy exchanges produce a faster pace than lengthy monologue.
2. *The delivery* – Fast, high-pitched, interrupted sounds provide a rapid pace; compared with slow, low-pitched ones.
3. *Production treatment* – The rate of camera movement, switching, performer moves.

The eye can maintain a quicker pace than the ear. While the eye can assess, classify, evaluate almost immediately, the ear has to piece together consecutive sounds to interpret their overall meaning.

While a fast *visual* pace is readily assimilated, it is usually at the expense of less attention to the accompanying sound; unless visual changes are so rapid that the viewer ignores their information and just listens! Where emphasis is to be on the sound, visual pace generally needs to be relaxed.

Timing

There are two kinds of timing:

Mechanically – timing refers to duration checks that ensure a program keeps to schedule.
Artistically – timing is choosing the right moment and duration for an

action – exactly when to cut, the speed of a transition, the pause duration between a comment and a retort.

Inept timing lays wrong emphasis. It can ruin a gag, over-emphasize mechanics, and disrupt continuity.

Visual clarity

If a picture is to get its message over quickly and unambiguously, your audience must be able to see relevant details easily and clearly. Aim to avoid confusion, ambiguity, obscured information, restricted visibility, distractions and similar visual confusion.

Fig. 15.22   Viewpoint and clarity
A good camera viewpoint can mean the difference between: (1) important parts of the subject being hidden, or (2) a clearly visible demonstration.

■ *Viewpoint*   A poor viewpoint can make even the commonest subjects look unfamiliar. Occasionally you may want to do this deliberately. But you should generally aim at clear unambiguous presentation; even if, for instance, it becomes necessary for a demonstrator to handle or place items in an unaccustomed way to improve shot clarity.

■ *Distractions*   Poor lighting treatment can distract and confuse, for it can hide true contours, cause planes to merge, and cast misleading or unmotivated shadows (especially from unseen people). It can also unnecessarily create hot spots, lens flares and specular reflections.

Strong tonal contrasts can distract, as can strongly marked detail. Where someone stands in front of a very 'busy' background, the cameraman may inadvertently focus harder on the background (or seem to) than on the subject itself. Close inspection of eyes, necktie, hair, etc., will show us if this is happening.

Slightly defocused details, particularly lettering that we cannot read easily, can sidetrack our attention. For similar reasons, strongly colored defocused background objects are best excluded from shot wherever possible.

Confusing and frustrating techniques

How often, when watching regular TV productions, do you experience total frustration or antagonism at the way the show is being handled? Here is a list of frequent annoyances:

1. Important subjects cannot be clearly seen – they are soft-focused, masked, or shadowed, or merge with the background.
2. Someone points to detail – it is too small or fuzzy to see.
3. An intriguing collection of items fills the table – we are shown only a couple.
4. The demonstrator shows the host a particularly interesting item – the camera never sees it in detail.
5. An item is promised us later in the show – but time runs short and it is eliminated.

Fig. 15.23   Ambiguity
1. In a flat picture, visual ambiguity can arise whenever lines or tones in one plane merge into those of another; as when adjacent patterns or adjacent tones are similar or where scenic lines continue.¹ 2. Take care to avoid items in the set becoming extensions of the performer.

6. Titling or graphics are shown – but too briefly for us to read or examine properly.

7. A demonstrator shows us how to prune a tree – but the camera gets a close shot just as he finishes.

8. We are watching interesting action – but it is cut short and now we watch a talking head instead.

9. We can hear the events taking place off camera – but the camera is still on this voluble announcer.

10. The speaker who says to camera, 'I'll be with you in just a moment' – why isn't he ready?

11. The interviewer who asks questions (quoting from notes), but is not really listening to replies.

12. The interviewer who gives the *guest* information about himself!

13. The interviewer who asks the guest questions which require only 'Yes' or 'No' replies.

14. A too-brief glimpse of a subject – followed by the commentator talking about it instead.

15. Someone speaks in a group – but the camera dwells on the previous person. (They have not yet lined up a shot of the new speaker!)

16. Wrongly cued performers – the action has already started; or action has finished but the shot remains.

17. The shot that leaves us wondering what we are supposed to be looking at or where we are now.

18. The lost opportunities when a film crew goes on location – but mid-shots of a speaker against nondescript backgrounds predominate.

Interest or concentration patterns

Throughout any production, audience interest and concentration will fluctuate; growing and subsiding. Tension and excitement build up and relax. The trick is to arrange these responses so that they come when you need them most.

Fig. 15.24   Background contrast
Hand held items are often shot against clothing. Ensure that this background is not similar in hue and tone, or too distracting. If necessary hold it against a more suitable back-ground.

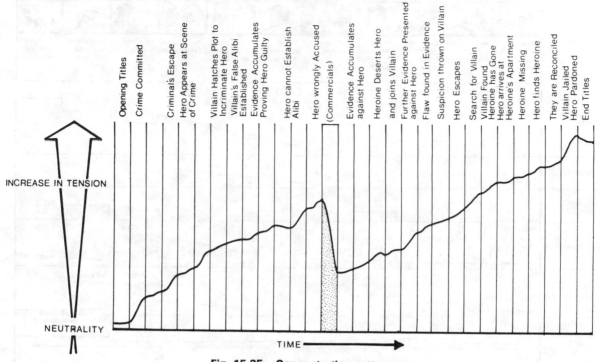

Fig. 15.25   Concentration pattern
Showing audience concentration throughout program.

Directors and writers rely on experience and intuition rather than analysis, to blend the various contributory factors:

1. *Script construction* – the order and duration of shots, their dramatic strength, plot outline, etc.
2. *Interpretation* – the performance, its delivery, etc.
3. *Production treatment* – staging, camera treatment, editing, audio treatment, etc.

But by outlining this reaction pattern as a rough graph, you can see how the overall impact changes throughout the production and how the separate factors combine.

In the well-worn story line of Figure 15.25 you can see where one seeks to build tension; where it will be allowed to fall. You aim to grip audience interest at the start of the show, introducing suitable variations, and building to an encouraging peak just before commercial breaks. You can see the bid to recapture interest immediately afterwards . . . and so on to the finale.

Both strengthening and relaxing tension require some care. After a lull, a peak appears greater. But after a long relaxed period, a highly dramatic peak can be intrusive, so that the viewer becomes overaware of his own sudden reaction; responding with laughter rather than shock. A climax may even pass him by, unless he is emotionally preconditioned to receive it.

Preferably, you build interest, concentration, or tension, in a

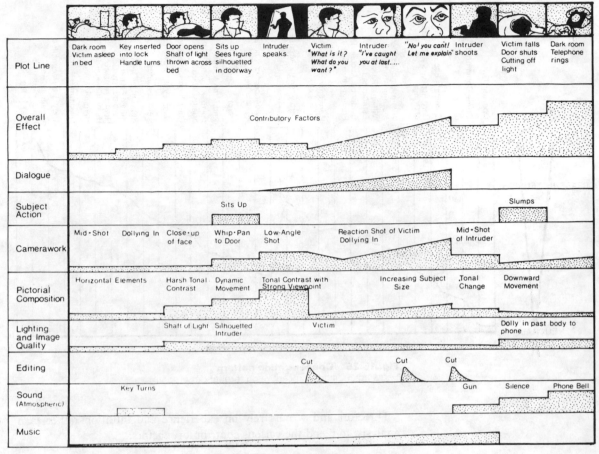

Fig. 15.26   Scene analysis
Various factors contribute to the effect of each scene.

progressive series of peaks. But too slow a development can allow interest to wane. Too many climaxes eventually produce no climax at all.

Relaxation after an interest peak can lead to indifference. Again, sudden tension release can precipitate amusement, after the nervous strain of concentration.

Where action or storyline follow a recognizable pattern, the viewer may grasp the point before the director has time to finish making it! To avoid this happening, you can disguise the obvious through careful treatment; or if this is not possible, at least bypass all superfluous detail (using filmic space and time).

Sometimes attention will wander despite great visual activity. And when quickening pace or high mobility follow a slow episode (e.g. a fast-cutting film clip after slow-speed studio shots), the viewer often finds himself *inspecting* the fast scene rather than stirred by its tempo.

If you present an excess of information or provide facts too quickly, the earnest student may feel frustrated and confused at his inability to note them. But a general audience is more likely to absorb a few random aspects and then relax when they have seen enough (not, as some believe, becoming bored when they have grasped its full import).

Visual padding

Although there are occasions when you can make effective use of silence, a blank screen is an anathema! Yet many subjects have no *direct* visual element. Consider discussions, poetry, music – the emphasis is on *sound*. What does the viewer gain from *seeing* people perform! He sees expressions, instrumental fingering, etc., but these are the mechanics. They have nothing intrinsically to do with the material itself, its significance or purpose (i.e. the argument or musical effect). In fact, the pictures may actually cause *distraction* as he watches the performers – becoming preoccupied with their appearance, expressions and mannerisms.

■ *The visual problem*   For some programs, directly appropriate visuals are not obvious:

1. *Abstract subjects* – philosophical, spiritual, social concepts.
2. *General, non-specific subjects* – humanity, transport, weather.
3. *Imaginary events* – hypothetical, fantasy.
4. *Historical events* – before photography, or unphotographed events.
5. *Forthcoming events* – future projects.
6. *Filming is not possible* – photography is prohibited or subject inaccessible.
7. *Filming is impracticable* – photography is too dangerous, meaningful shots not possible.
8. *Concluded events* – event now over and has not been photographed.
9. *Appropriate visuals too costly* – would involve distant travel, copyright problems.

■ *Possible solutions*   When the director cannot show the actual subject being discussed, he often has to provide a suitable alternative picture – a kind of *visual padding* or 'screen filler'.

The most economical solution, and the least compelling, is to introduce a *commentator*; who *tells* us about what we cannot *see*, as he stands at the now empty location (historical battlefield, site of crime, outside the conference hall).

Inserts in the form of photographs, film clips, VT excerpts, paintings, drawings (typically used for courtroom reports), can all provide illustrative material. Occasionally, a dramatic re-enactment is feasible.

When discussing future events, you can show stills or library shots of a *previous occasion* to suggest the atmosphere, or show the principles (celebration days, processions).

You may show a *substitute* subject (not the animal that escaped but one just like it), hoping your audience does not mistakenly assume that they are seeing the actual subject.

Occasionally the camera can show the *absence* of the subject: the frame of the stolen painting; where the castle once stood.

Associated subjects are frequently used. We visit the poet's birthplace, often using stock tourist location shots. However, they may not be strictly applicable (wrong period), inaccurate (wrong part of city), or irrelevant

Fig. 15.27 part 1   Subject illustration – pictorial treatment
Where pictures are not readily available, or a more imaginative effect is required than
the direct approach, various substitutes are possible.

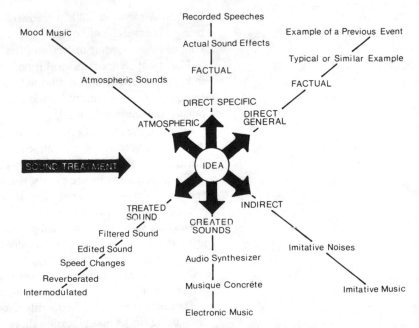

Fig. 15.27 part 2   Subject illustration – sound treatment
Some possible alternatives to direct sound.

(not architecture, but social conditions influenced his poetry). But, apart from family album snapshots or newspaper cuttings, nothing else is available!

When using library (stock) shots or stills, there is always the danger, that available shots will become overfamiliar through repeated use. This is particularly likely with historic material, or unexpected tragedy (assassination, aircrash).

Some forms of visual padding suit a variety of occasions. The same waving wheatfield can epitomize food crops, daily bread, prosperity, agriculture, the war on insect pests . . .

Abstracts can be pressed into service at almost any time! Atmospheric shots of rippling water, shadows, light reflections, into-sun flares, defocused images, shooting up into a tracery of leaves . . . all have very regular use!

Table 15.4   Continuity

	If you are shooting discontinuously, or out of sequence (for later correct-order editing), several kinds of continuity problems can develop.
Technical continuity	The quality of intercut shots of the same action should match: similar color, brightness, contrast, tonal balance; light direction; shot height; perspective.
Pictorial continuity	Atmospheric effect should be consistent: e.g. weather conditions – not raining in one shot, dry in a reverse shot.
Environmental continuity	The location should appear consistent from different viewpoints.
Spatial continuity	The audience can lose their sense of direction, e.g. on reverse cuts. Space and distance can change with varying lens angle.
Physical continuity *Action continuity*	The appearance of people and the scene, should not change noticeably between successive shots, e.g. clothing, set dressing, props, etc.
Performance continuity	If you repeat an action sequence (to provide different shot lengths or viewpoints for intercutting), performers should have similar expressions and make similar gestures in each version. (Check VTR replay.)
Time continuity	There should be appropriate signs of time passing during scenes. Check how food, cigarettes, clocks, candles, etc. change.
Event continuity	Take care to avoid accidental jumps in time or place, when parts of continuous action are missing. (Use cutaways.) Avoid accidentally duplicated action. Avoid rediscovering people in a scene after they have apparently exited; or having a person unexpectedly relocated after an intermediate shot.
Relationship continuity	Avoid shot mismatches that jump-cut the subject around the screen.
Attention continuity	Make sure that centers of attention are reasonably related between shots.
Audio continuity (technically)	Ensure that audio volume and quality are compatible between successive shots.
Audio continuity (artistically)	Maintain similar atmosphere between shots in an edited scene: reverberation, background noises, effects, room tone, balance, etc.
Dialogue continuity	Uninterrupted speech when shots change during dialogue.

Illusion of time

Motion-picture editing has long since accustomed us to concepts of filmic space and time:

Filmic space – intercuts action that is concurrent at different places. As a soldier dies . . . his son is born back home.
Filmic time – omits intermediate action, condensing time and sharpening pace. We cut from the automobile stopping . . . to the driver entering his apartment.

Where all the intervening action has no plot relevance, the viewer would often resent a slow pace, stating the obvious.

■ *Time lapses* You can use several devices to indicate the passage of time. Explanatory titles are direct and unambiguous, but other subtler techniques are generally preferable. For short time lapses:

1. Slow fade-out, new scene slowly fades in.
2. Cutting away from a scene, we assume time has elapsed when returning to it.
3. A time indicator (clock, sundial, burning candle) shows passage of time.
4. Lighting changes with passing time (a sunlit room gradually darkens).
5. Dissolve between before/after shots of a meal, fireplace, etc.
6. Transition between sounds with time association – nocturnal frogs and owls, to early morning roosters and birdsong.
7. Defocus shot, cut or mix to another defocused shot and then refocus.

For longer time lapses:

1. A calendar sheds leaves or changes date.
2. Seasonal changes – from winter snow to spring flowers.
3. Changes in personal appearance – beard growth, ageing, fashion changes.
4. New to old – dissolving from a fresh newspaper . . . to a yellow crumpled discarded version.

■ *Flashbacks* A familiar device, the *flashback* turns back time to see events before the present action for reminiscive, explanatory or comparative purposes. Typical methods include reversed time-lapse conventions (e.g. the old becomes new again), or explanatory dialogue during 'mist', edge diffusion, ripple or defocus dissolves. Nowadays, a very brief *flash cut-in* (½–2 second long) conveys recognition or moments of memory recall.

Interscene devices

As well as the usual editing transitions (cut, dissolve/mix, wipe) and their derivations (defocus and ripple dissolves), you can use various interscene devices to link sequences.

Fig. 15.28 part 1   Cheated substitutes – the desired sequence
A fugitive climbs a cliff to escape pursuers. The viewer sees the formidable cliff, and his climb – but he dislodges a rock, and they look up.

1. *Blackout* – a performer moves up to block out the lens. He (or another subject) moves away, revealing a new scene. A balloon is used similarly, being burst to show the new scene.
2. *Pan away* – the camera turns from the action area to a nearby subject. Panning back, we now see different action (or appearance), for time has passed.
3. *Bridging subject* – associative material interconnects two scenes: shots of wheels turning to imply travel, swirling mists to form an atmospheric transition.
4. *Decorative bridge* – abstract forms in light or shadow between scenes. Moving patterns – kaleidoscope, spirals, whip-pan. Digital video effects are increasingly used here: mosaic tile, posterization treatment, explosions, etc.
5. *Matching shots* – the close-up ending one scene (wrist watch) dissolves to a matching shot (bus station clock) in the next.

Deliberate disruption

The idea of deliberately cutting away from the main action, to look at incidental happenings nearby, may seem somewhat incongruous. Yet, if appropriately introduced, this disruption offers valuable production opportunities. Providing the viewer does not feel that he is missing vital

Fig. 15.28 part 2   Cheated substitutes – the studio procedure
The studio set-up is simple: A gravel-strewn floor, a photograph of a cliff-face, and a surface-contoured flat over which the fugitive crawls (shot is canted to suggest vertical climbing).

information or is robbed of exciting action, the technique can heighten interest and enthusiasm.

■ *Cutaway shots (intercut shots)* By cutting from the main action to *secondary activity* or *associated subjects* (e.g. spectator reactions), you can:

1. Join shots that are unmatched in continuity or action.
2. Remove unwanted, unsuccessful, dull or excess material.
3. Suggest a time lapse, to compress or expand time.
4. Show additional explanatory information (*detail shots*).
5. Reveal the action's environment.
6. Show who a person is speaking to; how another person is responding (reaction shots).
7. Show what the speaker is seeing, talking about or thinking about.
8. Create tension, to give dramatic emphasis.
9. Make comment on a situation (cutting from a diner to a pig at trough).

Interviews can be shot using a continuous intercut multicamera set-up or as a one-camera treatment. A separate series of cutaway shots (*cutaways, nod shots*) are often recorded *afterwards*, in which the interviewer and interviewee are seen in singles or over-shoulder shots, mutely smiling, nodding, 'reacting', looking interested. When edited in (to disguise cuts, continuity breaks, or to add visual variety), the subterfuge appears quite natural. Without such intermediates, any continuously held shot would *jump frame* when edited (dissolves may improve the disruption).

Cut-in or *inserts* may also be used, reshooting parts of the action from another camera set-up (different shot size, or angle).

■ *Reaction shots/partials/cut-in shots* By skilfully concealing information, you can prime the imagination and arouse curiosity. Instead of showing an event, you show its effect.

1. *Reaction shot* – the door opens . . . we see the victim's horror-stricken face, not the intruder.
2. *Partial shot* – a switch-blade opens . . . is moved out of frame . . . we hear the victim's cry . . . then silence.
3. *Cut-in shot* – we watch the victim's cat drinking milk . . . to sounds of a fight, and a body falling . . . the victim's hand comes into frame, upsetting the milk dish.

This technique can provide maximum impact with minimum facilities, conveying information by implication rather than direct statement. It aims to intrigue and tantalize. Ineptly introduced, though, it can frustrate.

Illusion of spectacle

Budgets do not generally permit lavish staging. Yet occasions arise when you want to create an impressive illusion of space, grandeur, and spectacle. Several methods are available.

Fig. 15.29   Crowds
Crowds can be simulated by selected viewpoints: 1. Showing part of the crowd.
2. Using foreground (real, dummy, cut-outs).   3. Inserting people electronically
into a recorded scene.

■ *Library (stock) film shots* By intercutting existing filmed library
shots with limited studio action (often close shots) it is possible to build
up extremely convincing illusions. Where highly dramatic spectacle is
required, as in battle scenes, hurricanes, volcanic eruptions, mobs,
earthquakes, floods, this is usually the only solution.

However, available library shots may not be exactly suitable for your
purpose (contents, quality, viewpoint, time of day, unwanted or spurious
aspects included). It might even be necessary to reorganize the studio
treatment to suit the library shot!

■ *Direct imitation* A complete or *partial* replica of part of the scene
(e.g. a stone wall) is intercut with location material or library shots (the
actual castle).

Fig. 15.30   Staging distractions
Various distractions can appear in shot. Here is a particularly disastrous collection!
1. Unexplained, distracting object in shot.   2. Cable in shot.   3. Visible surface
damage on flat.   4. Shadow of someone out of shot.   5. Wall-picture not straight.
6. Light reflection.   7. Camera reflection visible in table picture.   8. Multiple
shadows from lamp fitting.   9. Distracting light patch.   10. Wall mirror appears as
'halo.'   11. Wrinkle in background surface.   12. Shooting off the set!
13. Obtrusive foreground prop.

■ *Indirect imitation* Here an environment provided by electronic insertion (chroma key, CSO), rear projection, photo backings, or glass shot, etc., is conjoined with a localized studio setting. For example: an automobile in the studio is inserted into a filmed shot of a highway; an impressive ceiling (a graphic) appears to be part of a studio set.

■ *Cheated substitute* Montage can create an illusion by intercutting small representative parts of the action, to convey a composite impression. Ingenious, imaginative, and most effective if properly handled, you must ensure that the component parts are completely integrated. For instance, you can build up a dramatic impression of a battle simply by rapidly intercutting close shots of details in war photographs, to an audio background of battle noises.

16 Production organization

How any director organizes his show, varies with local procedures, the nature of the production, and his own experience and temperament. Consequently, there are approaches ranging from the 'spontaneous' to the meticulously planned. Much depends, too, on the artistic and operation standards you demand, and the production crew's experience.

Unplanned productions

Total unpredictability is not adventurous. It creates needless stress and haphazard results. Television necessarily involves teamwork. If people do not have a clear idea of what is happening, you must not be surprised when there is no chair for the extra guest, the film insert is not ready, lighting is inappropriate, the camera has a wrong shot, or you cannot hear the speaker.

The amateur often collects material, then considers how to use it. The professional invariably starts with a plan of campaign, however broad, and obtains or arranges material to these concepts; modifying as necessary.

Unrehearsed formats

Even where you cannot rehearse a production, you will usually find that the situation fits some familiar format. So you can arrange suitable staging and camera positions, and allocate probable shots. It is possible to precheck potential shots and lighting, using available people. Then, when talent appears, you can quickly preview them to check over voice levels, make-up, lighting, and costume.

If the format is less definite (e.g. a dance troupe arriving just before air time), it is a matter of choosing typical strategic viewpoints (front and cross shooting), then allocating cover shots and close shots to cameras for a defined working area (not forgetting to tell the performers of any necessary movement limits!) The show itself largely involves recognizing effective shots as they are offered; taking action detail and group shots in a balanced ratio.

Regular formats

There are a number of regular formats: interviews, panel discussions, piano and instrumental performances, singers, and newscasts. These are usually familiar to the production team and meaningful shooting variations are limited. What the performer is saying (or playing) is more

311

Fig. 16.1 part 1   Regular formats – piano recital
The basic range of pictorially attractive shots is limited when presenting a piano performance.

important than straining to achieve new and original shot development. Consequently, such productions follow recognizable lines, so that the director often starts off with planned viewpoints and then introduces a particular treatment as it becomes desirable.

Planning for regular productions may largely be a matter of coordinating staff and facilities, ensuring that film or VT inserts are available (with known timings and cue points); graphics, titles, etc., are prepared, and any additional material organized. The production itself may be based upon a series of key shots and spontaneous on-the-fly decisions.

Fig. 16.1 part 2   Regular formats – formal interview
In a formal interview, the number of effective shots is relatively few.

ABOVE THE LINE COSTS
Writing, Performing, Production Elements

Cast
Performers
Music · Script
Floor Manager
Writer · Script Editor
Choreographer · Musicians
Production Personnel
(Producer, Director, Assistants)
Insert Materials (Stock Film, etc.)
Offices · Rehearsal Room
Announcer · Office Services

BELOW THE LINE COSTS
Physical Elements Involved in Mounting the Production

Make-Up · Costumes · Graphics · Prompters
Titling · Transportation · Storage · Labor
Scenic Design · Scenery · Construction · Properties
Studio Servicing · Engineering Personnel · Filming
Editing · Videotape Recording · Remote Pick-ups (O B's)
Special Effects · Sound Effects · Stage Manager
Studio Facilities & Personnel (Technical Operations Crew, Cameras,
Sound, Video, Lighting)
Additional Technical Facilities Etc. Etc.

Fig. 16.2   Budget
Accurate cost estimation and accounting are essential in TV organization, despite the great diversity of the various contributions. Budgets are usually related to the concepts of 'above' and 'below' the line. These differentiate between the 'writing, performing, and production elements', and the various 'back-up' services and physical elements involved in mounting the production.

Complex productions

Whether you are shooting in the studio or on location, time is money and must be used efficiently. While smaller shows may get by with a preliminary talk-over a few days before the production date; for more complex projects, comprehensive planning is essential. The team must be briefed and organized, and this requires discussive agreement; for there are sundry factors to consider, such as time estimates, costing, manpower, safety, union agreements, etc.

■ *Planning preliminaries* Planning begins with *script study*; the director reading and visualizing with his budget, facilities, and personnel in mind.

Some directors rely on the set designer to produce an environment for action and then arrange performers within this setting. Others indicate the strategic features or staging format they require, and from that briefing the designer interprets and builds workable arrangements.

After preliminary discussion, the designer produces a rough scale plan of the various settings; often on separate pieces of overlay (tracing) that can be moved around the studio staging plan for optimum layout. He may include sketches, reference photographs, and preliminary elevations.

Table 16.1　Stages in production procedure

Program concepts	Idea potentials, objectives, potential audience, market, saleability, probable duration.
Executive decisions	Selecting *above-the-line* personnel (production: director, writer, etc.). Budget allocation. Production scheduling (deadlines). Preproduction publicity.
Scripting	Theme, coverage, style, research/advisor. Script editing (evaluating content and practicability). Script conference/rewrites. Director's visualization.
Organizing talent	Contacts, auditions, interviews, casting, contracts. Organization/preparation of performers. Read-through, rehearsals, costume/make-up preliminaries.
Organization of inserts	Any *pre-studio* photography, filming, taping. (Arrangements for shooting these: copyright clearances, facility fees, access permissions, permits, insurance, scheduling, staffing, editing, etc.). Selection of illustrative inserts (film clips, VT, stills). Graphics and titles. Musical inserts (on disc, on tape, performed live). any equipment for demonstrations (construction or hire).
Staffing	Coordinating services of *below-the-line* personnel (technical, operational, facilities).
Production paperwork	Requisitions. Scripts (draft, rehearsal, and camera script). Rundown sheet, camera cards, etc.
Organizing artistic services	Staging, costume/wardrobe, make-up.
Organizing technical services	Cameras, lighting, audio, telecine, VTR, special effects.
Organizing facilities	Loan/hire of equipment. Storage, transport, catering, accommodations (dressing rooms). Prompters, audience arrangements (tickets, seating, warm-up).
Pre-studio rehearsals	Rehearsal of dialogue, moves, action; treatment preparation.
Studio rehearsals	Camera rehearsals (finalization of action, video, and audio treatment).
Videotape recording	Straight-through, discontinuous, or compilation recording.
VT editing	Off-line selection, organization, and editing of video recording. Audio sweetening.
Review and transmission	Evaluation of recording
Post-production activities	Logs/reports. Publicity/billing/promotion. Correspondence, ratings.

Shot 1 – Cam 1
Shot 2 – Cam 2
Shot 3 – Cam 1
Shot 4 – Cam 3

Fig. 16.3　Action treatment
The plan summarizes the camera treatment for a brief scene (see text).

Those responsible for studio operations including technical organization, cameras, lighting, audio, make-up, costume, etc., may be involved at these early stages.

■ *Treatment breakdown* Clearly, there are many ways in which the director could set about devising his production treatment. So much depends on individual experience, methods, and the kind of show involved. A typical approach is to closely analyze the script, and within the staging format to visualize potential treatments for each situation. The director then systematically blocks out movement and camera shots, to build up a continuous, effective presentation. The same situation can often be tackled in various different but equally successful ways. Let us look at an example for a dramatic production:

Table 16.2   Typical considerations in technical planning

Talent	Cast discussed, re costume and make-up requirements (styles, fitting, etc.).
Staging	Style, treatment of sets.
	Staging plan: details of set structures, scenic changes, storage, audience seating.
	Special visual effects (physical, video, lighting).
	Special props.
	Safety precautions, regulations, etc.
Action	Director indicates possible performer positions, action, business.
Cameras	Number of cameras, types of mountings, main positions for each scene, probable moves.
	Any camera accessories (special lenses, etc.).
	Specialists estimate feasibility of anticipated treatment (checking sufficient working space for cameras/booms, time for moves, cable routing, etc.).
Lighting	Discussion of lighting treatment feasibility, relative to: scenic design, action, sound pickup, time/equipment/manpower availability.
	Discussion of pictorial effects, atmosphere, etc.
	Discussion of picture matching to inserts (film or VT).
Audio	Similar discussion to *'Lighting'*.
	Considering audio pickup methods, potential problems.
	Audio inserts discussed (prerecorded library effects, spot effects, music).
Video effects	Chroma-key (CSO), electronic treatment.
Artwork/graphics/titles	Displays, graphics, maps, charts, models, etc.
Further technical facilities	Equipment organization, re filming or pre-studio videotaping.
	Technical resources required: telecine, videotape, video disc, slide scanner, picture monitors, prompters, cuing facilities, etc.
Scheduling	Pre-studio shooting/recording. Experimental sessions.
Pre-studio rehearsals	Read-through, block action, dry run (technical run).
Studio rehearsal/recording	Setting (staging and lighting).
	Camera rehearsal (times and arrangements, meal breaks).
	Technical periods (line-up, relight, reset).
	Recording periods (continuous, discontinuous, rehearse/record).
Editing	Scheduling and facilities. Audio sweetening. Post-production video effects.

Returning husband enters door, wife has unexpected guest.

This could be broken down as:

1. Husband enters door, hangs up hat ... MLS shows who it is, yet orientates audience.
2. Wife looks up, greeting him ... Medium 2-shot showing her with guest.
3. Husband turns and sees guest ... CU of husband's reaction.

Fig. 16.4 Equipment stencil
Scale stencils are used to mark the floor plan, with equipment positions.
1. Camera/Sound boom stencil.   2. Typical furniture stencil.

4. Guest rises, walks to greet husband . . . From med. 2-shot; pans with guest, dollying in for tight 2-shot of guest and husband.

The interpretation could have been simpler. Its impact would have been different.

1. Husband enters door, hangs up hat . . . Over-shoulder long shot between wife and guest, showing entrance. Watch husband's reactions, tightening shot as he walks to guest.
2. As guest stands . . . Cut to frontal 2-shot of guest and wife greeting him. Zoom in to guest. Intercut CU of guest and husband.

Having decided on a particular treatment, the director now arranges camera and audio coverage for these shots. He will often use a 'shot plotter' (protractor or transparent triangle) showing the lens-angle coverage, estimating and marking the camera positions needed (1A, 1B, 2A, etc.), and locating a sound boom (A1). The resultant rough production plan (camera plan), together with his script margin action notes or sketches, form the basis for all rehearsals. Even the biggest productions can be analyzed into shots or sequences in this way (see Figure 16.6, page 322).

■ *Production planning meeting* Once a complete provisional floor plan has been prepared by the designer, the specialists, involved in studio operations meet with the director and designer. They examine the staging proposals and production treatment; evaluate, discuss, anticipate practical problems, and so on. They outline their own proposed contributions – lighting treatment, audio effects, costume details, etc.

Following this meeting, they then carry through their own organization procedures (documentation, costing, manpower, scheduling, equipment selection), and the designer issues the agreed *staging plan (floor plan, ground plan, setting plan)*.

The production planning meeting forms the basis for efficient economic teamwork. Problems anticipated and overcome at this stage, prevent last-minute compromises. Camera cable routing, for example, is a typical potential hazard. Cables get snarled up, can impede other cameras, or drag around noisily. So directors may move around scale card cutouts of cameras (perhaps cord-attached to simulate cables) when devising their camera plans.

Much depends, of course, on the type of show you are considering, how it is to be recorded, elaboration of treatment, any special set-ups (chroma key), rehearsal time, editing facilities, etc.

In a *live* or live-on-tape show, you must allow time for people, cameras, and sound booms to move between situations; time to cover any costume or scene changes, and to reposition equipment or furniture. Discontinuous shooting overcomes such problems; although continuity and editing factors then arise.

The script

■ *Semi-scripted show* For ad-lib shows, discussions, interviews, variety, compilation shows, and demonstrations, it is normal to use *outline scripts*. This script lists the talent involved, facilities being used, graphics (slides), film and VT inserts (identifying sections, giving durations). Dialogue is only included in detail for introductory announcements, and commentary containing cue-lines (for cueing inserts, editing breaks, or redeploying cameras).

■ *Fully-scripted show* Here the script develops in several stages:

1. *Preliminary script/draft/outline script/writer's script* – Initial submitted full-page script (dialogue and action) before script editing.
2. *Rehearsal script* – Script prepared for TV and used for pre-studio rehearsal. Script details the locales (settings), characters, action, talent directives, dialogue (Table 16.3).
3. *Camera script* – A revised script for camera rehearsals, augmented with details of production treatment: cameras and audio, cues, transitions, stage-instructions, set changes (Table 16.4).

Fig. 16.5   The Camera Plan
Position of Cameras 1, 2, 3, 4 are successively marked (1A, 1B). Positions of Sound booms A, B, are successively marked (A1, A2).

TV scripts follow several 'standard' layouts. The preferred version uses two vertical columns, with picture treatment (cameras, switching) on the *left*, action and dialogue on the *right*, together with stage instructions and lighting/effects cues. Some studios prefer a *single-column* cinematic format, with transitions in a left margin, and all video and audio information in a single main column. Directors often hand-mark this version with their own instructional symbols indicating transitions and shots. But for more complex productions, this is less easily followed than a two-column format.

The *full script* is not, as some people believe, an artistically inhibiting document that commits everyone concerned to a rigid plan of procedure. It can be modified as the need arises. It simply informs you about what is expected at each moment of the production. Studio rehearsal time is too precious to use up explaining basic mechanics as you go. Far better to have a detailed script that shows the exact moment for the lighting change, to cue the film, or introduce the superimposition. The full script is a plan of campaign, that has details added to it as the production develops.

For some types of show, the outline script is quite sufficient; in fact, any attempt to include 'pseudo information', such as the entire dialogue

Table 16.3   The rehearsal script

SCENE	INT./ EXTR	LOCATION	TIME OF DAY
3.	INT.	LOUNGE	NIGHT

(GEORGE ENTERS. WALKS TO TABLE SWITCHES ON LAMP.)

GEORGE: (CALLS) The lights are OK in here.
It must be your lamp

(GEORGE TAKES GUN FROM DRAWER.)
SLIPS IT INTO HIS POCKET: PULLING OUT TELEGRAM. HOLDS IT UP.

'SORRY CANNOT COME WEEKEND. BRIAN SICK. WRITING . . . JUDY.'

(HAND SCREWS IT UP AND THROWS INTO FIRE.)
(DOOR OPENS: EILEEN ENTERS.)

EILEEN: Really, these people are too bad. They promised to be here tonight. Look how late . . .

GEORGE: It's probably the storm that has delayed them. They'll be here all right.

(EILEEN SITS ON COUCH: GEORGE JOINS HER.)

EILEEN: If Judy knows you're here, it'll take wild horses to keep her away.

GEORGE: How many more times do I have to tell you . . .

EILEEN: Why do you keep pretending?

/ LIGHTNING FLASH /

GEORGE: I've warned you. You'll go too far.

for a film insert would usually be pointless. (The duration and 'in and out cues' would suffice.)

When is it necessary to fully script a production?

1. When the dialogue is to follow a prescribed text, that is to be learned, or read from a prompter or script.
2. Where action is detailed, so that people move to certain places at particular times and do specific things there. (This can affect cameras, sound, and lighting treatment.)
3. When there are carefully timed inserts (film, videotape) that have to be cued accurately into the program.

Table 16.4   The camera script

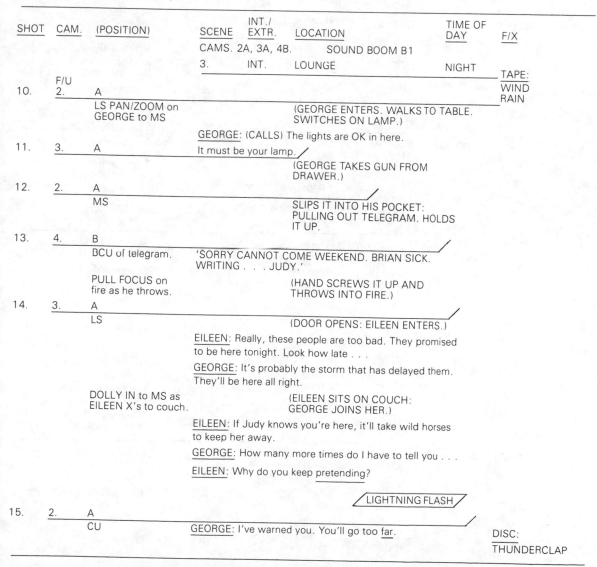

SHOT	CAM.	(POSITION)	SCENE	INT./ EXTR.	LOCATION	TIME OF DAY	F/X
			CAMS. 2A, 3A, 4B.		SOUND BOOM B1		
			3.	INT.	LOUNGE	NIGHT	
10.	F/U 2.	A					TAPE: WIND RAIN
		LS PAN/ZOOM on GEORGE to MS			(GEORGE ENTERS. WALKS TO TABLE. SWITCHES ON LAMP.)		
			GEORGE: (CALLS) The lights are OK in here.				
11.	3.	A	It must be your lamp. /				
					(GEORGE TAKES GUN FROM DRAWER.) /		
12.	2.	A					
		MS			SLIPS IT INTO HIS POCKET: PULLING OUT TELEGRAM. HOLDS IT UP. /		
13.	4.	B					
		BCU of telegram.	'SORRY CANNOT COME WEEKEND. BRIAN SICK. WRITING . . . JUDY.'				
		PULL FOCUS on fire as he throws.			(HAND SCREWS IT UP AND THROWS INTO FIRE.) /		
14.	3.	A					
		LS			(DOOR OPENS: EILEEN ENTERS.)		
			EILEEN: Really, these people are too bad. They promised to be here tonight. Look how late . . .				
			GEORGE: It's probably the storm that has delayed them. They'll be here all right.				
		DOLLY IN to MS as EILEEN X's to couch.			(EILEEN SITS ON COUCH: GEORGE JOINS HER.)		
			EILEEN: If Judy knows you're here, it'll take wild horses to keep her away.				
			GEORGE: How many more times do I have to tell you . . .				
			EILEEN: Why do you keep pretending?				
					/ LIGHTNING FLASH /		
15.	2.	A					
		CU	GEORGE: I've warned you. You'll go too far.				DISC: THUNDERCLAP

Table 16.5   TV script abbreviations

Many organizations duplicate the *rehearsal script* on white paper. Operational information is added to the original stencil to provide the *camera script* on yellow paper.

All *camera shots* are numbered in a fully scripted show. *Inserts* are not numbered (film, slides, VT, titles, graphics), but are identified in the audio column. Where possible, cutting points are marked in the dialogue with a slash mark ____/ underlining back to the camera number.

Various abbreviations are widely used:

Equipment				
CAM	Camera	B	Balop
MIKE MIC	Microphone	T	Telop
		CP CAP	Caption
BOOM	Sound boom	G	Graphic
F/P FISH	Fishpole	ROLLER	Roller caption (crawl)
VT VTR	Videotape	TC	Title card
		PIC	Pictorial graphic
F	Film	PIX	(photo caption)
TC TK	Telecine	RP BP	Rear projection Back projection
SL	Slide	CPU PROJ	Caption (slide) projection unit
CS	Caption Scanner		
TJ	Telejector	VD	Video disc

Position				
L/H, R/H; C/S, U/S; D/S; P/S, O/P; B/G, F/G:		X	Move across.
Picture left-hand, right-hand; Centre stage, upstage, downstage; Prompt side (RHS facing the stage). opposite prompt (LHS facing stage); Background, foreground.		POV	From the point of view of person named.
		O/C	On camera.

Cuing				
Q, I/C, O/C:	Cue, in cue, out cue.	ROLL, RUN:	Start cue for film (telecine) or VT.
Pull, flip, Graphic (caption) animate:	animation.	C/S	Change slide.
S/B:	Standby		
FX:	Cue effects.		

Cameras				
BCU, CU, MCU, MS, MLS, LS, LVS. (See Chapter 12).		D.I.:	Dolly in.
		H/A, L/A:	High angle, Low angle.
2–S, 3–S	Two-shot, three shot.	N/A, W/A	Narrow angle, Wide angle
AB:	As before, i.e. shot as previously.	P/B, D/B:	Pull back, Dolly back.
O/S, X/S:	Over-shoulder shot.	FG/BG	One person foregd; another backgd.
FAV.	Favor (make prominent).		

Switching (vision mixing)				
CUT:	Not marked, but implied unless other transition marked.	LOSE 2:	Cut out Cam. 2 from a super or key.
		FI, FO:	Fade in, Fade out.
MIX (DIS):	Mix. (Dissolve)	T:	Take. (Moment for a transition).
WIPE:	Wipe.		
SUPER (S/I):	Superimpose.	S/S	Split screen.
KEY (INSERT):	Electronic insertion (chroma key, CSO).	CK:	Chroma key

Audio

F/UP:	Fade up audio.	Spot FX:	Sound effect made in studio.
FU:	Fade audio under.	STING:	Cue strong musical chord emphasizing action.
P/B:	Playback.		
F/B:	Foldback (audience address).	OS; OOV:	Over scene; out of vision (audio heard where source not shown).
DISC: CART: CASSETTE: S/TAPE: GRAMS:	Recorded audio insert.	REVERB	Reverberation added.
		B/G:	Keep audio in background.
ANNCR:	Announcer.	OPT; MAG:	Film audio: Optical; Magnetic.
ATMOS:	Atmosphere (background sounds).	SOF: SEP MAG:	Sound on film. Separate magnetic track.
		SOT:	Sound on tape.
		SIL:	Silent.

General

TXN:	Transmission.	POS, NEG:	Positive, Negative.
SEQ.	Sequence.	MON:	Monitor.
P/V;	Preview.	ID:	Station Identification.
ADD:	An addition (to a story)		
PBU:	Photo blow-up	MOS; VOX POP:	Man-on-street; interview.
PRAC:	Practical.	EXT:	Exterior.
PROP:	Property.	INT:	Interior.
		LOC	Location.

4. When the duration of a section must be kept within an allotted time bracket, yet cover certain agreed subject points. (The speaker might otherwise dwell on one point, and miss another out altogether.) Even where post-production editing is available, it is not always possible to remedy uneven subject-coverage.

5. Where there are spot cues, e.g. a 'lightning flash' and an effects disc of thunder at a point in the dialogue.

So you will find fully-scripted approaches in newscasts, drama productions, operas, comedy shows (situation comedy), documentary-type presentations and major commercials. Where dialogue and/or action are spontaneous, there can be no script; only an outline of routine (e.g. discussions). A formal talk is scripted.

The more fragmentary or disjointed the actual production process is, the more essential is the script. It helps everyone involved to *anticipate*. And in certain forms of production (rehearse/record; total chroma key staging) anticipation is essential for tight scheduling.

In a complex production that is videotaped out of sequence, the production crew may be unable to function meaningfully without a full script, which makes it clear how shots/sequences are interrelated, and reveals continuity. The lighting director may, for example, need to adjust the lighting balance for a scene, so that it will intercut smoothly with a different viewpoint shot yesterday.

So the full script can be a valuable coordinating document, enabling you to see at a glance the interrelationship between dialogue, action, treatment, and mechanics. During planning, of course, it helps the team to estimate how much time there is for a camera move, how long there is for a costume change (perhaps a recording break will be necessary), whether re-arranging shooting order will give the necessary time for a make-up change, the scenes during which the 'rain' should be seen outside the windows of the library set (i.e. the water spray turned on and the audio effects introduced) . . . and the thousand and one details that interface in a smooth-running show.

The full script is used differently by various members of the team. The director uses it to develop his treatment, control timing, etc., and to demonstrate to the rest what he requires. Thoroughly familiar with it (hopefully!) he refers to his script for certain treatment and cuing details. His assistant(s) follows it carefully, checking dialogue accuracy, noting

Table 16.6   Breakdown sheet/show format/running order

DRAMA PRODUCTION

Page	Scene (Sequence)	Shots	Cameras/Audio (layout across set)	D/N Day/ Night	Cast (Performers)
1	FILM – 1 (40sec) OPENING TITLES (20sec)		SOF (SEP. MAG.) 4A. S. TAPE (RAIN)		
1	INT. DINING ROOM	2–9	1A. 4A	N.	GEORGE
3	2. INT. LOUNGE	10–27	4B, 2A, B1, 3A.	N.	GEORGE EILEEN
		R E C O R D I N G B R E A K			
10	3. EXT. GARDEN	28	B2, 3B	D.	JUDY GEORGE
10	4. EXT. STREET	29	1B. Slung.	D.	BRIAN
11	5. INT. CAFE	30–43	2B, 4C, A2	Eve.	BRIAN JUDY GEORGE

ETC . . .

DEMONSTRATION PROGRAM   (TOTAL DURATION: 15 MINS.)

Sequence No.	Item (Sequence segment)	Cameras/F/VT	Seq. dur.
1	OPENING TITLES – SIG. TUNE.	4A, 1A,	07 sec
2	PROG. INTRO.	2A, 3A,	30 sec
3	TIMBER FELLING.	VT.	24 sec
4	PREPARING WOOD.	1B, 2B.	2 min 30 sec
5	CARVING DEMO	1C, 4B, 3B.	8 min 00 sec
6	TIMBER IN BUILDINGS.	FILM.	2 min 58 sec
7	CLOSING LINK	3A	22 sec
8	END TITLES – SIG. TUNE	4A, 1A,	09 sec
			15 min 00 sec

where retakes are needed, timing (durations) sections, perhaps cuing contributory sources from the script, as well as 'calling out shots' on intercom ('Shot 24 on 2, coming to 3'). The switcher follows the script in detail, preparing for upcoming transitions, superimpositions, effects.

Others such as the cameramen, boom operators, electricians, may use the script as a detailed reference point when needed, but use simplified outlines (breakdown sheet, camera card) as they memorize their operations.

Auxiliary information

In addition to the script, various supplementary summaries may be necessary:

■ *Synopsis* An outline summary of characters, action, plot. Appended to a dramatic script; particularly when shot out of sequence, or to coordinate a series.

■ *Fact sheet/run-down sheet* Summarizes information about a product, or item for a demonstration program; or details of a guest for an interviewer. Provided by a researcher, editor, or agency for guidance.

■ *Breakdown sheet/show format/running order* Lists the events or program segments in order, showing allowed durations, participants' names, cameras and audio pick-up allocated, setting used, video and audio inserts, etc. (Sometimes ambiguously called a run-down sheet.)

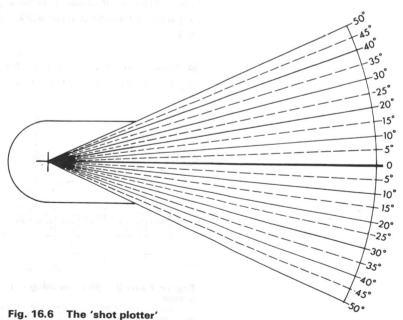

Fig. 16.6   The 'shot plotter'
The horizontal lens angles are marked on this protractor. Laid on a scale floor plan, they show the shot coverage for any angle. (Vertical angles for use on elevations, are ¾ horizontal angle.)

station has its own procedures for booking studios, equipment, facilities, services, manpower, etc. The director may become involved directly in ordering props, graphics, titles, etc., or simply inform specialists. Various requisitions concerning costume, make-up, staging, lighting, video, audio, VTR, filming, editing, are normally handled by the specialists.

Calculating shots

Many directors prefer to work empirically, from mental concepts, rough notes, and experience. They make 'guesstimates', or wait until they can guide the cameramen and see which shots are practical. They improvise instinctively and draw inspiration from the occasion. This is fine, as long as time is available to experiment, improvise and coordinate the production team. But as a general practice, it is preferable to plan as fully as possible; modifying, correcting and improving during camera rehearsal and subsequent editing.

■ *Why measure?* Preliminary planning can provide you with the answers to a lot of your camera problems long before even preliminary blocking:

What shots are available on this immobile camera?
Am I going to shoot off the set?
Can I get the shot from here?

Table 16.7   Camera card

CAMERA THREE		'DEATH COMES ONCE'	STUDIO B	
SHOT No.	POSN.	(LENS ANGLE*)	SCENE/SETTING	
11	A	13°	SC. 2.	LOUNGE CU GEORGE pockets gun from drawer pulling out telegram.
14	A	35°		LS EILEEN enters DOLLY IN to MS as she X's to couch.
19	A	20°		BCU GEORGE'S eyes.
23	A	13°		BCU EILEEN screams.
25	A	20°		CU GEORGE puts gun in drawer.
		QUICK MOVE TO GARDEN		
28	B	35°	Sc. 3	GARDEN MLS follow GEORGE carrying body tightening, depressing to L/A shot: ZOOM IN to hand as he stops.
		MOVE TO RHS LOUNGE		
44	A	50°	Sc.	LOUNGE LS DETECTIVE enters. PAN with him into MS as he goes to phone.

*Optional

What will relative sizes (proportions) be?

How large must we make the graphic in this setting?

Where do I position people for this chroma key effect?

Why *guess* whether it will work on the day, when you can check it out now?

The tools are simple enough: a scale floor plan and a transparent triangle or protractor representing the horizontal lens angle. Wherever you place this 'shot plotter' on the floor plan, it shows what the camera sees from that viewpoint. If the angle falls outside the marked-out setting, you are shooting off (Fig. 16.6).

■ *Shot proportions* The edges of the lens angle represent the left- and right-frame edges. Any object that touches both lines fills the screen width – whether a small close item, or a large distant one.

To make a subject fill one-third of the screen width, just mark on a paper strip a length *three times* the subject's width. At the distance this marker fits across the angle, the subject will exactly fill one-third of the screen width. Conversely, if a subject is a known distance away, measure the scene width there and divide this by the subject width to find proportions.

In Figure 16.7, you have a quick shot-check table showing the distances for 'standard' shots on a 25° lens. For other lens angles, distances are inversely proportionate:

$$50° = {}^{25}\!/_{50} = \times \tfrac{1}{2} \text{ table distance.}$$

$$40° = {}^{25}\!/_{10} = \times 2.5 \text{ table distance.}$$

$$40° = {}^{25}\!/_{40} = \times 0.6 \text{ table distance.}$$

Lens Angle	Width at 3m Distance	Width at 10ft Distance
5° —	0.26 m	10 in
10° —	0.53 m	1 ft 9 in
15° —	0.79 m	2 ft 7 in
20° —	1.06 m	3 ft 6 in
25° —	1.33 m	4 ft 5 in
30° —	1.61 m	5 ft 5 in
35° —	1.89 m	6 ft 4 in
40° —	2.18 m	7 ft 4 in
45° —	2.49 m	8 ft 4 in
50° —	2.80 m	9 ft 4 in
55° —	3.12 m	10 ft 5 in
60° —	3.46 m	11 ft 7 in

Fig. 16.9   Checking your camera's angle

1. *To find the angle of your lens:* Place two small objects on a crossline 3 m/10 ft away, moving them so that they just appear within the left-right frame edges. Measure how far apart they are and check in the table, the angle that covers this width.

2. *To set the shot-box to a particular lens-angle:* Look up the *required angle* in the table and find the screen-width it takes in at 3 m/10 ft away, place them this distance apart (e.g. for 30° they must be 1.61 m/5 ft 5 in apart). Adjust your lens to just take in the objects at the frame edges, and it is now at the required angle. Adjust shot-box preset, or note zoom setting. You could make up a regular zoom-lens line-up graphic for adjusting all lens angles at this distance.

For a useful formula that you can apply to your particular zoom lens system, multiply its maximum focal length (in mm) by the corresponding horizontal lens angle at that setting (e.g. 110 mm × 5° = 550).

Then, when you want to find the lens angle given by a particular focal length (e.g. 55 mm) simply divide this 'standard factor' by that figure (e.g. 550 ÷ 55 = 10°). When you need a certain lens angle (e.g. 25°), divide the factor by 25, and you will find that you need a focal length of 22 mm.

17 In production

Any production benefits from some kind of rehearsal prior to recording or live transmission. These rehearsals take several forms.

Pre-studio rehearsal

Complicated productions particularly gain from pre-studio rehearsal. Even a table demonstration can be discussed, practiced and checked beforehand; perhaps in a *preparation room* near the studio.

For larger shows (drama, comedy), it is essential to work out mechanics, practice dialogue and action, and coordinate performance. So these productions are often rehearsed in halls (outside rehearsal rooms) some two or three weeks before studio date. Meanwhile, the studio is scheduled for other programs.

Pre-rehearsals begin with a *briefing, read through,* or *line rehearsal,* in which the director outlines his interpretation. The cast becomes familiar with the script, the other actors, and the required characterizations.

The rehearsal hall floor is taped or chalked with a full-size layout of the studio setting. Doors, windows, stairways, etc., are outlined. Stock rehearsal furniture substitutes the actual studio items and action props (telephone, tableware) are provided. Rehearsing in this mock-up, actors become accustomed to the scale and features of their surroundings; vertical poles, chairs, dummy doors, marking the main architectural limits.

The director arranges performers' positions, grouping, action, to suit his treatment. He rehearses in sections: the cast learning lines, practicing performance, moves and business; until the entire show runs smoothly, ready for its studio debut. Segments and overall timing are checked (and controlled) throughout, allowing for subsequent non-action inserts — titles, film, VT, graphics, announcements, etc.

During rehearsals, the director scrutinizes action through his viewfinder from potential camera positions, adjusting details as necessary.

A few days before the studio date, the specialists concerned with technical operations watch a complete rehearsal (technical walk-through/technical run) checking and anticipating problems, envisaging camera and boom treatments. Following this meeting, facilities are finalized and the lighting prepared.

Studio rehearsal

Before a studio rehearsal, the staging crew supervised by the set designer, erects and dresses the settings. Lighting units are rigged; and guided by

Table 17.1   Initial blocking hints

Timing	A preliminary read through gives only a rough timing estimate. Allow time for business, moves, recorded inserts, etc. Anticipate potential script cuts if an overrun is evident. Many productions include sequences that can be dropped, reduced, or expanded to trim timing.
Briefing performers	Ensure that performers have a clear idea of the program format, their part in it, and their interrelationship with other contributions. Ensure that performers have a good notion of the setting; what it represents, where things are.
Props	Provide reasonable substitutes where real props are not available. Sometimes only the actual item will suffice. Where unfamiliar costume is to be worn (cloak, hoop skirt, space helmet), a rehearsal version is preferable to dummy motions.
Directing performers	Maintain a firm attitude towards punctuality, inattention, background chatter during rehearsals, to avoid time wastage and frustration. Check that performers' positions are consistent and meaningful (they do not stand 'on' a wall). Avoid excessive revisions – of action, grouping, line cuts, etc. Wrong versions can get remembered, new ones forgotten. Warn performers where they are in close shots, to restrict their movements; perhaps indicating which camera to play to.
Shot arrangement	Use a portable viewfinder to arrange shots. Even a card cut-out frame or a hand-formed frame is better than unaided guesses. Always think in terms of *shots*, not of theatrical-styled groupings, entrances, exits, business. At script stage, form ideas about shots rather than arranging 'nice groups' and trying to get 'good shots' during rehearsal. When setting up shots in a rehearsal hall, do not overlook the scenic background that will be present in the studio. Check shot coverage with plans and elevations. Consider depth of field limitations in close shots or deep shots (close and distant people framed together). Think in terms of practical studio mechanics. You may rapidly reposition your viewfinder, but the move may be impossible for the studio camera.
Audio and lighting	Try to bear audio and lighting problems in mind when arranging positions and action. For example: where people are widely spaced, a sound boom may need time to swing between them, or have to be supplemented.

the lighting director, are adjusted to cover their plotted areas. Camera and sound equipment are positioned. The performers arrive, seeing the staging for the first time. The show is ready to begin.

Directors organize their studio rehearsals in several ways, according to the complexity of the production, available time, performer experience, and criticality of results. Given the opportunity, you might like the luxury of:

1. *Dry run* (*walkthrough*) – actors perform, familiarizing themselves with the studio settings, etc., while the studio crew watch, learning the format, action, and production treatment.
2. *Camera blocking* (*stagger through*) – initial camera rehearsal, coordinating technical operations, discovering and correcting problems.
3. *Predress run-through* (*continuous run-through*) – 'polishing' rehearsal, proving corrections.

4. *Dress rehearsal (dress-run)* – hopefully fault-free 'on-air' quality performance.
5. *Videotaping/transmission* – final optimum performance.

In reality, many productions have little more rehearsal time than the show's running duration, and the second and fifth stages have to suffice. So a continual watch on progress, relative to available rehearsal time, is essential.

Rehearsal procedures

■ *Camera blocking/stagger through/first run/stopping run*   Here the director controls operations from the production control room, only 'going to the floor' when personal on-the-spot discussion is essential. Otherwise, his eyes and ears are the picture monitors and loudspeaker. All communication with his crew is via the *intercom* (*production talkback*) system; the *floor manager* cuing and instructing the talent through his intercom guidance.

Many directors use the *whole method*, and go straight through a sequence (segment, scene) in camera rehearsal, continuously guiding until a serious problem arises to require stopping and correction. The director discusses problems, solutions and revisions; then re-runs the sequence with corrections. It should now work.

This method give a good idea of continuity, timing, transitions and operational difficulties. But, by skimming over the various shortcomings before the 'breakdown point', quite a list of minor corrections may develop.

Other directors, using the *stopping method*, stop action and correct faults as they arise – almost shot-by-shot. This precludes error adding to error, ensuring that everyone knows exactly what is required throughout. For certain situations (chroma key treatment), this may be the only rational approach.

However, this piecemeal method gives the impression of slow progress, and can feel tedious and nit-picking. The continual stopping makes checks on continuity and timing more difficult. Later corrections are given as notes after the run-through.

■ *Floor blocking* Using this method, the director forsakes the production control room and works from a studio picture monitor. Guiding and correcting performers and crew, he calls out required transitions to the switcher in the control room, watching results on his monitor screen. This is the luxury of delayed decisions!

This technique is often used by directors who find visualizing difficult, feel remote from operations in their orthodox position, and prefer direct contact to relaying instructions.

The director often returns to the control room to run each floor-rehearsed scene. During videotaping, the show may be shot as segments, scenes, or continuous action.

Where a set-up is particularly complicated or discontinuously recorded, the system may have some advantages. But it has all the weaknesses of the 'stopping method' plus low crew cohesion. When they *all* hear the same intercom instructions, crew members can coordinate more effectively. At worst, this method wastes a great deal of time, and because the director has not been watching channel previews or listening to audio while on the floor, continuity and video/audio relationships may be below optimum.

■ *Rehearse/record* This is really a form of 'floor blocking', in which the director sets up a sequence, rehearses it, then immediately records the corrected result. Each sequence may need to be relit, cameras repositioned and scenery reset or cheated. The separate videotaped sections are later edited together with appropriate transitions and bridging sound.

Ideally, this pseudofilmic technique could provide optimum results for each shot. But in practice, the process can be extremely frustrating and time consuming. Normally the effectiveness of lighting, scenery, make-up, costume, etc., is checked on camera, and improved or corrected while another scene is being rehearsed, or during a studio stand-down. In a *rehearse/record* situation, such changes have to be made immediately, so that the scene can be shot – and this leads to many compromises. To save time, a director may even record the first camera rehearsal with all its imperfections, in case it can be used! A videotape channel is continuously tied to the studio. Themes and variations are shot for later selection, and repeat action may be necessary to ensure editing continuity. Considerable poststudio videotape editing is necessary. Audio sweetening becomes a major consideration.

Rehearsal problems

During the course of rehearsal, various problems regularly arise. Here, in summarized form, are typical situations.

■ *The shot*

1. *Subject detail not sufficiently visible* – Move subject/camera closer. Zoom in. Shoot subject in a series of close detail shots or localized insets (magnified view within longer shot). Is greater detail available? (Very close shots of some subjects are confusing or reveal no further information – unsharp photographs.) Is detail defocused? Is subject shadowed or obscured?

2. *Extreme close-ups of details required* – Problems arise due to limited focused depth, unsteady camera, subject moving in/out of frame. Use higher light intensities (levels) to permit stopping down. Use wider lens angle. Locate item on firm surface (use position marks). Use photoenlargement of detail.

3. *Subject's shape does not fit screen aspect ratio* – Take a long shot of total subject, then pan/tilt over detail or intercut closer shots. If a series of

Table 17.2   Effective studio rehearsal

Unrehearsed or briefly rehearsed studio production	*Director's assistant* checks that available production information is distributed (breakdown sheet/running order). Also checks contributory graphics (titles, slides, floor captions) and film/VT inserts are correct. Notes word cues for inserts, timings, announcements.
	Director with floor manager, technical director, lighting director, cameras and sound crew, arranges basic performer and camera positions (floor is marked). Even a basic plan aids coordination. He outlines action or moves, and shot\ coverage. Lighting is set.
	If talent is available, line up shots and explain to them any shot restrictions, critical positions, care needed in demonstrating items, etc. (Otherwise use stand-ins for shot line-up and brief talent on arrival.)
	Check that performers, crew and contributory services (prompter, film channel, etc.) are ready to start.
	If full rehearsal is impractical, carry out basic production checks: rehearse 'tops and tails' of each segment with intermediate links (e.g. announcer's in-cues/out-cues, to cue film or VT inserts); check any complicated action or treatment. Check any errors or problems.
Intercom and the director	Remember that the production team is interdependent. A quiet, methodical, patient approach is as infectious as an acrimonious one. Be firm but friendly, Avoid critical comments on intercom.
	How detailed intercom instructions need to be, depends on the show's complexity and crew experience. Aim at a balanced information flow, avoiding continuous chat and comment. (A mute key cuts the circuit when necessary.)
	Preferably call cameras by numbers, guiding all camera moves (and zooms) during rehearsal, warning the crew of upcoming action and movements.
	Examine each shot, if necessary, modify positions, action, movement, and composition.
	Consider *shot continuity*. Alterations may affect earlier shots, too.
	Remember, the crew and performers are *memorizing*. Their aids are the production paperwork and your intercom reminders/instructions.
	Do not be vague. Make sure that your intentions are understood. In correcting errors, explain what was wrong and what is wanted. Not 'Move him left a bit' but 'He is shadowing the map'. Do not assume performers will see and correct any problems.
	Avoid excessive changes or revisions, or there will be hesitations and mistakes.
	Correct operational and performance errors, even in early camera rehearsal. Misjudgments and inaccuracies should be noted directly they occur (e.g. camera in shot, shooting off, late cue, wrong lines, wrong shot, wrong mike). But avoid an overinterrupted rehearsal, or timing and continuity will be lost.
	If a cameraman offers alternative shots (e.g. to overcome a problem), briefly indicate if you accept or disagree, and why.
	Where practicable, at the end of each sequence ask if there are any problems, and whether anyone wants to rehearse that section again.
	Remember, various staging and lighting defects may be unavoidable in early rehearsal. Certain details (set dressing, light effects) take time to complete. Some aspects need to be seen on camera before they can be corrected or finally adjusted (overbright lights, lens flares). Shot readjustments during rehearsal often necessitate lighting alterations.
	Never repeat a segment without indicating whether it is to be *changed* (move faster next time), or is to correct an *error* (late cue), or to *improve* the performance/operations.
	Ensure that everyone knows when shots have been deleted or added (e.g. Shot 2A, 2B, 2C).
	At the end of rehearsal: check timings, give notes to performers and crew on any errors to be corrected, changes needed, problems to be solved. Check whether they have difficulties that need your aid.
	At least one complete uninterrupted rehearsal is essential for reliable transmission.
	At the end of videotaping, give details (including shot numbers) and reasons for any retakes.

items are involved, do similarly or recompose the shot (move them together, arrange in depth, or shoot more obliquely).

4. *Unsatisfactory framing* – Subject cut off by frame edge. Shot too tight or loose. Subject too high in frame or off-center (unbalanced). Unsuitable headroom.

5. *One subject masks (obscures) another* – Reposition subject and mark floor. (Check that this does not spoil earlier shots.) Reposition camera (e.g. arc or truck/crab).

6. *Subjects appear too widely spaced apart* – Move subjects closer together, shoot obliquely, or intercut single shots.

7. *Subject appears too large or small relative to others in shot* – See Table 4.3.

8. *Subject appears too prominent* – Reduce shot size, alter composition, or increase camera height.

9. *Background objects or scenic lines 'grow out' of subject* – Reposition camera or subject. Move, cover or remove background items. Reduce their prominence by lighting or defocusing.

10. *Unwanted distortion* – Adjust lens angle to nearer 'normal' (25°) and change camera distance accordingly, reposition subject or change viewpoint.

11. *Colors have similar monochromatic values* – Lighten/darken areas concerned. Change hue or materials (surface texture). Put black outlines round areas of similar tone.

■ *Performers*

1. *Out of position* – Check if they have toe marks or location points. Move them and remark floor (instructing performers). Reposition camera.

2. *Performer working to wrong camera* – Floor manager signals. Draw attention to tally (cue) light on camera. Switch shot allocation to the 'wrong' camera.

3. *Dialogue errors (cuts lines, dries/fluffs, or freezes and needs prompt, wrong lines)* – Use prompter, cue cards, etc. Give audible prompt. Is prompter working, script OK? Misunderstanding? Retake sequence, or insert cutaway shot and dub audio retake into audio track of VT.

■ *Scenic problems*

1. *Check staging for distracting features* – Overbright surfaces or reflections. Can relighting cure? Reangle, use dulling spray, repaint, cover over, scrim over or remove.

2. *Colors or tones unsuitable* (e.g. subject merges with background) – Modify background, lighting or subject (e.g. change costume).

3. *Background blemishes* (dirty marks, tears, scrapes, wrinkles, etc.) – Rectify, refurbish, cover over or relight.

4. *Ugly or distracting shadows on background* – Performers or scenery too close to background? Relight or modify shot.

■ *Operation hazards*

1. Camera shooting off set – Modify shot, extend scenery or add foreground masking.

2. *Lens flares* – Raise camera viewpoint, improve lens shade (hood), shield off camera or raise lamp height. Alter shot.
3. *Unwanted subjects in shot* – Have their positions changed since last rehearsal? Alter framing, camera position or lens angle. Rearrange shot, remove unwanted items. Mask/cover items. Leave items unlit.
4. *Boom mike in shot* – Check whether boom operator is aware. Warn him before cutting from close to distant shot. Tighten (reduce headroom) or recompose shot. Alter sound pickup method.
5. *Boom shadows* – Check with audio/lighting personnel if avoidable. Consider modifying shot – tighter shot or change viewpoint. Alter sound pick-up or lighting.
6. *Cables in shot* – Check for distracting cables in shot – audio, lighting, monitors, cameras.
7. *Graphics/captions/titles* – Check they are straight, level and undistorted. Can all be seen (no cutoff) and read? Time to read?

■ *Editing/video switching/vision mixing*

1. *Transitions appropriate?* Suitable type? Timing and rate of transitions OK?
2. *Any distractions?* Any reverse cuts, jump cuts, position jumps, instant changes in size, direction, frame height? Any loss of orientation or direction on cuts? Any image confusion during supers or mixes?

Floor manager

The *floor manager* (FM) is a person of many parts. On larger productions, he or she may, with an assistant (AFM), join the show at its onset and assist with organization, local liaison, location shooting, and sometimes substitute for the busy director at prestudio rehearsals. Alternatively, the FM may join the production in the studio for camera rehearsals.

During studio preparations for camera rehearsal, the FM checks all *non-technical* aspects of the show, confirming the team's readiness. Progress checks ensure that there are no staging hangups (i.e. action props work, scenery and furniture are in planned positions, doors do not stick . . . etc.); that no fire, safety or union regulations are being contravened. He guides the floor crew/stage hands, relative to operating graphics, studio/title cards, cue cards, scenic moves, effects cues; etc.

Around this time, arriving performers may need to be welcomed, checked in, and accommodated; and told when and where they are required. Ensuring punctuality and the observation of scheduled times are important aspects of the FM's duties; whether for rehearsal starts, *turnarounds* at the end of a rehearsal (returning equipment, props, scenery, to opening positions), or studio breaks (meals).

■ *Rehearsal* As the director's contact man on the studio floor, the FM wearing his earphones, listens to the director's intercom (talkback) and then passes this information on to the talent. He anticipates problems, rearranges action and grouping, furniture positions, etc., as the director

Fig. 17.1 Floor manager signals
1. Stand by . . . go ahead.   2. Speed up, faster pace, quicker tempo (speed according to increase required).   3. Slow down, slower pace, stretch it out (indicated by slow 'stretching' gestures).   4. OK, you're all right now, its OK (confirmation signal).   5. Keep talking (open/close break movement).   6. We're/ you're on time, on the nose.   7. FM TO CAMERA. Are we on time? How is the time going?   8. You have . . . time left (illustrated – 2 min and ½ min).   9. Wind up now, conclude action.   10. Cut it, stop, finish, omit rest of item.   11. You are cleared. You are now off camera, and can move or stop action.   12. Speak more loudly. 13. Volume up, louder.   14. Volume down, quieter (sometimes preceded by 'Quiet' signal).   15. Quiet, stop applause.   16. Get closer to mike.   17. Come nearer, come downstage.   18. Go further away, go upstage.   19. Stop, keep still. 20. Turn round (in the direction indicated).   21. Move to camera left. 22. Tighten up, get closer together.   23. Open up, move further apart. 24. You're on that camera, play to that camera (sometimes with turning head gesture).   25. Play to the light indicated. (When actors are shadowing, point to light source and to area of face shadowed.)   26. Commercial break (brush right hand over left palm – spreading butter on bread).   27. FM TO AUDIENCE: You can applaud now (may be followed by louder sign).   28. Stop. (For applause, widespread action, etc.). Some use this sign ambiguously: slow to stop; fast to increase.

indicates, marking the floor where necessary. He supervises staging and property changes.

Only the FM will normally stop floor action, on the director's instructions. (The director only exceptionally uses the studio-address loudspeaker/loudspeaker-talkback, to talk directly to performers). The

FM talks back to the director over studio mikes, his own miniature 'reverse-talkback' transmitter, or by gestures in front of preview cameras. Being on the spot, he can often correct problems not evident to the remote director.

A good FM combines calmness, discipline and firmness, with diplomacy and friendliness; putting talent at ease. Always available yet never in shot. He maintains a quiet studio, yet appreciates that various last-minute corrective jobs must progress. He investigates any delay, aiming to clear it; or if rehearsal is likely to be halted, suggests an alternative sequence that is ready instead. Later, the FM, may welcome and guide any studio audience, relative to the show format and their contributions.

■ *Taping/transmission* In checking and making ready for 'air time' or videotaping, the FM confirms that all studio access doors are shut, talent and crew standing by in opening positions, the ident slate has accurate details (which he reads during the VT countdown), that studio monitors are showing pictures, etc.

During the show, he is cuing talent, keeping a wary eye on all about him, listening to intercom guidance, anticipating hazards, and generally smoothing proceedings. At the end of taping, he holds talent and crew until results have been checked; announcing and preparing any necessary retakes, finally 'releasing the studio' (performers and crew). He checks on safe storage of any valuable or special props or equipment and ends his duties with a logged account of the production.

Guiding performers

How much guidance performers need, varies with their experience and the complexity of the production. But you must always ensure that talent realizes exactly what you want them to do and where to do it. A preliminary word may be enough, or a painstaking rehearsal may prove essential.

■ *Inexperienced talent* Having welcomed talent, put them at ease, and outlined their contribution, they are best supported by an experienced host who guides and reassures them. Have them talk and demonstrate to the host rather than the camera, for he can steer them by questions and ensure that subject positions suit the shots.

We all feel daunted by unfamiliar conditions, mechanics, and disciplines; self-confidence is essential for good performance. So keep problems to a minimum, with only essential instructions to talent. Avoid elaborate action, discourage improvisation, and have minimal rearrangements.

Even slight distractions may worry inexperienced talent. Sometimes a small cue card or a list of points held beside the camera, may strengthen their confidence. However, few inexperienced people read scripts or prompters 'naturally'; but instead have a stilted, ill-at-ease delivery.

The balance between insufficient and excessive rehearsal, is more

Fig. 17.2   Guiding the performer
Show them where to stand: using (1) a locating point, or (2) toe marks. (3) Keep other action and monitors out of their eyeline.

crucial with inexperienced talent. Uncertainty or over-familiarity can lead them to omit sections during transmission. Sometimes the solution lies in either taping the item sectionally or in compiling from several takes.

■ *Professional talent*   You will meet a very wide range of experienced professional performers in TV production – actors, anchormen, hosts, link men, commentators, introducers, presenters, and MCs (Master of Ceremonies).

Familiar with studio routines, they can respond to the most complicated instructions from the FM, or an earpiece intercom (switched talkback) without the blink of an eye, even under the most trying conditions – and yet maintain cool command of the situation. Comments, feed questions, timing and continuity changes, item cuts, ad-libbing padding, are taken in their stride.

The professional makes full use of a prompter displaying the full script – this means that cameras must always be within reading distance. His performance (action and positions) is accurately repeatable and he will play to particular cameras for specific shots, making allowances for lighting problems (e.g. shadowing) or camera moves.

Cueing

To ensure that action begins and ends at the instant it is required, precise cueing is essential. If you cut to performers and then cue them, you will see them waiting to begin or watch action 'spring into life'. Cue them too early before cutting and action has already begun. So *'cue and cut'* is normal practice.

Wrong cueing leaves talent bewildered. If they have finished their contribution and you have not cut away to the next shot, they may stand with 'egg on the face', wondering whether to ad-lib or just grin! Wrong cueing can mean that film or VT runs out to a blank screen, or we see run-up leaders flashing by on transmission. VT editing may compensate for poor cueing and disguise sloppy direction.

■ *Methods of cueing:*   (See Fig. 17.1)

1. *Hand cues* – Given by the FM (or relayed by the AFM), these are the

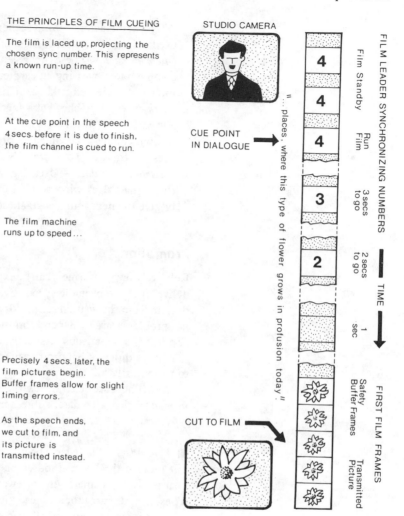

THE PRINCIPLES OF FILM CUEING

The film is laced up, projecting the chosen sync number. This represents a known run-up time.

At the cue point in the speech 4 secs. before it is due to finish, the film channel is cued to run.

The film machine runs up to speed...

Precisely 4 secs. later, the film pictures begin. Buffer frames allow for slight timing errors.

As the speech ends, we cut to film, and its picture is transmitted instead.

STUDIO CAMERA

CUE POINT IN DIALOGUE

CUT TO FILM

FILM LEADER SYNCHRONIZING NUMBERS ——— TIME ———

Film Standby / Run Film / 3 secs to go / 2 secs to go / 1 sec / Safety Buffer Frames / Transmitted Picture

FIRST FILM FRAMES

"...places, where this type of flower grows in profusion today."

Fig. 17.3   Principles of film cueing

standard methods of cueing action to start or stop. Sometimes a performer cannot watch for cues (during an embrace) and a tap on foot or shoulder may be used instead.

2. *Word cues* – An agreed go-ahead word or phrase during dialogue, commentary or discussion, may be used to cue action or to switch to an insert. We note *out cues/out words* (last spoken words) at the end of a recorded insert (VT or film) to ensure accurately timed switching to the next item.

3. *Monitor cues* – Commentators and demonstrators often watch recorded inserts on a nearby picture monitor, taking a go-ahead cue from certain action. Alternatively, the may use a *time cue*, counting down (e.g. from 10 seconds) from a cue point. Most inserts have a few seconds without strong action or speech as *run-in* (*top*) and *run-out* (*tail*) to cushion/buffer the cueing.

4. *Light cues* – Performers can take a cue from the *camera tally* (*cue*) *light* (illuminated as the camera is switched to line). For announce booths or

when cueing actors behind scenery, small portable *cue lights* are often used; where the standby 'flick' is followed by a steady 'action light'.

5. *Intercom cues* – These are given direct to a performer (newscaster, commentator) wearing an earpiece – interrupted feed-back, program interrupt, switched talkback (Chapter 6).

6. *Clock cues* – A go-ahead at a specific time.

7. *Buzzer cues* – Used in some organizations, for intercom between film/videotape areas and the production control room. (One buzz: 'Yes' or 'Start'. Two buzzes: 'No' or 'Stop'.)

8. *Electronic cue dots* – Used by networks at program change points, these small black/white squares in corner frame cue program out-time, or give the next source a go-ahead cue.

Prompting

Relatively few performers can be expected to learn a script accurately and deliver it at a repeatable speed. Even the most experienced are liable to deviate from the written script, 'dry' (forget) or 'cut' lines. Whether this is a problem, largely depends on the show format, whether live or taped and if it is spontaneous or strictly scripted.

While a quiet verbal prompt may suffice (perhaps using a muting key to temporarily kill the mike), more sophisticated methods are generally needed. There are generally two types of prompters – *reminder notes* (*aide mémoires*) that give data, subject heads, or show format; and *continual references* giving entire script or lyrics.

■ *Reminders*   These have been written on shirt cuffs or nearby scenery, but more orthodox methods range from small hand notes to the clip boards used by many interviewers, commentators, and anchormen. These boards carry their notes, questions and research information.

For brief information, cards can be held near the camera by floor crew (cue card, goof sheet, idiot card), or smaller *flip cards* (*flippers*) suspended under the camera head.

Fig. 17.4 part 1   Prompting – direct methods
1. Handwritten prompt cards usually held near the camera, may contain dialogue or reminder notes. (Cue-cards, idiot board, goof sheet.)   2. Camera flip cards usually carry brief reminders.   3. A roller-script (speed remotely controlled) may be attached to the camera, or floor-located.

Fig. 17.4 part 2   Prompting – video prompters
1. Video prompters use a 45° clear glass sheet at the camera lens, reflecting a picture-tube display of the script: from a nearby script-scanner (monochrome TV camera shooting a miniature roller script), or a computer-stored script. Simpler prompters reflect a wide paper roller script with 'jumbo' type.   2. The camera lens shoots through the glass sheet at the subject. The reader appears to be looking straight at the lens and the audience. (Other systems can result in an off-camera stare.)   3. Where the speaker does not need to speak directly to the camera, the prompter script video may be fed to floor video prompters or monitors.

■ *Script*   A talking head reading a desk script does not make good television. It is dull and lacks 'spontaneity'. But a regular script ensures accurate timing. Consequently, many shows use a *roller prompter* (mechanically or electronically operated) that provides a continuously rolling copy of the script at or near the camera lens.

The vary-speed display is remotely controlled (by the talent or an operator) and typically has some 20 words visible in an 8-line frame. To disguise eye movements or a fixed stare, the performer 'casually' changes his head position while reading. Off-camera prompters can lead to a 'shifty eyed' presentation, for the speaker has to continually glance away from the lens axis.

Prompters may inhibit shot variations because cameras carrying prompters need to be close enough for comfortable reading. Where only selected cameras have prompters, we must ensure that one of these is always near the speaker.

Production timing

Whereas a *closed-circuit* program needs only approximate timing a *live transmission* must fit its allocated time slot exactly. Overruns can result in end cut-off or cause scheduling problems. In live *composite productions*, where various contributory sources *'opt-in'* or *'opt-out'* (temporarily join or leave) the main presentation to insert their own material accurate timing is imperative.

Scripts may be roughly timed by reading aloud and allowing for any mute action, business or inserts. Many run at around a minute a full page. During rehearsal each segment or scene is timed, and subsequently adjusted to suit a timed show format/running order (estimated, permitted or actual).

Table 17.3   On-air intercom

Intercom (talkback) instructions reveal the split-second teamwork involved in efficient TV directing. Although local terminology and personnel vary, the following intercom talk from an actual show certainly reflects the spirit of the occasion.

Director's assistant	*Director*
Stand-by studio. Going ahead in 1 minute . . .	(FM alerts studio and gives countdown)
Stand-by film. (Acknowledging buzz from film channel).	Start VT. Show slate (identifying board) on 4.
Stand by announcer.	
Roll film . . . 4–3–2–1–Zero.	Fade up film. Music (on audio tape).
On film for 1 minute . . . Stand by 1	Super 1.
Shot 1.	
On 1 . . . Stand-by 2.	Take music under. Cue Announcer. (Cue light in announce booth).
Coming to end of film. counting down . . . 30 seconds – 20–10–5–4– 3–2–1–0.	Bring up music. Cue Peter (FM cues talent). Take 2 (cut to Cam. 2). Take music under.
On 2. Shot 2 . . . 1 next	He's going to sit. Go with him . . . Dolly in slowly to CU . . . Hold it there . . . Super slide title (guest's name) . . . take out super. Steady 1 . . . a bit tighter . . . good . . . take 1.
On 1. Shot 3 . . . 2 to graphic.	
Inserting 2 . . . Stand-by disc (grams)	Wipe in 2 . . . fine . . . take 2 out.
Clear 2 (after combined shot).	Go disc. Stand-by Joan (FM alerts talent).
Stand-by 3 . . . Coming to 3	Music under. Cue her on and cut. He'll exit left.
On 3. Shot 4 . . . Stand-by 2 . . . Extra shot 4A.	
On 2 . . . We're 15 seconds over (overrun).	Coming to 2 . . . Mix to 2 . . . She's going to open the box . . .
On 2 . . . Shot 4A . . . Stand-by VT	Cue Joan to open it (FM cues) . . . we're tight for time . . . Drop Shot 5.
Shot 5 is *out* (to be omitted).	Give her a wind-up . . . run VT.
Coming to VT . . . 4–3–2–1–0.	Cut to VT.
On VT for 2 minutes 7 seconds.	
1 minute left on VT . . . Coming out of VT in 30 seconds.	
Out words . . . 'on the road'.	
Stand-by 2 for Shot 6.	
Stand-by studio. Coming out of VT.	
20–10–5–4–3–2–1–0.	Hold it 2. Cut to 2.
On 3. Shot 60 . . . Clear 1 to crawl (roller titles).	He's going to move to the door and wave. Give him ½ minute.
Stand-by tape (audio). Stand-by 1 for Shot 61.	(FM signals talent) Wind him up . . . go crawl, go tape.
On 1 and 3 . . . Off the air;	Super 1. Take out 3 . . . Go to black at end of phrase.
Stand-by for retakes	Right everyone. That was great. We'll just check VT (VTR spot-checked). OK. Thank you very much. We have a clear.

Fig. 17.5   Forward and back timing
1. *Forward timing (front timing):* Duration timing (estimated and real) as the show proceeds.

(Desired durations)	Running stop watch reads (from prog. start)	Clock start time	Clock end time	Item running times (actual duration)
Intro 30″	30″	19.15.00	19.15.30	30″
Item A 10′	10′ 33″	19.15.30	19.25.33	10′ 03″
Item B 8″	18′ 30″	19.25.33	19.33.30	7′ 57″

2. *Back timing:* A 'remaining time' measurement, showing the amount of time before the production ends.

Item duration	Clock time (item starts)	Remaining time
Item X 1′ 0″	20.23.00	2′ 0″
Item Y 30″	20.24.00	1′ 0″
Item Z 30″	20.24.30	30″
End titles, Out time	20.25.00	00.00

■ *Intermittent timing* When rehearsal is halted for any reason, the stop-watch time is noted. Rehearsal recommences at a point *before* the fault and the watch is restarted when the fault point is reached. A videotaped production can usually be edited to reduce excess; its associated *time code* providing duration or elapsed time checks throughout.

■ *Shortening inserts* A live transmission needs continual timing surveillance to obviate over- or underrunning – particularly with unscripted material. If one segment *overruns (spreads)*, another may have to be shortened. Where prerecorded inserts (film or VT) are involved, their durations and *out-words* should be precisely known. However, they offer little time flexibility; particularly if accompanied by recorded dialogue. We can only shorten them on the air by omitting their start (a *late-in*) or end (an *early-out*), or even omitting an insert entirely (*dropping*).

To assist cuing when excerpting from existing material (e.g. a complete speech), we should note both the *run-in* (precue) dialogue and the *in-cue* (in-words).

■ *Back cueing* To ensure that recorded play-out music finishes precisely at program fade-out, time the music from a recognizable cue point to its conclusion (say 1 min 35 seconds). On transmission we start the music from that cue point at 1 min 35 seconds before program out-time, fading it up when required. (Dead-pot/backtime.)

Table 17.4   The director's instructions

To cameras	Opening shots please.	Cameras to provide initial shots in the show (or scene).
	Let's line up Shot 25.	Adjust that camera's shot and subjects, for composition required in Shot 25.
	Ready 2: Stand-by 2.	Stand-by cue for Cam. 2.
	Give me a single; 2-shot; 3-shot/group shot/cover shot.	Isolate in the shot the single, two or three persons specified./A shot including a group of people./A wide shot taking in all likely action.
	Zoom in (or out).	Narrow (or widen) zoom lens angle.
	Tighten your shot.	Slightly closer shot (slight zoom in).
	Get a wider shot	Get the next wider standard shot, e.g. from CU change to MS.
	2 match to 3.	Cam. 2 relate to or fit into Cam. 3's shot (using viewfinder 'mixed feeds').
	More (or less) headroom.	Adjust space between top of head and top of frame.
	More (or less) looking room.	Adjust space between angled or profile face and side of frame.
	Center (frame-up).	Arrange subject in picture center.
	Lose the hands.	Compose shot to avoid seeing hands.
	Cut at the hands.	Frame to just keep hands in shot.
	Pan left (or right).	Horizontal pivoting of camera head.
	Tilt up (or down)/pan up (or down).	Vertical pivoting of camera head. (Strictly, 'pan' should apply only to *horizontal* action, but term's misuse is very widespread.)
	Dolly back/pull back/track back.*	Pull camera mounting away from the subject.
	Dolly in/push in/track in.*	Push camera mounting towards the subject.
	Creep in (or out).	Push in (or pull out) very slowly, imperceptibly.
	Truck left (or right)/crab left (or right). *	Move mounting to the left (or right).
	Arc left (or right).	Move mounting round subject in an arc.
	Ped up (or down)	Raise (or lower) column of pedestal mounting.
	Crane up (or down)/boom up/ (sometimes elevate or depress).	Raise (or lower) crane arm or boom.
	Tongue left (or right)/crane/ slew/jib.	Turn crane boom to left (or right).
	Tongue in (or out)/crane/ boom in.	Crane positioned across the scene, move boom to and from subject.
	Focus up 3.	Warning to a camera 'standing by' that is defocused.
	Lose focus on the boy.	Let the moving boy become defocused, remain sharp on other subject(s); *or* deliberately defocus on the boy.
	Pull focus on the girl.	Change focus deliberately from previous subject, to the girl.
	Follow focus on the boy.	Maintain focus on moving boy.
	Split focus.	Focus equally sharply between main subjects.
	Focus 2/two, you're soft.	Criticism that Cam. 2's shot is not sharply focused.

You're focused forward (or back)	Focused at a point too near the camera (or too far away – e.g. background sharp while nearer subject is unsharp).
Rock focus 2. (Focus check).	Focus to and from the subject to check optimum sharpness.
Stand by for a rise (or sit).	Person is about to stand up (or sit down).
Follow him over/hold the boy.	Keep subject in shot (well composed) as he moves.
Let him go.	Do not reframe. Let him pass out of shot.
Lose him.	Recompose (or tighten shot) to exclude him.
Cam. 2, you're on lights.	Cam. 2 has lamps or strong reflections in shot (liable to damage the camera tube).
Clear on 3/you're cleared 3.	A 'clear', usually after a combined shot (super, chroma key); Cam. 3 can move to its next position.
Release 3 to captions.	A 'clear' directing camera to next position.

To the floor manager		
	Opening positions please.	Performers (and equipment) in position for start of show (or scene).
	Stand him by/give him a stand-by.	Alert him in readiness for a cue.
	Cue action/cue 'Bob'.	Give sign for action to begin (perhaps name person or character).
	Hold it.	Stop action/performance; to correct an error.
	Freeze there.	Stop movement exactly at that point; hold it quite still.
	Back to the top/take it from the top.	Begin again at the start of the scene; repeat the rehearsal.
	Pick it up from Shot 20.	Recommence rehearsal from Shot 20.
	Would they just walk it?/Go through it?	Without dialogue or performance, actors move through their various positions.
	Clear 2's shot.	Something/someone is obscuring Cam. 2's shot.
	Tighten them up.	Move them closer together.
	Move him downstage (upstage).	Move him toward (away from) the camera.
	Move her camera left.	Move her to *left* of the camera's shot (i.e. stage *right*).
	Give him a mark.	Draw a toe mark or show him a location point.
	Give her an eyeline.	Show her the direction in which to look.
	He'll take a word cue.	He will begin action on hearing certain dialogue.
	Give him a light/flash him.	Operate a cue light.
	Have him take a beat (or two) before he moves.	He should delay for a silent count of one (or two) before moving.
	Have him play to his key.	He should face his main light (key light).
	Show David 3/he's on 3.	Indicate to him which camera is shooting him.
	He's to work to/play to 3.	He should face Camera 3.
	Ask him for more (less) voice.	To speak louder (more quietly).
	Show him the mike.	Indicate the mike picking him up.
	Speed him up.	Tell him to go more quickly (i.e. time is short).
	Stretch him/tell him to spread.	Tell him to go more slowly (i.e. there is time to spare).

	Tell him to pad/keep talking	Tell him to improvise until next item is ready. (Often a hand signal, thumb and extended fingers touch and part.)
	Give him 2 minutes . . . 1 minute . . . 30 seconds.	He has 2 minutes left (followed by countdown on fingers).
	Give him a wind/wind him up.	Signal him to finish.
	Give him a hard wind/quick wind.	It is essential for him to stop immediately. (Faster signal.)
	Kill him/cut him.	He is to stop immediately.
	Give him a clear.	We have left him. He is free to move away (or relax).
	Lose the flowers.	Remove (kill) the flowers (for the shot or scene; or take them away entirely).
To audio (sound mixer)	Fade up sound/fade up boom.	Fade up from zero to full (general or specific source).
	Stand by music (disc/grams, tape, effects, etc.).	Warning before cue.
	Cue music/go music.	Go-ahead for music (live, disc or audio tape).
	Creep in music/sneak in music.	Begin very quietly, gradually fading up audio.
	Down music.	Reduce volume (level) of audio.
	Music under/music to background.	Keep music volume low, relative to other sources.
	Hit the music.	Begin music, at full volume.
	Up music.	Increase volume of music, usually to full.
	Sound up (or down).	General instruction to increase (or decrease) overall volume.
	Kill (cut) the music.	Stop the music.
	Fade sound.	Fade out all program sound.
	Fade tape (disc, film sound, etc.).	Fade out specified source. Usually leaving other sources.
	Cross fade; mix.	Fade out present source(s), while fading in the next.
	Segue (pronounced 'seg-way').	One piece of music immediately follows another without a break.
	Cue tape.	Start audio tape replay.
To switcher (vision mixer)	Take 1/cut to 1/cut 1.	Switch to Camera 1's picture.
	Fade up 2.	Bring Cam. 2's video-fader from zero to full.
	Stand by to fade 2/ready to fade 2.	Prepare to fade Cam. 2's picture out.
	Fade/go to black/fade out.	Fade selected camera's video fader down to zero.
	Stand-by to mix (dissolve) to 3.	Warning before mixing cue.
	Mix (dissolve) to 3.	Mix from present camera(s) to Cam. 3's picture.
	Supering 3/ready to super 3.	Warning before super cue.
	Super 3/superimpose/add 3.	Fade Cam. 3's picture up, adding to existing sources.
	Take 2 out/lose 2.	Remove (usually fade) Cam. 2's picture, leaving the rest.
	Wiping 3 over 2.	Stand-by for wipe.
	Wipe to 3.	Using prearranged pattern, Cam. 3's picture obliterates present picture.

	Ready black . . . go to black.	Stand-by . . . fade picture to black.
To captions (graphics)	Flip, animate (de-animate). Change caption. Go crawl (roller).	Cuing caption changes. ('De-animate' indicates 'return to preanimation position'.)
To other source	Cue telecine/roll film/run TK .	Start film projector (similarly for *videotape*, although some organizations ROLL film and RUN VT.).
	Go ahead PARIS.	Start cue for remote source in PARIS.

British/European terms.

18 Imaginative production

Pictorial function

Most pictures are factual, showing subjects in a familiar undistorted fashion, without any predominating emotional appeal. Yet, by judiciously arranging these same subjects, by careful composition, and a selective viewpoint, you can modify their entire impact and give them quite a different implied *significance*. You *interpret* the scene.

You can deliberately distort and select reality, so that your presentation bears little direct relationship to the actual situation; you may do this to create a dramatic illusion . . . or to produce an influential force (advertising, propaganda).

Abstracting further, you can stimulate emotions and ideas, simply by the use of movement, line, form, etc., which the viewer personally interprets.

Most TV production aims at the direct reportage of events. But there are occasions when we seek to stimulate the audience's imagination; to evoke ideas that are not conveyed directly by camera and microphone. In this chapter we shall examine these concepts and how they can be used.

■ *Picture usage*   The purposes for which pictures are employed are, of course, extremely varied. Some of the more common uses are:

1. *Factual* – Conveying information directly.
2. *Environmental* – Establishing location. (Big Ben suggests London.)
3. *Interpretative* – Visual associations, conveying ideas, thoughts, feelings. (Plodding feet suggest weariness.)
4. *Symbolic* – Symbols associated with people, events, etc. (Old Glory to symbolize USA.)
5. *Imitative* – Imitating appearance or action. (The camera 'staggers', as a drunk reels.)
6. *Identifying* – Features associated with particular people, events, etc. (Trademarks, logos.)
7. *Recapitulative* – Recalling subjects met earlier.
8. *Coupling* – Linking events, themes, etc. (Pan from toy boat . . . to water . . . to ship at sea.)
9. *Montage* – An interplay of successive images, or a juxtaposition of subjects.

Production rhetoric

Rhetoric is the art of persuasive or impressive speech and writing. Unlike everyday conversation, it stimulates our imagination through style and technique, by inference and allusion, instead of direct pronouncement, by appealing to our inward ear and eye. The rhetoric of the screen has similar roots, that film makers such as Hitchcock have explored over the years to great effect.

The analysis that follows is more than a concise list of facts. It is a distillation of production techniques with exciting persuasive potentials, techniques that have moved audiences to tears, of laughter and of pity; that have held them in tense expectation. Translate these principles into living illustrations and we see how the camera can, without a word of dialogue, convey the whole gamut of human responses.

An example: A veteran performer ends his brave but pathetic vaudeville act amid gibes and cat-calls. He bows, defeated . . . we hear hands clapping . . . the camera turns from the sad lone figure . . . past derisive faces . . . to where his aged wife sits applauding.

Summary of devices

Regard this analysis as a series of fingerposts, pointing the opportunities to build up original situations of your own. The summary outlines the principles involved. The examples that follow show those principles in action.

1. Making a *direct visual contrast.*
   (a) Of the picture quality – brightness, clarity, tonal contrasts.
   (b) By editing, contrasting the shot duration, transitions used, cutting rhythm.
   (c) Contrasting camera treatment – shot sizes, viewpoint height, camera movement, composition.
   (d) Through the subject itself. Creating a change that reveals new information, altering the picture's significance, e.g. by introducing a subject movement (the blonde turns . . . to reveal it is a man in drag); by cutting to a new viewpoint (the formally dressed butler . . . is wearing sneakers); by lighting. Contrasting the movement of one subject with another (contrasting energy with langour). Contrasting subject associations, i.e. the mood, qualities, properties, state, of one subject with another (new with old). Contrasting subject form (building construction with its subsequent demolition).
2. Making a *direct audio contrast.* Contrasting the sounds' relative volume, pitch, quality, reverberation, speed, rhythm, duration, methods of transition, composition, sound movement, association.
3. We can *directly contrast the picture and its sound.* By comparing any aspect of (1) with another in (2) (e.g. a picture of starving children singing *Pennies from Heaven*).
4. Similarly, we can make a *direct comparison* between two ideas, situations, etc. for visual comparison, audio comparison, picture and sound compared.
5. Showing identical subjects with *different associations.*
   (a) Identical or similar subjects having different purposes, values, significances, etc.

(b) The original purpose (or associations, etc.) of a subject has become changed.

6. Linking a variety of subjects, through *common association*.

7. *Juxtaposing apparent incongruities*.

8. *Implication*. Hinting at a situation without actually demonstrating it. Examples range from filmic time to censorable innuendo.

9. *Unexpected outcome*.
    (a) Climactic build-up to an unexpected outcome.
    (b) Anticlimax, following a build-up

10. *Bathos*. A fall in significance; from the sublime to the ridiculous.

11. *Deliberate falsification or distortion*. 'Accidentally' causing the audience to misinterpret.

12. *Imitative interpretation*.
    (a) Between subjects.
    (b) Between mechanics and subjects.

13. *Associative selection*.
    (a) Direct, using part of a subject to represent the whole.
    (b) Recalling a subject by referring to something closely associated with it.
    (c) Symbolism – using a symbol to represent a subject.

14. *Deliberate overstatement*. Excessive emphasis on size, effort, etc., for dramatic strength.

15. *Deliberate understatement*. Preliminary underemphasis, to strengthen the eventual impact of size, effort, etc.

16. An *unreal effect* seeming to evolve naturally.

17. A *natural effect* introduced through *obviously contrived* means.

18. *Repetition*.
    (a) Of sound.
    (b) Of picture.

19. *Sequential repetition*.
    (a) A series of sequences, all beginning with the same shot, associations, etc.
    (b) A succession of similar circumstances.

20. *Successive comparison*.
    (a) Showing the same subject in different circumstances.
    (b) Showing the same subject is different manifestations.

21. *Pun*. Play on a subject's dual significance.

22. *Irony*. A comment with an inner sardonic meaning, often by stating the opposite.

23. *Modified irony*. An ironic modification of the real significance of a subject, situation, etc.

24. *Dramatic irony*. The audiences perceiving a fact that the character involved is unaware of.

25. *Personification*. Representing an inanimate object as having human characteristics.

26. *Metaphorical transfer*. Transferring the properties of one subject to another.

27. *Flashback*. Jumping back in time, to a point earlier than the narration has reached.

28. Referring to *future events* as if *already past or present*.
29. Referring to *the absent as if present*. Usually relating concurrent events by montage.
30 Referring to *the past as if still present*.
31. *Cutaway*. Deliberately interrupting events to show concurrent action elsewhere.
31. *Fade-out on climax*. Fading at the crucial moment in action:
    (a) To leave the audience in suspense.
    (b) To prevent the climactic peak being modified by subsequent action.
33. *Double take*. Passing by a subject casually . . . then returning to it quickly, having suddenly realized its significance.
34. *Sudden relevation*. Suddenly revealing new information that we were not previously aware of . . . immediately making the situation meaningful.
35. *Incongruity*. Where a character:
    (a) Accepts an incongruous situation as normal.
    (b) Exerts disproportionate effort to achieve something.
    (c) Displays disproportionate facility (i.e. exaggerated speed, etc.)
    (d) Is unable to perform a simple act.
    (e) Imitates unsuccessfully.
    (f) Does the right thing – wrongly.
    (g) Caricature.

Examples of production rhetoric

These are, of course, only the bare bones of opportunity. You can take any of the devices listed, and apply them in many quite different ways. For example, let us take (10) BATHOS. Here is the basis of the 'banana-skin' and 'custard-pie' jokes, and our reactions when the tattered hobo dusts off the park-bench before sitting. In the following examples you will see how readily these ideas can be introduced.

1. (a) A sudden mood change, by switching from bright gaiety . . . to macabre gloom.
       Contrasting a soft-focused dream-like atmosphere . . . with the hard clear-cut state of harsh reality.
       Contrasting the airiness of a high-key scene . . . with the restrictiveness of heavy chiaroscuro treatment.
   (b) Contrasting the leisurely pace of prolonged shots . . . with fast-moving short-duration shots.
       Contrasting the peaceful effect of a series of fades . . . with the sudden shock of a cut.
       Contrasting the jerky staccato of rapid cutting . . . with the deliberation of a slower cutting rhythm
   (c) Contrasting the size of a giant aircraft . . . with its diminutive pilot.
       Contrasting an individual's dominance in close-up . . . with his relative insignificance within his surroundings.

Contrasting the subject strength from a low-angle shot . . . with its inferiority from a high-angle viewpoint.

Contrasting a forward aggressive move . . . with a backward recessive move.

Contrasting the resctriction of limited depth of field . . . with a spacious deep-focus shot.

Contrasting the normality of a straight-on shot . . . with the instability of a canted shot.

    (d) The only refuge on a storm-swept moorland is revealed by a lightning flash . . . as a prison.

2. Contrasting the busy crowds' noise by day . . . with the hush of the empty street at night.

Contrasting realistic . . . with unreal sounds.

3. A hippopotamus lumbers along, in step with delicate ballet music.

4. A pair of lovers embrace . . . and the camera tilts up to show a pair of lovebirds.

A soprano's high C . . . merges into the scream of a factory siren.

A helicopter hovers . . . to the sound of a bee buzzing.

5. A favorite record which has been played at a party, is later used to cover the sounds of a murder.

6. Shots of sandcastles, rock pools, beach ball; sounds of children's laughter, sea-wash, suggest the seaside.

7. Shots of a massive French locomotive . . . end with the shrill, effeminate toot of its whistle.

8. Suspecting that he is followed, a fugitive leaves a café . . . the sound of feet joins his own in the empty street.

9. A thief grabs a valuable necklace . . . it breaks . . . the pearls scatter.

It is spring. Migrant ducks arrive and land on a lake . . . but skid on its still-frozen surface.

10. After ceremonial orders, a massive gun is fired . . . producing a wisp of smoke and a pop.

11. South American music, a striped blanket on sun-drenched stone, a bright straw hat, cactus . . . but only a sunbather in a suburban garden, listening to the radio.

12. Someone is speaking to a deaf person . . . we see his lips in close-up, but without sound.

An upward movement . . . accompanied by rising-pitch sounds.

13. (a) The name on a ship's life-belt identifies the vessel – TITANIC.

     (b) The guillotine used to epitomize the French Revolution.

     (c) A shot of the Golden Gate bridge to represent San Francisco.

14. A close shot of an auctioneer's gavel descending.

15. A smoker casually throws aside a cigar-butt. A fire starts . . . which develops into a devasting forest blaze.

16. As we watch a moving picture . . . a large hand appears and turns it over like the page of a book.

17. Watching a street fight as a distorted reflection in the chromium wheel-trim of a nearby automobile.

18. A seacher shouts the lost person's name . . . it echoes and re-echoes.

An angry crowd closes round a central figure. Close shots cut alternately between the accused and individuals in the crowd.

19. A successful concert tour is shown by the artist taking a series of similar curtain calls.
20. A succession of shots show the same policeman in a variety of situations; directing traffic, guiding a sightseer, rescuing a would-be suicide, making an arrest . . .
21. A parrot at an open window whistles for food . . . a passing girl turns at the 'wolf whistle'
22. It is a power blackout. The lost traveler strikes a match . . . and sees a poster – 'Save Energy'.
23. A newspaper advertisement shows extraordinary bargains . . . then we see it is an old copy, used to line a drawer.
24. A mountaineer climbs . . . unaware that his rope is fraying.
25. An animated coffee-pot describes the great coffee it makes.
26. An elephant that flies ('Dumbo').
27. An old woman tells of her childhood . . . brief shots showing her life as a girl.
28. Looking at the projected plans of a ship . . . we hear the launching festivities.
29. A superimposed montage showing a missing man surrounded by headlines; radio announcers telling of his disappearance.
30. A derelict ballroom echoing to the sounds of bygone dances.
31. The fugitive escapes down a side alley. But just as we see that his way is blocked, the shot changes to show his pursuers.
32. A little man arrogantly challenges a person sitting nearby . . . who stands and towers over the challenger. The picture cuts to another scene.
33. Walking past a poster of a wanted robber, a man suddenly stops, reacts, and returns to it. He realizes that its picture looks like himself.
34. Entering a room, we see someone reading . . . a close viewpoint reveals the dagger-hilt protruding from his back.
35. A man takes off his hat . . . and eats it.

Imaginative sound

Although the aural memory is less retentive it is generally more imaginative than the eye. We are more perceptive and discriminating towards what we see. Consequently, our ears accept the unfamiliar and unrealistic more readily than our eyes, and are more tolerant of repetition. A sound-effects recording can be reused many times, but a costume or drapes design may become familiar after a couple of viewings.

In many TV shows the audio is taken for granted, while attention is concentrated on the visual treatment. Yet, without audio the presentations can become meaningless (talks, discussions, interviews, newscasts, music, game shows, etc.): whereas without video the production would still communicate.

Audio can explain or augment the picture, enriching its impact or appeal. Music or effects can suggest locale (seashore sounds), or a situation (pursuing police heard), or conjure a mood (gaiety, foreboding, comedy, horror).

A non-specific picture can be given a definite significance through associated sound. Depending on accompanying music, a display of flowers may suggest springtime, a funeral, a wedding or a ballroom.

Sound elements

■ *Voice* The most obvious sound element, the *human voice*, can be introduced into the presentation in several different ways:

1. A single person addressing the camera, formally or informally.
2. An off-screen commentator (voice over) providing a formalized narrative (e.g. travelogues); or the spontaneous commentary for a sports event.
3. We may 'hear the thoughts' of a character (reminiscive or explanatory narration) while watching his silent face, or the subject of his thoughts.
4. Dialogue – the informal natural talk between people (actual or simulated), with all its hesitance, interruptions, breaking off, overlapping; and the more regulated exchanges of formal discussion.

■ *Effects* The characteristic sound picture that conjures a particular place or atmosphere, comes from a blend of stimuli: from action sounds (e.g. footsteps, gunfire), from environmental noises (e.g. wind, crowd, traffic), and from the subtle ways in which sound quality is modified by its surroundings (reverberation, coloration, distortion).

■ *Music* Background music has become near-obligatory for many programs. It can range from purely melodic accompaniment to music that imitates, or gives evocative or abstract support. You can even use musical instruments to create audio effects (creaks, clicks, whines, etc.).

■ *Silence* The powerful dramatic value of *silence* should never be underestimated. However, silence must be used with care, for it may too easily seem to be just a loss of audio.

Continued silence can suggest such diverse concepts as: death, desolation, despair, stillness, hope, peace, extreme tension (we listen intently to hear if the marauders are still around).
Sudden silence after noise can be almost unbearable:

A festival in an Alpine village . . . happy laughter and music . . . the tumultuous noise of an unexpected avalanche engulfing the holiday makers . . . then silence.
Sudden noise during silence creates an immediate peak of tension:

The silently escaping prisoner knocks over a chair and awakens the guards (or did they hear him after all?)

Silent streets at night . . . then a sudden scream.
Dead silence when the audience has been following action that would

logically lead to a tremendous noise can give a scene a taut unreal quality:

To a crescendo of sound, intercut shots of two locomotives traveling towards each other at speed on the same track . . . they crash in silent slow-motion.

The explosive charge has been set . . . the detonator is switched . . . nothing happens . . . silence.

Sound emphasis

You can manipulate the relative volumes of sounds for dramatic effect; emphasizing particular sources, cheating loudness to suit the situation. A whisper may be amplified to make it clearly audible, a loud sound held in check.

You may establish the background noise of a vehicle and then gradually reduce it, taking it under to improve audibility of conversation. Or you could deliberately increase its loudness so that the noise drowns the voices. Occasionally you may take out all environmental sounds to provide a silent background – for a thoughts sequence, perhaps.

You can modify the aesthetic appeal and significance of sound in a number of ways.

For *factual sound* you can use:

1. *Random* natural pickup (e.g. overhead street conversations).
2. *Selective pickup* of particular sources.

For *atmospheric sound:*

1. By choosing certain natural associated sounds, you can develop a *realistic* illusion. (Cockcrow suggests it is dawn.)
2. By deliberately distorting reality, you create *fantasy* to stimulate the imagination. (A Swannee whistle's note suggests flight through the air.)
3. By *abstraction*, the pitch and rhythm of sounds can evoke ideas and emotions without direct reference to naturalistic phenomena. (Film music, cartoon sound-tracks, musique concrète.)

Sound usuage

As with picture usage, this can be extremely varied:

1. *Factual* – Conveying information directly (normal speech).
2. *Environmental* – Establishing location (traffic noises imply a street scene).
3. *Interpretative* – Of ideas, thoughts, feelings (a slurred trombone note as a derisive comment).
4. *Symbolic* – Of places, moods, events (air-raid siren denoting an attack).
5. *Imitative* – Of a subject's sound, character, movements (music imitating a cuckoo's call).
6. *Identifying* – Associated with particular people or events (signature tunes, leitmotif).

7. *Recapitulative* – Recalling sounds met earlier.
8. *Coupling* – Linking scenes, events, etc. (Musical bridges between scenes.)
9. *Montage* – A succession or mixture of sounds, arranged for dramatic or comic effect. (A bassoon and piccolo duet.)

Off-screen sound

When someone speaks or something makes a sound, it might seem logical to show the source as a matter of course. But it can be singularly dull if we do this repeatedly: she starts talking, so we cut and watch her.

You can use *off-screen* sound in many ways, to enhance program impact:

1. Having established a shot of someone talking, you might cut to see the person they are speaking to and watch their reactions, or cut to show what they are talking about. The original dialogue continues, but we no longer see the speaker. So you can establish relationships, even where the two subjects have not been seen together in the same shot.
2. Background sounds can help to establish location. Although a mid-shot of two people occupies the screen, the audience interprets that they are near the seashore, a highway, a sawmill.
3. Off-screen sounds may be chosen to intrigue us, or arouse our curiosity.
4. A background sound may introduce us to a subject before we actually see it, informing us about what is going on nearby or is going to appear (e.g. the wheezy spluttering of an approaching jalopy).
5. Tension can build as a character recognizes and reacts to a sound that the audience cannot interpret. Again, tension grows when a character hears a sound (that we also hear) but cannot understand its significance. Alternatively, we may realize the significance of a sound that the character has not heard or understood.
6. Off-screen sounds can exaggerate or emphasize our impressions of a scene (a crowd, traffic); perhaps indicating them even where none exists.
7. By deliberately *overlapping* sound you can create a linkage between scenes; introducing the next scene's audio before you cut to it. For example, an old man reminiscing at dinner: 'In those days, Vienna was a city of wonderful music.' While watching him, we hear a waltz in the background . . . the picture dissolves to show a soirée.
8. The background sound may create audio continuity, although the shots switch rapidly. Two people walk through buildings, down a street . . . their voices are heard clearly throughout at a constant level.
9. An audio montage of several different sources, may be used to suggest thoughts, dreams, etc.

Substituted sound

Surprisingly often, instead of reproducing the *original* sound, we shall deliberately devise a substitute to accompany the picture. There are several reasons for this approach:

No sound exists – as with sculpture, painting, architecture, inaudible insects, prehistoric monsters.

Sometimes the actual sounds are *not available, not recorded* (mute shooting), or *not suitable*. For example: absence of birdsong when shooting a country scene; location sounds were obtrusive, unimpressive, or inappropriate to use; a location camera may obtain a close shot of a subject (using a narrow-angle lens) that is too distant for effective sound pickup.

The sounds you introduce may be just *replacements* (using another lion's voice instead of the missing roar), or *artificial substitutes* in the form of effects, music, synthesized or treated audio.

Background music and effects should be added cautiously. They are easily:

1. Disproportionate (too loud or soft).
2. Hackneyed (too familiar).
3. Over-obvious (imitating every action – 'Mickey Mousing').
4. Obtrusive (surging into slight gaps of silence).
5. Out of scale (overscored music).
6. Inappropriate (have wrong or misleading associations).

Controlling sound equipment

Various working principles are generally accepted in sound treatment:

1. The scale and quality of audio should match the picture (appropriate volumes, balance, audio perspective, acoustics, etc.).
2. Where audio directly relates to picture action, it should be synchronized (like movements, footsteps, hammering, other transient sounds.)
3. Video and audio should normally be switched together. No audio advance or hangover on a cut.
4. Video cutting should be on the beat of the music, rather than against it; preferably at the end of a phrase. Continual cutting in time with music becomes tedious.
5. Video and audio should usually begin together at the start of a show; finishing together at its conclusion, fading out as a musical phrase ends.

Audio analysis

We all recognize that some sounds seem exciting, martial, happy . . . while others are melancholy, soporific, wistful. Is this entirely fortuitous, or are there working principles to guide our audio selection? Experience suggests that there are.

If you analyze a series of sounds creating a particular emotional impact, you will find they have many common features. The Table 18.1 shows some 42 sound characteristics and typical associated responses. These effects can, of course, combine in various complex ways. For example,

Table 18.1   Analysis of sounds and their effect

	Sound characteristics	Associated with
Volume	1. Loud sounds	Big, strong, assertive, powerful, energetic, rousing, earnest.
	2. Soft sounds	Small, soothing, peaceful, gentle, subdued, delicate, little energy.
	Against a quiet background	Alerting, persuasive.
Pitch	3. Pitch	Often suggests physical height.
	4. High-pitched sounds	Exciting, light, brittle, stirring, invigorating, elating, attractive, distinct, sprightly, weak.
	5. Low-pitched sounds	Powerful, heavy, deep solemn, sinister, undercurrent, depression.
Key	6. Major	Vigor, brightness.
	7. Minor	Melancholy, wistful, apprehensive.
Tonal quality	8. Pure, thin (e.g. flutes, pure string-tone)	Purity, weakness, simplicity, sweetness, ethereal, daintiness, forthright, persuasiveness.
	9. Rich (possessing strong overtones, harmonics)	Richness grandeur, fullness, complexity, confusion, boisterous, worldly, vitality, strength.
	10. Edgy, brassy, metallic	Cold, shrill, gay, bitter, snarling, vicious, forceful, hard, martial.
	11. Full, round tone (e.g. horn, saxophone, bowed basses)	Warm, rich, mellow.
	12. Reedy (e.g. oboe, clarinet)	Sweetness, nostalgic, delicate, melancholy, wistful.
	13. Sharp transients (a) High-pitched (e.g. xylophone, breaking glass)	Thrilling, exciting, horrifying.
	(b) Low-pitched (e.g. timpani, thunder)	Dramatic, powerful, significant.
Speed and rhythm	14. Slow	Serious, important, dignified, deliberate, ponderous, stately, somber, mournful.
	15. Fast	Exciting, gay, hopeful, fierce, trivial, agile.
	16. Simple	Uncomplicated, deliberate, regulation, dignity.
	17. Complex.	Complication, excitement, elaboration.
	18. Constant	Uniformity, forceful, monotonous, depressing.
	19. Changing	Vigorous, erratic, uncertainty, elation, wild.
	20. Increasing (Accelerando)	Increasing vigor, excitement, energy or force; progressive development.
	21. Decreasing (Rallentando)	Decreasing vigor, excitement, energy or force; concluding development.
Phrasing	Repetition of sets of sounds:	
	22. Regular repetition	Pleasurable recognition, insistence, monotony, regulation, co-ordination.
	23. Irregular repetition	Distinctiveness, personality, disorder.
	24. Strongly-marked accents	Strong, forceful, emphatic, rhythmical.
	25. Un-accentuated sounds	Continuity, lack of vitality.
	26. Interrupted rhythm (Syncopation)	Character, vigor, uncertainty, unexpectedness.

Duration	27. Brief, fragmentary	Awakening interest, excitement, forceful, dissatisfaction.
	28. Sustained	Persistence, monotony, stability, tiredness.
	29. Staccato	Nervous vitality, excitement.
Movement	30. Movement pattern	Movement pattern of sound suggests corresponding physical movement, e.g. upward – downward – upward – glissando pitch changes suggesting swinging movement.
	31. Upwards	Elation, rising importance, expectation, awakening interest, anticipation, doubt, forceful, powerful.
	32. Downwards	Decline, falling interest, decision, conclusion, imminence, climatic movement.
Pitch changes	33. Sudden changes (a) rise (b) fall	Increasing interest, excitement, uplift. Force, strength, decision, momentary unbalance.
	34. Slow changes (a) rise (b) fall	Increasing tension, aspiration, rising motion. Saddening, depression, falling motion, reduced tension.
	35. Well-defined pitch-changes	Decision, effort, brightness, vitality.
	36. Indefinite pitch-changes (e.g. slurs, glissando)	Lack of energy, indecision, sadness.
	37. Vibrato	Instability, unsteadiness, ornamentation.
Volume changes	38. Tremelo	Uncertainty, timidity, imminent action.
	39. Crescendo	Increasing force, power, nearness, etc.
	40. Diminuendo	Decreasing force, power, nearness, etc.
Reverberation	41. Dead acoustics	Restriction, intimacy, closeness, confinement, compression.
	42. Live acoustics	Openness, liveliness, spacious, magnitude, distance, uncertainty, the infinite.

from Table 18.1, it is obvious that a sound containing the features – 1, 4, 9, 10, 13, 15, 19, 20, 23, 24, 26, 27, 31, 33a, 35, 39, 42 must necessarily produce an exciting, vigorous impact. On the other hand, one containing features – 2, 5, 8, 11, 14, 16, 18, 21, 22, 28, 32, 34b, 36, 41 must be a sad, peaceful, sound.

■ *The effect of combining sounds*   When we hear two or more sounds together, we shall often find that they *interrelate* to provide an emotional effect, that changes according to their relative loudness, speed, complexity, etc.

Overall *harmony* – Conveys completeness, beauty, accord, organization.

Overall *discord* – Conveys imbalance, uncertainty, incompletion, unrest, ugliness, irritation.

Marked *differences* in relative volume, rhythm, etc – create variety, complication, breadth of effect, individual emphasis.

Marked *similarities* – Result is sameness, homogeneity, mass, strength of effect.

Focusing attention

Audience attention is seldom divided equally between picture and sound. One aspect usually dominates. However, you can transfer concentration between ear and eye. For example, a movement will emphasize a remark made immediately afterwards. Dialogue before a move gives it emphasis.

The ear is particularly drawn to certain types of sound:

1. Loud sounds, increasing volume.
2. High-pitched sounds (around 1000 to 4000 c/s).
3. Sounds rich in overtones (harmonics); edgy, metallic sounds; transients.
4. Fast sounds, increasing speed or rhythm.
5. Complex rhythms.
6. Briefly repeated phrases, syncopation, strong accents.
7. Short-duration or staccato sounds.
8. Aural movement.
   (a) Especially increases in volume, pitch, etc.
   (b) Clear-cut, unexpected, violent, changes.
   (c) Interruption, vibrato, tremolo.
9. Reverberant acoustics.
10. Marked contrast.
    (a) Between the principal and background sounds.
    (b) Between the sound and the picture (i.e. their associations, composition, etc.).
11. Marked similarity.
    (a) Between sounds (e.g. one source echoing another).
    (b) Between sounds and picture (e.g. simultaneous upward movements in both).

We can transfer aural attention to another subject by:

1. Giving the original subject's sound pattern (rhythm, movement, etc.) to the new source.
2. Weakening the original subject's attraction and strengthening the new source.

Fig. 18.1 Interaction between sounds
1. Towards a common focal point – suggesting conflict, concentration. 2. Away from a common focal point – suggesting divergence, broadening. 3. Contrasting sound movement – suggesting diversity, variety, interdependence. 4. Parallel sound movement – suggesting similarity, unanimity.

3. Linking action e.g. having the pattern of the original sound change to that of the new subject, before stopping it.
4. Transferring aural movement through e.g. by carrying over a solo sound, while changing its background.
5. Cutting to a shot of the new source alone.
6. Changing the original composition lines e.g. whereas upward sounds lead attention towards high notes, downward sounds lead attention towards lower notes.
7. Dialogue attracting attention either to its source or to its subject.

Selective sound

In recreating the atmosphere of a particular environment, the trick is to use sound *selectively* if you want the scene to carry conviction, rather than try to include all typical background noises. You may deliberately emphasize, reduce, modify or omit sounds that would normally be present; or introduce others to convey a convincing sense of location.

The selection and blend of environmental sounds can strongly influence the interpretation of a scene. Imagine, for example:

The slow even toll of a cathedral bell accompanied by the rapid footsteps of approaching churchgoers.

In developing this scene, you could reproduce random typical sounds. Or, more persuasively, you might deliberately use audio emphasis:

1. Loud busy footsteps with a quiet insignificant bell in the background.
2. The bell's slow dignity contrasted with restless footsteps.
3. The bell's echoing notes contrasted with the staccato impatience of footsteps.
4. The booming bell overwhelming all other sounds.

Table 18.2   Selective sound treatment

Sound selection	Interpretation
Scene: After a long hopeless day seeking work, a cripple returns through emptying streets.	
All sounds audible – of subject and background.	His footsteps sound amidst traffic and crowd noise.
The subject alone is heard.	His stumbling footsteps echo through quiet streets.
The subject plus selected background sounds.	His slow tread contrasts with the brisk steps of passers-by.
General background sounds alone.	Traffic noises. Passers-by.
Significant background sounds alone.	The laughter and gaiety from groups he passes; contrasting with his abject misery.
Interpretative sounds, not directly originating from the scene.	His echoing footsteps become increasingly louder and distorted. By progressively filtering out the higher audio-frequencies, his labored tread becomes emphasized.
Significant selected sounds from another *scene* (providing explanation or comment).	Voices of people refusing him work, echo in his brain.

So you can use the same sounds either *environmentally* or *atmospherically*; to suggest hope, dignity, community, domination . . . simply through selection, balance, and quality adjustment.

As you saw earlier (*substituted sound*), instead of modifying a scene's natural sounds, you might augment them or replace them by entirely fresh ones.

Audio-visual relationships

The picture and its audio can interrelate in several distinct ways:

1. *The picture's impact may be due to its accompanying audio.* A close-shot of a man crossing a busy highway . . .
   - (a) Cheerful music – suggests that he is in lighthearted mood.
   - (b) But automobile horns and squealing tires – suggest that he is jaywalking dangerously.
2. *The audio impact may be due to the picture.*
   - (a) A long shot of a wagon bumping over a rough road . . . and the accompanying sound is accepted as a natural audio effect.
   - (b) But take continuous close-ups of a wheel . . . and every jolt suggests impending breakdown!
3. *The effect of picture and audio may be cumulative.*
   A wave crashes against rocks . . . to a loud crescendo in the music.
4. *Sound and picture together may imply a further idea.*
   Wind-blown daffodils . . . birdsong, lambs bleating . . . can suggest Spring.

19 Visual effects

We use 'effects' to create an illusion. It may be simple and unobtrusive, or elaborately impressive. In more extreme applications, our audience will realize that there must have been some subterfuge, but many effects are subtle and their methods undetectable.

'Effects' are used for very *practical* reasons too: for convenience, economy, safety, reliability – and when a particular visual impact is not possible in other ways.

Pictorial effects are achieved by various means:

1. *Special effects* such as fire, explosions, fog, are a specialist craft, and best left to the expert. In amateur hands, the results can be uncertain, unconvincing or dangerous.
2. *Staging effects* include scenic illusions such as false perspective, scale changes (Chapter 8).
3. *Lighting effects* range from environmental impressions such as sunsets, to illusory effects – passing vehicles, water ripples, firelight (Chapter 7).
4. *Mirror effects* to reposition the camera viewpoint or multiply images.
5. *Projection effects* using front- or rear-projection images.
6. *Camera effects* using optical attachments.
7. *Foreground effects* in which the camera shoots through a foreground device.
8. *Electronic effects* resulting from manipulating or controlling the video signal.
9. *Temporal effects* involving the speeding, slowing or freezing of time.

Fig. 19.1   Basic laws of reflection
1. Light is reflected at an angle (R) equal to the angle of incidence (I). The *normal* is a line perpendicular to the mirror surface and starting from where the beams meet. The *incident* and *reflected* rays and the *normal* lie in the same plane.   2. The reflected image appears laterally reversed and as far behind the mirror as the subject is in front. The camera focuses on the subject image, not the mirror surface.

Fig. 19.2 part 1   Changing the viewpoint with mirrors – using a single mirror
1. Overhead (top) shot – image inverted and laterally reversed.   2. Reverse-angle top shot.   3. Very-low-angle shot.

Fig. 19.2 part 2   Changing the viewpoint with mirrors – using two mirrors
1. Overhead shot.   2. High-angle shot.   3. Low-angle shot.   4. Low-level shot (mirrors may be mounted separately, fixed in a portable periscope stand, or attached to the camera mounting).

Mirror effects

Mirrors are a simple straightforward way of creating certain illusions. Although vulnerable to marking, surface-silvered mirrors are preferable to rear-silvered types, which produce a tinted less-sharp image. Mirror-plastic, ferrotype or chromium sheeting, are successful for less critical applications where distortions can be tolerated or are required.

Mirrors are mostly used for overhead shots (demonstrations, piano, dancers) and for low-angle (periscope) shots. They can be time consuming to adjust and usually permit little camera movement. The mirror size needed increases with the camera/mirror distance and when using oblique mirror angles. Large mirrors are heavy and expensive items.

Having adjusted any mirror set-up during rehearsal; ensure that camera, mirror, and performer positions are clearly floor marked.

Where the lateral reversal (mirroring) is unacceptable, a further intermediate mirror or reversing prism can be introduced to correct the effect. While monochrome cameras can be either laterally or vertically reversed electronically, only the latter is possible directly with most color cameras. (Digital video effects systems where available, may provide lateral or horizontal reversal.)

Fig. 19.3   Area seen in a mirror
The easiest method of planning a mirror position and judging what it reflects, is to cut out a paper triangle of the lens angle (e.g. 25°), folding it at the anticipated mirror position and placing this on a scale floor plan. This indicates mirror size and distance required. (The smaller the mirror, the closer it must be to the camera.)

■ *Pepper's ghost*   An old theatrical device, the camera shoots through

Fig. 19.4   Mirrors to extend space
The camera's effective distance can be increased, to obtain a longer shot than studio space permits.

an angled sheet of clear glass or semi-transparent mirror (pellicle), which reveals the direct scene and/or a reflected scene, according to their relative lighting intensities (see Fig. 19.9).

The idea is widely used with display dioramas in museums (comparing before and after conditions). In television, we find it in *shadow boxes* which present a series of graphics simultaneously to one camera; cuts, superimpositions, dissolves between them being achieved by lighting changes.

The device is a useful aid to shadowless lighting for multiplane animated graphics. It also provides the background image for *reflex projection* systems (see Fig. 19.14).

Rear (back) projection *(see Fig. 19.10)*

Here the camera shoots action against a translucent screen of 'frosted' plastic; a film or slide being projected onto its rear side.

Once used extensively in motion pictures and monochrome TV, rear projection has been largely replaced in film by process work (matting during optical printing), or reflex projection; and in color TV by electronic insertion (chroma key, CSO).

Fig. 19.5   Multiple images
For multi-reflections, you can arrange mirrors: 1. Angled – the smaller the mirror-angle, the more the images (number = 360/angle).   2. Parallel mirrors.   3. Triple mirrors.

However, rear projection still has some useful applications in TV studios. As well as being used for pictorial rear projection, the translucent screen can be used to display silhouettes, shadows or pattern effects.

Front projection

We can project still or moving images directly onto a light-toned background, or even onto action for decorative or scenic effect.

Basic light patterns (from metal stencils) are most effective, but under typical full-lighting conditions, subtle half-tones and low-key images are disappointing. Geometric patterns and shapes, clouds, etc., are regularly

Fig. 19.6   Split screen reflection
A horizontal reflector (foil, mirror, clear glass) across the lens can provide reflected images, mirage or water-reflection effects.

Fig. 19.7   Mirror shot
Here a subject is shot together with a background mirror. The result is a combination of the direct and reflected images.

Fig. 19.8   One-way mirrors
The thin reflective coating on this one-way mirror makes it appear transparent (with a considerable light loss) from the rear unlit side (Cam 1); but as a normal mirror in the brightly-lit scene (Cam 2).

Glass Sheet

Fig. 19.9   Pepper's ghost
The out-of-shot person (B) is reflected into the lens as a transparent ghost within the main subject picture. Depending on the relative illumination, you can see A or B, or both (B ghostly).

projected onto cycloramas; and used to simulate natural light and shadow effects (window shadows). Scenic projectors can provide certain moving images (flames, sea-swell, snow) that are effective enough under favorable conditions. See Fig. 19.13.

Given *sufficiently sensitive* cameras and no spill light to dilute the image (so reducing its clarity and contrast), further interesting effects are possible, e.g. an announcer with newsprint projected onto his face, dancers against black drapes who are illuminated only by striped lighting.

Reflex projection

In this system (also called *front axial projection* or simply *front projection*) the background is projected directly along the TV camera's lens axis, via a half-silvered mirror, onto a special background screen material. The secret lies in this *highly directional* surface, comprising millions of minute glass beads, each reflecting nearly 92 per cent of the projected background image back to the camera. (The principle of this Scotchlite sheeting is identical to that used in many reflective traffic signs and night-safety clothing strips.) See Fig. 19.14.

Normal subject lighting cannot dilute the background image (unless placed near the camera) thanks to the screen's directionality. Where the front projected *background* image falls onto the performer or foreground subjects, it is swamped by action lighting and so is not visible on camera. Shadows from it are cast directly behind subjects and so are unseen by the camera, providing the system is accurately aligned, and the lens angles of the camera and projector are comparable.

Although not a foolproof system, it can provide near-miraculous effects for both film and TV cameras. Its limitations include: mirror light losses; lighter subject tones can be reflected in dark screen areas, causing edge haloes; the system must be aligned to avoid dark subject edges; and the studio camera must be *static* in most applications.

If pieces of reflex screen material are cut out and positioned to match objects or planes in the background picture (e.g. wall, tree, couch, archway), the studio performer can seemingly walk 'behind' them very convincingly.

Camera filters

Filters of various kinds can be clipped over the front of the lens or inserted in a *filter-wheel* holder within the camera.

■ *Neutral density filters* These have various light transmissions (Chapter 3) and are used to prevent gross overexposure when working under strong sunlight.

■ *Corrective filters* When there are changes in the color temperature of light sources these filters can be used to compensate e.g. when moving from daylight to tungsten-lit areas.

Fig. 19.10   Rear projection
1. A slide or film image is projected onto one side of a matte translucent screen. On the reverse side, a camera shoots action for which the screen image provides a background.   2. The rear-projected image can be used as a complete scenic background with foreground set-pieces, furniture, etc.; or (3) used to supplement a built set; (e.g. window backing); or (4) to extend a built set.

Fig. 19.11   Folding the light path
By folding the light-path with a mirror, floor space can be saved. Using a second mirror even greater compactness is possible, but with a further loss of clarity.

■ *Star filters* These are clear discs with closely scribed grid patterns. Diffraction effects produce multi-ray patterns (typically 4, 6, 8) around highlights from flames, specular reflections, and lamps. (Sunburst versions may have some sixty rays!) The rays' directions change as the filter is turned.

■ *Diffusion discs* Available in various densities, these filters provide

Fig. 19.12   Background distortion
Unless the studio camera is perpendicular to the flat two-dimensional background picture, distortion occurs. Similarly, the projector must be dead square to the screen to avoid distortion.

—Enclosed
Glass Disc

Fig. 19.13   Scenic projector
An enclosed glass disc with painted or
photographed patterns is rotated at an
adjustable speed by a small motor.
This device is attached to a projector
spotlight and focused onto a background to simulate moving clouds,
snow, water patterns, etc. The low
image-intensity usually restricts the
usable image-size.

general image softening through fine surface scratches or dimpling on a clear disc. Nylon or muslin net or hose may be similarly used. Sharp detail is reduced and highlights develop glowing haloes. To produce localized softening or distortion, a clear glass disc can be lightly smeared with grease or oil where required – usually round the edges. The effect can be ethereal, or woolly and irritating. But never treat the actual camera lens, for this would damage its special surface coating!

■ *Low-contrast filters* When used, these desaturate and mute colors, while softening contrast.

■ *Fog filters* Made in different densities, these create image diffusion from slight mist to dense fog, with strongly haloed highlights.

■ *UV (haze) filters* When used on daylight exteriors, these help to reduce haze blur due to ultra-violet light.

■ *Night filters* These are graded neutral density or blue-tinted filters (denser at the top) used to simulate night or evening scenes. By heavy filtering (particularly the sky areas) and considerably reducing overall exposure, it is possible to shoot 'night scenes' during daylight ('day for night' shooting) – thereby saving money and avoiding lighting problems.

■ *Color filters* These are rarely used on *color* TV cameras, as hue changes can be introduced electronically. In monochrome, they facilitate lightening/darkening the tonal reproduction of parts of the spectrum.

Table 19.1   Rear projection/BP

Advantages	The system is adaptable and simple to use.
	The background image is visible to performers.
	Compact screens can provide backgrounds outside small scenic openings (e.g. automobile windows).
	Rear projection can provide displays panels in settings to show graphics, titles, microscope shots, film clips, etc.
Disadvantages	Studio space is wasted due to the projector-to-screen distance (*throw*) required, especially for large screens.
	Projectors occupy floor space.
	Projector noise may be audible.
	Subject illumination may spill onto the screen, diluting its image. (A black scrim layer over the screen may improve matters.)
	The projected image may be: insufficiently bright, have a central hot spot or edge darkening.
	Only slides or film can normally be projected. (Film is susceptible to vertical *hop* and horizontal *weaving*). Projected TV images are seldom of suitable quality when shot by the studio camera.
	The rear projected picture's apparent sharpness will vary with the studio camera's focusing and depth of field.
	Matching of the projected background and foreground subject/scene may pose problems: perspective, scale, light direction, contrast, color quality, etc.
	Problems can arise in matching audio perspective and quality to varying projected backgrounds.

Fig. 19.4   Reflex projection
1. In Reflex (axial) Front Projection, the background scene is projected along the lens axis, via a half-silvered mirror, onto a highly directional glass-beaded screen. Actors' lighting swamps the image falling on them.   2. People appear *in front* of the background scene.   3. If people move behind a surface covered with beaded material, they will appear *behind* corresponding areas of the background scene (walls, trees, etc.).

■ *Polarizing filters*   These are occasionally used to reduce strong reflections or flares from smooth or shiny surfaces such as glass or water. (They have little effect for rough materials.) Polarizing filters can be used to darken an overbright sky without affecting overall color quality; although light loss is inevitable (e.g. 75 per cent loss). The filter's properties derive from its crystalline structure, which enables it to discriminate against light reflected at around 35°. By rotating the filter, you can selectively reduce or suppress particular reflections.

Lens attachments

A variety of add-on devices can be attached to the lens to modify the image:

■ *Multiple images*   These can be produced by prismatic or multifaceted

Fig. 19.15   Prismatic lenses
The number and position of images is determined by the facets on the lens. The peripheral images move round as the lens is turned but remain upright.

Fig. 19.16   The Kaleidoscope
1. Shooting through a three- or four-sided mirror-tube, produces an upright central image surrounded by angled reflections, that move round as the tube turns.   2. Two angled mirrors provide multiple converging images. (Number of images equals 360 divided by angle of mirrors.) Surface-silvered mirrors are needed to avoid spurious ghost images.

lenses. One form splits the screen into a series of repeat-image strips. Another has a static central image facet surrounded by a series of repeat versions, while a further form provides a ring of merging images. Their image patterns can be repositioned or rotated about the center by a small handle (or motor control), the images remaining upright; unlike those from the simple *kaleidoscope* mirror tube.

■ *Image distortion*   Methods available for distorting the image include shooting through molded ripple or patterned glass, via a flexible mirror, or water dish, or a foil tube giving peripheral effects. Fisheye lenses cover a wide angle of view (e.g. 100°–360°), providing extreme geometrical (curvature) distortion.

■ *Image rotation*   Several mirror or prismatic attachments enable you to rotate, invert, or tilt the picture. Apart from ceiling walking, you can simulate floating in free-space, flying, cliff climbing and other feats – the easy way. The most frequent use, however, if for *canted* (*dutch angle*) shots in which the picture is horizontally tilted for dramatic effect. If the image is to be rotated continuously, this must be done smoothly and at a suitable speed.

■ *Split-field close-up lenses*   These are used to overcome extreme depth-of-field problems, for they can provide sharp images of both close, *and* distant subjects simultaneously.

Fig. 19.17   Ripple distortion
1. The camera shoots into a shallow mirror-bottomed water tank, giving an inverted ripple image.   2. The camera shoots into a mirror periscope containing a water-filled glass tray. Ripples can be made to flow across the picture, finally breaking it up altogether. If an opaque liquid is poured into the tray, the picture blots out with a fluid wipe.

Camera mattes (gobos)

For many years, solid or transparent foreground devices have been used in motion picture making to create composite visual effects. Although often replaced in TV by electronic insertion methods, they still remain a useful facility. These *mattes* (masks) or *gobos* ('go-between') take several forms. (The term 'gobo' is also used for a black surface that masks off lights or cameras appearing in shot.) See Figure 19.20.

■ *Foreground matte*   At its simplest, this is just a plain surface with a

Fig. 19.18 part 1   Tilting the picture – using mirrors
Tilted shots can be obtained from (1) elevated or (2) depressed angles using canted mirrors. Shooting via a 45° mirror (3) attached to the lens system, causes the scene to cant as the camera tilts.

Fig. 19.18 part 2   Tilting the picture – using prisms
1. The Porra prism (a pair of reversing prisms). Rotating one of the prisms causes the image to rotate. A similar device can be constructed from two sets of double mirrors.
2. Image inverter prism (straight-through reversing prism). Rotating the assembly causes the picture to revolve.   3. A device similar to 2 uses a three-mirror assembly. Lateral reversal takes place.

Fig. 19.19   Split-field close-up lens
A half-lens (½ to 3 diopters) provides a sharp image of a close object, although the main lens is sharply focused on a distant subject; so simulating a considerable depth of field. The broad band of confused focus at the border, is arranged in a subject-free area.

hole in it, through which distant studio action is seen. Painted black, it provides a soft-edged isolating *vignette* (stencil) selecting part of a scene, for example:

To superimpose or insert somebody's head into another shot.

To create a shaped border, simulating a telescope, binoculars, keyhole. See Figure 19.20.

To provide localized *chroma key insertion*, a colored foreground matte board (e.g. blue) is used. See Figure 19.36.

The foreground matte may be used to introduce a *decorative border*, or a *framed opening* (picture frame), or a *realistic* scenic effect (a window). Often the camera dollies forward and 'enters' the scene as it loses the matte. *Cartoon gobos* are 'funnies', where the performer appears behind the cut-out section of a comic drawing, or pokes his head through a hole.

■ *Insertion matte* Sometimes the foreground matte is intended to merge imperceptibly with the background scene, e.g. a foreground photograph with a cut-out area, or a painted *glass-shot* putting a matching ceiling 'onto' a studio setting. The scale, perspective, lighting, colors, tones, etc., of 'foreground' and background must be matched accurately to be really convincing and action must not normally move behind the matte opening (or it will disappear). When using insertion mattes, we must have considerable depth of field or overall sharpness may not be feasible.

Foreground miniatures (models) are occasionally used to extend the scene, but these are usually rudimentary – foliage, saloon swing doors, drapes, pillars, arches. *Transparent mattes* can provide a decorated foreground plane showing titling or graphics (a world map, shop window sign, patterns, etc.); the camera pulling focus from the foreground to the background scene.

Fig. 19.20   Foreground mattes
This is a foreground surface (plain or decorated), through part of which the distant scene is visible. It has several purposes: 1. Selectivity isolating an item, e.g. for localized superimposition.   2. A pattern vignette, e.g. keyhole effect.   3. Scenic foreground, e.g. a window through which camera shoots. A breakthrough frame parts to enable the camera to dolly 'through' the foreground.   4. Insertion, e.g. a studio subject is apparently inserted into an area within a foreground graphic.   5. A glass-shot, e.g. positioning a foreground painted ceiling 'on' a studio setting.

Electronic effects

The pictorial opportunities that electronic effects can provide are endless. The more you use them, the more will you discover fresh applications for both realistic and abstract picture treatment. They combine practical economies with a fascinating magic that never palls.

■ *Superimpositions* As we saw in Chapter 6, when two picture sources are faded up together, their pictures intermix. The relative strengths of their images are *additive* and can be adjusted, but:

1. Where *black* appears in either shot, the other shot's detail appears firm and solid.
2. Where *white* appears in either shot, the other shot's detail appears diluted, paled out. A peak white can burn through another shot's detail.
3. Where different hues appear in both shots, they form a new color mixture (e.g. $R+G=Y$).

■ *Black level adjustment* By electronically darkening the lowest picture tones until they crush to a solid overall black (batting down on blacks, sitting down) you can:

1. Ensure that 'black' materials (black drapes, black title cards) reproduce as a firm black without wrinkles or shading.
2. Prevent slight tonal variations and construction being seen in hand-animated graphics – e.g. to make a black strip (with white titling) merge with its black background card.
3. Make parts of a subject disappear – e.g. a black-gloved hand against black drapes will disappear while light-toned objects that are held, remain visible.

To make a near-*white* tone merge with a white area, you increase exposure so that lightest tones merge (burn-out, clip off) at white-clipper video limits.

■ *Picture weave/electronic ripple* Many switchers include a device that introduces a sideways ripple into a picture. Its rate and strength are adjustable. Straightforward picture weave is used to simulate flashbacks, or in transformations. But combined with multiple wipe patterns (Fig. 6.12 part 4), you can break the picture up to provide a variety of undulating, decoratively-shaped transitions.

■ *Negative picture* Electronic switching enables you to reverse picture *tones* (reverse polarity) so that they become *negative*. White reproduces as black, black as white. This is a useful facility for changing standard white-on-black titling to black-on-white (to improve clarity on light backgrounds). It can also be used to produce negative images or to reproduce negative monochrome film.

■ *Complementary picture* Color can be transformed into its complementary hues – red, green, and blue become cyan, magenta,

Normal   Weave

Fig. 19.21 Electronic weave/ripple effects
An S-distortion (of variable strength and speed) is created electronically by varying the line-trigger pulse.

yellow. This system enables us to directly transmit negative color film. Reversal can be used dramatically, too: transforming smoke, clouds, steam; creating black highlights glistening in a white sea; black lightning in a white sky.

■ *Camera channel adjustment*   The color TV camera channel requires careful adjustments for optimum picture quality. But, by making certain changes from standard line-up, you can obtain some interesting visual effects:

1. Reduction of the camera tube's beam current (*beam limiting/ debeaming*) causes light tones to lose sharpness and intensity, and wash out (*puddle*).
2. The *video gain* or the *black level* controls of the RGB channels can be altered to give or correct a color cast in light or dark tones, or overall. So you can provide color effects that would otherwise require extensive colored lighting (suggesting moonlight, firelight, candlelight).

■ *Video feedback*   TV cameramen soon discover that by shooting a picture monitor showing their own output, they can obtain interesting repeat-image effects. When you mix this camera's repeat-video with that from *another source* (in the studio switcher) and feed this combination back to that picture monitor, all manner of interesting multi-effects develop. (Two or more cameras can be used.) This technique can produce a variety of dynamic patterns, transformations and surround images.

Interesting effects are obtainable, too, if you take a defocused shot of a subject on a picture monitor and superimpose it on the original picture. The resultant halo creates a convincing aura around 'supernatural' beings.

If positive and negative images of a subject are intermixed, a strangely 'solarized' image results, that can be further processed by video feedback.

Keyed insertion (electronic matting)

Electronic insertion processes can provide in an instant, illusions that in film making involve costly expertise, laboratory apparatus, and time. Nowadays TV production switchers have many of these associated effects facilities ready at the touch of a button! They have become an everyday tool, offering challenging opportunities.

■ *How it works*   Electronic insertion is an ingenious interswitching process, used to selectively combine different picture sources. It is virtually a process of 'cutting a hole' in one picture and inserting exactly a corresponding piece of another picture. (Seldom putting one picture *over* another.)

As you know, a TV picture is normally formed by scanning the scene's image in a series of horizontal lines. The switcher selects which source is sent to line. However, suppose we had an instantaneous electronic switch

Fig. 19.22   Inter-source switching
1. If an electronic switch changes from Cam 1's picture to Cam 2's output halfway through each line period, the resultant *split screen* combines those parts of the shots.
2. If the switching moment is earlier in the line, the division is displaced left.
3. Occurring later in the line, the division is displaced right. The shots may be composed to suit the division being used; or the division located to suit the composition.   4. If the apparatus is arranged to select the top half of Cam 1's picture, switching to Cam 2 for the remainder of the frame, the result with these particular shots is nonsensical.

available, so that the system switches itself between sources *during* this scanning process. We might, for instance, begin *each* scanning line by showing Cam. 1's picture but half way through that line switch to Cam. 2's shot instead. (Switching back to Cam. 1 at the end of each line.) Because of this interswitching, the resultant transmitted composite would show the left half of Cam 1's picture and the right half of Cam. 2's picture. (You will recognize this particular example as a split-screen effect.)

Altering the exact switching moment, repositions whereabouts the division appears in the frame. If we *gradually alter* the switchover moment, a *moving* division, a *wipe* is produced; in this example, a horizontal wipe movement.

This intersource switching is initiated automatically by a *keying* or

Fig. 19.23   Special-effects generator (SEG)
The SEG provides voltages of variable waveforms (square, parabolic, triangular, etc.). These control the exact switching pattern of the keying amplifier, so producing a series of geometrical matte shapes.

matting signal we apply to the system. This signal can be produced in several ways and may be:

1. An *external key or matte* – from a separate specially generated waveform (SEG, camera matte, prepared film).
2. An *internal key or matte* (self-keying) – derived from a selected tone or color in one of the pictures involved (chroma key).

If sources are instantaneously *interswitched*, there will be a sharp hard-edged division between their pictures. If the insertion circuits rapidly *mix* (dissolve) between them, the result is a soft edged (diffused) transition with one source merging into the next at the borders.

■ *Tonal and color mattes* Depending on the equipment used, you can actuate any keying process by:

1. A *tonal matte* (*luminance key, insert key*) – The system switches from the background picture to the foreground shot, wherever it sees a black (or white) matte – however this is derived.
2. A *color* matte (as in chroma key or CSO) switches only where it sees a particular hue (usually blue).

External key

■ *Special-effects generator (SEG)* This produces a series of electronic waveforms. Its output is used as an external keying signal to interswitch sources. Depending on the shape and frequency of the waveform used, so the picture divisions will differ. If its switching sequence continually repeats, the pattern appears stationary. If it gradually alters, the divisions will move across the frame and/or change the divisions' shape. The effects produced are entirely independent of the pictures involved.

The interswitching divisions produce by the SEG are invariably *geometric*. They have the following features:

1. They can be controlled in *speed* (fader lever or *autowipe*).
2. They can be *directed* (expand/contract, up/down, left/right).
3. Their *symmetry* and *position* are controllable (wipe center selection by a joystick positioner control).
4. The pattern can be adjusted and left as a static *insert* (*inset*).
5. The *edges* may be hard (sharp) or soft (diffused).
6. A border (black, white, color) can be placed around the insert.

Fig. 19.24 Wipes
Wipes can be controlled in various ways: (1) direction; (2) position; (3) symmetry; (4) edge sharpness. Changes can be made at any speed. (See Fig. 6.12)

Graphic
Matte

Fig. 19.25   Camera matte
The graphic in front of the matting camera (3) results in a video signal which inter-switches Cam 1 (flowers) with Cam 2 (girl) in a heart-shaped mask form. Wherever complex, non-geometrical matte shapes are required (e.g. tree-branch patterns, flower shapes, decorative screens, etc.), camera mattes are used.

7. The pattern may be made to *weave* (ripple) at an adjustable speed and strength.

8. Spotlight pointer, or magnifying-glass effects (central enlargement), can draw attention to a feature (Fig. 19.33).

■ *Physical mattes*   Instead of using electronically operated waveforms (SEG), intersource switching can also be derived from a physical matte (mask) – 'separate key mode' – provided by:

1. A *camera matte* – a graphic placed in front of a TV camera.
2. An *electronic rostrum camera* (masking scanner, inlay desk). (Fig. 19.26).
3. *Prepared film or VT masks*. (See vignette/surround matte, page 382).

Fig. 19.26   Electronic rostrum camera (inlay desk)
Using this external keying apparatus, even elaborate masks are practical.   1. TV camera – the overhead monochrome TV camera shoots a back-lit white panel. Cut-out card, inked or painted shapes, provide a matte for the keying signal.   2. Picture tube – the matte is placed or drawn on a *cel* (clear plastic sheet) or glass, over a picture tube displaying a plain white picture (raster) – a flying-spot scanner. The phototube picks up a constant scanning output (i.e. peak white video) except where interrupted by the matte. Adjustment of the scanning width or height alters the effective matte shape. Zooming produces matte size changes.   3. Keying signal – this is fed to the montage amplifier, where it inter-switches between the cameras' outputs.

■ *Camera matte* Here a studio camera shoots a graphic with the required matte shape (mask, key) e.g. a black silhouette on a white background (or vice versa). The video from this masking camera is used solely to operate intersource switching (via a *keying amplifier*). Its picture as such is not used. Even if the matte is of a complicated shape (a map silhouette), it will key a corresponding area from one chosen picture into another.

The key could equally well be derived from a static matte in a *slide scanner*:

Cam. 1 shooting a brick wall photograph.
Cam. 2 shooting a striped surface.
Matting slide – Title slide.
Matted result – Lettering in striped paint, on a brick wall.

Moving camera mattes are also possible:

Cam. 1 – A cloud scene.
Cam. 2 – Glittering reflections (defocused tinsel).
Cam. 3 – Silhouette of dancer in studio, used as a matte.
Matted result – A glittering shape dancing amongst clouds.

Self-keying (self-matting internal key)

The most sophisticated method of keying requires no *prepared* matte/mask or waveform. Instead, it continually examines the video from the master or foreground shot and wherever the system detects a specified tone or hue (depending on the process used), it switches instead to another picture – the background. In this *common-key mode*, therefore, the matting signals originate from the master picture itself.

If you are using a *tonal-keying*/luminance keying process wherever the chosen tone (black or white) appears in the foreground shot, a corresponding part of a background is seen instead in the composite

Fig. 19.27　Self-keying/self-matting
Wherever a selected *tone* (or *hue* if you use *chroma-key/CSO*) appears in the *master shot* (the subject or foreground shot), a corresponding part of the background shot is seen instead. The system switches back to the master shot for all other tones (or hues) in that scene. *Background* scene tones or hues do not affect keying in either system.

Fig. 19.28   Choice of system
External key does not normally allow foreground subjects to move *in front of* background features. The subject disappears when it moves outside the matted area.   1. This is appropriate when people are to move behind walls, trees, etc.   3. It is incongruous if they were to get out of a vehicle matted in by external key. *Any* tone or color may be used in foreground and background scenes. (Switching is due to a separate matte.)

Self-keying relies on hues (or tones) within the master (subject/foreground) shot. So subjects cannot normally move *behind* background features.   2. The effect can be incongruous in certain situations (people may appear to stand in space).   4. Where appropriate, the technique is convincing. The subject itself should not contain (or reflect) the keying hue (or tone). The background may contain any colors or tones.

picture. So areas of the keying *tone* must only appear in the *foreground* scene where you require insertion; otherwise you will see spurious breakthrough. The background would be visible through a black necktie! Any tone may appear in the *background* scene, however. This *tonal keying* process can be used in monochrome *and* color TV systems.

Using a *color keying process* (chroma-key, CSO color separation overlay), wherever the selected keying/switching *hue* appears in the master scene, the background is switched in instead. Again, any color or tone may appear in the background scene. The *color* keying process can only be used in a color system.

Using keyed insertion

Some applications for keyed insertion are obvious; other are extremely subtle. Certain effects can be achieved by either external or self-keying methods. Others are only possible using specifically designed equipment. In the following section, we shall look at the most frequently used processes.

■ *Inserted titles*   Printed information has often to be introduced into a picture to supply identification or to add data. This titling can be provided by camera title cards, a photoslide, or an electronic alphanumeric character generator, and inserted in several ways:

1. *Superimposition* may result in 'transparent' lettering; tone and color varying with the background.
2. Where the switcher has a *non-additive mix* (NAM) facility, the source

with the *lightest* tones (usually titling) inserts 'solidly' into the associated picture.

3. *Keyed insertion* permits lettering of any tone or hue to be solidly punched into a background picture, without interaction effects.

However, even an inserted letter becomes indistinguishable if its tone or color exactly match its background. To improve clarity you can:

1. Use a *border generator*. Edge-keying electronically creates an edge shadow outline around lettering. This can be black (black edge), white, or of selectable color; the width of this surround being constant throughout, or adjustable to produce contouring (drop shadow). It is even possible to use the original lettering as a matte and transmit its outline instead.

2. Change the lettering tone or color by *infilling* it with a different one; e.g. white lettering is used to produce a matte, which keys in any chosen color; the result being colored titling.

Table 19.2 Keying methods compared

	Advantages	Disadvantages
External key (Using SEG, camera matte, slide matte)	Simple to operate and adjust.	Complex scenic mattes (ceiling insert) may require accuracy in construction and adjustment
	Reliable and definite in action.	
	No spurious breakthrough between pictures.	*The camera set-ups for recording must usually be identical to rehearsed version.
	Any tones/colors usable in foreground subjects *and* background shots.	*Normally, foreground and background cameras should remain static. Any film must be free from hop or weaving in static scenes.
	Only the matted area is inserted into the composite.	
	No mutual degradation of picture quality (unlike *superimpositions*).	*In pictorial insertions, foreground and background shots should match in perspective, proportions, scale, lighting. etc.
	Studio area required for insertion may be confined.	*The *whole* of one picture source cannot normally be inserted into *part* of another shot (*see Fig. 19.30*).
	Sharp matte edges keep edge ragging to a minimum.	But appropriate or accidental cut-off or disappearances can arise.
	Subjects disappear behind matted areas. Appropriate when moving *behind* walls, objects . . .	
Self-keying/self-matting (using chroma key, CSO)	Operation is automatic.	Similar to *external key* disadvantages marked *.
	No mattes/masks have to be prepared.	The keying/matting tone or color must only be present where 'background' is required. Shadows or reflections may cause spurious breakthrough.
	Subject movement is not confined (but may need restriction, to suit background scene).	Edge ragging, color fringing, arise.
	Various tones or hues can be used, for differential keying.	When inserting into long shots, a large studio area may require chroma key background and floor unless keying foreground matte/gobo is used.
	Foreground subjects always move *in front* of background and cannot be cut off by matte or inadvertently disappear . . .	But the effect may not be appropriate and foreground matting flat or external matte may be necessary also.

Fig. 19.29   Title insertion
1. Titles introduced by *superimposition* are satisfactory against plain backgrounds (preferably white letters against black), but otherwise, mutual interaction reduces evenness and clarity.   2. *Inserted* letters cut through all picture tones; but for tilting against similar tones (white on white, gray on gray) black-edging is desirable. 3. Sometimes an *inset area* (mid-gray presenting black or white titling) is more distinctive. It does not require a border. But the overall effect may be intrusive.

3. Using *double re-entry switching*, you can introduce texture or patterning into titles.

A *background generator* (field generator, colorizer, color synthesizer) produces color electronically, that may be used to colorize background and/or titling independently. *Cycling* can cause this color to self-change throughout the spectral range. In addition, lettering may be rhythmically blinked or flashed if required.

■ *Display screen* Keyed insertion can simulate a wall-screen in a setting, to display illustrations, photoenlargements, maps, etc.

1. *External matte* (using a box wipe inset or a camera matte) is easily introduced into any shot. While avoiding chroma-key problems, this

Table 19.3   Chroma key; internal key/self-keying

Check for *unwanted areas of keying color* in the master scene, that could cause spurious switching and background breakthrough, e.g. blue clothing or articles, nearby chroma key surface color reflecting onto subject, blue reflections in eyeglasses, shiny surfaces, etc.

Watch for *deep shadows* (particularly subject's) falling on chroma key surfaces, patchy lighting, unevenly painted or draped chroma key surface. These can all lead to spurious breakthrough, ragged edges, etc.

To give a performer an accurate *eyeline*, have him look towards a distant colored lamp.

In a total chroma key situation (blue background and floor), place discs of chroma key hue on the floor to give talent *location marks*.

Where a person (or object) has to be keyed in *correct scale/perspective* into a background scene, at various distances, use the following technique: Lock off the *background* camera, and watch its picture displayed on a picture monitor. Mark reasonably accurately scaled vertical lines (wax pencil, felt pen) on this scene, that are proportionate to a person standing in those positions. Using a normal lens angle, take a long shot of the chroma key area so that the foreground performer matches the nearest marker (in location and height). Then move him to the farthest position.

If the perspective and camera height are correct, he will match the marker. If he looks shorter than the distant marker, zoom in and dolly back a little, and repeat near and far matching again for optimum results.

If the subject appears to move upwards disproportionately as he goes to the further position, lower the subject camera's viewpoint slightly.

If the subject camera overshoots or sees cameras, boom, lights, obscure them with a chroma key camera matte or a localized wipe.

2   Subject Cut Off

3

4

5

Fig. 19.30   Display screen
1. A 'wall display' screen can be simulated by self-matting (chroma key). 2. External keying can only be used when nothing moves into this area.   3. A 'screen' may be used to include a distant guest in a studio interview.   4. This is achieved by using a corresponding chroma key area in the main shot.   5. Care must be taken that the person to be inset is in proportion and position for the display screen.
To insert the whole of one picture into part of another, a picture monitor must be used (or a digital effects unit). Monitors should be shaded from reflected or spill light, color-adjusted (yellow bias), preferably using a dark screen (black matrix) tube. Quality unavoidably deteriorates.

method does restrict performers, who *must not* move in front of the matted area (*cut-off* problems).
2. *Self-keying* requires a chroma-key panel in the setting (a blue panel or blind, a blue light patch), this keying hue being excluded from the rest of the master scene.

■ *Inset/Insert*   You normally introduce a *detail insert* into a wider shot by wiping in and holding the required shape (e.g. to show a close-up soloist within a full orchestra long shot, a box or iris wipe is positioned in the selected part of the screen). A hard-edged inset is usually preferable, to prevent image confusion – perhaps with a colored border to emphasize demarcations. Occasionally a soft (diffused) edge is unobtrusively effective – for a dream montage or a 'thinks' bubble (Fig. 19.24).

Main Scene   Detail Shot   Matte   Composite

Fig. 19.31   Inset
To introduce close-up detail while retaining the main shot, an inset can be used (created by any method).

■ *Vignette/surround matte*   You can use keyed insertion to provide decorative surrounds or borders to an insert subject, or to form symbolic shapes (keyhole, telescope, binoculars, heart). Geometrical patterns are available on the SEG.
    By blanking out parts of the shot, you can exclude unwanted subjects. The support stand of a world globe could be matted out, so that it appeared in 'free space' – perhaps inserting a skyscape into the now black surround.
    Regular opening titles sequences (film or VT) can include chroma key color patches in the pictures, into which live studio shots of 'today's guest' can be inserted.

1   2

Fig. 19.32   Surround matte
Mattes can be used: 1, to mask off unwanted material in the shot, or 2, to simulate a vignette.

Fig. 19.33 Indicators
Visual indicators in the form of an arrow, ring, spotlight (devised electronically or by any matting method), can identify specific detail.

■ *Indicators* Many switchers include facilities for inserting indicators, that draw attention to specific information – in maps, charts, diagrams, photographs. Arrows, surround-rings, spotlight effects (a lightened disc on darkened background) are widely used, and located by joystick positioning; often with a 'blink' option.

■ *Appearance/Dissapearance* This is simply achieved, by switching or fading the insertion in and out.

■ *Multisplit screen* This is a method of showing information from several shots simultaneously, by dividing the screen into 2, 3, 4 or more sections (with or without border lines).
Individual segments may show:

1. *Different views* of the same situation (reactions and prize giving at a game show).
2. A *montage* of concurrent events (different rescuers moving to the disaster area).
3. *Sequences* (steps in the development of a product).
4. *Groupings* of subjects with a common significance (all members of the team).

The multisplit screen can be achieved by: (see Fig. 19.34)

1. *Sequential insertion* (Quad overlay) – The switcher treats pictures in turn; matting out a chroma-key area, passing the matted result on to combine with the next source (with its chroma-key area), matting from

Fig. 19.34 part 1   Type of split screen
Several forms of divided screen are widely used: 1. Split screen.   2. Triple split.
3. Quad split.   4.   Multi-split.

Fig. 19.34 part 2   Methods of creating split screen effects
Several methods are used: *sequential switching* – the system selecting each source in turn for a certain period. *Sequential insertion* – after the first picture has been treated, part of a further picture is matted in. The next source is inserted into that composite . . . and so on. Other techniques include VT build-up (see Fig. 19.42), or digital image-processing.

Table 19.4   Electronic insertion terms

Background	The picture into which the foreground subject is electronically inserted. Can usually contain any tone or color.
Blink, flasher	Blinks a keyed insert (tilting, symbol) at an adjustable rate.
Character generator, alphanumeric generator	Equipment synthetically generating lettering, numerals, signs.
Chroma-key process	Several systems exist, including: 1. Fast switching chroma key, using *encoded* composite video signals (e.g. video coded into NTSC form with syncs). 2. Similar system using direct RGB (decoded) video signals (more precise, less noise or spurious switching). 3. *Ultimatte*, which derives separate black matted images, that are then superimposed in an additive mix.
Chroma keyer	Equipment controlling chroma-key operations. 1. Selects hue of keying color. 2. Selects input for chroma-key treatment. 3. Selects edge-switching (hard, soft. color).
Color synthesizer, colorizer, color field generator	Equipment generating color synthetically, by applying selected voltages to the RGB channels.
Cycling	Synthesizer cycles through spectral colors (or flashes the luminance/brightness level).
Downstream key, title key	Provides titling insertion while the main effects system is already in use (e.g. for chroma key). It inserts titles or any external key into the switcher's *line output*. May be used to fade program to black.
Double re-entry, cascade re-entry	The output of one mix/effects-bus amplifier (A/B) can be re-entered into another (C/D) for successive additional treatment. So we can mix to or from combined shots (keyed-in titles, split screen, supers, chroma key). Also, a key from an external matte source may be used to create a matted area in one shot, that is filled in by another camera's background.
Edge key, border generator, black-edge	Introduces a black, white, or color border; or derives an outline on any matted-in subject.
External key	Interswitching between two sources, actuated by a *separate* video source (SEG, camera matte).
Foreground	The subject inserted into the background shot. In chroma key, contains the keying color.
Hard key	Sharp-edged matting. Imperfections (tearing) are very visible at subject edges.
Hue control	Adjusts the actual color used for keying matte (usually blue, yellow or green).
Internal key, self-keying, self-matting	Interswitching between two sources, using a tone or hue within the subject picture itself to provide the key (fed into a mix/effects bus).
Key edge	Controlling keying amplifier gain for the chroma key insertion of *transparent materials*. (*Linear keying*).
Key fill	Selects the source or color of infill for insert titling.
Key level, clipper, clipping level, clip control, threshold level	Adjusts the exact brightness (luminance) in the foreground matte, at which the background shot is inserted. Adjusted on preview to suit each shot. If incorrect, tearing, spurious breakthrough occurs.

Linear keying, transparent matte, proportional keying	A facility enabling transparent subjects to be inserted, while permitting background to be seen 'through' them.
Luminance	Control of brightness level (in monochrome) or saturation (in color).
Luminance key, tonal key, inlay	A self-matting process, in which a selected tone (black or white) in the master/subject shot is replaced in the composite picture by a corresponding area of the background shot.
Matte, key	A shape (mask) supplying a signal to a keying amplifier, causing it to switch from one source to another in the matted area, integrating the respective images. Can be derived from a camera-picture, or specially generated electronic waveforms.
Mode	Selects the function of the *bank fader lever*. The same lever may be used to: 1. MIX (LAP DISSOLVE) between buses (banks). 2. MASK KEY for wipe-pattern movement. 3. MIX KEY to fade in a key (matte) signal. 4. To provide a pattern transition between A and B buses.
Non-additive mix (NAM), peak mix mode, white insert mode, insert key	A circuit facility in which the lightest tones of one picture are inserted solid (opaquely) into another source's picture. Used for title insertion.
Pattern direction	Selects direction of movement with operation of fader control.
Pattern edge	Adjusts pattern's edge sharpness (hard, soft-edged) or width.
Pattern generator	Selection of interswitching patterns used for wipes and insets.
Pattern symmetry	Adjusts pattern shape and proportions.
Pattern weave	Adjusting a weave or ripple effect – speed, amplitude (extent), frequency (rate), direction, position, pattern shape.
Polarity, key reversal	Determines whether white or black is used for keying.
Position	Joystick positioning a pattern in the frame.
P/V (preview) bus key	The *preview bus* signal mattes a hole in the A bus picture and fills it with the B bus video.
Quad split	Simultaneous display, dividing the screen into four separate images. (SPLIT or VAR adjusts the division proportions.)
Sequential effects amplifier	Matting in a series of steps to produce a complex composite.
Shadow keyer	Subject shadows falling on the chromakey surface are normally lost with basic chromakey systems, or cause spurious tearing. 'Natural' shadow insertion is possible using special shadow-keying circuits.
Soft key	Diffused-edged matting (often adjustable). Edge imperfections are less visible; images can be blended together at borders.
Special effects generator (SEG)	Apparatus generating a series of electrical waveforms (square, sawtooth, triangular, parabolic), at line and field rate, from which switching patterns are derived; for wipes and inserts.
Spotlight	Background brightness reduced around a disc matte (joystick positioned).
Undercut	Switching in which the main subject picture is retained, while the background scene is changed. (Opposite of *Overcut*, in which the subject changes, appears, disappears, while the background remains.)

this combination, and so on. (Each insertion could use a different keying hue if required.)

2. *VT build-up* – Recording a split screen pattern; then reproducing the tape and matting in a further segment(s).
3. *Digital video effects* – Capturing a frame, reducing the image size, and positioning it beside other frozen images, in a multiframe store.

Chroma-key insertion techniques

Chroma-key has endless applications; especially when combined with other video effects. You can simulate total reality, or create magical, stylized, decorative displays. The opportunities are endless; the economies considerable. But you need to apply chroma-key carefully, keeping in mind its problems and limitations, if you are going to achieve convincing, accurate results. Forethought and careful planning can save a great deal of rehearsal time. So we shall look in some detail here at many of its potentials and its pitfalls.

■ *Compatibility* Foreground and background usually need to match in *pictorial* inserts: scale, perspective (lens angle, height, eyeline), color quality, contrast, light direction, etc. Incongruities can arise too, if the depth-of-field is restricted in foreground subjects, yet the inserted background appears quite sharp.

If the inserted foreground camera pans or tilts, the subject will appear to slide around the background. If you dolly or zoom the foreground camera, scale will be upset as the subject grows and shrinks. Unless you want such effects, therefore, foreground and background must normally remain stationary.

However, if foreground and background cameras move in synchronism, realistic pan/tilt/zoom changes are often possible. In simpler situations, skilled cameramen may actually coordinate their cameras' movements and achieve effective results. But the most reliable

Fig. 19.35 Background insertion
1. Substituted background – Using a self-matting/self-keying (usually chromakey) surface behind the subject, a different background can be substituted of plain tone or hue (perhaps color synthesized), decorative or pictorial. 2. Camera matte – This selects part of the studio scene, matting it into a background scene (graphic, photo, film, VT).

Fig. 19.36 Typical chroma-key set-ups
1. A chroma-key backing permits an 'exterior' to be inserted from a photograph.
2. Where (a) the floor is not in shot or (b) the studio floor area is required and foreground objects are to be included, a simple chroma-key flat is sufficient. 3. For longer shots, or where people are to appear higher in the frame, or the studio floor is to be substituted, a continuous chroma-key background and floor covering is necessary. 4. A camera matte in chroma-key hue masks off most of the studio, and inserts the visible area into the background scene. This method also avoids the need for large keying areas when inserting into long shots. The chroma-key surface must be evenly lit, and free from shadows, folds, etc., to give good clipping overall.

synchronism becomes possible if foreground and background cameras are ganged by electronic servo devices (as in 'Magicam' process). Then the foreground camera can tilt/pan/zoom and the background camera shooting a photograph, graphic, or model will move proportionately. In an alternative arrangement, the background derives from a static camera shooting a servo-controlled graphics stand or a rear-projection device (slide or film) – 'Scene-Sync' (Fig. 19.40).

Results can be extremely convincing as the foreground camera follows action and adjusts shot length. However, the background camera must turn on a correctly adjusted pivot center and its displacement rate match the relative lens angles used. Where possible, you should avoid visually critical situations; scenes involving perspective and parallactic movement (relative displacement of planes at different distances).

■ *Color fringing and edge ragging* Color fringes (of the keying hue) can

Background Scene

Chroma·Key Backing and Floor

Walks in front of Wall

Foreground Matte Matches Wall in scene

Walks behind Wall

Fig. 19.37 part 1   Foreground mattes – matting flat
A flat of chroma-key hue can be positioned within the chroma-key set-up to coincide with a wall in the photo background, so enabling a performer to 'move behind' it.

Background Scene   Normal Insertion   Camera Matte   Insertion + Camera Matte

Fig. 19.37 part 2   Foreground mattes – camera matte
Normally, when subjects are chroma-keyed into a scene, they appear in *front* of the background. But by introducing an *additional matte* (e.g. a silhouette camera matte as an external key), to suppress the chroma-key insertion in that area, you can make subjects 'move behind' parts of the background scene. Such matting can be switched in and out to allow moves in front and behind background objects.

Photo Background   Chroma·Key Backing Floor Matching Areas in Studio   Composite Result

Fig. 19.37 part 3   Foreground mattes – relating to background objects
By appropriately positioning suitable items in the chroma-key set-up (blocks, parallels, stairs, etc., painted in the keying hue), people can apparently sit, lean, climb, or put objects on features in the background shot.

develop round the borders of keyed-in subjects for several reasons: colored spill light, reflected keying hue, optical-flare problems, and inherently poor color detail (restricted band width). The often recommended 'remedy' of using yellow backlight only alleviates the problem, and is likely to tint the subject yellow! Some chroma-key systems are less susceptible to color fringing than others. Soft-edge keying can diminish the effect, but for total suppression special circuits (hue suppressors/ fringe eliminators, exclusive hue matrix) may prove necessary. Unfortunately, these may modify the reproduction of certain color mixtures.

When inserting fine detail (hair, lace, fur, feathers) or vague, unsharp

Fig. 19.38   Matching camera height
The height, angle of tilt, and lens angle, of the studio camera should be identical to that used to photograph the background scene, if distortion is to be avoided. Often the errors are not obvious.   1. Unmatched viewpoints.   2. Matched viewpoints.

subjects (smoke, steam) you will encounter edge ragging or break-up due to indecisive switching action, without such electronic compensation.

■ *Keying surface and hue* Strictly speaking, the actual color of the matting surface in the foreground scene should exactly match the keying hue chosen for the system – whether a colored surface or colored lighting is used. And it should present an even surface brightness overall. In practice, set-ups deviate considerably from this ideal and work successfully. Most studios use colored cyc cloths, flats, stretched cloth, painted floor cloths, and their brightness and spectral distribution can vary noticeably. The matte can, of course, originate equally well from graphics, film, videotape, or any other video source.

Although any *keying hue* may be used, this color must not be present in the foreground picture, or you will see spurious break-through and the background will appear instead. If you were to dress someone in clothes of the keying hue, they would progressively disappear. So total or localized 'invisibility' is readily achieved!

A highly saturated *blue* (approximately 'cobalt') is widely used for the keying hue, because it is chromatically most distinguishable from fresh colors and least likely to arise in foreground scenes. But where blue subject matter is unavoidable, yellow or green keying hues are often used instead. Circuitry can be so color specific (*exclusive hue*), that even close colors or color mixtures do not trigger spurious switching. Matting systems that rely on color comparison processes, rather than the direct color-keying method of chroma-key (e.g. *Ultimatte*), are less susceptible to breakthrough problems.

Fig. 19.39   Matching eyelines
1. The foreground subject matches its background's perspective only when the television camera's eyeline coincides with the eyeline of the background.
2. Background eyeline *above* subject eyeline.   3. Background eyeline *below* subject eyeline.

Fig. 19.40 Ganged backgrounds
By using a servo-controlled inter-connection ('ganging') between the subject (master) camera and the back-ground (slave) camera, the latter pans, tilts, and zooms automatically as the subject camera follows the action. Alternatively, the background graphic itself may be moved vertically/hori-zontally by servo systems (SCENE-SYNC SYSTEM) using a static slave camera.

■ *Shadow chroma-key* The chroma-key system extracts everything from the foreground scene that is not *blue* (if that is the keying hue) and inserts it into the background scene. So a person's shadow falling onto some foreground scenery will be keyed-in but not their floor shadow (a shade of blue). Performers' shadows falling onto a keying surface can actually cause irregular switching (reduced key matte strength), so we often avoid or illuminate them to prevent this.

Without floor shadows, however, inserted people may appear to 'float' and the illusion is spoiled – particularly where shadows are evident in the background scene. With shadow-key circuitry a natural shadow can be *simulated*. It detects the lower brightness (luminance) of the shadow on the keying surface, deriving a matte from it of adjustable sharpness and density, and introduces it transparently over the background scene. Extremely convincing, even its position can be relocated to match the background by including keying surfaces in the foreground scene.

■ *Transparent/translucent insertion* Basic chroma-key insertion tends to block out detail beyond transparent materials (glass, smoke) or show spurious triggering (tearing, ragging). By using suitable circuitry (*linear/proportional keying*) it becomes possible to 'see through' a glass surface in the foreground shot and key it into the background scene without spurious effects.

■ *Moving backgrounds* Where a photostill us used for the background scene, you should avoid any 'frozen' features (waves, smoke, people) drawing attention to the falsity. When keying into moving backgrounds from film or VT, you should make sure that sequences last long enough

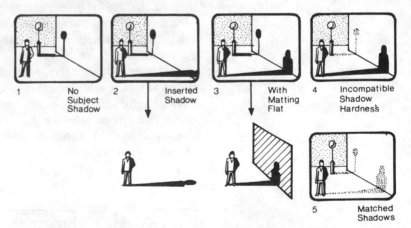

Fig. 19.41 Shadows *(see Table 19.4 – Shadow keyer, p. 385)*
1. Chroma-key insertion relies on color to actuate switching, but does not normally differentiate between different intensities of the keying-hue (i.e. shadows on the chroma-key surface). So subject shadows are not inserted. 2. Special extra circuitry permits 'shadows' to be produced (actually luminance-derived mattes), but the shadow falls along the floor and may be inappropriate. 3. If a carefully-positioned matting flat is used in the chroma-key set-up, so as to coincide with planes in the background picture, the subject shadows falling on it seem to be on the photographed wall. 4. The inserted shadow's sharpness must be comparable with that of the photo background. 5. Given compatible shadow direction, contouring and hardness, a totally convincing illusion is possible.

Fig. 19.42   VT build-up
1. Using chroma-key, extra subjects can be inserted into videotape to provide action build-up e.g. a series of separate recordings (passes) using the same person in different costumes. 2. Multi-camera shooting can be integrated to produce simultaneous multi-images of the same subject.

for the foreground action and are suitably synchronized (e.g. a 'moving' automobile's background).

■ *Foreground pieces* With care, you can introduce subjects in the foreground scene, so that they blend with the background shot into which they are inserted. Furniture, scenic units (pillars, walls), foliage, properties, can be used by performers to achieve a totally convincing integrated effect. Also, by carefully positioning a foreground piece, you can even cover an obtrusive or unwanted feature in the background scene picture.

Complex insertion *(see Fig. 19.37)*

■ *Moving 'behind' background subjects* When you want people in the foreground scene to 'move behind' subjects in the background picture, you can use either *keying areas* or *external mattes*. If you exactly align an area of keying hue (e.g. blue) in the foreground scene, with a subject in the background shot, you effectively 'detach' that item in the background picture. Make a blue matching flat in the studio correspond with a wall in the background photograph and a performer can paste a bill on it, or walk behind it in the chroma-keyed composite! Using blue-covered risers (blocks) parallels (rostra), treads (stairs), a person can apparently sit, lean, climb, place objects on the background items!

Where your performer is to move behind fine detail (tracery, open screens, foliage, fences) in a background photograph, you can use an *external matte silhouette* that inhibits the chroma-key insertion, letting the background through instead. A suitable silhouette can be traced from the background picture or the projected image of a background slide. As this inhibiting matting signal can be switched in or out, a person can walk behind (matte in) or in front of (matte out) the background feature at choice.

Fig. 19.43   Mirror effects
1. A demonstrator stands before a 'magic mirror' displaying a series of changing images. In fact, the mirror reflects a cloth of keying hue, so turning it into a self-matting area, into which subjects are inserted (from slides projected on obliquely-angled screens).   2. A person walks through a mirror. In fact, an opening in a blue flat is hung with a curtain of thin blue strips and corresponds to another camera's mirror flat.

■ *Video build-up* You can key a person into a background, replay the composite, and then key him into that. So far, he has become twins! You could then continue inserting into composites (with quality deteriorating at each dubbing) to provide any number of different insertions of the same performer; thus generating a barber-shop quartet, choir, or orchestra! One ingenious example showed a man sitting beside himself, taking a tiny figure (of himself) out of his pocket . . . and so on!

Solid superimpositions can be used (supers against black background), but chroma-key insertion offers most flexibility. Using magnetic video disc, varispeed VT, or digital processors, the movement of inserted subjects can be adjusted (fast, slow, freeze, reverse motion).

Color synthesis

Any color can be simulated in a TV system, without a TV camera, by supplying appropriately proportioned voltages to the red, green and blue video channels.

The color synthesizer (colorizer, color field generator) produces these voltages either for switch selection or joystick control (paintpot). The latter is a hemispherical device with a central joystick and provides rapidly variable changes in the R–G–B balance.

This synthesized color can be used as a source for electronic insertion: lettering infill, title backgrounds, background insertion, and decorative effects (Chapter 13).

■ *Multilevel synthesis* This keying process switches in a chosen synthesized color wherever a particular tonal level appears in the treated picture. So for example, in a two-tone system, a white on black slide can be reproduced as a red on yellow picture. Both economical and adaptable, this is a regularly-used facility in many studios; titling being prepared in monochrome and then video processed.

Using *multilevel digital synthesis*, greater elaboration is possible. The picture is analyzed into perhaps eight tonal levels, each of which can be colorized to a different hue or tint. So a multitone graph becomes transformed into a multihue display. A normal varitoned picture (monochrome or color) becomes strangely posterized in synthetic colors; akin to a colored contour map. The same device may be used to produce *tonal*

Fig. 19.44 Sequential keying (sequential insertion, cascade insertion, quad overlay)
Each picture is keyed in 'on top of' the previous combination, to build up an overlapping composite.

Fig. 19.45   Multi-hue chroma-key
Several keying hues are used in turn, each keying in a particular video source. So different pictures appear on this rotating multi-colored block.

Fig. 19.46   Outline effects
The outline of a girl dancer transforms into the outline of a tree. To obtain this: Camera 1 shoots a white on black silhouette of the dancer, gradually zooming in until the white shape fills the screen; while Camera 2 is close on the white tree silhouette, gradually zooming out. The combined effect is fed through a border generator and the outline transformation develops.

coarsening, reducing half-tones to eight or less gray scale levels, or to solid areas of black and white, and provide mosaic effects.

Digital video effects

The current TV camera produces a fluctuating voltage (the video signal) which is a direct *analogue* corresponding to the scene's light and shade. However, there are many technical advantages in transforming the video into a different form, through digital analysis. To the engineer, this provides exciting opportunities using digital picture processors to improve picture quality (image enhancement), reduce picture noise (snow removers), improve apparent definition (edge enhancement), stabilize picture synchronism from mobile recorders, build switchers (vision mixers) that accept non-sync and synchronous sources, permit multigeneration dubbing without quality deterioration. Also to provide more compact higher quality equipment such as standards converters, teletext facilities, electronic still stores, time-base correction, etc., etc.

Digital analysis is remarkably simple in principle. It checks the strength of the video signal at regular intervals and stores away these samplings in numerical form (binary digits – i.e. an on-off pulse code representing numbers). Now, instead of fluctuating video, we have a store of numbers representing the brightness and color of each tiny area (element) of the picture. These 'quantized' stored digitally coded signals can be recalled (or replaced) at will and reconstituted into the original picture.

The particular advantage of what otherwise seems a tortuous transformation, is that we now have random access to each stored element of the picture! Normally, picture information would be taken from the store in its original order. But the equipment can now manipulate the video according to the rate and order in which it reads this information: repeating parts of the picture, sampling in reverse order, skipping information, changing the sampling rate . . . and here lies the magic of digital effects!

Temporal effects

Once *real time* has been recorded, you can control the speed at which this action is reproduced; using film, VT, video disc, or digital processing.

■ *Fast motion*   Fast motion effects can be introduced for various reasons:

1. Speeding up subject movement and time scale.
2. To exaggerate energy for comic effect, pixillation, or dramatic force (fast-moving clouds).
3. To shorten an action's normal duration.
4. To reveal the development of a slow process – time lapse shots speeding plant growth.

Table 19.5   Digital video effects

DVE systems manipulate the visual image in many ingenious ways. Terms are not universal, and like the effects themselves, are continually being invented. Many results are obtained by combining several separate effects.

1. *Aspect ratio change*	Picture holds its non-standard shape, as it is zoomed or positioned.
2. *Audio activation*	Effects change at an audio rate.
3. *Auto freeze*	Picture freezes at selected frame intervals, producing a strobe effect.
4. *Auto key tracking/key follow*	A compressed keyed-in area (e.g. wall patch) automatically fits as the master shot-size changes (zoom in/out).
5. *Auto sequence*	Stores a selected effects sequence on floppy disc, to run automatically on selection.
6. *Bounce*	Combined 'flys, zooms, swings'.
7. *Breakthrough/videomelter*	One picture dissolves (in tonal order) into another.
8. *Burns*	Feedback (output back to input) creating swirling, flaring, multilayering, etc.
9. *Cover*	One picture moves over, overlaps another.
10. *Crop*	Moves picture frame edges in selectively, to mask the picture.
11. *Cube*	Rotating cube with different picture on each face.
12. *Decay*	Picture contrast/brightness reducing at adjustable rate.
13. *Effects dissolve*	Smooth vari-timed transitions between two dissimilar effects.
14. *Elastic sheet*	Differential shape-changes.
15. *Expand*	Vertical/horizontal growth of image size.
16. *Explosion*	Picture breaks into many diverging fragments.
17. *Flip/flip-over*	Picture flipped over horizontally/vertically; a selected No. of times; continuously; at a vari-angle.
18. *Fly*	Picture zooms up from nothing, to any position on screen while spinning.
19. *Freeze frame*	A single picture selected from a sequence and held.
20. *Glow*	A glow effect created around key signals.
21. *Hall of mirrors*	Repeated overlapped images of diminishing size.
22. *Image positioning*	Places the image anywhere in the frame.
23. *Image size changes*	Overall image compression, expansion.
24. *Image trail freeze ('Teletrak', 'Action Trak')*	Composite shot, showing path of subject movement, by freezing images at regular intervals.
25. *Key pattern*	Picture shape changes to conform with an external matte; e.g. a star
26. *Magnifying glass*	Localized area of picture enlarged; 'false zoom-in' effect.
27. *Mirror image*	Horizontal and/or vertical reversal, inversion.
28. *Mosaic tile*	Divides picture into an array of small tile-like colored rectangles.
29. *Multimove*	Series of segments or frames moving.
30. *Multi-image freeze/multifreeze*	Array of frozen images from one input.

31. *Multisegment* — A checkerboard of frames showing different subjects, or different stages of the same subject's action.

32. *Negative polarity* — Luminance or color, changed to negative version.

33. *Non-linear movement* — Slow start . . . accelerate . . . slow down.

34. *Ooze* — Change picture frame to amorphous shapes; e.g. circle, creates fisheye effect.

35. *Orbit* — Circular, elliptical, corkscrew image movement around the screen.

36. *Page turn* — Picture appears to turn over like a page.

37. *Pan/tilt* — Total picture moves horizontally/vertically around screen.

38. *Perspective changes* — Pseudo perspective effect, introducing trapezium distortion along horizontal and/or vertical axes.

39. *Pong* — Reduced frame bounces around as it reaches screen edges.

40. *Posterization* — Pictures reproduced with only a few tonal values (adjustable).

41. *Push-off* — Frame moves off the screen.

42. *Push-pull wipe* — A new frame pushes the present picture off the screen.

43. *Roll-up* — Picture curls to form a tube (right edge to left edge). Perhaps another picture revealed on 'reverse face'.

44. *Rotate* — Image appears to turn around X, Y, Z axes.

45. *Shape* — Forms the flat picture into a geometrical shape (still or revolving); e.g. sphere, cylinder (barrel roll), cone, cube. Perhaps with a different image on each face.

46. *Skew* — Partial rotation.

47. *Slide* — Push-off, push-over wipe.

48. *Snapshotting/blink* — Display of a series of 4–16 reduced frames, progressively updating.

49. *Spin* — Continuous rotation clockwise or anti-clockwise at variable speed.

50. *Split* — Splits the screen into segments, which independently wipe to new sources.

51. *Split wipes* — Picture breaks into 2, 3, 4 segments, wiping them off the screen (horizontally, vertically, diagonally.)

52. *Squeeze/compression* — Vertical or horizontal reduction of image size, compressing the image.

53. *Star trail* — Moving subject is followed by a trail of 'stars' (random pixels).

54. *Strobe title* — Flashing image.

55. *Swing* — Image moves to and fro in a curved path.

56. *Swoop/scoop* — Curved path movement.

57. *Trail* — Moving video frame passes over a frozen frame, creating a 3-D effect.

58. *Tumble/roll* — Similar to a continuous flip.

59. *Video outline* — All luminance values changed to e.g. white, with all edges black.

60. *Zig-zag* — Series of reduced pictures move around, collide, overrun, explode from frame center.

61. *Zoom* — Image expands/contracts from full frame to zero on screen.

In film this is achieved by shooting at less than 24 fps and reproducing at normal projection rate of 24 fps; or by regularly omitting frames.

■ *Slow motion*   The uses of slow motion include:

1. Slowing subject movement and time scale.
2. To exaggerate movement, form or pattern.
3. To allow rapid movement to be discerned (hummingbirds' wing-beats).
4. To emphasize movements, giving it force and importance (emphatic body movements).

In film, slow motion is achieved by shooting at more than 24 fps and reproducing at normal speed, or repeat printing alternate frames (stretch/skip frame). In television, slow motion is achieved by magnetic video disc or by slow replay of helical VTRs.

■ *Freeze frame*   Stopping action during its course, to show development or prevent completion. Achieved by still-frame VTR, magnetic video disc, digital effects processing, or by repeat-printing the required film frame.

■ *Reverse motion*   Reproducing action backwards for comic, magical, or explanatory effect – a demolished building reforms, articles wrap themselves up, scattered lettering arranges itself.
    Video disc is generally used. Film can be reversed by: feeding it into telecine tail first and electronically inverting, running in reverse, or reverse printing. Some VTR systems provide reverse replay.

■ *Animation (single-frame, stop frame)*   Achieved on film or VTR, by recording a single frame at a time and changing the subject a little for each. When reproduced in quick succession, the shots develop a group significance – usually creating apparent movement. Thus you can animate cartoons, puppets, still-life.
    Photoanimation uses a series of photographic prints as the basis for treatment, rephotographing them after progressively adding titling, retouching, sectional movement, etc. Thus various process effects can be achieved economically, including complex wipes, spins, phantom sections and explosions.
    Video rostrum cameras are increasingly used for animation treatment (often combined with digital video effects) for promotion material, advertisements, graphics.

■ *Cyclic motion*   Recurrent repetition of an action; achieved by a film loop or conjoining a series of identical copies of a sequence.

■ *Extended and contracted time/space*   By editing-in a repeated part of an action sequence (from another viewpoint, to avoid an obvious jump cut), we create the impression that space or time are extended. Similarly, by editing-out action (with a viewpoint change or cutaway shot) we contract space and time.

■ *Transformations* By animation; or by stopping action during recording (with locked-off cameras), then modifying the scene and continuing recording. When the sections are joined together, we can, for example, make trees burst into bloom and a man turn into a mouse!

20 On location

Until the advent of relatively lightweight TV equipment, video programming originated in television studios, larger mobile control rooms, and lightweight mobile vans that covered smaller scale field events. All used standard broadcast-quality TV cameras. Film crews with 16 mm cameras covered most news reporting, documentaries, and high-mobility situations.

Then, in the early 1970s, competitive broadcasters turned to new lightweight TV cameras and VTRs (mostly designed for closed-circuit and industrial use). This move greatly increased production flexibility. Highly mobile units now set fresh standards in newscast topicality. Spurred by events, rapid technological advances provided increasingly higher quality, and lightweight TV cameras began to supplant film-shooting for various program purposes.

Initials proliferated, to designate applications:

EJ – Electronic journalism.
ENG – Electronic news gathering.
EFP – Electronic field production.
ESG – Electronic sports gathering.

The facilities we need, depend largely on the type of program material involved. A large-scale remote may require a formally organized set-up to coordinate the production on site (e.g. major sports coverage). For improvised snatch shots in a disaster area, high mobility and a low profile are essential. So broadcasting organizations often have a comprehensive systems range.

Large mobile control room (location production unit)

■ The biggest vehicles used for remotes are usually mounted in large truck or trailer form. The unit provides a full broadcast standard production control center with complete video and audio facilities (switcher, audio and lighting boards, audio and video recorders, caption scanner, etc.). Occasionally a small mobile studio is attached. The sizable production and operation team controls up to five broadcast-standard cameras dispersed about the site; more perhaps, for a complex situation, supplemented by mobile portable cameras.

The unit may be used too, as a *drive-in control room* for a temporary studio; or alternatively, equipment may be removed from the vehicle and installed within a site building (e.g. for conferences). Program material may be relayed to base by microwave links for direct program insertion, taping, or provide a complete live production. For large-scale telecasts in which on-site program-control is essential, this traditional *remotes* (*outside broadcast*) approach has considerable merits.

Remotes van

A more compact system uses a small control room in a lightweight van. This contains full broadcast-standard equipment for one or two studio-type or lightweight cameras. Basic switching, monitoring, and audio facilities are provided. The program material may be videotaped (1 in helical or U-Matic) for subsequent editing at base; or microwave transmitted to base.

Typical applications include EFP (for documentary and drama inserts), ESG, and some ENG.

Lightweight truck/small van units

Fitted with one or two *broadcast lightweight cameras* and a helical-format VTR (1 in), this type of mobile vehicle has proved highly adaptable for ENG, EFP, ESG, and commercials. Versatile designs often include arrangements for roof-mounted cameras, a cab hatch, and/or a rear platform for flexible camera viewpoints.

Program material is recorded on the internal VTR, and/or microwave transmitted to base.

The vehicle may also be used as a *satellite unit*, transmitting back to a mobile control room, e.g. traveling at speed around a horserace track, cycle-race circuit, etc.

Station wagon/small van units

Designed to meet the demands of rapid news-gathering techniques, this unit carries one or two 'braodcast ENG' cameras and a small-format helical recorder. The cameras may feed audio/video to the support vehicle by cable or small microwave transmitter. The program is video-taped and/or transmitted to a central relay station (at a high vantage point) from which it is retransmitted to the news center. There the signals are processed (timebase correction, image enhanced, color corrected, noise reduction) and videotaped.

Portable units

These range from 'utility versions' using a small industrial-quality hand-held color camera feeding a ¼ in shoulder-slung VTR, to broadcast-quality *combo-cameras*. Although results from simpler systems are below broadcast standards, news-gathering opportunities may outweigh sub-standard picture quality.

Program handling

Program material (audio and video) can be handled in several ways for field production:

1. Videotaped in the field and delivered to base by courier or when the unit returns. A growing technique involves single or two-camera shooting with a VTR per camera and without a switcher; all editing being a postproduction operation.
2. Videotaped on site and transmitted to base via a suitable relay station. In remote areas, where local topography prevents a line-of-sight transmission path (dead spots due to hills or ridges), it may be necessary to drive to a known good transmission point to replay to base.
3. Transmitted live to base over microwave links (ocassionally via helicopter or satellite stations) for live broadcast.

Fig. 20.1   Field transmission
The illustration shows one typical method of handling program material.   1. *Camera* may be hand-held or tripod mounted, its video being fed to a 'window unit'. Local mike connects to camera's audio pick-up socket.   2. *Window-unit* is a lightweight battery-operated transmitter. Range 1–8 kms (1–5 miles) in line-of-sight contact with support vehicle (13 GHz).   3. Coaxial or fiber-optic cable from camera to support vehicle.   4. Portable VTR.   5. Portable dish reflector of 60–120 cm (2–4 ft) diameter, or microwave antenna (telescopic mast) transmits audio/video from support vehicle to central relay station. Range is 16–24 kms (10–15 miles). (Transmitter 10–20 W, 2–7 GHz, circular polarization.) (In certain situations a helicopter may serve as a relay point.) Satellite up-links are increasingly used between the remote unit and production center for live ENG.   6. Remote signal is picked up on 4-horn remotely controlled 360° dish antennae system on a distant high building. The signal from the uplink receiver is up-converted to 7 GHz, for transmission to news center.   7. At news center, signal correction is introduced (digital timebase correction, image enhancer).   8. Two-way communication system from news center (program and engineering coordination) to field unit (450 MHz). *Remote pickup broadcasting frequencies*. FCC: 150–170 MHz (VHF); 450–456 MHz (UHF) 2, 2.5, 7, 13 GHz. Europe: Also 66–73 MHz, 76.5–108 MHz.

While some mobile units are essentially self-contained, others such as ENG teams maintain continuous two-way VHF communication with base for engineering and production control. When the team is remote from their vehicle, it serves them as a repeater station (receiving and transmitting) for their program audio/video and control.

Most organizations videotape the incoming material (after timebase correction and image enhancement), onto 1 in helical VTRs, for subsequent editing.

ENG editing

The production demands of ENG are considerable and special organization has evolved to meet its particular needs. In some systems, the mobile crew (reporter/director, engineer/operator) is closely co-ordinated from the news center through two-way radio communication. The center provides news evaluation, late-breaking information, updating, talent cues, production timing, and interrupted feedback. The editorial coordinator serves as field producer, continually examining story progress and giving editorial guidance.

The program material is transmitted from site to the base news center (via a relay point), where it may be continuously taped; both as a 'work-print' copy for editorial purposes and a master reference copy storing the material.

Although time code is widely used for editing (single-frame accuracy), some organizations count VT control track pulses instead (6–8 frame accuracy) for technical convenience.

In one system, an *editor* reviews, the 'work-print' copy, assessing edit-decision points, logging in-out times and audio cues. Freeze frame facilities precise location. An *assembler* using this edit decision list enters the precise frame numbers into the VT editing equipment. Computer-controlled VT equipment locates these points in the master reference tape, dubbing off the selected sequences for broadcast – perhaps with a

Fig. 20.2 Typical ENG organization
1. Incoming program material scrutinized, controlled by News Coordinator. 2. Video recordings prepared with time-code: helical work-print for editing decisions and quad master copy.   3. Decision booth where editor (writers/reporters) examines incoming material; log in-out times (time-code) of required excerpts, audio cues for edit points, etc.   4. Dub editing by assembler from editor's instructions (commentary, graphics, titles added), on to tape cart (cartridge) player using computer-controlled selection.   5. Cart player with edited version of program; one cart on air, others cue up ready.

corresponding back-up version. Either reel-to-reel or cartridge (cart) systems are used. The latter providing automatic replay of a series of cart stories from a special recorder/reproducer.

The unaffected original unedited master reference tape remains available for any revised editing of the material (revamping) for later newscast.

During the dubbing process, commentary may be added from an adjacent announce booth; titles can be inserted (multifont electronic character generator); and graphics added (a back-up from an *electronic still store* providing illustrations from digitally-stored graphics in computer memory files.

Types of field camera

TV cameras used in the field come into four broad categories:

1. *Larger studio camera* – designed to state-of-the-art parameters, with full broadcast specifications
2. *Portable broadast cameras* – in more compact mobile form, often using multi-module configurations that offer various facility options (different lens systems, viewfinders). These are used for both studio and portable field-work.
3. *Lightweight cameras* – designed for ENG/EJ applications, where emphasis is on reduced size and hand-held use.
4. *Small hand-held low-cost cameras* – designed for CCTV, industrial applications, but used for certain ENG assignments.
5. *Combo/VRC cameras* – Shoulder-mounted units providing broadcast quality pictures and VT recording.

Field camera equipment

Basically, a complete field TV system includes:

The camera (lens, picture generation circuitry, sync circuits, intercom); picture monitor, cables, mountings. *The audio channel* (microphone, amplifier, monitoring earphones, audio recorder); video recorder; power supplies; lighting units.

These sections are usually arranged in separate units: handled by the cameraman and his assistant, contained in shoulder-slung bags, a back-pack, a trolley-pack, or be located in a support vehicle. Trailing interconnecting cables can be a regular problem.

■ *Mountings* Camera mountings used in field production are varied and adaptable: lightweight pedestals, tripods (fixed or rolling), lightweight platforms, fixed cameras (platforms, towers, roof-sites), hydraulic hoists (cherry pickers), helicopters used as camera platforms (and as microwave relay stations).

Portable cameras may use lightweight tripods, body harness (brace), be shoulder-mounted, or hand-held.

Fig. 20.3   Field camera mountings
Some typical methods of mounting the TV camera in the field: 1. Roof-top tripod at
vantage point.   2. Camera on frame or tower.   3. Lightweight pneumatic pedestal.
4. Lightweight tripod. (3 and 4 may have wheeled bases.) 5. Portable cameras.
6. Van with hatch, roof, rear-platform cameras.   7. Hydraulic platform.
8. Helicopter.

■ *Electronics and power* Lightweight and hand-held camera equipment is usually battery powered (rechargeable battery belt containing
silver-zinc/nickel-cadmium cells), with options for the use of an on-board
generator, inverter supplied by the vehicle generator, a battery system, or
power lines (mains supply).

■ *Lens systems* Although lightweight cameras can support large zoom
lenses when pedestal mounted, lighter systems are necessary for hand-
held cameras (6:1 or 10:1). For some purposes, weight-saving fixed-angle
(non-zoom) lenses are preferred.

The handling and focusing problems we met earlier when discussing
zoom-lens operation (Chapter 3) are inherent. They are particularly
troublesome when trying to maintain steady hand-held shots at narrower
lens angles.

■ *Automatic video control* Studio conditions can usually be controlled
closely. But portable cameras working in the field shoot under varying,
often unpredicted conditions. So it is essential to be able to readjust the
camera simply and rapidly, to maintain optimum picture quality.

Various automatic control circuits help here:

1. *Automatic iris* – prevents gross over- or underexposure; but adjusts
   the lens aperture as light levels and scenic tones change . . . whether
   this is artistically desirable or not. If a bright surface or a light comes
   into shot, the camera stops itself down and lower tonal detail is lost;
   even if that contains the main subject tones! When using manual
   control, an indicator often shows when technical exposure is correct;
   but cannot of course, allow for the *effect* you are aiming at.

Fig. 20.4   Portable cameras
Mobile camera designs include: 1. Shoulder-mounted (battery belt supply).
2. Hand-held camera cabled to a back-pack. Cameras with microwave transmitters
may work up to e.g. 1500 meters from the base unit.   3. Body-brace support for
camera cabled to control equipment on a trolley-pack (transmitter or VTR).
4. Small hand-held camera attached to shoulder pack VTR.   5. Combo cameras.

2. *Autoblack* – sets the black balance, to prevent grayed or crushed
   blacks.
3. *Autowhite* – readjusts to a chosen 'white' reference in the scene (e.g.
   white card), to compensate for changes in lighting color temperature.
4. *Scenic-contrast control* – adjusts the camera's gamma (exposure
   contrast) for improved shadow detail under high- or low-contrast
   conditions.

■ *Time-base correction* Complete synchronism is essential if TV
pictures are to be transmitted and reproduced without color errors; or
even total loss of color, and picture displacement.

A small portable helical VTR offers considerable economy and
portability for ENG projects. But although its output produces
satisfactory pictures when reproduced on a picture monitor (which
adjusts to the varying sync pulses), the video from such a machine is too
unstable for use with a precisely synchronized TV system. Particularly
when editing or using picture combinations (super, insertions) the
irregular speed fluctuations, arising from tape travel and mechanical
imperfections, would cause color loss and image break-up.

This problem can be overcome by using *digital correction*, which
compensates for even substantial errors and produces stable pictures of
improved quality from small-format VTRs.

Digital time-base correctors function by storing up the video
information from the VTR (notwithstanding the information rate
variations) and clocking it out of store again at precisely timed intervals,

in perfect synchronism with the station sync-pulse rate. Certain other imperfections may be improved too, such as low color detail and video noise (although not the chroma delay inherent in 'color-under' helical systems). Under poor lighting conditions the digital noise reducer ('snow remover') works wonders to reduce the disturbing background (although low-light lag remains). It may also remove grain from televised film.

21 Video engineering

The disciplines and complexities of television engineering do not normally involve the program maker. He is more concerned with what the equipment can or cannot do, and with using it effectively. However, there are certain engineering areas where a basic understanding will help you to appreciate the TV system's idiosyncracies and to achieve optimum performance.

Video control (shading)

Although scenery and lighting can build up an atmospheric effect, how successfully this is conveyed by the camera will depend on the video equipment and how it is adjusted.

It is really a matter of standards. The very act of producing pictures *at all*, may be sufficient for some purposes – e.g. surveillance. But to produce pictures that are consistently attractive and persuasive requires forethought, skill and patience. To obtain optimum picture quality, you must do more than just point a camera at a scene. Appropriate control is necessary, otherwise shadows can become clogged and detailless; the lightest tones may merge; successive pictures may jump in brightness; and some shots may look 'washed out', while others are overcontrasty.

In the studio, you can help to ensure good picture quality, by carefully selecting tones, and lighting, wardrobe and so on. But on location, where the situation is less easily adjusted, it may be necessary to avoid shots that produce unacceptable results, such as an overexposed exterior seen outside the window of a room. Alternatively, you may be able to introduce compensatory lighting.

'Picture processing' in the form of video control (shading) is necessary to get the most from the TV system. Ideally all video sources (cameras, film, slides, tape) should be continuously monitored and their pictures suitably adjusted. But this is often neither practical nor economic, so four basic approaches to the control of TV picture quality have evolved. These are preset, automatic, shader and video control operator.

Pre-set control

Here the equipment is adjusted during a technical *line-up*, and its working limits set (exposure, black level, etc). This involves placing test cards in front of cameras to check equipment performance and adjusting circuits for optimum definition, tonal gradation, geometry, etc. Computerized *auto set-up* is also used.

If at the selected *f*-stop there is any over- or underexposure, then you must adjust studio lighting or change subject tones (e.g. alter clothing).

Otherwise you just have to tolerate defects. Lighting with this method generally needs to be even overall and of low contrast. This technique may be quite adequate for simpler presentations and where staffing is kept to a minimum.

Automatic control

In this method, after technical line-up, automatic control circuits are switched in which respond to extreme picture tones. Detecting a bright area, they will stop the lens down until 'correct exposure' is obtained; opening up when the general levels fall. So too, they can adjust the *black level* (set up) of the video signal to ensure that the darkest areas are reproduced as black. Therefore, any gross errors are avoided.

For many types of presentation, results can prove quite satisfactory. But, unfortunately, any automatic compensation can be fooled. The darkest tones in shot may not be black . . . but autoblack could set the picture down and shadow detail would be lost. A person's face should appear of *similar* brightness when shot by two adjacent intercut cameras. But automatic controls react to *all* picture tones, whatever their significance. With light backgrounds to one shot and dark to another, face tones would not match. Bring a newspaper up into a shot and the lens stops down, so a face becomes darker. Have another person move into shot wearing a lighter or darker costume and the picture may change.

Automatic systems are useful safety devices under varying or unpredictable light conditions, even if artistic results are quite arbitrary. Set a *preset lens aperture* for a bright interior and then move into a dim interior; we now have a gross underexposure and can see nothing! Set the stop to correctly expose this interior and the bright exterior is now totally overexposed (washed out). The camera tube (or film) cannot accommodate such a brightness range. We have to select what we want to see best. In these circumstances, an *automatic iris* will 'correct' the exposure by opening and closing – however arbitrarily, and produce usable results. *Skilled* manual adjustment can anticipate, and be artistically sensitive; for unlike the film camera, the TV camera enables us to see and immediately correct results.

Shader

This system is widely used in network studios and remote trucks (mobile control rooms for OBs). The video engineers, who service and align the video equipment, sit at the *camera control units* (CCUs) adjusting the camera lens aperture (remotely controlled), the *black level* (*set-up, sit, sit-up*) and *video gain*, to suit each shot. Camera color balance can also be adjusted.

Video control operator (video control)

Here a specialist video operator remotely controls all the camera equipment at a central video console (vision control desk). He adjusts lens-aperture and black level, with a combination control knob for each channel. Color balance (TARIF) controls are provided for film and caption scanner sources, corresponding controls being available for the camera channels. Video and lighting controls are also closely coordinated. All equipment is lined-up and serviced by video engineers (studio engineers).

Exposure control

The main operational function of video control (shading) is to ensure that the camera tube is suitably exposed – technically and artistically.

The TV camera tube, like emulsion, can only accept a limited tonal range. If the scenic tonal contrast is restricted and you suitably adjust the lens aperture (*f*-stop, iris), your picture will reproduce these tones effectively.

But many scenes exceed this tonal range, especially if lighting is contrasty, and fall way beyond the camera's limits. Then you must set the *f*-stop to provide optimum reproduction of what you consider to be the most important tones. This situation arises for instance, in strongly sunlit exteriors where you cannot expect to reproduce detail and tonal gradation in both highlights and shadows. In the studio, by ensuring that the lightest tones are not overbright nor the shadows too dark, a full tonal range can be reproduced.

Most shots are exposed to provide good reproduction of *faces* although this may mean that more extreme tones are lost. You may be able to compensate for this loss – for example, by illuminating deep shadows sufficiently to bring them within the system's limits, and so make detail visible.

Black level

The video equipment has two inherent limits within which the video signal must be contained; these are reference white and reference black. Generally, the peak whites in the camera's video signal are adjusted to correspond with the reference white level (by exposure and video gain), while the blackest picture tones are adjusted to meet the reference black level (by a black level control). Beyond these limits, any tones are 'clipped off' electronically and reproduced as solid white or black.

This black level adjustment (*set-up, sit*) can be adjusted operationally, to suit the picture. When raised (*setting up/sitting up*), the darkest picture tones 'gray-out' – without revealing any more shadow detail – as all reproduced tones are lifted. On lowering the black level (*setting down/ sitting down/batting down on blacks*) the reproduced tones are reduced so that the darkest tones become crushed to a firm, detailless black – without revealing more detail in the lightest tones.

Further controls

■ *Video gain* This adjusts video amplification and can be increased under adverse light conditions to boost the video – but at the expense of greater picture noise.

■ *Gamma*   The subtlety or coarseness of tonal gradation is influenced by a system's *gamma*. Where it has *unity gamma* (a gamma of one) the video signal strength is proportional to the subject tones. If a device such as a vidicon camera tube has a low gamma (below unity e.g. 0.65) the result is thin, reduced tonal contrast. A high gamma device (e.g. a color picture tube with gamma 2.2) provides coarse, exaggerated tonal contrast. Fortunately these effects can be compensated by the use of gamma correction circuits.

Normally one aims at unity gamma, to avoid color distortions (hue shift) that would otherwise occur. Gamma adjustment may be introduced though, to compensate for otherwise uncorrectable errors when reproducing color film – 'TARIF'; or to compensate for extreme tonal contrasts in ENG/EFP (electronic news gathering/electronic field production) presentations. In monochrome systems, gamma is sometimes adjusted to deliberately modify tonal quality, or to give greater clarity in shadows or lighter tones. Picture noise increases with gamma correction.

■ *Color balance*   Preset adjustment of the video gain and black level of each camera's red, green, blue channels, enables the video engineer to ensure color fidelity throughout the tonal range. This avoids, for example, bluish or greenish blacks, or pinkish whites. These controls may also be adjusted to improve intercamera color matching, to compensate for light quality changes during a remote telecast (color temperature variations), or for deliberate effect.

Artistic aspects of video control

You can make a picture more attractive or effective by appropriate video adjustments:

■ *Surface brightness*   This often alters with lighting angle and camera viewpoint. So in multicamera shooting, changes in effective tonal values can arise. (Improved by exposure or black level adjustments.)

■ *Subject tones*   Where these exceed the system's limits, judicious adjustments can disguise these limitations. For instance, opening the aperture when we need to see shadow detail or reducing exposure when an overbright area would be intrusive.

■ *Overall lighting*   Flat lighting produces pictorially uninteresting pictures and skilled lighting directors avoid it. Although uneven lighting can lead to certain problems, such as accidental shadowing, or a performer moving out of his key light, video adjustments can often alleviate matters by compensatory exposure.

■ *Difficult detail*   Where we want to see details in very light or very dark-toned subjects, appropriate video adjustments show them more clearly. For example when looking at a book page, reduced exposure and lower black level improve clarity. Otherwise the page might well block out and appear blank!

■ *Subject brightness changes*   Our impression of a subject's brightness varies with the amount of light falling upon it, and with background tones – looking lighter against dark backgrounds and darker against light tones. So in intercut shots we could become overaware of subject brightness changes. Again, judicious control can compensate for this subjective effect.

■ *Long and close shots*   Distant shots generally appear more dynamic if they have strong tonal contrasts, while closer shots are coarsened by contrast. When a series of viewpoints are intercut in a continuous scene, it can prove more practical to simulate these changes by subtle adjustments to black level (setting down long shots), than to adjust lighting.

■ *Some additional adjustments*   Video control can enhance the pictorial impact considerably in various ways:

Controlled overexposure can be used to simulate dazzling sunshine. *Underexposure* in night scenes prevents overbright highlights. *Increased tonal contrast* emphasizes harshness (squalid environments). *Reduced tonal contrast* to aid high-key treatment, misty effects. Deliberate *white-crushing* to obtain even-toned white areas; deliberate *black crushing* (the most regular technique) to merge darkest tones to a solid black – consolidating background tone for black backgrounds to title cards, or for black drapes.

Table 21.1   Inherent picture defects

Line beating (strobing)	Localized flickering regularly encountered with close horizontal stripe patterns in clothing, fabrics (checks, stripes), line engravings, close mesh, etc. Can be reduced by altering the shot size or by slight defocusing. Effect is due to subject lines coinciding with picture scanning lines. Interference effects (cross-color) can arise too, producing a color fringing effect on fine stripes (Table 21.3).
Stroboscopic effects	When the movement of rotating wheels or pulsating light, coincide with the TV picture scanning rate of 60 per second USA (50 per second Europe) they will appear stationary. Slightly faster or slower speeds can cause wheels to apparently rotate forwards or backwards.
Interlace break-up	When viewed closely, a TV picture's interlaced line structure breaks up as we look up or down the frame. Line structure becomes coarser and vertical definition halves. Evident on fast crawl titles and extensive titling ('panning-up') shots.
Horizontal break-up	During panning or fast horizontal movement, strong vertical lines or detail breaks up into displaced sections. Due to the inherent time lag between scanning the odd and even fields of the picture (1/60 or 1/50 second).
Highlight flicker	Sometimes visible on very bright highlights, particularly when viewed in dark surroundings; although the picture repetition rate is too fast to be detected under normal conditions.

■ *Color values* Changing a camera's color balance slightly, you can compensate for unwanted *subjective* color bias effects, e.g. when a subject's color appears warmed or paled against strong background hues.

You can introduce color bias deliberately, to create the impression of sunset, firelight, moonlight, gaslight; either bymisaligning the R, G, B channels' gains (amplification); or with a camera having color temperature settings, using a false high Kelvin setting to warm the picture, or a low setting to cool it.

The television camera tube

Although the electronic intricacies of your TV camera tubes are really only the concern of the video engineer, their performance can have a direct influence on staging practices and production opportunities. Some of the shortcomings are inherent; others aggravated or emphasized by the way you use them.

From the earlier vidicon camera tube, a number of sophisticated designs have evolved. These have, with varying success, overcome many of the technical problems that degrade picture quality. (See Table 21.3.)

Table 21.2   Basic electronic adjustments – line-up

	While the camera shoots special geometric charts and tonal step wedges, picture and waveform monitors are scrutinized to check the following:
Electronic focus	Focuses the camera tube's scanning beam for sharpest picture detail.
Beam current	Controls the scanning beam strength. This is set to prevent lightest picture tones blocking off to detailless white areas (i.e. to discharge target's white elements). Too high a beam loses picture clarity, giving excess video noise. Too low a setting and no video is generated.
Target volts	Set for optimum tonal contrast. If too low, camera needs more light (larger *f*-stops or higher illumination) to compensate for weaker video – but image lag (trailing) is less. In the *vidicon*, target voltage adjustment is used as manual or automatic sensitivity control – instead of continual aperture adjustment.
Black level (sit)	Adjustment relating darkest picture tones to system's video level representing black. May be automatically and or manually maintained. Virtually moves all reproduced picture tones up or down the tonal scale.
Video gain	Ensures video amplification similar for each camera channel (1 volt overall).
Alignment	Camera tube beam's scan pattern adjustment (geometry).
Scan width and height	Adjust scan limits on camera tube and obtains 4:3 aspect ratio.
Vertical/horizontal shifts	Enables tube's scanned area to be centralized.
High peaker/aperture correction	Circuitry enhancing apparent picture sharpness by emphasizing higher video frequencies. (But increases video noise.)
Neg/pos switch	Picture tones (hues) as in scene, or 'phase-reversed' for negative effect.
Local/remote switch	Switches lift, black level and target controls from CCU to remote control point.

Table 21.3   Spurious visual effects

Certain picture defects are created or aggravated by unsuitable staging, lighting, and video operation; while other are inherent.

After images (sticking, image retention)	Faint well-defined image remaining on the screen after the subject has moved away; especially of light-toned areas and highlights. Particularly bad on ageing camera tubes, and under cold conditions.
Background	Blemish, spot, patch, on a particular camera-tube. May be due to target damage or deterioration, or a low-grade camera-tube. Also a general unevenness over the light-sensitive area. In solid-state arrays (CCD) isolated spots are difficult to avoid.
Blooming (puddling)	Camera tube overload causing overbright areas to be reproduced as grossly enlarged areas of blocked-off white. Reduced by tube design: anticomet tail gun (ACT), highlight overload protection (HOP), or automatic beam optimizer circuits/dynamic beam control circuits.
Burn-in	Spurious after-image of light or bright reflection, temporarily (sometimes permanently) 'stuck on' to all of a camera's subsequent shots. Vidicon and plumbicon tubes are *not immune*, so avoid sustained shots of strong highlights.
Color response	Ideally, reproduced colors should be completely accurate. However, apart from design compromises, inaccuracies inevitably arise (analysis errors, unbalance, drift), throughout the system, from camera-tube to picture-tube. Many are corrected during line-up process.
Cross-color	A 'rainbow' interference effect seen on fine stripe or check patterns caused by luminance information intruding into chrominance signal.
Cross-luminance	Bands of crawling dots seen at sharp color transitions. This is due to chrominance information intruding into luminance signal.
Definition (resolution)	Maximum resolution of detail is not generally possible over the entire picture area, on camera-tubes, or picture-tubes. It deteriorates away from the frame center; although in broadcast equipment it still remains well within required standards.
Edge effect	With plumbicon and vidicon tubes, circuits compensating for definition fall-off (*aperture correction*) can produce false black edging round high-contrast borders – even crispening distant detail that would naturally be soft focus. Does not sharpen low-contrast borders.
Exposure time (lag)	Smearing or trailing seen behind movement, particularly on high-contrast subjects in low-key scenes. Evident on vidicon film channels during night scenes. In color systems, colored trailing or hue changes may be seen.
Flare	*Optical*: Overall reduced contrast; graying (set-up) of picture; spurious light-streaks or patterns, due to internal reflections (light scatter) within lens system, and camera-tube face-plate. Caused by light shining directly into lens (backlight). *Electronic*: Excess highlights in the scene causing localized blooming around this area of the picture (charge redistribution effect).
Geometric distortion (non-linearity)	Cramping, stretching or bending of picture due to electronic (scanning/sweep circuits) or optical shortcomings. Includes S-curvature, trapezoidal, barrel and pincushion distortions.
Microphony	Strong horizontal streaks arising when the camera is jarred, vibrated, or near strong sound sources (explosions, gun shots, singers, trumpets). Susceptibility to microphony depends on camera-tube and camera design.
Performance stability	Most camera systems (like picture monitors) take some time to warm up and become stable (drift, color balance, etc.). To avoid/reduce cold start-up problems, cameras may be left on 'standby' (i.e. camera heaters kept warm); but this consumes battery power. Performance variations may only be obvious on comparing several monitor displays or cameras showing the same subject, and when editing together shots taken at different times (!)

Picture noise ('snow')	Overall fluctuating grain due to random electronic disturbances. Always present in the TV picture: it becomes particularly noticeable in dark scenes. At worst, develops into a 'snowstorm' overall. Chroma noise varies with hue.
Registration	The red, green, and blue picture images should coincide exactly over the entire frame area. In practice, *registration errors* arise (mainly at edges/corners); known as *convergence errors* on the picture tube. *Note:* If error disappears on cutting to another source, it is faulty camera registration. If the same error is visible on all sources' pictures, in same part of picture, it is a convergence error on the monitor.
Sensitivity	When light levels are below optimum, and lens aperture has been fully opened, video gain may have to be increased (often switchable on camera). This will improve video signal strength, turning a dim flat picture into a brighter contrasty one (with increased video noise!), but cannot compensate for any picture defects arising from the lack of sufficient light to the camera-tube (e.g. lag, smearing).
Shading	Localized lightening/darkening or color shading of parts of a camera's picture (electronic or optical causes). Most noticeable on plain light-toned surfaces. Reduced by corrective electronic shading signals.
Streaking	Black or white streaks extending across the picture beside high-contrast subjects (stair treads, venetian blinds). Usually due to overload or low frequency losses in video channel.

■ *The Vidicon* (Antimony trisulphide target). This is a cheap, reliable, long-lived, simply-adjusted camera tube that is widely used in closed-circuit TV systems (CCTV) as well as in film and caption (slide) scanners. Its low sensitivity (needing high light levels) and *lag* (image smearing on movement) restrict its applications. Its spurious background shading can be troublesome.

■ *The lead oxide camera tube* (Plumbicon – Philips; Leddicon – EEC; Vistacon – RCA). This is currently the major pick-up tube in color TV cameras; offering a higher sensitivity than the Vidicon, a more constant tonal response (unity gamma) and low spurious signals (less shading). Its response at the red end of the spectrum was poor (now improved in 'extended red' versions) and picture noise was 'high in the reds.' It has a tendency to lag, although less than the vidicon and is considerably improved by *bias light* – a technique where the camera tube is internally illuminated. The tube overloads to create *blooming* (*puddling*) – grossly enlarged white blocked-off areas in overbright regions (skies) and disturbing *comet tails* behind moving highlights. Later tube designs, using highlight overload protection (HOP) or anti comet tail (ACT) guns, have largely overcome this problem. *Separate target mesh tubes* have improved detail resolution, highlights and geometry.

■ *The Saticon* (Hitachi/NHK; RCA). An extremely promising camera tube, with a target layer of selenium arsenic tellurium which is more stable and long-lived than the lead oxide target. It provides higher definition (resolution) and has a more uniform spectral response. Its performance in 18 mm form has proved comparable with larger cameras using 25 mm plumbicons. Image lag is noticeably better than vidicons; with a white comet rail rather than the usual red or green.

■ *Further tube designs*   These brief technicalities do remind us that the electronic camera is still evolving. Under optimum conditions of suitable light level and contrast, results can be superb. When conditions are less than ideal, the program material may be important enough to disregard even appallingly bad picture quality (under ENG conditions). But we always need to be aware of the final image quality.

Synchronization

As we saw in Chapter 2, the TV scanning process is kept in step from camera to picture tube, by specially generated *synchronizing (sync) pulses*. A color system is particularly critical, and requires stable precise sync pulses (for scanning accuracy), and *color burst* signal (for hue accuracy) for optimum reproduction.

A master SPG (sync pulse generator) supplies these pulses to the entire video equipment in studio or station. So all the equipment is *synchronous* (scanning in unison). Your switcher can accept any synced source (camera, film island/telecine, caption machine), and intercut, mix, superimpose, insert, chroma-key between their pictures.

External video sources (remotes) on the other hand, operate from their own synchronizing generators. Although these are producing identical types of pulses, they will not be exactly in step with the stations, pulses (*out of phase;* wrong *timing*). If you feed such a *non-sync source* into most production switchers, you will get totally unacceptable pictures (having displacement, tearing, break-up, roll, extreme color errors).

Where the production switcher design permits, you can *cut* to non-sync sources (*hot cuts*), but still cannot mix or combine their pictures with other local video sources. Only certain switcher designs (digital systems) allow you to combine 'sync' and 'non-sync' sources.

■ *Synchronizing systems*   To match two independent video sources' synchronization, several ingenious electronic systems have evolved. The earliest and simplest was *Genlock*; which adjusts the timing of the local pulses to get them into step with the remote (non-sync) source. This system of slaving works well, as long as the remote's syncs are not interrupted or distorted, for then, *all* local equipment run from these genlocked pulses would 'lose syncs'.

VTR sources present another allied problem. Although the original sync pulses were recorded along with the picture, these are somewhat irregular or replay, due to mechanical irregularities in the tape machines. Some form of synchronizer is needed that will accept these randomly changing syncs, and adjust them to match local pulses (a delay process).

A range of *timebase correction* equipment is available that provides automatic compensation for synchronizing inaccuracies on VTR replay. The more elaborate *field or framestore synchronizers* include digital storage (memory) circuits that allow information to be written into the store at any rate, and read out at a stable synchronous speed. (If the incoming video is interrupted, the system may hold a still frame of the action, and recommence when the signal is re-established; so preventing picture breakup on air.) These units often offer additional facilities, such as: freeze frame, digital enhancement, drop-out compensation, noise reduction, color correction . . .

Standards converters, which are used primarily to convert TV signals from one system to another (e.g. NTSC to PAL), may also be used to ensure source synchronism.

■ *Composite signals* – *and switcher operation* A *composite signal* consists of the total video (picture) information together with inserted sync pulses at the end of each scanned line and field. Depending on local facility design, the video system may be supplied with either a full composite signal or a *non-composite* version (video information only, no sync pulses).

Table 21.4   Picture monitor checks

	Picture quality can only be judged on correctly adjusted, high-grade monitors, without spill light or reflections diluting the picture. Here are general methods of checking performance. Allow time for warm-up before adjustments.
Gray scale (all picture monitors)	Feed a *gray scale* (from camera, slide, or electronic generator) to all monitors. Adjust BRIGHTNESS (BRILLIANCE) to ensure *black* merges with blank screen-face. Adjust CONTRAST for maximum white brightness without line defocusing and good half-tone reproduction. Ensure all monitors' pictures are similar. Replace gray scale (tonal step wedge) with a monochrome picture containing good tonal variations. Compare all monitors' gradations and highlight brightness.
Color monitors	As above. Examine gray scale reproduction for traces of color cast throughout tonal range. They should be neutral grays (good color tracking). Circuit adjustments may be necessary. Recheck using same color picture on all monitors. The picture should contain facial tones and pastel hues (desaturated and not primary colors, or color bars).
Picture size/shape	Check that the screens show *all* of the TV picture (no edge cut-off) in correct 4 by 3 proportions.
Focus	Scanning lines should be sharp over entire picture, reproducing maximum detail on camera test chart.
Linearity	Picture should not show serious geometrical distortions (cramping, stretching). Check linearity with cross-hatch (grille, square lattice) generator – this produces thin white lattice on black background.
Color defects	Check reproduction of cross-hatch for color fringing (*convergence errors*) along pattern. In practice some spurious color edges may be unavoidable. Check overall for: *color balance* (warm or cool?). *desaturated color* (washed-out, low contrast?), *oversaturated color* (overstrong color, high contrast?), hue shift (predominant overall color), and color shading (*purity* errors).
Black level	Picture *black* should be constant; not varying with picture tones, or reproducing as gray in low-key scenes or when faded to black. (Variations are due to equipment design or fault condition.)
Off-air pictures	Probably appear noiser and less sharp than direct off-line pictures. They may have displaced multiple images (ghosts, reflections) and ringing, due to multipath reception of transmission; and/or interference patterns (herringbone, stripes, edge tearing).

Certain production switchers are self-compensatory, accepting composite and non-composite inputs. Others only permit you to *fade to black* by sliding split A-B faders to out, when controlling *non*-composite video. If this fade-out is attempted with *composite* signals, the switcher

Table 21.5   Video engineering terms

Synchronizing pulses	Sync pulses from the master control sync pulse generator (SPG) keep the entire TV system in step – from camera to receiver (preventing picture tearing, roll, etc.).
Line (horizontal) drive pulses	Synchronize line scanning rate.
Field (vertical) drive pulses	Synchronize field scanning rate. (Twice each total picture or frame.)
Mixed syncs	The total, combined sync pulse information used to synchronize the system.
Blanking	Special pulses used to suppress video output from the camera, to enable sync pulses to be inserted. The scanning process retraces to the beginning of the line or field during blanking.
Timing	Video signals take measurable time to travel along distribution cables inside the studio complex. If such cable-connected sources (e.g. film, VTR) at different distances from studios/master control are not suitably compensated, their pictures arrive with slight horizontal displacement or cut-off. (Important consideration for multisource picture combinations.)
Color information	
Color subcarrier	A constant carrier frequency that is modulated to encode information.
Reference color burst	A brief burst of the above subcarrier, introduced into the synchronizing information to stabilize color reproduction.
Coder (encoder)	Circuitry (matrix) converting a camera's red, green and blue video signals into a single luminance/chrominance encoded form (NTSC, PAL, or SECAM) for distribution and transmission.
Decoder	Circuitry (matrix) converting the coded video back into separate RGB video to drive the receiver or monitor circuits.
Equipment	
Distribution amplifier (DA)	Video amplifier boosting signal strength prior to distribution, to compensate for subsequent losses.
Processing amplifier/stabilizing amplifier	Corrects errors developing in the video signal. Used to reshape, reinsert, or separate sync pulses from the composite signal (i.e. video plus syncs).
Image enhancer (IA)	Circuitry used to improve apparent picture definition, reduce video noise.
Termination	To match a picture monitor to its video cable, a termination resistance is introduced at its video input. This avoids signal losses, distortions and reflections. Only *one* termination is required for a succession of looped-thro monitors.
Color bar generator	An electronically generated color test pattern, comprising vertical bars displaying white, yellow, cyan, green, magenta, red, blue, and black. Used for video system checks.
Standards converter	Electronic equipment used to enable pictures televised by one TV system (e.g. 525-line NTSC – USA, Japan), to be reproduced by another incompatible system (e.g. 625-line PAL or SECAM).

loses color. In such designs, you must select a *black-level button*, and mix to this 'non-channel' to simulate a fade-out.

Some switcher designs present severe video overloads when peak-white or light-toned areas are combined through mixing or superimposition. If your switcher does not incorporate protective circuits (processing amplifiers), you must avoid fading up channels fully in such circumstances.

Glossary

■ **A & B rolls** Method of assembling recorded material (film or videotape) on two machines running concurrently in sync, to permit fast interselection or combination optical effects. In *A-B film cutting*, shots are joined in sequence until a combination shot is required (mixes, supers, inserts), when the additional shots are assembled on the second roll. Opaque blanking is included in each roll, where only the alternative roll's shot is being used. A *checkerboard method* is widely used to provide invisible editing splices between shots (as well as combined transitions) on narrow-gauge films. Here odd number shots are assembled on 'A' roll, and even shots on 'B' roll. The film printer alternately selects between them, the joins being hidden by the opaque leader.

■ **Acoustics** *(see Fig. 10.5)* Higher frequency sound waves travel in straight-line paths. So they are easily deflected and reflected by hard surfaces; and are absorbed by porous fibrous materials. Lower frequency sound waves (below 100 Hz) spread widely, so are not impeded by obstacles and are less readily absorbed.

As sound waves meet nearby materials they are selectively absorbed and reflected; the reflected sound's quality being modified according to the surfaces' nature, structures and shapes. Studios are carefully proportioned and their walls covered with suitable absorbent materials (fiber panels, rockwool, mineral wool, seaweed quilting) to prevent unwanted sound coloration and to reduce reverberation (small TV studios 0.3–0.5 second; larger TV studios 0.7–1 second). The acoustic characteristics of scenery, furniture, drapes, people, further modify audio quality.

■ **Animation** Creating an illusion of movement – by inter-cutting stills, using graphics with movable sections, using step-by-step changes in a static subject (objects, models, drawings, photographs, etc.), or control wire activation.

■ **Aperture correction** Electronic correction to compensate for the loss of definition due to inherent spread of the scanning beam in the camera tube.

■ **Audio enhancement** Thanks to developments in semiconductor technology, sound signals can be treated in a number of ingenious ways: processed either by *analogue* (charge transfer capacitance devices), or by *digital* systems. These convert and selectively retrieve the stored result. Each has its advantages.

Various effects can be achieved, including:
variable reverberation, echo, doubling/double-tracking (close repeats), delays, chorus, chords, tunelling, phasing, Haas effect (shifting stereo images), hollowing, sweep effects, Doppler effect (pitch changes), arpeggio, vibrato, spin (feedback), flanging (original with delayed version of changed strength and phase), time compression, expansion.

■ **Automatic assembly** The VT editing process is time-consuming, and several methods have developed to assemble the program automatically from instructions. In *auto assembly* the computer-aided editor files edit decisions, translates and carries out edits and effects, in sequence.

Linear assembly (Mode A) performs the edits in the order of the *edit list*. As the unedited material is usually shot out of order (execution order), this can involve several reel changes and VTR setups.

In *reel sequential assembly (Mode B)*, the edit list is scanned, and those sections available in the reels currently loaded on the VTRs are carried out (no overlaps or overlays are permissible).

In *look-ahead assembly*, any VTR not actually being used readies itself (i.e. finds the next edit-point, pre-rolls ready to run-up and record), so saving preparation time.

■ **Automatic tracking** A system on some VTRs for ensuring that the replay head (which is mounted on a deformable piezo-electric element) accurately retraces the recorded video track when replaying a helical recording; particularly when replaying a tape recorded on another machine of the same type. This avoids picture quality variations (of detail, chrominance, saturation), noise bars (due to playing guard tracks), or disturbed synchronism. Video playback head position is automatically adjusted as the recorded track is sampled for maximum signal. This arrangement also allows full color at varying tape speeds; avoiding picture breakup during stop action, jogging, fast/slow motion. (*Ampex –* AST: automatic scan tracking. *3M –* ATF: automatic track follow. *Sony* – dynamic tracking).

■ **Azimuth** Magnetic recording/reproducing systems (audio and video) use heads that scan the passing surface with a fine slit. In audio systems, the head's slit is at right angles to the tape edge. If the slit of the reproducing head is not at exactly the same angle to the track as the original recording's (i.e. the same *azimuth*), there will be a corresponding reduction in the audio output. Azimuth checks (like cleaning and demagnetizing) should be a regular part of recorder maintenance.

Helical VTR systems deliberately *angle* a pair of video heads (e.g. ±6°) so that two separate tracks can be recorded on the same portion of tape without mutual interference. Neither head reproduces the other's track signals, because their azimuths are different. This principle has been taken further in a VHS system with Hi-Fi audio (*depth multiplex recording – see Consumer video formats*). Here high-quality stereo sound (in FM form) is recorded along exactly the same track as the *video*, with ±30° heads, angled at 120° to the video record, so providing independent outputs! (The standard audio edge-track is also recorded; lower-quality mono sound.)

■ **Backing track** A prerecorded track providing musical accompaniment for a performer who, listening on earphones (or a playback loudspeaker), is recorded on his individual mike.

■ **Banding** Can occur on quad or segmented-head recorders, dividing the picture into a series of wide horizontal bands, if head responses are uneven (e.g. a head clog) or are not automatically compensated.

■ **Bands** In a videotape recorder, an FM carrier is generated which is then modulated with the video signal. It is this modulated carrier that is recorded on the tape; the video component itself being recovered during replay. However, spurious interference effects can arise in the process (close bands or stripes, noise effects) depending on the FM carrier-frequency band is used. A *low band* 2.5 MHz is suitable only for monochrome. A *high band* 3.58 MHz is suitable for color, but liable to a fine moiré pattern in colored areas, especially red. *Super high band* 8 MHz considerably reduces the problem.

■ **Beeper** An identification audio signal sometimes used at the start of a recorded section (videotape, audio tape, or disc band) to aid sound cuing.

■ **Bias current** An ultrasonic current (e.g. 75–120 kHz) is combined with the audio in the record head; this effectively linearizes the tapes magnetic characteristic. Its strength is adjusted to suit particular tape materials. The bias setting is a compromise between distortion and high note response.

■ **Bias light** Many camera tubes suffer from *lag*, which creates movement-blur, an ectoplasmic smearing (*trailing, beam lag*) and color fringes behind moving high-contrast subjects under low-light conditions. This effect is considerably reduced by internally illuminating the camera-tube target (e.g. with miniature pea-lamp). A similar lag effect can occur when a camera-tube is slow to charge (*build-up*) during movement from low tones to a bright surface area.

■ **Blimp** Padded sound proofing cover for a film camera. This prevents camera noise from being picked up by a nearby mike, and heard in the background; a particular problem when shooting interiors with live acoustics.

■ **Bridge** Words or music introduced to tie together two dissimilar items. *Also* the shorting together of RGB channels on a picture monitor to produce a black-and-white picture.

■ **Bulk eraser** A large electromagnet which demagnetizes an entire tape spool, ensuring that any previously recorded program is completely wiped.

■ **Camera cables** TV cameras can be connected to video equipment by various means:
coaxial cable, triaxial cable (co-ax plus outer screen), multi-conductor/multicore cable, fiber-optic cable, radio mini-link, laser link, infra-red link. Each method has its advantages, but typical factors to be considered include: cost, bulk, weight, damage vulnerability, interference pick-up. Whereas *multicore* may have a length limit for a particular camera of e.g. 1800 ft, with *triax* the camera could be 6500 ft from base, and with *optical fiber* 7000 ft away. Fiber-optic cables weigh only around 5 lb per 1000 ft.

■ **Cans** Earphones; headphones.

■ **CATV** Community antenna TV. The TV signal is distributed over a given area by coaxial cable.

■ **Charge-coupled device** *(See Solid-state image sensors)* The charge-coupled device (CCD) is a solid-state image sensor that uses a small silicon chip containing thousands of individual elements, each independently charged by a part of the lens image. This small device is rugged, consumes low power, and is potentially cheap.

■ **Cinching (windowing)**   Slippage between tape layers on a loosely wound spool, causing physical distortion and even tape damage.

■ **Closed circuit**   Production being recorded, reviewed, etc., *locally*; as opposed to programs being *broadcast* for public viewing (off air, or cable). Closed-circuit television (CCTV) is the general term for non-broadcast TV.

■ **Coding**   Electronic process of encoding RGB video signals into an NTSC or other color system. (*Decoder:* circuitry for transforming the encoded signal into its RGB components.)

■ **Color bars**   Video test signal presenting a series of vertical bars of fully saturated color: white, yellow, cyan, green, magenta, red, blue, black.

■ **Color characteristics:**

Achromatic values (*gray scale*) – progressive scale of brightnesses, from black through grays to white.

Brightness – the subjective quantity of light received from a subject. Often used to denote 'luminosity' (US).

Hue – the predominant sensation of color; e.g. red, orange, yellow.

Lightness – perceived brightness of surface colors.

Luminance – the true brightness of a surface. Snow has high luminance, black velvet a low luminance.

Luminosity – perceived brightness of light sources.

Saturation (chroma, intensity, purity) – the extent to which a color has been diluted with white. The pure undiluted hue is fully saturated (100 per cent saturation), e.g. red. Dilution pales the color, e.g. red desaturates to pink.

Shade – a hue mixed with black.

Tint – a hue diluted with white.

Tone – a grayed white.

Value – in the Munsell system, indicates subjective 'brightness'.

■ **Color definition**   The eye cannot readily detect fine color detail. Therefore, to save bandwidth in color TV systems, full detail is transmitted in *luminance* only – 4.2 MHz; i.e. 320 lines horizontal resolution – NTSC 525/60 (5.5 MHz. PAL. 625/50). Color information is deliberately restricted: I bandwidth (orange to cyan) 1.6 MHz; Q (green to magenta) bandwidth 0.8 MHz. The effect is of lower definition color 'overprinted' with tonal detail. Colors are transmitted in the proportions 30 per cent red, 59 per cent green, 11 per cent blue, to produce a suitable monochrome tonal balance.

■ **Color recording**   Several different techniques are used to record color information on video tape: 1. recording a composite signal (*chrominance modulated subcarrier*); 2. *direct recording* of R G B components; 3. *color-under recording (see Color-under)*; 4. *dual-track recording*; recording luminance and chrominance (*color difference signals*) on separate tracks.

■ **Color temperature**   Defined by reference to a black-body radiator. If such a non-reflective body is heated, the spectral distribution of the resultant light changes with its physical temperature (0 Kelvin = 273° C). This figure gives a good guide to the color quality of light sources. A tungsten halogen lamp (quartz lamp) burns with a color temperature of around 2600–3500 K.

■ **Color under** The detailed information in a fully encoded color TV signal (i.e. NTSC, PAL, etc.) cannot be recorded accurately at the slower videotape speeds of small-guage VTR systems (U-Matic, VHS, Betamax, etc.). Instead, an ingenious *color-under* system is used. In principle this involves recording brightness (luminance) and color (chrominance) information simultaneously on two adjacent carriers (FM, AM), using filters on replay to distinguish between them. However, there are problems in differentiation, and various visible defects arise: detail loss (above about 2 MHz), chroma noise, moiré patterns, edge sparkle, color displacement, ringing (edge repeats), 'cartooning' (plain areas lack texture). *See Image enhancement.*

■ **Combination cameras** Various incompatible forms of camera systems incorporating a VTR are available (called 'combos; VCRs; camcorders'). Based on the VHS system, but with different electronics, are the *ARC* (Ampex), *Hawkeye* (RCA), *Recam* (Panasonic), *ProCam* (JVC), and Ikegami versions with a Matsushita-design recorder. This system is widely referred to as *M-Format* (*M-wrap*) due to the tape path shape, or as *Chromatrak*.

Sony's *Betacam* system or *CTDM-format* uses a Betamax-type cassette, (used also in Thompson-CFS *Camescope*). The Bosch Fernseh produced *QuarterCam* (*Lineplex*) system uses ¼ in CVC tape (allied versions by Hitachi and Philips).

Although generally based on domestic recorder formats, broadcast quality has been achieved by: faster tape speed (hence better detail, lower noise), separately recorded encoded color components (chrominance) and luminance; which avoids the spurious patterning/cross-color effects of color-under systems. Although tapes carry luminance track, color track, 2 audio tracks, control and timecode tracks, their arrangements and form differ considerably between formats. Typical tape duration is 20 minutes. Performance is approaching 1 in C-Format VTRs.

■ **Compact disc** Digital audio disc (DAD) recordings use a universal format on 4.7 in (120 mm) single-sided discs (60–75 mins max duration). Audio is digitally recorded as a pattern of shallow depressions (pits) along a fine-groove in-out spiral track. (These correspond with regular samplings of the original fluctuating audio signal/analogue signal.) This track is replayed by a contactless laser/optical pickup system. Audio quality is exceptionally high, a wide frequency range, virtually without rumble, flutter, wow, background noise; a high dynamic range >90 dB); low distortion (<0.05 per cent peak).

■ **Compatible** When video or audio signals are generated by one system or piece of equipment and reproduced effectively by another, the second is said to be *compatible*.

■ **Consumer video formats** A wide range of features are available in these low-cost helical-scan VTRs, including: off-air recordings;

channel selection; video input (for video cameras); tracking control (adjusts replay for best track-following); audio dub (change or add audio track); noise reduction; cue/review controls, shuttle search (fast picture search forwards/backwards); pause/still (freeze-frame); remote control (cable, infra-red); timer (auto switch on-off); auto rewind at tape end; auto program marker (signal locates starts or cue points); tape-used/elapsed time indicator; tape-left indicator.

Dual-speed VHS models are available (lower quality on half-speed). Some recorders have stereo sound capability. Typical maximum duration at normal speed 3 hrs 35 min (Beta) to 4 hrs (VHS).

The *Beta* and *VHS* provide very comparable results. Certain design features are similar: color-under processing, tilted-azimuth heads. Others are quite individual: e.g. the tape path (U-form in Beta; M-form in VHS), and tape handling (tape remains laced up during all operations in Beta; but retracts for fast winding in VHS). Beta formats seem less susceptible to tape tangle through humidity changes (tape sticking to head-drum) than the U-Matic system.

VCRs with advanced audio systems offer very high-quality stereo sound output. They use *depth multiplex recording*, in which the two audio heads lay down an FM signal of relatively low frequency, deeply penetrating the tape. The video heads immediately follow them along the same track (different azimuth), erasing and replacing the top level of the FM audio recording with a higher frequency video signal. This creates a 'two-layer' effect, with virtually no interference between recordings.

■ **Crossed gray scale (chipchart)** A standard test graphic comprising two opposed horizontal nine-step tonal gray scales (from 3 per cent to 60 per cent reflectance).

■ **Crossing the line** Discontinuity or position-jumps in the frame, caused by intercutting viewpoints on either side of the 'imaginary line' ('action line').

■ **Cut-back** During editing, returning to the main scene after a series of interpolating close shots.

■ **Date** A system of sound distribution used by PBS (Public Broadcast Service) network, in which audio is digitally encoded for distribution and decoded at the local receiving station. Usable for stereo simulcasts (simultaneous TV and high-fidelity FM stereo radio transmission), the system can relay four audio channels in addition to the mono TV sound.

■ **Decibel (dB)** A logarithmic unit indicating ratios of powers, voltages or currents, and used to express transmission levels, gains and losses. The human ear (like the eye) does not respond proportionally to changes, but follows a 'power law'. A decibel represents the smallest perceptible change in audio level.

■ **Degaussing** Demagnetizing. Tape recording heads must be periodically degaussed to prevent magnet build-up from increasing tape hiss. Video tape is usually bulk erased before reuse.

■ **Diode-gun Plumbicon** Camera-tube design providing a precisely focused electron beam, improving picture resolution, and reducing lag.

■ **Diopter** A *diopter lens* is a simple supplementary lens placed over the main camera lens, to alter its effective focal length. Mainly used for closeups of small objects.

The *diopter* is the measurement of the power of a single lens; one hundred divided by its focal length in centimeters. So a lens of power +15 diopters has a focal length of

100/15 = 6.66 cms (66.6 mm).

+ indicates that the lens is converging; − that it is diverging.

■ **Dope sheet** Film cameraman's sheet giving basic story information, location, exposure data, footage, instructions.

■ **Drop-out** Magnetic tape surface defect or damage causing momentary disturbance of reproduced video, resulting in small localized information gaps in a line (black flash, color loss). To disguise this brief loss of FM signal pick-up from the tape, a *drop-out compensator* can insert stored picture information from a corresponding part of the previous line. (This term is also used for the information loss, *noise band* at end of line/frame scanning in helical recording.)

■ **Dubbing sheet** A chart prepared by the film editor for the *dubbing mixer* (sound recordist) showing the exact relationships of the various contributory sound sources in the final mixed track.

■ **Ducker/voice-over ducker** An audio-fader circuit that automatically reduces the volume of e.g. music ('backgrounds' it), to enable an announcement to be heard; its level being restored as the speech stops.

■ **Dupe neg** A duplicate negative prepared from a positive print – when the original negative is not available, or to protect the original negative, or for special effects work. By using *color reversal intermediate film*, duplicate negatives of the original color negative can be prepared, so eliminating one printing stage (reduced grain, improved color reproduction and sharpness).

■ **Electronic cinematography (EC)** Video cameras designed to produce typical 'film look' picture quality. Used for shooting 'motion pictures' that will subsequently be transferred to film for screening. These cameras are intended to handle and perform like 35 mm cine cameras. They have the merits of both media, viz: the advantages of videotape over film stock, continuous monitoring, with interchangeable lens systems (prime and zoom), T-stops, the familiar angles of film camera lenses, and facilities for a separate focus-pulling operator.

Other design features include extended dynamic range, soft clip (i.e. a *knee* in the exposure curve, instead of the hard/sharp cut-off of highlights in the normal TV white clipper/white limiter). The inherent characteristics of TV camera-tubes remain, of course.

■ **Electronic still store (ESS)** Photographic slides are costly, vulnerable, bulky, need manual sorting and loading, etc. So magnetic video disc stores of various designs are increasingly used, that provide a library of still video pictures. These pictures, which include photo library stills, artwork, titles, etc., can be derived from video cameras, slide scanners, character generators, computers.

Storage capacity may range from a few hundred to several thousand frames. Sometimes a number of work stations can load from one central library store. Individual stills are coded and may be selected at random, or arranged to play through in a programmable sequence.

As stills selection from store can be almost instantaneous, several can be shown in rapid succession to create animated effects. An index of descriptions/titles can be displayed on a monitor screen, and may enable a simultaneous multi-segment picture (e.g. 64 'slides') to be displayed (*browse mode*).

■ **Exposure curve (transfer characteristic)** Only where a picture system's output is directly proportional to the light input (unity gamma) will tonal reproduction be strictly accurate. Most systems have a linear (straight line) portion to their characteristics, but are less responsive to changes at exposure extremes. Lightest tones are therefore progressively compressed at the upper end of the exposure curve (knee, shoulder), while shadow detail merges at the lower end (toe).

■ **Fibre optics** A cable of fine glass filaments conveys intensity-modulated light from light-emitting laser diodes in a miniature transmitter, to light detectors, which transform these light pulses into corresponding electrical signals (video and audio).

The advantages of optical fibers include: lightweight, small-diameter cable, no electromagnetic interference, no crosstalk between fibers, low losses, no radiation, no picture degradation, no equalization needed, wide bandwidth, independent of line-of-sight and weather conditions (unlike external radio links), rapidly routed, very robust (withstands vehicles, trampling, wet, mud, sand, snow, etc.).

■ **Flash cutting** A sequence structured from a series of very brief shots, each lasting only a few frames.

■ **Flying erase head** In a standard helical scan recorder a fixed erase head wipes the tape width, so erasing parts of *several* tracks simultaneously. It cannot erase one complete track at a time, so precludes precision editing. To overcome this problem, recorders designed for *insert editing* have an auxiliary *flying erase head* fitted just before the record head (on the head wheel). A *flying reproduce* head provides simultaneous confidence playback during recording.

■ **Focal length** The distance from the camera-tube target to the lens' optical center when the lens is focused at infinity – far distance.

■ **Forced processing** When a film is developed at a higher temperature or for a longer period than normal, its effective *speed* (sensitivity) is increased; although contrast, graininess and fog are emphasized. Reversal films 'push' more successfully than negative film material. This technique is resorted to when light levels are too low for normal exposure.

■ **Gamma** Gamma is a logarithmic measurement of reproduced tonal contrast, relating light input to the resulting picture density. In *photography*, gamma defines the tangent of the maximum slope (straight portion) of the processed emulsion's characteristic curve. In *television*, gamma measurement relates light input to voltage output, or voltage input to light output. The effects of a series of processes combine (cascade). Thus a camera tube having a low gamma (vidicon 0.65) relates to a color picture tube (around 2.2) to produce an overall gamma of 1.43 (0.65×2.2), which can be electronically corrected (0.7) for overall unity (1.43×0.7) gamma.

■ **Gate** A metal masking plate with a rectangular hole, against which the film is held stationary (during exposure in the camera to form individual *frames*, or while being projected). Unsteadiness of the image during projection (*gate float*) may be discernible as horizontal weave, or vertical judder (*hop*). This movement, together with extraneous blemishes (sparkle, dirt, 'hair in the gate') often reveals that a televised image originates from film rather than a video camera

■ **Glitch**   General term for any brief electrical disturbance in a picture.

■ **High-definition television (HDTV)**   Today's broadcast color TV standards were conditioned largely by the need to provide systems compatible with existing black-and-white (monochrome) services. Far higher picture quality is achievable, and NHK/Sony have demonstrated a high-definition color system using 1125 lines, 60 field-scanning rate, with a picture of 5:3 aspect ratio, interlaced 2:1, with the video bandwith increased from the present 4.5 MHz to 30 MHz.

Although the process is incompatible with existing TV systems, it has been used effectively in closed-circuit and 'film-making' applications. Definition is higher than moving 35 mm motion picture film, and scanning lines are not discernible at ×3 picture height.

■ **Highlight overload**   Camera tubes are liable to block-off on bright areas, the edge overspill of charges affecting darker picture tones nearby. Spurious *comet tails* also develop behind moving lights or speculars.

Special camera tube design reduces these problems, by enriching the scanning-beam density (during line blanking/retrace periods) to discharge extreme highlights on the target. The camera tube's exposure curve (light transfer characteristic) develops a *knee*.

Automatic beam-optimizing circuitry is variously termed: *highlight overload protection* (*HOP*), *anti comet-tail gun* (*ACT*), *dynamic beam control* (*DBC*).

■ **Hyperfocal distance**   When the lens is focused at infinity (∞), focus remains sharp from infinity to a plane near the camera. When focused at this *hyperfocal distance* (H) the scene is sharp from about distance ½H to infinity.

$$\text{H in meters} = \frac{(\text{focal length in cm})^2 \times 100}{\text{lens } f/\text{stop number} \times 0.05}$$

■ **Image enhancement**   Electronic correction and improvement of video signals by a *video processor*. This includes processes such as crispening edge sharpness (high frequency synthesis), edge color fringe removal, color displacement correction (chroma/luma delay), reduced noise ('snow remover'), suppressing 'ringing' at edges, and improved small image detail, sync regeneration.

■ **Imaginary line (action line or axis, center line, vector optical axis)**   An audience's impressions of space and subject positions within a scene come from various visual clues appearing in the picture. The director must take care not to confuse these concepts by using incompatible viewpoints, avoiding puzzling repositioning or exits.

If you switch across an *imaginary line* established by the action (direction of look and/or movement of performers), disconcerting position changes (jump cuts) and loss of orientation can occur. This is a particular hazard in discontinuous or multicamera shooting. No problems arise when dollying across the line, changing the line's direction by regrouping or moving subjects, or when altering eye-lines. But you can seldom *cut* across it unobtrusively. *See also Fig. 15.11.*

■ **ITFS**   Instructional television fixed service. Transmission on 2500 MHz for PTV (Public Television) using short-range closed-circuit television transmission.

■ **ITV**   Instructional TV. Program material produced for formal educational systems.

■ **Lighting measurement:**

Lumen – a unit of light output (luminous flux).

Lux, foot candle – units of incident light intensity falling on a surface (illumination).

Nit, foot lambert – units of surface brightness; reflected light intensity (luminance).

Nanometer, micron, angstrom – all units specifying wavelengths of light (e.g. identifying spectral colors) and other electromagnetic radiation.

Kelvin – a unit of color temperature.

■ **Liquid gate (wet printing)**   Printing system in which the film passes through a liquid at the point of exposure. This system is used mainly for printing from badly scratched originals and gives a final print which is virtually free from blemishes.

■ **Lockup time**   The time taken from starting a VTR (or telecine) for it to reach a stable running speed. Some helical recorders use *standby idling* (for recording) and *timebase correctors* (on replay) to reduce startup time and picture instability.

■ **Longitudinal video recording (LVR)**   System recording 48 video and 96 audio tracks bidirectionally in a series of parallel tracks along the tape on 8 mm wide videotape moving at 400 cm/s (160 ips) past fixed heads, changing direction and switching tracks every 2½ min.

■ **Low-frequency extender (line extender)**   Audio equipment permitting regular phone lines to be used for 'broadcast-quality' commentary speech, by suitable frequency shifting, filtering, etc., to remove clicks, pops, hum, and compensating for limited audio bandwidth.

■ **Matte box**   A bellows or box mounted in front of the camera lens. It holds camera mattes (masks), gelatine filters, as well as providing an efficient lens shade (sunshade hood).

■ **MATV (master antenna system)**   Distribution system derived from a single antenna, to service any area from a single building to an entire community.

■ **Mired (microreciprocal degrees)**   Unit derived to classify a color filter, or the color temperature of a light source. It enables easy calculation of the color shift required to modify a light source's color quality. Mired value equals one million divided by the Kelvin value e.g. 2500 K = 400 mired.

■ **Multivision (multiscreen)**   A large presentation using an assembly of adjoining screens to form a large composite single or multiimage display. Sometimes indicates several images appearing simultaneously in the same frame.

■ **Munsell color frame**   System of notation defining color through a set of charts showing *hue* (5 principal and 5 intermediate hues), *value* (brilliance) in a scale of 10 steps from black to white, and *chroma* (saturation).

■ **Narration**   Voice-over (explanatory or commentary). Non-synchronous speech accompanying a picture.

■ **Nemo**   Remote pick-up.

■ **Noise reduction (NR)**   *(See Chapter 10).* The major audio background noise reduction systems are incompatible. Audio recorded with a given system must generally be reproduced by the same method; although some can be played satisfactorily, through suitable equalization adjustments on any reproducer (Dolby B, C; CBS Type CX). Each system has its associated compromises (e.g. need for careful alignment, or performance limitations).

In the complex *Dolby A* system used for professional recording, the audio frequency spectrum is filtered into four sections (bands). Each is individually treated, boosting very quiet signals, while leaving louder ones virtually unaffected. When decoded on replay, the original relative audio levels are restored, and background noises correspondingly reduced.

The simpler earlier *Dolby B* system is succeeded by *Dolby C* with improved noise reduction. Widely used for audio-cassette recording, it uses pre-emphasis; the frequency at which the boosting begins, depending on the volume at that moment. There is corresponding de-emphasis on replay.

During audio taping, the strength of the fixed bias current applied to the recording head is normally a technical compromise. (Lower bias improves high notes, but worsens bass distortion, modifying the system's overall response.) The *Dolby HX* (*headroom extension*) adjusts the tape bias automatically, according to the high frequency energy content of the program, to produce lower distortion levels overall.

The relatively straightforward *dBx* system does not split the audio spectrum, but applies routine pre-emphasis/de-emphasis to the program, The Telefunken *Telecom* and *High-com* systems have similar features to Dolby A, but with a constant compression.

Further facilities for reducing unwanted background noise include *noise gates* which selectively suppress low-level signals; and *notch filters* which reduce a narrow selected part of the audio spectrum (e.g. hum reduction).

■ **One and a half heads (1.5 heads) principle**   A separate head records the vertical information near the lower edge of the tape, thus retaining VIRS, VITS, teletext.

■ **Optical effect**   A filmed visual effect, created in an optical printer.

■ **Optical printer**   A special film-printing machine in which a filmed image is projected onto the film stock rather than printed by contact with it. The projected image can be independently exposed to provide optical transitions, superimpositions, size changes, freeze frame, step printing, speed and direction changes, skip frame, multiimage, traveling matte, image position changes, image distortions, etc.

■ **Out-take**   A shot or scene rejected during editing.

■ **Overcranking**   Filming at a higher speed than normal, to produce a slow motion effect when projected at normal speed (24 fps).

■ **Overlapping sound**   An introductory editing treatment used when flat cuts join two dissimilar scenes. The sounds of next scene are heard before the vision switches.

■ **Overrun**   To exceed a prearranged duration.

■ **Overscanning**   If a picture on a monitor is expanded so that its edges are lost beyond the surround mask, it uses the full picture-tube screen, and appears subjectively to be larger. But in fact all the picture information around the edges is being lost – sometimes including subtitles. In any production area, monitors should be *underscanned* to show the entire TV frame (*raster*) including corners; for this will reveal when any unwanted subjects are peeking into shot (mikes, another camera, distracting items); and also display certain technical defects more clearly (e.g. sync problems shown by ragged picture edges).

■ **Padding (fill)**   Improvised action/dialogue introduced when a program is underrunning, or *stretching* available material to fill the allotted time.

■ **Panning head/Pan head**   Several designs are widely used. The *fluid panning head* uses layers of high-viscosity silicon fluid to dampen head movement. The head is adjustable, and very smooth in action.

The *friction head* relies on surface friction (stiction) between parts to control pan/tilt action. Cheapest and simplest, but not always easily controlled, due to excess friction at the start of movement. Larger TV cameras may be supported on *cradle heads* based on this principle. Although balance is fairly good as the camera's centre of gravity is distributed, its tilt range is limited, and the friction setting (drag) changes in use.

A *cam head* incorporates cams on either side of the head, overcoming these problems.

Geared heads which incorporate gearing to control movements are larger and less flexible. Mainly used for heavy film cameras.

■ **PBS**   Public Broadcasting Service. Network for public television supported by the Corporation for Public Broadcasting (CPB).

■ **Perspective distortion**   Perspective effects strongly influence one's interpretation of space. Where the camera's lens angle and your viewing angle to the screen are comparable, you see 'natural perspective', showing proportions and spatial impressions similar to those of everyday life. When a *camera moves* towards a subject to obtain a larger image (i.e. a closer shot), perspective remains consistent, the proportions of subjects are compatible, their relative positions and spacing changing as you approach.

Zooming, on the other hand, simply alters the overall magnification of the lens image, so these natural effects do not result. Although by reducing the lens angle you can fill the screen with a distant subject – so suggesting that it is close – the resultant image is generally dissimilar from the impression you would actually get at a close viewpoint. Instead, subjects show characteristics you normally associate with *distance*: depth in the picture appears foreshortened, and there is often considerable overlapping. Sizes do not diminish naturally with distance. You interpret such incompatibilities as *spatial compression*. A *spatial exaggeration* effect arises when a very wide camera lens angle is used. (The illusion of natural perspective can be restored by changing your viewing distance proportionally to the lens angle used.)

■ **Pickup**   A loose term for any separate shots recorded after the main program to be inserted during VT editing. They may be *corrective* (e.g. to enable action, dialogue, technical errors to be removed), or *detail inserts* (e.g. showing close-ups, local action, reactions, etc.) that could not be shot during the original take.

■ **Picture monitors**   One's opportunity to assess picture quality and video equipment performance largely depends on the standards and adjustment of the picture monitor. Where monitor performance drifts (loses focus, convergence alters, color balance changes) or reproduction varies with picture content, judgment is very arbitrary.

Various types of picture tube are used *(Fig. 2.6)*. While delta-gun dot-mask (shadow mask) tubes provide generally superior pictures, their convergence drifts with time (so subjects seem to develop color fringes). PIL tubes have improved convergence stability, but coarser resolution.

In black matrix screens, the phosphor dots are laid down on a low-reflectance black background, so that less light is reflected from the screen surface. The picture-tube's resolution depends on the closeness and size of the screen's dot: from typical broadcast tubes (pitch of 0.47–0.63 per in), to high resolution (0.43), and ultra-high (0.31).

Typical picture-tube performance is around: White 25 fL (max) to black ½ fL (minimum limited by flare and dispersion in glass). Maximum contrast of 50:1 is possible, but 15:1 in a lighted room is more typical.

■ **Picture quality**   A subjective grading scale may be used to assess video or audio quality (CCIR/CCITT).

Quality	Grade	Impairment
Excellent	5	Imperceptible defects
Good	4	Perceptible, but not annoying
Fair	3	Slightly annoying
Poor	2	Annoying
Bad	1	Very annoying

■ **Pilot tone**   VTR development in which a special frequency is recorded (1.5 times the color subcarrier) to provide constant monitoring and correction of the system's chrominance, as well as checking scanning synchronizing errors for improved time base correction.

■ **Pixillation**   Jerky fast motion effect created by regularly omitting frames from film shot at normal speed. *Also* an animation effect obtained by conjoining a series of still frames.

■ **PLUGE**   Electronically generated image used to adjust picture monitors to a uniform standard. Picture comprises a vertical white bar, an area of reference black, and two reference tones slightly higher and lower than the reference by 2.5 IEEE/IRE units (Institute of Electrical and Electronic Engineers). The monitor is adjusted so that the darker patch merges with reference background, the brighter patch still remaining visible.

■ **Post syncing** The process of recording sound (speech, sound effects) to synchronize with an existing picture – as when replacing original dialogue with a different language, closely following the original lip movements; or when fitting convincing new sound to a mute print.

■ **Pressure zone microphone** A form of high-quality electret mike. Its flat base plate contains a narrow slot through which sound reaches a diaphragm. Reflected and direct waves are in phase in the *pressure zone*, so that when the mike is placed against a large reflecting surface, it becomes non-directional.

■ **PTV** Public television (ETV, Educational TV). Non-commercial TV, citizens group TV.

■ **Quadruplex (quad, transverse) VTR** Now obsolescent, this high-quality system uses a 2 in wide magnetic tape moving at 38 cm/seconds. A full-width erase head demagnetizes the tape, which passes a transverse headwheel with 4 recording/replay heads. Mounted 90° apart, these scan across the tape in turn recording a series of parallel transverse video tracks (effective writing speed 3800 cm/s or 1500 ips). Each track records 16 lines in 525 systems (20 lines, 625 systems). Interhead switching ensures continuous recording/replay. The audio, control and cue tracks are located along the tape edges *(see Fig. 12.1)*.

■ **Rostrum camera** Two basic forms are used: (1) A vertical TV camera shoots an animation table, where successive drawings (or cels) are displayed on a horizontal surface; top lit, or illuminated by a light-box underneath. The results are recorded on a VTR or magnetic video disc. (With *two-frame animation*, changes are made after every other exposed frame.) In sophisticated designs, camera movement, zoom, table position changes (N/S, E/W), exposure rate, etc., are computer-activated. (2) Another system projects a video recording of live action (a frame at a time) onto a glass screen, where it is traced on a cel to derive an animated cartoon.

■ **Simultaneous contrast (spatial induction)** A visual illusion in which the apparent tone, color and size of an area is modified by its background. A light-toned area appears lighter and larger against a dark background; a dark area even darker against a light one. Similar interaction arises in color, where an area may look cool (bluish) against a dark background, and warm (red/yellow) against light tones. A colored background may modify the appearance of the foreground subject, often biasing its color towards a complementary hue. Juxtapose red and blue, and the red will seem quite orange while the blue has a greenish tinge. A strongly colored subject may similarly influence a neutral background tone.

■ **Single system sound** Audio recorded directly onto film sound track (or integrated VTR), using a mike on top of the camera. Automatic gain circuits control audio levels. In *double systems* a separate camera and synchronized audio recorder are used; picture and sound being combined during editing, or reproduced in sync on separate equipment (*double headed*).

■ **Slate (clapperboard, clapstick.** *Fig. 11.1*) An identification board used during filming. Shown before a shot; or inverted if taken at its end. The hinged top section is brought down quickly to produce a loud noise, which enables the separate picture and soundtrack (double system) to be synchronized during editing. Electronic *time code* systems of synchronizing are increasingly used.

An electronically generated *'slate'* with a time-remaining clock is widely used as a VTR 'slate'/leader.

■ **Slides**

Standard 35mm slide format – mount 50×50 mm (2×2 in) mount; aperture 36×24 mm; aspect ratio 3:2.

Superslide format – similar mount size; aperture 40×40 mm (1.6×1.6 in).

■ **Slide scanner** An optical projector or flying-spot scanner used to televise transparencies. Plastic-mounted slides are fitted into pairs of drums, discs, or trays (typical capacities of 36–40). Selection may be sequential (instantaneous) or random (delayed) from the production switcher position. Scanners do not usually permit size and position adjustments of the image.

■ **Solid-state image sensors** Solid-state image conversion devices such as *charge-coupled devices* (*CCD*), *silicon diode arrays, MOS* (*metal oxide semiconductor*) *image sensor,* now replace traditional tubes in some camera designs.

A CCD solid state image sensor uses a postage-stamp-sized silicon chip, containing thousands of individual elements, each independently charged by light from part of the lens image.

Among the advantages are: long life, low power consumption, instant startup, unaffected by nearby magnetic fields, free from after-images, no geometric distortion. No burn-in, or sticking, or highlight overload, or comet trailing, and lag is negligible. Picture noise is low. Registration is no problem. Sensitivity is high, and color response good. The camera is lightweight, resistant to vibrations and jarring. On the other hand, definition is less than desirable, background blemishes (holes, spots, uneven background) are difficult to avoid over the picture area, and blooming has proved a serious problem.

■ **Sound in syncs** A system in which audio is digitally encoded, and introduced into the composite video signal, during the line syncs period. Thus both video and audio can be transmitted on one carrier, instead of requiring two separate transmission systems.

■ **Staging** The design and arrangement of scenic elements (scenery, furniture, props) to create a practical and artistically suitable working environment; permitting appropriate action, shots, sound.

■ **Staircase (step wedge)** Video test signal generated to provide a series of distinct brightness steps from black to white.

■ **Standards converters** Used primarily to convert composite picture signals originating from one TV system (e.g. NTSC) to another incompatible system (e.g. PAL).

Conversion problems include: motion judder/blur, color errors, horizontal edge-flicker. Various degrees of design sophistication exist, but six-field storage equipment provides more accurate movement rendition, is free from drift, and includes such operational features as freeze-frame, noise reduction, technical corrections (blanking errors, head-switching, frame break-up).

■ **Standupper**   Shot of a reporter addressing the camera at a location.

■ **Stringer**   Local freelance cameraman or reporters.

■ **Synchronizer**   A film-editing device enabling the synchronism of the picture and separate soundtrack(s) to be maintained as the sections are run forward and backward. It consists of two or more *gangs* (sprocket wheels) mounted on a common revolving shaft. Sound heads permit the replay of audio tracks, while the picture is visible on a viewer screen.

■ **Teletext (Oracle, Ceefax, Antiope, Telidon)**   Systems for the digital transmission of written information and diagrams during vertical interval period – for selective display of data on visual display units or home TV receiver.

■ **Television systems**   All color TV pictures are distributed or transmitted in coded form (not as separate RGB signals).

NTSC (National Television System Committee) The three primary color video signals (RGB) are transformed by a coder into a *luminance* (brightness) signal conveying the tonal values, and two special *chrominance* or color difference signals (I and Q). I and Q signals are used to simultaneously modulate the chrominance subcarrier; its strength (amplitude) varying with a color's saturation at that moment, and its phase changing with the hue (quadrature modulation). The resultant complex transmitted wave therefore contains both chrominance and luminance information. Color errors can arise in the path from transmitter to receiver (phase errors). Corrective receiver circuits increasingly use *VIR* signals to regulate these errors. Overall bandwidth 4.2 MHz. Color subcarrier 3.58 MHz.

PAL (Phase alternating line) Basically a similar system, but one of the color difference signals is reversed in phase on alternate line, so that slight color errors due to phase shift are averaged out. (Greater errors become visible as *Hanover bars.*) Overall bandwidth 5.5 MHz. Color subcarrier 4.43 MHz.

SECAM (Sequential color and memory) Similarly derived, but here the chrominance signals are transmitted one at a time sequentially, on alternate lines of each field to average out phase errors. (A delay line stores and reinserts color information).

All three systems can exhibit 'herringbone' (moiré) or 'crawling dot' patterns.

■ **Time code**   This is a specially generated digital code based on the 24-hour clock; recorded with a video or audio program, to provide continuous shot identification. The original standard time code (*longitudinal time code – LTC*) is widely used, in NTSC and EBU forms.

It is recorded on a separate tape-edge track (*cue track*). However, readout is not reliable at the very variable tape speeds (slow, fast, intermittent) found in sophisticated VT editing systems, and readout ceases altogether when the tape stops.

In a new format (*vertical-interval time code – VITC*), the code is recorded in the vertical interval (retrace) period, and read out by the video heads, so is always available with the picture at all tape speeds.

Whereas the LTC format, codes at *frame-rate*, decoded at the end of the video frame, the VITC format is a *field-rate code*, decoded at the start of each video field, and odd/even fields are indentified. Unlike the LTC format, where picture and its corresponding time-code pickup points are displaced along the tape (offset), the VITC is read with its picture.

A time-correction factor known as *drop frame* (108 frames per hour) may be used in 525-line NTSC systems, to compensate for the error of 3–6 seconds per hour. (The system scans at 59.9 Hz, using a 60 Hz power supply.)

■ **Time base correction**   Any disturbance of synchronizing pulses in a color system can cause such picture defects as jitter, frame roll (vertical), skew or hooking at the top of frame, scalloping at edges, hue and saturation errors. (Helical scan recorders are very susceptible to such irregularities.) Ingenious circuitry can reduce such scanning errors by using delay lines (as in analogue *time base correctors*, TBC), or by digital storage of a full frame of video information (as in *frame synchronizers*). Sophisticated digital correctors have overcome certain problems in video switching and remote source synchronizing, and in satellite transmission.

■ **Time compression**   Circuitry that strategically adjusts the length of pauses on replay of a taped program, by just a few milliseconds, enables the overall duration to be adjusted automatically by e.g. 3–6 mins in a 30-minute show (10–30 per cent contraction). Tape transport speed is guided by a digital controller, which speeds up the tape very slightly, without obviously changing the audio pitch, or perceptible visual disruption. This facility allows precise program duration adjustment to a fixed time-slot, without having to edit the tape unduly.

■ **Translator**   Equipment used to extend the service area of a TV station, by receiving the transmitted signal, boosting it and retransmitting at increased power.

■ **Transmission numbers (T)**   The *f*-stop number is based on physical aperture size, and disregards light transmission losses and reflections between lens elements. *T-stops* are based on the actual amount of light passed by the lens system. In practice, these systems are comparable.

■ **Traveling matte**   A film printing process in which a matte or mask silhouette is derived from a subject image, to block out a selected area of another picture. This permits the subject (or other material) to be introduced into that area.

■ **Traveling shot**   Any shots from a moving camera (e.g. tracking shot).

■ **UHF**   Ultra high frequency. TV transmission band *above* channel 13, 470–890 MHz. (UK bands IV, V.)

■ **Undercranking**   Filming at a lower speed than normal to produce fast motion when projected at normal speed (24 fps), or to provide increased exposure on a static scene where light levels are low.

■ **VHF** Very high frequency. TV transmission band covering Channels 2–13, 54–216 MHz. (UK bands I, II).

■ **Video discs** Originally a general term used for 'magnetic video discs' (analogue-recorded television composite video; no audio. *(See Fig. 12.3)*.

Several different incompatible systems of digitally recorded video discs (CED video discs) have evolved, carrying permanent program material.

Their market success has been variable, especially when competing with existing small-format videotape systems (which can be wiped and reused). Video discs can, however, have certain unique storage merits.

Video discs have a variety of potential applications, with various degrees of user-interaction:

Continuous replay (e.g. 'long play' of a film); *selective replay* (frame search, freeze frame, vari-speed); *still store* (thousands of individually selectable still frames); *inter-active routing* (user-selected sequences from a menu); *disc computer interfacing* (computer-selected stills, sequences, animation).

Video disc formats include *Selectavision (RCA, Hitachi – discontinued)*, *Laservision (Philips – MCA)*, *VHD (JVC)*. Information is stored digitally on a metalized disc surface, in the form of a pattern of pits on a fine spiral. These are read capacitatively by a contact stylus passing over them, or optically by a reflected laser beam (Laservision).

■ **Videotape standards**

SMPTE Type C (non-segmented) – The videotape wraps round most of the split head-drum. The upper drum, with a single record/play head mounted on it, rotates at field rate (60/50 rev per second). This rotating head loses tape-contact at the end of each scan, so misses 10 picture lines (12 in 625/50 system), which are either replaced by a timebase corrector store, or recorded on a separate track by an additional *sync head* just in front of the *record head*. (The 16 or 19 lines this head records overlaps the missing segment, so compensating for changes in tape tension, slow motion, and still frame modes.)

Where broadcast-quality slow motion or a still frame is required, an extra video head is included, mounted on a piezo-electric element, to ensure optimum tracking accuracy (*auto scan/dynamic tracking*). Along the tape edges are located 3 (4) audio, and 1 control track. Full information in the TV vertical interval (blanking) period can be recorded where it contains control and logging data (e.g. for activating auto opt-out, advertisement logging). In Europe an extra head can be fitted to record the vertical interval information, or an extra high-quality fourth audio track.

In general, audio tracks 1, 2 are used for main program sound (for stereo: *SMPTE* record sum and difference signals; *EBU* record left- and right-hand channels). Gyroscopic errors that may arise (due to the large head-drum) if the machine is moved violently while recording may not be within the range of a timebase-corrector on replay; but scanner servos do help to reduce replay errors.

SMPTE Type B (segmented) – The videotape wraps round 190° of the small-diameter low-mass head-drum. Its two heads together record the *total* picture information, without loss or disturbance during the line-retrace/blanking period. The small mass of the head-drum enables lighter, more compact design, high speed stability, and immunity to shock or gyroscopic effects if recording while mobile. Simple tape threading (lace-up) reduces tape friction. The high writing speed makes tape quality less critical. The shorter track length (80 mm) provides more accurate tracking and interchange compatibility. However, there is less room for confidence heads on the head-drum, and the possibility of head-switching problems (banding). Along the edges of the tape, there are four independent longitudinal tracks: audio (two); time-code; control track. (There are differences between the SMPTE/NTSC and EBU/PAL formats.)

■ **Viewfinder**   The camera viewfinder displays a monochrome (rarely color) picture of the camera output. It is often switchable, to show the line (transmission) output of the switcher, or videotape replay, or to superimpose another camera's picture (e.g. to align mutual graphics). As well as normal brightness and contrast adjustments, viewfinder picture sharpness may be exaggerated ('crispness') to aid camera focusing.

The viewfinder on studio cameras is typically 5 in (12.5 cm), 3½ in (9 cm), 7 in (18 cm); while handheld cameras use a 1½ in (40 mm) magnified screen viewed through an eyepiece. The viewfinder's position may be adjustable.

Within the viewfinder assembly, there are usually indicators showing; for example, current lens data (focal length/lens angle), exposure, VT running, battery condition, filter, tally light.

■ **Viewing conditions**   Preferred viewing conditions recommended by CCIR include – viewing distance 4–6 times picture height; peak screen luminance 60–80 cd/m^2; blank screen 0.02 of peak white.

■ **VIRS (Vertical Interval Reference Signals)**   These   special signals are inserted into the vertical interval period (i.e. while the scanning process returns to top left screen after tracing a complete field). They fall outside the normal picture area and are transmitted just before picture information begins (visible as a dot pattern along the top edge of frame). They can provide reference data to enable receiver screen tint and hue to be adjusted automatically to levels specified at the source. Also, they can provide identification of program source, point of origination, time and date of original broadcast.

■ **VITS (Vertical Interval Test Signals)**   These specially inserted signals (see VIRS) are used for technical measurement, monitoring, performance correction of transmission systems.

■ **Volume indicators** *(see Fig. 10.22)*   Our ears do not react in a simple way to changes in sound strength. Because their response is *logarithmic*, our judgment of volume varies according to whether a sound is quiet or loud. But audio equipment has a *linear* direct response to sound amplitude. Consequently, it can be difficult to judge by ear whether the dynamic range of the sounds we are controlling needs adjustment to suit the audio channel.

To assist audio control, several types of volume indicators are used to prevent *over-modulation* (*overload distortion* as the audio signal exceeds the system's limits) or *under-modulation* (as very weak audio becomes intermixed with random background noises).

The widely used *VU meter* is a cheap simple indicator of program *loudness*, i.e. how strong the sound appears to the *ear*. It has 'decibel' and 'modulation' scales (*volume units*) showing the audio system's limits. The continual rapid needle movement can be confusing and tiring to watch. The indicated readings for steady sounds (tone) are accurate, but much less reliable for fluctuating audio, and very inaccurate for loud transient sounds (e.g. percussion), that can read low, so that the sound system overloads and distorts. Normal range used: −20 to 0 dB. Speech: −14 to 0dB. True undistorted maximum modulation reading is around 50 per cent on the meter.

A *peak program eter* (*PPM*) responds to the audio signal's *peaks*, so gives a better indication of system overload. Readings are accurate for steady sounds, transients, and for complex audio, so reveal any possibilities of overload distortion. However, unlike the VU meter, the PPM's readings do not necessarily relate to the impression of loudness we actually hear. Normal range used: 2 to 6 (each scale step is 4dB).

Various forms of *visual display* are becoming popular as peak-volume indicators, including: bargraphs of LEDs (light-emitting diodes), gas discharge devices, plasma displays, and light patterns on video monitors.

■ **VT − freeze** There are occasions during videotape replay when one wants to freeze a moment in an action and present it as a still picture. An unfamiliar problem can arise. (Remember, each TV picture *frame* is made up of two interlaced scans; an odd and an even *field*.)

Still pictures may be grabbed from the moving TV image in two different ways: by replaying a single *frame*, or repeating a single *field*. Recorders may offer the option of either.

For a high-definition freeze, the single *frame* is used, because it contains the full picture information of both the odd and the even fields that make up a complete picture.

However, if the subject is moving very rapidly while shooting, the separate images in the odd and even scans will appear displaced, and produce position-flicker in the combined freeze frame. In this situation, it is preferable to use the still *field* option, in which the freeze just repeats an interlaced image of one field. There is now no flicker, but because its accompanying field is missing, vertical detail is reduced.

■ **Waveform monitor (WFM)** A small oscilloscope tube displaying a fluctuating line which traces the variations of the video signal, sync pulses, and insertion pulses. Individual picture lines can be selected and examined (line strobe).

■ **Wild shooting** Shooting mute pictures for a sound film; appropriate sound being added later.

■ **Wild track** Sound recorded independently of vision (non-sync sound).

■ **Work print (cutting copy)** The initial check prints of the camera original (dailies, rushes) are edited together to form the work print, from which initial editing decisions are made. A *rough-cut* then a *fine-cut* are developed. Identifying numbers every 20 frames along the film edge (edge-numbers) aid in conforming camera original to the final edited work print.

■ **Wrap (wrap up)** To finish activities.

■ **Zoom microphone** A specially designed camera-mounted microphone, containing electret capsules, which combine to provide adjustable coverage. This ranges from 'omni-directional' (equal sensitivity in all directions), to 'ultra-unidirectional' (narrow-angle). The apparent closeness of the sound can nominally be adjusted to match different zoom-lens settings: viz. 'close' sound for close-ups. 'distant' sound for long shots. The arrangement is very arbitrary, but a useful compromise for a one-camera unit.

Bibliography

TV production

Bretz, R. *Techniques of television production*. McGraw-Hill, New York.

Chester, G., Garrison, G. R., Willis, E. E. *Television and radio*. Meredith Corpn., New York.

Millerson, G. *Effective television production* – 2nd ed. (Media Manual). Focal Press, London and Boston.

Stasheff, E., & Bretz, R., Gartley, J. & L. *The television program*. Hill & Wang, New York.

Zettl, H. *Television production handbook*. Wadsworth Pub. Co. Inc., Belmont, California.

Staging/scenic design

Millerson, G. *Basic TV staging* – 2nd ed. (Media Manual). Focal Press, London and Boston.

Wade, R. J. *Designing for TV*. Pelligrini & Cudahy, New York.

TV lighting

Millerson, G. *TV lighting methods* – 2nd ed. (Media Manual). Focal Press, London and Boston.

Millerson, G. *The technique of lighting for television and motion pictures* – 2nd ed. Focal Press, London and Boston.

Samuelson, D. W. *Motion picture camera and lighting equipment*. (Media Manual). Focal Press, London and Boston.

Television sound

Alkin, G. *TV sound operations*. Focal Press, London and Boston.

Nisbett, A. *The use of microphones* – 2nd ed. (Media Manual). Focal Press, London and Boston.

Nisbett, A. *The technique of the sound studio* – 4th ed. Focal Press, London and Boston.

TV camerawork

Millerson, G. *Video camera techniques*. (Media Manual). Focal Press, London and Boston.

439

Make-up

Buckman, H.   *Film and television make-up*. Pitman, London.
Kehoe, V. J-R.   *The technique of professional make-up for film, television and stage*. Focal Press, London and Boston.

Film

Burder, J.   *16mm film cutting*. Focal Press, London and Boston.
Burder J.   *The technique of editing 16mm film* – 2nd ed. Focal Press, London and Boston.
Happé, L. B.   *Your film and the lab* – 2nd ed. (Media Manual). Focal Press, London and Boston.
Reisz, K. & Millar, G.   *The technique of film editing* – 2nd ed. Focal Press, London and Boston.
Samuelson, D. W.   *Motion picture camera techniques* – 2nd ed. (Media Manual). Focal Press, London and Boston.

Television studio

Bermingham, A., and others.   *The small television studio*. (Media Manual). Focal Press, London and Boston.

Special effects

Fielding, R.   *The technique of special effects cinematography* – 4th ed. Focal Press, London and Boston.
Wilkie, B.   *The technique of special effects in television*. Focal Press, London and Boston.
Wilkie, B.   *Creating special effects for TV and films*. (Media Manual). Focal Press, London and Boston.

Color

Evans, R. M.   *An introduction to color*. Wiley, N.Y.

Technical

Ennes, H. E.   *Television broadcasting*. Foulsham-Sams.
Robinson, J. F. & Lowe, S.   *Videotape recording* – 3rd ed. Focal Press, London and Boston.
Spottiswoode, R. (Ed.)   *Focal encyclopedia of film and television*. Focal Press. London and Boston.

Index

441